LABOUR LINES AND COLONIAL POWER

INDIGENOUS AND PACIFIC ISLANDER LABOUR MOBILITY IN AUSTRALIA

Aboriginal History Incorporated

Aboriginal History Inc. is a part of the Australian Centre for Indigenous History, Research School of Social Sciences, The Australian National University, and gratefully acknowledges the support of the School of History and the National Centre for Indigenous Studies, The Australian National University. Aboriginal History Inc. is administered by an Editorial Board which is responsible for all unsigned material. Views and opinions expressed by the author are not necessarily shared by Board members.

Contacting Aboriginal History

All correspondence should be addressed to the Editors, Aboriginal History Inc., ACIH, School of History, RSSS, 9 Fellows Road (Coombs Building), Acton, ANU, Acton, ACT, 2601, or aboriginalhistoryinc@gmail.com.

WARNING: Readers are notified that this publication may contain names or images of deceased persons.

LABOUR LINES AND COLONIAL POWER

INDIGENOUS AND PACIFIC ISLANDER LABOUR MOBILITY IN AUSTRALIA

EDITED BY VICTORIA STEAD AND JON ALTMAN

Australian
National
University

PRESS

Published by ANU Press and Aboriginal History Inc.
The Australian National University
Acton ACT 2601, Australia
Email: anupress@anu.edu.au

Available to download for free at press.anu.edu.au

ISBN (print): 9781760463069
ISBN (online): 9781760463076

WorldCat (print): 1111771294
WorldCat (online): 1111771094

DOI: 10.22459/LLCP.2019

Cover design and layout by ANU Press. Cover photograph by Henry King. Tyrrell Collection: Museum of Applied Arts and Sciences. Gift of Australian Consolidated Press under the Taxation Incentives for the Arts Scheme, 1985.

Contents

List of Figures

List of Abbreviations

ANU	The Australian National University
ARC	Australian Research Council
ASO	Aboriginal support officer
ATSIC	Aboriginal and Torres Strait Islander Commission
BAC	Bawinanga Aboriginal Corporation
CDEP	Community Development Employment Projects
CDP	Community Development Program
CSR	corporate social responsibility
CYP	Cape York Partnerships
FIFO	fly-in fly-out
LGA	local government area
LMAP	Labour Mobility Assistance Program
LMS	London Missionary Society
RGS	Royal Geographical Society
RSE	Recognised Seasonal Employer
SCV	Special Category Visa
SWP	Seasonal Worker Programme
TTTA	Trans-Tasman Travel Arrangement

Contributors

Jon Altman was a research professor at the Alfred Deakin Institute for Citizenship and Globalisation, Deakin University, Melbourne, until early 2019. He is an emeritus professor at The Australian National University (ANU) affiliated with the School of Regulation and Global Governance, Canberra. Since 1979, Jon has worked as an economic anthropologist with Kuninjku-speaking people in western Arnhem Land, looking at economic transformations in situations in which there are limited formal labour markets. Much of his research has focused on Indigenous employment issues nationally and, especially, the workings of Indigenous specific programs like the now defunct Community Development Employment Projects scheme.

Tracey Banivanua Mar was a historian of colonialism and a Pacific Islander scholar of Fijian (Lauan) as well as Chinese and British descent. Tracey's research interests included colonial and transnational indigenous histories with a concentration on Australia and the western Pacific. She published widely on race relations and the dynamics of violence in Queensland's sugar districts during the era of the Queensland–Pacific indentured labour trade, and nineteenth-century histories of Australian South Sea Islanders. At the time of her death in 2017, she was an Australian Research Council (ARC) Future Fellow (2014–15), working on two ARC projects examining the myriad strategies and interconnected networks established by indigenous peoples during the nineteenth century as they negotiated the effects of colonialism.

Lucy Davies completed her PhD at La Trobe University in 2018. Her thesis examined how Papuans' and New Guineans' travels shaped Australia's administration of Papua and New Guinea from the beginning of the twentieth century to independence. In 2012, she was a National Archives of Australia/Australian Historical Association postgraduate scholar and, in 2014, a National Library of Australia summer scholar. Her honours thesis examined the regulated trade of Papuan and New Guinean domestic workers to Australia in the mid-twentieth century.

Ruth (Lute) Faleolo is a PhD candidate with the Aboriginal Environments Research Centre and Institute for Social Science Research at the University of Queensland. As a New Zealand–born Tongan and Pasifika academic, she has a passion for the empowerment of indigenous and migrant communities through social, economic and cultural development. Ruth has a background in both education and social sciences qualitative research. Her PhD research focuses on the wellbeing of trans-Tasman Pasifika migrants of Samoan and Tongan descent in Auckland and Brisbane. Her research seeks to capture the voices, perceptions and experiences of these migrants using a mixed-methods approach that incorporates indigenous research methods.

Daniel Guinness is an anthropologist interested in the changing social relations and performances of masculinities in the context of globalised neoliberal labour markets, particularly those involving sporting migration. He has undertaken ethnographic field research in Fiji, Argentina, Australia, New Zealand and France. His postdoctoral research was funded through the European Research Council as part of the project 'Globalization, Sport and the Precarity of Masculinity', and was undertaken at the University of Amsterdam.

Fiona Haslam McKenzie is the co-director of the Centre for Regional Development at the University of Western Australia. She has a PhD in political geography. Fiona has extensive experience in population and socio-economic change, housing and regional economic development analysis. She has particular expertise in the socio-economic effects of different workforce arrangements for the mining industry on rural, regional and remote communities. She has published widely and has undertaken work for corporate and small business sectors, both nationally and in Western Australia, and for all three tiers of government. Fiona led the CSIRO Minerals Down Under Regions in Transition Project and the Regional Economies – Enduring Community Value from Mining division of the Co-operative Research Centre, Remote Economic Participation, in 2010–14.

Shino Konishi is a historian based at the University of Western Australia. She has long been interested in histories of exploration and cross-cultural contact. She is the author of *The Aboriginal Male in the Enlightenment World* (London: Pickering and Chatto, 2012) and coeditor of *Indigenous Intermediaries: New Perspectives on the Exploration Archive* (Canberra: ANU Press and Aboriginal History, 2015) and *Brokers and Boundaries: Colonial Exploration in Indigenous Territory* (Canberra: ANU Press and Aboriginal History, 2016). She is Aboriginal and identifies with the Yawuru people of Broome, Western Australia.

Helen Lee is professor of anthropology in the Department of Social Inquiry, La Trobe University. Since the 1980s, she has conducted research with the people of Tonga, both in their home islands in the Pacific and in the diaspora, particularly in Australia, with a focus on childhood and youth, cultural identity, migration and transnationalism. Recent books include *Mobilities of Return: Pacific Perspectives* (Canberra: ANU Press, 2017, coedited with Jack Taylor) and *Change and Continuity in the Pacific* (London: Routledge, 2018, coedited with John Connell). Her ARC Linkage Project (2015–19) looked at the effects of immigration status on Pacific Islanders in rural Victoria.

Scott Mackay is an independent scholar who completed his PhD in the University of Melbourne's Australian Indigenous Studies program in 2018. His thesis examined the places (real and symbolic) accorded to Pacific peoples within the construction of the Australian nation and production of Australian nationalism; how such places both reflect and inform the ways in which Australia engages with the Pacific region; and the extent to which Australia considers itself a part of, or apart from, the Pacific region. In 2016 and 2017, he received funding from the European Research Council for a project entitled 'Globalization, Sport and the Precarity of Masculinity', focusing specifically on Fijian men's and women's rugby experiences in Australia.

Timothy Neale is a senior research fellow at the Alfred Deakin Institute, Deakin University. His research concerns the intersections between biopolitics, settler–Indigenous relations, and environmental governance. Timothy is the author of *Wild Articulations: Environmentalism and Indigeneity in Northern Australia* (Honolulu: University of Hawai'i Press, 2017) and coeditor, with Eve Vincent, of *Unstable Relations: Environmentalism and Indigenous People in Contemporary Australia* (Crawley, WA: UWA Publishing, 2016).

Makiko Nishitani is a lecturer in anthropology at La Trobe University, Melbourne. She worked with Professor Helen Lee on the ARC Linkage Project 'Pacific Islanders in Regional Victoria: Settlers, Visitors, and Overstayers' (2015–19), and spent more than nine months in Mildura, Robinvale and surrounding areas conducting field work. She is actively engaged with the wider society beyond academia, having participated in a public hearing of the Australian parliament and a UN consultation on business and human rights to help make the voices of Pacific peoples who engage in farm work in Australia heard.

Sarah Prout Quicke is a human development geographer and researcher at the Centre for Regional Development, University of Western Australia (UWA). Her research examines population, development and social policy issues in Indigenous Australia and Africa, with particular focus on Indigenous mobility and migration, education and housing policy, and regional development in resource economies. Prior to her appointment at UWA, Sarah led the Indigenous mobilities research sub-theme on the Ministerial Council for Aboriginal and Torres Strait Islander Affairs 'Populations Project' at the Centre for Aboriginal Economic Policy Research, ANU. Sarah teaches in population, migration and social geography.

Lynette Russell is professor of Indigenous Studies (History) at the Monash Indigenous Studies Centre, Monash University. Her work is deeply interdisciplinary and collaborative, and her research outputs are focused on showing the dynamism of Aboriginal responses to colonialism, their agency and subjectivity. She is deputy director of the ARC's Centre of Excellence for Australian Biodiversity and Heritage. A widely published author specialising in Aboriginal history, Lynette has held fellowships at both Oxford and Cambridge universities.

Rachel Standfield is a lecturer at the Monash Indigenous Studies Centre, Monash University. Rachel is a historian of indigenous societies and race relations histories in Australia and New Zealand. Her work explores cross-cultural encounters, the agency of indigenous peoples as they encountered Europeans on their country, and how those encounters are encoded in colonial sources and national histories. She edited *Indigenous Mobilities: Across and Beyond the Antipodes* (Canberra: ANU Press and Aboriginal History, 2018).

Victoria Stead is an ARC DECRA senior research fellow at the Alfred Deakin Institute, Deakin University. She is an anthropologist with a focus on the Pacific, particularly Melanesia, and also regional Australia. Her research explores local negotiations of colonial relations and (post)colonial legacies, and processes of change related to land, labour, memory and belonging. Victoria is the author of *Becoming Landowners: Entanglements of Custom and Modernity in Papua New Guinea and Timor-Leste* (Honolulu: University of Hawai'i Press, 2017) and a co-author of *Sustainable Communities, Sustainable Livelihoods: Other Paths for Papua New Guinea* (Honolulu: University of Hawai'i Press, 2012).

Michael J. Stevens (nō Kāi Tahu ki Awarua) is a historian with the Ngāi Tahu Archive Team at Te Rūnanga o Ngāi Tahu. He is interested in knowledge born out of cross-cultural entanglement and colonisation in the long nineteenth century. He focuses primarily on southern New Zealand's colonial and maritime histories, especially as they relate to Kāi Tahu families and communities. Mike's work is noted for blending *whakapapa* (genealogy) and an attention to the specificities of place with a strong sense of British imperial history to shed light on the development of distinctive Māori social formations.

Preface

This volume has its origins in a two-day workshop convened in June 2017 at the Alfred Deakin Institute for Citizenship and Globalisation, Deakin University. Coming together as historians, anthropologists, geographers and sociologists, our twin aims were to consider both Indigenous Australian and Pacific Islander experiences of labour mobility in a comparative context, and to bring historical and contemporary experiences into conversation. In doing so, we sought to interrogate the nature of labour relations and discourses of labour within colonial projects, including in the governing and making of colonised subjects, as well as the making and governing of colonised territories. We sought, also, to expand the terms and scope by which Australian coloniality has often been conceived, thinking together about the settler colonialism of the Australian state, the colonial administration of the territories of Papua and New Guinea, as well as more diffuse (but nevertheless violent) forms of post- and neo-colonialism articulated through 'development' and border regimes. 'Coloniality' provided an analytical frame for holding together this expanded scope of vision at the workshop and, similarly, holds together the papers collected here. A focus on labour mobility experiences *within* Australia facilitates our particular comparisons between Indigenous and Pacific Islander people, and the particular inquiry into Australian coloniality.

What emerged from the two days of collegial exchange was a picture of particularity and diversity, but ultimately, also, of powerful continuities across time and among the experiences of diverse indigenous peoples. The labour lines that this book traces, then, are lines across both time and space—lines of connection that speak to the extended reach of both colonial power and indigenous world-making across the region.

To the extent that our project seeks to disrupt the disciplinary compartmentalising of Indigenous and Pacific studies, and to interrogate the transnational connections, networks, imaginations and flows in which Australian settler colonialism is enmeshed, it builds upon the recent work of others, most notably the Pacific historian Tracey Banivanua Mar. We were fortunate and privileged to have Tracey participate in our workshop just months before she passed away. Tracey's premature death came just as the full significance of her groundbreaking work—particularly her books *Violence and Colonial Dialogue: The Australian-Pacific Indentured Labor Trade* (Honolulu: University of Hawai'i Press, 2007) and *Decolonisation and the Pacific: Indigenous Globalisation and the Ends of Empire* (Cambridge: Cambridge University Press, 2016)—was being recognised. Tracey's paper at the workshop is included here as a posthumous contribution, having been finalised by her colleagues and friends Kalissa Alexeyeff, Lucy Davies and Alan Lester. We extend our sincere thanks to them for their support.

We also wish to thank everyone who participated in the original workshop. In addition to the contributors to this volume, participants included Tiffany Shellam, who played a key role in organising the workshop, and also Shannyn Palmer, Kirstie Close, Julia Martínez, Melinda Hinkson and Elizabeth Watt, and John Connell, who acted as our discussant. For a variety of reasons, none sinister, their workshop contributions are not included in this volume. Thanks also go to the Alfred Deakin Institute for their financial support of the workshop and publication, and to Rani Kerin and her colleagues in the Aboriginal History series at ANU Press. We are also appreciative that two anonymous reviewers wholeheartedly supported our project while also providing constructive comments for some revisions. Finally, we thank the Indigenous and Pacific Islander communities and individuals who have responded positively to our inquiries, from whom we learn, and about whose lives and labour lines we are privileged to write.

Victoria Stead and Jon Altman
Melbourne

1

Labour Lines and Colonial Power

Victoria Stead and Jon Altman

> The Government's policy of buying stations and building large
> settlements—at considerable cost to the taxpayers—and then
> encouraging large numbers of natives to congregate on these
> places enjoying Government sustenance with a minimum of work
> has not helped the employment problem ... It would be easier,
> in our opinion, to 'blackbird' a boat load of Kanakas, than to pry
> loose a couple of native stockmen from some of these Government
> settlements.
>
> Jim Martin, secretary of the Cattleman's Association, 1961.[1]

In 1961, faced with low wages and poor living and working conditions,
Aboriginal workers were leaving the northern Australian pastoral
industry. Responding to the resultant labour shortage, the secretary of
the Cattleman's Association of North Australia declared indignantly that
the Aboriginal workers had not 'walked off' but, rather, had been 'put
off'. In comments printed on the front page of the *Northern Territory
News*, under the heading 'Natives "Lazy"—Cattlemen Say', he invoked
long-running, racist stereotypes about the quality of Aboriginal labour,
the alleged poor work ethic of Aboriginal people and the perceived
immobility in which these moral failings were seen to be rooted.[2] His racist
comments were, of course, oblivious to the irony that what the labour

---

1   'Natives "Lazy"—Cattlemen Say', *Northern Territory News*, 18 April 1961, 1.
2   Konishi, 'Idle Men'.

crisis in fact demonstrated was both the deep reliance of the industry on Aboriginal labour, and the capacity and willingness of Aboriginal people to enact agency *through* their mobility. Invoking the 'blackbirding' of Melanesian workers through the Pacific labour trade—a trade that had formally concluded six decades prior—the cattleman's comments likewise referenced (and exhibited) both the intertwined enactments of colonial power against both Indigenous and Pacific Islander people, and the reverberating presence of historical labour relations, discourses and identities.

The colonial complexes of race, labour and mobility evident in the cattleman's comments (and in the events that prompted them) reverberate throughout Australian colonial history and into the present. Today, increases of so-called 'low-skilled' and temporary labour migrations to Australia—including via dedicated seasonal labour schemes targeted to Pacific Islanders[3]—occur alongside calls for Indigenous people to 'orbit'[4] from their remote communities in search of employment opportunities. These trends reflect the prevailing neoliberalism within contemporary Australia, as well as the effects of structural dynamics within the global agriculture and resource extractive industries. However, they are also, often, reflective of the rich cultures and histories of mobility,[5] and the diverse 'worlding' practices of those who move,[6] as well as of forces that compel movement. Drawing together historians, anthropologists, sociologists and geographers, this edited collection critically explores experiences of labour mobility (and immobility) by Indigenous peoples and Pacific Islanders, including Māori, within Australia. We seek to locate these new expressions of labour mobility within historical patterns of movement, including longer-term migrations, mobilities and diasporic settlements; in doing so, we also seek to comment on the contours and continuities of Australian coloniality in its diverse articulations.

---

3   Maclellan and Mares, 'Remittances and Labour Mobility in the Pacific'; Mares and Maclellan, 'Pacific Seasonal Workers for Australian Horticulture'; MacDermott and Opeskin, 'Regulating Pacific Seasonal Labour in Australia'.
4   Pearson, 'The Cape York Partnership Plan'. See also Neale, this volume; Pearson, 'Radical Hope: Education and Equality in Australia'; Pearson, *Up from the Mission*; cf. Altman, 'What Future for Remote Indigenous Australia?'.
5   Carey and Lydon, *Indigenous Networks*; Fijn et al., *Indigenous Participation*; Hau'ofa, 'Our Sea of Islands'; Taylor and Bell, *Population Mobility and Indigenous Peoples*.
6   Stead, 'Mobility and Emplacement'; Wilson and Connery, *The Worlding Project*.

Contemporary experiences of labour mobility by both Pacific Islander and Indigenous peoples unfold within the context of long and troubled histories of Australian colonialism and postcolonialism. Thus, contemporary labour migrations of Pacific Islanders through the Seasonal Worker Programme (SWP)—oriented particularly to the agricultural and horticultural sectors—have dark historical echoes in the 'blackbirding' of South Sea Islanders to work on sugar plantations in New South Wales and Queensland in the late nineteenth and early twentieth centuries, as well as in wider patterns of labour, trade and colonisation across the region.[7] The antecedents of contemporary Indigenous labour mobility, meanwhile, include forms of unwaged and exploitative labouring on government settlements, missions, pastoral stations and in the pearling industry,[8] and also agentive and purposeful labour migrations, including by Indigenous intermediaries accompanying colonial explorations.[9] Complex colonial histories and power relations inflect the contemporary encounters of both Pacific and Indigenous peoples with capitalist industry in Australia, as well as with the Australian state. They reverberate through past and present-day reckonings of class and race that posit certain types of work as undesirable for 'local' (white) labour, and through migration regimes that enact forms of precarious labour market access that are, for some, uncoupled from any possibility of citizenship.

The experiences of Indigenous and Pacific peoples speak to core, if diverse, expressions of Australian coloniality. These include the ongoing power relations and intercultural dynamics of settler colonialism, and also the kinds of racially structured hierarchies and North–South inequalities that Latin American and other postcolonial scholars have theorised as 'global coloniality'[10] and that inform and inflect the ongoing making of 'Australia' and its regional positioning. Aníbal Quijano offers the idea of the 'coloniality of power' as a means of identifying the pervasive reverberations of colonialism through the present.[11] Approached in this way, coloniality speaks to a system within which *race*, in its intersections with gender and other hierarchies, underpins foundational hierarchies that perpetuate unjust divisions of labour and that sustain the subordination of some for the benefit of others. As an analytical frame, the notion of

---

7   Stead, this volume.
8   Sharp and Tatz, *Aborigines in the Economy*; Martínez and Vickers, *The Pearl Frontier*.
9   Konishi, Nugent and Shellam, *Indigenous Intermediaries*.
10   Mignolo and Escobar, *Globalization and the Decolonial Option*; Quijano, 'Coloniality of Power'.
11   Quijano, 'Coloniality and Modernity/Rationality'.

coloniality provides a productive basis for comparisons between different expressions of colonial power (e.g. settler and non-settler colonialism and postcolonialism), as well as for holding together shifting modes of colonial domination across time. In the context of Australia, we deploy the notion of coloniality to think through both the particularities and commonalities of diverse forms of racialised and oppressive power enacted by the state, including frontier and settler colonialism (on the Australian continent), colonial rule (of the territories of Papua and New Guinea), and hierarchical and paternalistic engagements with other Pacific states, including through ideas and practices of 'development'.

In considering Indigenous Australian and Pacific Islander experiences of labour mobility in relation to one another and longitudinally, this book generates new insights into the nature of that coloniality, as well as into the material, imaginative and affective responses of those who labour on, and through, country. In bringing together Pacific and Indigenous Australian experiences, the book also seeks to push against the disciplinary and epistemological structures that have, with notable exceptions,[12] delineated these from one another as the subjects of the largely separate fields of Aboriginal/Indigenous studies and Pacific studies. In doing so, it builds on and extends a growing body of historical scholarship that has emphasised trans-local Indigenous networks and political activity.[13] A particular focus on Australian coloniality and labour mobility experiences within Australia is also intended as a response to the large existing literature on Pacific Islander labour mobility to, and within, New Zealand.[14]

The incursions of the Australian state and capital into Aboriginal and Torres Strait Islander lands and waters, as well as into the wider Pacific region, were (and remain) interconnected exercises of coloniality. The nineteenth-century exploitation of Islanders' labour through the Pacific labour trade was predicated on the dispossession of Aboriginal people in Queensland, and the colonial forms of violence nurtured on the frontier—often wrapped up in discourses of 'larrikinism' and tough settler identity—were the foundation for the material and discursive violence enacted against Islanders.[15] While distinctions between different forms of

---

12   Banivanua Mar, *Decolonisation and the Pacific*.

13   Carey and Lydon, *Indigenous Networks*; De Costa, *A Higher Authority*.

14   For example: Hammond and Connell, 'The New Blackbirds?'; Loomis, *Pacific Migrant Labour, Class and Racism*; Grainger, 'From Immigrant to Overstayer'; Macpherson, Spoonley and Anae, *Tangata o te Moana Nui*; Teaiwa and Mallon, 'Ambivalent Kinships?'.

15   Banivanua Mar, *Violence and Colonial Dialogue*.

coloniality are analytically useful—and, indeed, we sometimes distinguish within this collection between settler colonialism, the direct colonial administration of Papua and New Guinea, and other forms of colonial intervention within the Pacific—it is also the case that both throughout Australia, and throughout the region, the violence of colonialism has been enacted through multiple, changing and often interconnected modalities. For instance, as Ann Curthoys and Clive Moore have argued, the use of Torres Strait Islander labour from the latter half of the nineteenth century can be seen as much an extension of Pacific colonialism as of Queensland colonial labour relations.[16] Particularly in the pearling and bêche-de-mer industries, Torres Strait Islander labour was used alongside Pacific Islander and Asian labour. Across colonial Queensland and the Torres Strait, racism towards Aboriginal, Chinese and Melanesian people was both cotemporaneous and co-produced.[17] Colonial settlers themselves were frequently moving back and forth throughout the wider region from 1788 into the nineteenth century in a cycle of 'constant intercolonial movements'.[18] When the Pacific labour trade and indenture system were concluded at the end of the nineteenth century, Archibald Meston forecast self-sustaining missions on reserves to provide enough Aboriginal workers to replace the Pacific Islanders facing deportation.[19] These interconnected and mutually productive expressions of coloniality are explored powerfully in Tracey Banivanua Mar's chapter in this volume, which examines the 'inseparable bind' between land and labour in the colonial project of Benjamin Boyd, a white pastoralist who arrived in New South Wales in the mid-nineteenth century. Boyd's use of indentured Pacific labour, Banivanua Mar shows, was bound up in the colonial fantasies of transformation of Aboriginal land into 'productive property'.

Still, while these articulations of coloniality were interconnected, there were important differences in the ways that Aboriginal and Pacific Islander labour were managed. The reserves system that figures like Meston championed, for instance, provided a particular mechanism of control and centralisation from within which Aboriginal people could be pressed into cheap labour.[20] They also worked to contain those who did not, or would not, work for the colonists, or indeed whose labour was

---

16 Curthoys and Moore, 'Working for the White People'.
17 Evans, Saunders and Cronin, *Race Relations in Colonial Queensland*.
18 Curthoys and Moore, 'Working for the White People', 6.
19 Curthoys and Moore, 'Working for the White People'.
20 Evans, *'A Permanent Precedent'*.

undesired. As Patrick Wolfe has argued in his comparative study of race and colonialism, initial attempts by colonists to recruit Indigenous labour were often quickly abandoned:

> In principle, it is not good policy to incur reliance on a population that one is simultaneously seeking to eliminate, nor to promote the survival of the bearers of sovereignties that exceed the settler import.[21]

Thus, indentured Pacific labour became a desirable labour force, as its use helped to avoid settler reliance on Aboriginal labour. The use of indenture as a mechanism for facilitating and controlling some Pacific labour has also meant that this labour has historically been easier to track and quantify, allowing the more casual use of Aboriginal labour—often forced, unpaid or paid in rations—to 'slip quietly through the cracks of the historical record'.[22] This interplay between imported and local labour, and between strategies of confinement and transportation, remind us that labour mobility must also, necessarily, be considered in relation to immobility and constraint, and to both the denial and the refusal of movement. The issue of indenture also raises important distinctions between different groups of Pacific people, with Melanesian labour subject to indenture in a way that Polynesian labour largely was not. One effect of this has been that Māori and other Polynesian labour has, like Aboriginal labour, been far less visible in historical record.

In attending to the intersections of Pacific Islander and Aboriginal and Torres Strait Islander labour mobility, both historical and contemporary, contributors to this volume ask: For what, and whose, ends have Pacific people and Indigenous Australians laboured, both historically and today? Where, and in what ways, do past and present experiences of labour mobility by Pacific and Indigenous Australian peoples resonate, diverge and intersect? What are, or have been, the responses of Indigenous and Pacific peoples to labour mobility, and to the forms of intercultural encounter that labour mobility produces? In exploring these questions, the papers in this collection move between mission history, the mid-nineteenth-century origins of the Pacific labour trade, contemporary fly-in fly-out mining labour, seasonal labour in the horticultural sector and more. Underlying this diversity, strong commonalities of experience

---

21   Wolfe, *Traces of History*, 25.
22   Curthoys and Moore, 'Working for the White People', 4.

emerge, including the role of labour relations in colonialist efforts to produce and discipline particular kinds of Indigenous and Pacific Islander subjects; the ambivalent role of regulation in both ameliorating and reproducing colonial inequalities; and the complex interplay of coercion and agency as Indigenous and Pacific Islander people variously seek out, resist and negotiate experiences of labour mobility.

Producing Indigenous and Pacific Islander Subjects

Labour is materially, and also symbolically and subjectively, productive. White colonists and the Australian state have attempted to produce Indigenous and Pacific Islander people as particular kinds of subjects to make them exploitable as workers and, conversely, have exploited Indigenous and Pacific Islander workers in their attempts to produce them as particular kinds of subjects. As Banivanua Mar has shown, racialised stereotypes of Melanesians, cast in terms of moral and physical threat and reproduced within literary traditions of savagery and cannibalism, were part of the way that Melanesians were produced through the nineteenth century as 'colonizable, oppressable, and exploitable'.[23] The shifting codings of Pacific workers that she documents through the nineteenth century—as variously lazy and hard-working, passive and savage, menacing and benign—echo in the racialised, often contradictory, ways in which contemporary Pacific Islanders are depicted in media, political and public discourse, whether in the context of their labour (e.g. through narratives about Islanders as well suited to difficult horticultural work), their perceived *failure* to labour (e.g. in narratives about welfare dependency) or indeed through the pervasive stereotypes of young Pacific Islanders as delinquent, violent and trouble-making (and thus as unproductive subjects in the making).[24]

While recognising the ambivalence that Wolfe attributes to the use of Indigenous labour by early colonists, labour has nevertheless been similarly implicated in colonial attempts to create and govern Aboriginal and Torres Strait Islander subjects. Labour, as Henry Reynolds documented in *With the White People*, was valued both economically and as a way of civilising

---

23   Banivanua Mar, *Violence and Colonial Dialogue*, 3.
24   Stead, 'Doing "Social Cohesion"'.

Aboriginal people.[25] This civilising project reverberates today through the coercive labour regime installed by the Australian Government in the wake of the 2007 Northern Territory National Emergency Response (the 'Intervention'). As Jon Altman, Melinda Hinkson and others have extensively documented, the Community Development Program (CDP) that was launched in 2014 is profoundly ideological and normative in its character, bound up as it has been in the Intervention's wideranging but acute moral panic about perceived dysfunction in remote Indigenous communities.[26] As the 200-page report that called for the establishment of the CDP, *The Forrest Review: Creating Parity*, declared baldly:

> Idle hands and a lack of the dignity that work brings have contributed to the dysfunction of many remote communities. Compounding the pernicious effects of welfare, remote Australia is now an easy target for those peddling drugs, illegally sold alcohol and gambling. Full-time Work for the Dole activities from day one of unemployment will keep people active.[27]

Thus justified, the CDP has enacted extensive programs of work, enforced through punitive systems of penalties for noncompliance, that see Indigenous people labouring for an hourly rate of AU$11, far below the minimum wage. In contrast to Reynolds' observations about Aboriginal labour on colonial frontiers, though, economic value is of little consideration here. Most of the 'jobs' into which Aboriginal people are corralled are unsustainable—'make-work' valued exclusively for its governing and disciplining effects, as Jon Altman elaborates in his chapter in this volume, which takes as its geographical focus the communities around Maningrida in Arnhem Land.[28] Where the contemporary CDP does echo past labour regimes enacted upon Indigenous peoples is in its devaluing—indeed, its fundamental failure to recognise—*other* forms of work and labour beyond a particular capitalist, modern ideal. This is a theme that similarly emerges in other chapters. For instance, Shino Konishi documents the failure of the colonial explorer D. W. Carnegie to recognise the Aboriginal labour and forms of economy he encountered through the Gibson and Great Sandy deserts, a myopia that functioned in part to legitimate extreme cruelty towards the Aboriginal people he encountered. Meanwhile, Lucy Davies' insights into the characterisations

---

25   Reynolds, *With the White People*.
26   Altman and Hinkson, *Culture Crisis*.
27   Forrest, 'The Forrest Review', 197.
28   See also Altman, 'Modern Slavery in Remote Australia?'.

of Papuan and New Guinean female domestics as 'companions' rather than workers demonstrates that this selective privileging of particular conceptions of work and labour at the expense of others is similarly a feature of Australia's colonial engagements with Pacific lives and livelihoods, both within Australia and throughout the region.[29]

Other chapters provide different angles on the articulations of labour and colonial discipline. Scott Mackay and Daniel Guinness chart the experiences of young *itaukei* (indigenous) Fijians who travel to Australia under the promise of pathways into lucrative jobs within professional rugby, but instead find themselves exploited within low-paying manual jobs. Their labour experiences are rooted in the ethnicised divisions of labour that have characterised coloniality in both Fiji and Australia, and that frame the conditions of possibility for *itaukei* men. They are also, Mackay and Guinness show, reflective of contemporary neoliberal precepts that hold individual migrant workers responsible for negotiating the conditions of their employment. This logic holds those who do not secure lucrative professional sporting careers (which is to say, the vast majority) responsible for their own fates, and provides the legitimating discourse that sees them compelled instead into positions as cheap labour on the fringes of Australia's labour markets and migration regimes.

The contributions to this volume not only highlight the disciplining aims of various labour relations, but also the particular forms of disciplinary and colonial force enacted (or at least, attempted) through labour *mobility*. As Sarah Prout Quicke and Fiona Haslam McKenzie note in this volume, the mobility of Indigenous people has often been constructed as a factor in their ungovernability. Yet, both historical and contemporary practices have also sought to encourage or compel mobility as part of explicit attempts to govern and produce 'productive' working subjects. These forms of disciplining include the coerced movements of Indigenous people to settlements, as well as both historical and contemporary demands for Indigenous people to leave remote homes in pursuit of mainstream employment[30] (and the punishment through CDP labour or the denial of basic services[31] to those who refuse to leave). Timothy Neale, in this volume, provides a critical genealogy of the idea of 'orbiting', championed by Noel

---

29   Stead, 'The Price of Fish'; Stead, *Becoming Landowners*.
30   Konishi and Lui-Chivizhe, 'Working for the Railways'.
31   Helen Davidson, 'WA Plan to Close 100 Remote and Indigenous Communities "Devastating"'. *The Guardian*, 18 November 2014. www.theguardian.com/australia-news/2014/nov/18/wa-plan-to-close-100-remote-and-indigenous-communities-devastating.

Pearson as a model through which remote-living Indigenous people could (and should) move back and forth between culturally significant home communities and urban economies. Neale's observation, that orbiting bolsters the ideological privileging of the life of the migrant worker as the best 'lifestyle choice' for contemporary Indigenous people, is paralleled in key ways by the developmentalism championed by proponents of the SWP, interrogated by Victoria Stead in her exploration of Ni-Vanuatu temporary workers in north-central Victoria.

Regulation and Colonial Inequalities

A second thematic concern that runs through the chapters gathered here is the ambiguous role of regulation in both ameliorating and prescribing colonial exploitation and hierarchy in the context of labour mobility. As Shino Konishi shows in her account of Aboriginal people kidnapped and subject to gross mistreatment by the explorer Carnegie, the lack of legislative protections for Aboriginal and Torres Strait Islander people in the period of colonial settlement enabled highly exploitative labour relations. Further, as Sarah Prout Quicke and Fiona Haslam McKenzie observe in relation to contemporary fly-in fly-out (FIFO) labour, the fact that contemporary Indigenous workers are entitled to the same legislative protections as non-Indigenous workers has markedly reduced many vulnerabilities. Indeed, they note that Indigenous FIFO labour is, in many ways, facilitated by new kinds of legislative and regulatory frameworks, including those that require mining companies to foster Indigenous employment opportunities as part of their obligations within the context of native title. Nevertheless, the pervasive representational politics associated with the coloniality of power continue to structure Indigenous labour mobilities in ways that produce unique precarities and vulnerabilities.

It is not only the absence of regulation that produces colonial hierarchies and inequalities. As Julia O'Connell Davidson notes in relation to contemporary debt-financed labour migration and the host of mobile and exploitative labour relations that fall under the category of 'modern slavery', legal migration channels can be as likely as illegal ones to lock workers into severely unequal power relationships.[32] Nor does the legal/

---

32   Davidson, 'Troubling Freedom'.

illegal dyad map neatly onto that of protected/vulnerable, she argues; leaving home to work illegally in the informal sector can be a way of increasing personal freedoms for many migrant workers, albeit under risk of detection and deportation. This is the situation for many of the Pacific Islanders whose lives Makiko Nishitani and Helen Lee document in their chapter in this volume. Having initially travelled to Australia on SWP visas, which provide for specific hours and conditions of seasonal labour, some choose to overstay or 'abscond' from their designated places of employment, citing less exploitative and more profitable 'informal' work opportunities, in spite of the challenges and anxieties generated from living and working without documentation.[33] Historical antecedents to the regulated restraints of contemporary labour mobility schemes emerge in Lucy Davies' sensitive mapping of the experiences of Papuan and New Guinean women who travelled to Australia as servants, nursemaids and domestics for white women. Placing their labour into dialogue with the domestic labour of Aboriginal women, Davies argues that the regulation and government surveillance of these workers, often couched in terms of protections, was a response to the fear caused by the presence of Aboriginal and Pacific Islander women within the private spaces of white homes. In drawing attention to the gendering of colonial power, Davies thus calls attention not only to workers' movements between territories or across large geographical distances, but also to the intimate mobilities of labour across the borders of private and public spheres.

The regulated constraints on rights and belonging, and forms of variegated rights that characterise mobile labour regimes,[34] compel us to look beyond the kinds of exploitation and vulnerability produced by *illegality* to what Losurdo describes as the various 'exclusion clauses' that have always accompanied liberal pronouncements of rights and freedoms.[35] The regulated and racialised hierarchies enacted at the borders of nation-states affect Pacific Islanders entering Australia in ways that do not act upon Indigenous peoples; however, these 'exclusion clauses' nevertheless punctuate the exercise of colonial power against Indigenous lives. These are evident in the kinds of legislated inequalities that characterise the Northern Territory Intervention and the more recent CDP. Indeed, the dark irony of the CDP is that the author of the report that recommended its establishment, Andrew Forrest, is elsewhere lauded as a champion of

---

33 See also Lan, 'Legal Servitude and Free Illegality'; Mahdavi, *Gridlock*.
34 Anderson, 'Migration, Immigration Controls'.
35 Losurdo, *Liberalism*, 342.

freedom for his role as head of the Walk Free Foundation, an organisation that campaigns against 'modern slavery' in global supply chains.[36] Coercive labour conditions and exploitative remuneration make the CDP arguably a form of modern slavery. However, instead of being recognised as such, its foundations in intensely racialised, colonial representations of Indigeneity mean that it is legitimised and legally sanctioned.

Coercion and Agency

Images and discourses of slavery—modern or otherwise—have often ignited debates about the relationship between coercive force and workers' agency. As Victoria Stead argues in her chapter in this volume, these debates have long occupied scholars of the Pacific labour trade, as well as those concerned with contemporary forms of Pacific labour mobility. Discourses of slavery have also, she argues, gained popular traction among contemporary Pacific Islanders. Beyond technical or legalistic debates about the definitional parameters of slavery, the forms of meaning and historical awareness embedded in these discourses urge more nuanced attention to the lived experience of labour, and to the complex interplays of consent and coercion that also animate Tracey Banivanua Mar's chapter on the Islanders 'recruited' to New South Wales by Benjamin Boyd.

In contrast to the Pacific labour trade, the use of Aboriginal labour by Australian colonists began at a time when slavery was still legal in the British Empire. The initial clearances that accompanied colonial settlement were often followed by a subsequent enticement back of Aboriginal people to the fringes of those settlements as a labour force.[37] 'Aboriginal workers were never slaves in the strict sense', argue Curthoys and Moore, 'but neither were they free'.[38] In the context of Aboriginal labour in Queensland during the colonial period, Raymond Evans similarly makes a case for the 'striking parallel' between the conditions of slaves and 'unfree' Aboriginal workers, noting that the early colonists perceived Aboriginal workers in terms largely equivalent to those with which they regarded African slaves.[39] If the Pacific labour trade formally commenced in the aftermath of slavery's abolition, the racialised discourses, images and tropes that sustained this

---

36 Altman, 'Modern Slavery in Remote Australia?'
37 Curthoys and Moore, 'Working for the White People'.
38 Curthoys and Moore, 'Working for the White People', 4.
39 Evans, '"Kings" in Brass Crescents', 203.

perception of Aboriginal workers were nevertheless strongly paralleled by those that also sustained the exploitation of Pacific workers. As Banivanua Mar has shown, this exploitation was bolstered by narratives of white settler larrikinism, the 'siege mentality' of tropical settler colonialism and legitimising tropes of the 'the infectiousness of savagery'.[40] In the case of both Pacific Islander and Indigenous people, the substantive and experiential resonances of their historical labour conditions with slavery are articulated within contemporary self-understandings; further, they are affirmed by the kinds of labour that many continue to perform and the material and cultural conditions within which they work.[41]

Nevertheless, neither Indigenous nor Pacific Islander people have ever been simply passive recipients of colonial action. As Reynolds demonstrated close to 40 years ago, and as others have similarly shown, Aboriginal and Torres Strait Islander people were active agents in relationships with white settlers. White colonists undoubtedly did enact violence, force and punitive measures in the exploration and settlement of Australia. There were limits, though, to how much labour could be coerced. Many Aboriginal people in the period up until World War I worked intermittently, combining casual work with traditional food gathering, hunting and livelihood activities—an agentive combining of modern and traditional economies and ways of life that precedes and, in many ways, parallels the 'hybrid economies' that Altman describes in contemporary northern Australia.[42] Many Aboriginal and Torres Strait Islander people enacted agency in their roles as guides and intermediaries in the process of exploration,[43] as did Pacific Islanders who voluntarily recruited for periods of indentured labour, some choosing to sign on again when their initial periods of indenture were concluded.[44] Many Indigenous people continued to understand travel within their own epistemological frameworks, even if it was also shaped by colonialism, a point made by the contributors to Rachel Standfield's edited collection *Indigenous Mobilities: Across and Beyond the Antipodes*.[45] In their chapter in this volume, Standfield and Michael J. Stevens likewise draw attention

40 Banivanua Mar, *Violence and Colonial Dialogue*, 9, 37.
41 Curthoys and Moore, 'Working for the White People'; see also Stead, this volume.
42 Reynolds, *With the White People*; Altman, 'What Future for Remote Indigenous Australia?'.
43 Konishi, Nugent and Shellam, *Indigenous Intermediaries*; Shellam, Nugent, Konishi and Cadzow, *Brokers and Boundaries*.
44 Moore, *Kanaka*; Scarr, 'Recruits and Recruiters'; Shlomowitz, 'Markets for Indentured'; Shlomowitz, 'Time Expired Melanesian Labor in Queensland'.
45 Standfield, *Indigenous Mobilities*.

to the rich worldviews, social structures and epistemologies of movement that have long animated the travels of Kāi Tahu Māori, including to Australia. Kāi Tahu mobility, they argue, was and remains deeply informed by these cultures of movement, even as it has also involved forms of strategic response to historical circumstances and conditions of power and racialised inequality. Ruth (Lute) Faleolo similarly foregrounds Pasifika cultures and patterns of meaning in her exploration of the labour migration experiences of contemporary Tongan and Samoan trans-Tasman migrants. Highlighting holistic Pasifika concepts of 'a good and happy life'[46]—*moʻui ʻoku lelei* in Tongan and *ola manuia* in Samoan—Faleolo maps the complex ways in which Pacific labour migrants negotiate both the possibilities for betterment, and forms of racialised and regulatory obstacles, that their migrations entail.

Faleolo's attention to Pasifika migrating to Australia from New Zealand also highlights the particular place and role of New Zealand in Pacific Islanders' labour mobility experiences, including as a triangulating node in circuits that connect New Zealand, Australia and the Pacific Islands. For many of Faleolo's informants, as for the Kāi Tahu Māori who Standfield and Stevens discuss, the special migration relationship between New Zealand and Australia offers some reprieve from the regulatory regimes otherwise enacted at the border for Pacific Islanders seeking access to Australia. Stevens has also, elsewhere, demonstrated the ways in which Kāi Tahu Māori have pursued work within Australian maritime industries, both as an expression of Kāi Tahu lifeways and as an escape from their own dispossession by white settler society in Aotearoa/New Zealand.[47] Nevertheless, in each case, trans-Tasman migrants encountered other forms of racialised constraint that pushed back against their pursuit of wellbeing, *mana* (authority) and livelihood.

Rather than fall into unhelpful bifurcations of choice and coercion, freedom and force, the scholars in this volume—and the scholars on whose work this volume builds—insist on the possibility (indeed, the necessity) of recognising creativity, strategic decision-making and political resistance in ways that do not minimise the sharp edges of colonial power against which such expressions of agency were, and are, enacted.[48]

---

46 Faleolo, 'Pasifika Trans-Tasman Migrant Perspectives'.
47 Stevens, 'Māori History as Maritime History'.
48 Banivanua Mar, *Decolonisation and the Pacific*; Konishi, Nugent and Shellam, *Indigenous Intermediaries*; Carey and Lydon, *Indigenous Networks*; De Costa, *A Higher Authority*; Standfield, *Indigenous Mobilities*.

As Tracey Banivanua Mar puts it in her chapter in this volume, writing about the Ni-Vanuatu men and boys who found themselves transported to the colony of New South Wales in 1847: 'As active agents within a new world of differentially racialised opportunity and constraint, they created "labour lines", interweaving fates and creating entangled relationships of contingency that manifested new Oceanias.'

Outline of the Book

The interplay of force and agency emerges strongly in Chapter 2, Shino Konishi's 'Intermediaries, Servants and Captives: Disentangling Indigenous Labour in D. W. Carnegie's Exploration of Australia'. The history and contribution of Aboriginal guides to the exploration of Australia has long been recognised and even celebrated, Konishi observes, from the gifting of king plates to the erecting of memorials. Yet, the labour that Aboriginal people provided was more diverse than the iconic imagery of guides such as Wylie leading a lone explorer suggests. Approaching the colonial exploration of the Australian continent and its waters as a 'mobile enterprise', Konishi charts the 1896 expedition of D. W. Carnegie through the Gibson and Great Sandy deserts, drawing attention to the imaginings of both the explorers and Indigenous people involved. The use of colonised labour, she argues, was 'riddled with contradictions', both desired and derided. Konishi shows that Aboriginal labour and economy were not recognised by Carnegie and his men as work, with offers of reciprocal exchange and trade by some of those that they encountered in their exploration rejected in favour of more ruthless and coercive tactics, including the kidnapping of Aboriginal people to act as guides or to find water. Rather than see this behaviour as the result of desperation on the part of the colonial explorers (unfortunate but perhaps understandable actions by parched men in an inhospitable terrain), Konishi insists that we recognise it as flowing from particular forms of practice and understanding within which the patriarchal control of indentured and Aboriginal labour was part of the formation of settler masculinity.

In Chapter 3, Tracey Banivanua Mar attends to the intersections of coloniality in the Pacific and the dynamics of settler colonialism that Konishi's chapter articulates. In '"Boyd's Blacks": Labour and the Making of Settler Lands in Australia and the Pacific', Banivanua Mar explores the experiences and political agency of Ni-Vanuatu men and boys 'recruited' to New South Wales by the pastoralist Benjamin Boyd in 1847. Her analysis, and the history of Australian pastoralism, urge attention to the interconnections of land, labour and commerce within the settler colony and the wider region. Boyd's importation of Pacific Islander labour to work on his pastoral empire is generally remembered, if it is remembered at all, as a failed precursor to the Pacific labour trade that commenced two decades later. Reading through the gaps and biases of the colonial archives, Banivanua Mar attempts to reassemble the lived experiences of Ni-Vanuatu men and boys, including a group who absconded shortly after their arrival on Boyd's Riverina station and marched towards the port cities of Sydney and Melbourne. In doing so, she explores what their experiences tell us about the lines of labour that connected colonists across Australia and the Pacific Islands, suggesting that their stories demand a reconfiguration of the way we have come to understand the history of this relationship and, in particular, the scale and spectrum on which we have historically understood the Australian indentured labour trade.

The gendered dimensions of labour mobility, touched on in Konishi's discussion of settler masculinity, emerge again in Chapter 4 with Lucy Davies' examination of Papuan and New Guinean female domestic workers travelling to Australia in the mid-twentieth century. Arguing for the inclusion of Papuan and New Guinean servants within the broader historiography of Indigenous domestic labour, Davies maps the ambivalent effects of both regulation and affect. Not unlike Pacific Islanders involved in the early years of the Pacific labour trade, Papuan and New Guinean domestics travelled to Australia as indentured workers, were monitored closely during their time in the country and were expelled at the conclusion of their contracts. Regulatory processes associated with these labour migrations involved little consultation with the women themselves or with applications submitted by their employers, and few avenues were afforded them to exercise autonomy, express dissent and improve their working lives. Colonial descriptions of domestic servants as 'companions', of their wages as 'pocket money' and of their white employers as being akin to 'family', speak to particularly gendered ways through which Pacific women's labours were diminished and controlled, and to the ambiguous entwining of intimacy and colonial power.

In Chapter 5, 'New Histories but Old Patterns: Kāi Tahu in Australia', Rachel Standfield and Michael J. Stevens turn their attention to the relationships between historical and contemporary patterns of migration by Kāi Tahu Māori from Te Waipounamu on New Zealand's South Island.

Māori travel to the Australian continent began early in its European invasion, and has played an important role in migration to Australia throughout its colonial history, including a dramatic increase since the 1960s. Standfield and Stevens, who is Kāi Tahu, focus on the initial travel of Kāi Tahu people to Australia during the early to mid-nineteenth century to explore the ways that travel reflects Kāi Tahu worldviews, social structures and economic priorities. Asserting the centrality of mobility as foundational to Kāi Tahu identity—and also as something reconfigured through the experience of settler colonialism—they show how Kāi Tahu *rakatira* (chiefs) used mobility, the labour of their communities, and *iwi* (tribal) resources and trade goods to shape tribal wealth and bolster *mana*. This consolidated the Kāi Tahu position in terms of other tribal communities and influenced trade and other negotiations with the nascent state in early colonial New Zealand. Arguing for a *whakapapa* (genealogy)-based methodology, Standfield and Stevens seek to produce histories that speak to the concerns and desires of contemporary Kāi Tahu people, many of whom regularly visit or live permanently in Australia.

Shifts and continuities between past and present labour migrations remain a theme in Victoria Stead's chapter, 'Money Trees, Development Dreams and Colonial Legacies in Pasifika Horticultural Labour'. Stead considers the experiences of a group of Ni-Vanuatu workers employed through the Seasonal Worker Programme in the Shepparton horticultural industry, locating these in relation to the nineteenth-century 'blackbirding' of Ni-Vanuatu workers to the sugar plantations of north-eastern Australia, to consider the historical trajectories and complex ecologies of Australian coloniality in relation to the Pacific. Discourses about contemporary Pacific Islander seasonal labour in the horticultural industry frequently invoke a language of 'slavery', making direct connections to the exploitative, racialised and hierarchical labour relations that characterised the Pacific labour trade. At the same time, SWP labour is also actively and enthusiastically sought out by many Pacific workers, including as a pathway to 'development'. Mapping the messy convergences of development dreams and colonial legacies in the horticultural landscapes of north-central Victoria, Stead challenges the bifurcations of 'slavery' and 'freedom' within liberal thought as well as within much academic and popular commentary on Pacific Islander labour. This chapter suggests instead that we attend to the ambivalences of Pacific labour experiences, locating these in the context of long-running, known and felt histories of racialised inequalities.

A little further north-west from Shepparton, in Mildura and Robinvale, Makiko Nishitani and Helen Lee also examine the experiences of Pacific horticultural workers in Chapter 7, 'Becoming "Overstayers": The Coloniality of Citizenship and the Resilience of Pacific Farm Workers'. Nishitani and Lee's focus is on Pacific irregular migrants who work, often over many years, without work permits. The migrations of Pacific Islanders to rural Australia to work as seasonal labourers began in the 1980s, often motivated by the relative lack of surveillance of the industry.[49] Pacific irregular migrants include those who overstay their visas, work while on visitor visas that formally prohibit employment and abscond from the SWP. Examining the perspectives and experiences of Pacific irregular migrants themselves, both past and present, and the government's shifting responses to illegal workers, they draw attention to the ways in which different categorisations and conditions of legality and illegality are constructed. In spite of increases in surveillance and enforcement, many of Nishitani and Lee's informants continue to assess participation in the legalised SWP as posing greater risks of exploitation than the prospect of overstaying their visas and working irregularly.

In Chapter 8, Ruth (Lute) Faleolo focuses on the particular experience of Pasifika peoples migrating from New Zealand to Brisbane, Australia, in 'Wellbeing Perspectives, Conceptualisations of Work and Labour Mobility Experiences of Pasifika Trans-Tasman Migrants in Brisbane'. Drawing on interviews with Samoan and Tongan Pasifika and, as with Standfield and Steven's chapter, utilising indigenous methodology in her research, Faleolo highlights the significance of holistic Pasifika concepts of wellbeing—the Tongan concept of *mo'ui 'oku lelei* and the Samoan concept of *ola manuia*, translated as 'a good and happy life'—in motivating and informing the experience of trans-Tasman migrants. In contrast to the paternalistic developmentalism evident in the SWP, which are also evident in Konishi's considerations of colonial labour relations, Faleolo posits indigenous Pasifika developmentalist discourses within which labour mobility is an opportunity for progressive betterment, reflected in the importance accorded to achieving home ownership. Faleolo offers a gentle pushback against the notion of 'labour mobility', instead positing labour as one aspect of a multidimensional conceptualisation of mobility and its promises.

---

49   Nishitani and Lee, 'Invisible Islanders?'.

Urban Pasifika experiences of labour mobility are also the focus of Scott Mackay and Daniel Guinness's contribution, 'Coloniality of Power and the Contours of Contemporary Sport Industries: Fijians in Australian Rugby'. In contrast to many forms of Pacific labour mobility, which are oriented towards low-paying, so-called 'unskilled' labour, professional rugby offers the promise (if rarely the reality) of life-changing wealth and prestige. Individual and collective mobility aspirations, Mackay and Guinness argue, are intertwined with understandings and histories of what it is to be Fijian in a postcolonial nation and global world, and are highly influenced by gender and ethnicity. Mapping the 'economies of hope' that motivate young *itaukei* (indigenous Fijian) men to travel to Australia in pursuit of rugby dreams, Mackay and Guinness also chart the disappointments of those who do not secure professional contracts but rather find themselves confined to the margins of the Australian labour market, working as seasonal workers, manual labourers or religious workers as they also play for amateur or semi-professional rugby clubs. Their experiences highlight the intertwining of Australian and Fijian migration regimes, labour markets and social worlds, exposing the labour lines that must be traversed, and the contours of the global and domestic labour markets and economies of hope.

Chapter 10 takes us back to Australian Indigenous experiences, with Sarah Prout Quicke and Fiona Haslam McKenzie's study of Indigenous engagement in the resources sector through FIFO employment arrangements with a global mining firm. As with professional rugby contracts, FIFO labour promises big incomes. It is a form of labour mobility very much reflective of contemporary global neoliberal and neo-colonial market systems, although in other respects FIFO labour experiences are consistent with longer-running trends. In centring the localised experiences of Indigenous peoples in their narrative, Prout Quicke and Haslam McKenzie illuminate the scaled effects on Indigenous mobilities and lifeworlds of articulation into the operational spheres of transnational institutions. Key themes emergent in their discussion include the performance and transformation of kinship structures and customary economic practices in the context of market-based labour mobility. In this highly regulated, highly paid and highly formalised work environment, Indigenous workers negotiate complex calculations of benefits and cost, including long shifts in male-dominated, remote and arid environments, regular cycles of separation and reunion with family, disruptions to rhythms and routines, increased demands related to increased salary, and new forms of volatility and precarity.

In Chapter 11, Timothy Neale likewise attends to contemporary, neoliberal imaginings of labour mobility in 'Mysterious Motions: A Genealogy of "Orbiting" in Australian Indigenous Affairs'. Advocated by the Indigenous public intellectual Noel Pearson, the notion of 'orbiting' envisions circuits of movement through which remote-living Indigenous people could and should 'orbit' between urban 'real job' markets and their remote homes.[50] Neale argues that the origins, logics and effects of orbiting, which has been described as enabling the 'best of both worlds' for Indigenous people and has been positively received by policymakers, nevertheless remains mysterious. Locating the concept in relation to more critical analyses of diaspora and exile that have emerged in post-2000s Indigenous Australia,[51] Neale presents a genealogy of orbiting that tracks the shifting imaginaries of work, labour and governance informing Indigenous policy prior to, and now beyond, the ostensible end of self-determination.

Finally, in Chapter 12, Jon Altman extends the concern with new forms of Indigenous mobility considered by Neale, Prout Quicke and Haslam McKenzie, and in the contexts of Pacific workers by Stead, and Nishitani and Lee, in turning his attention to the forms of 'bureaucratic violence' enacted against those Indigenous people who resist neoliberal calls to move for employment. In 'Of Pizza Ovens in Arnhem Land: The State Quest to Restructure Aboriginal Labour in Remotest Australia', Altman focuses on those Indigenous Australians who have regained title to their ancestral lands. Subsequently, they wish to live at homelands and secure a livelihood that re-engages with pre-colonial forms that are fundamentally at odds with absent mainstream employment. Using his long-term field work at Mumeka in west Arnhem Land as an exemplar, he illustrates how, in the recent past, truly bizarre forms of enterprise, like pizza ovens, chicken coops and market gardens, have been underwritten by the recolonising state and a coopted regional Indigenous organisation to implement regimes to govern and produce acceptable Indigenous subjects. He highlights the emergence of the Australian Government's CDP as a form of bureaucratic violence that is predicated on an imagined incorporation of Indigenous labour into forms of capitalist enterprise that have never emerged in west Arnhem Land since colonisation 60 years ago. Altman's analysis points to labour regimes of coercion and punishment, regimes that are of the contemporary moment, but which

---

50   See also Neale, *Wild Articulations.*
51   Burke, 'Indigenous Diaspora'; Hinkson, 'Precarious Placemaking'.

resonate in powerful ways with the histories mapped through previous chapters. This concluding chapter bookends Konishi's opening, which argues that Aboriginal labour and economy were not recognised by nineteenth-century explorers like Carnegie as work. Altman laments the contemporary situation that replicates such myopia and that has seen the destruction of emerging and productive forms of plural economy. State projects promise capitalist improvement and the closing of employment gaps, but tragically fail to deliver anything for most staying at home except growing impoverishment and enhanced welfare dependence.

The interdisciplinarity reflected in this bookending, and throughout the volume, is highlighted in Lynette Russell's Afterword. 'Good and meaningful' history, she reminds us, requires such interdisciplinarity. Situating this project in the context of a transforming university sector as well as in relation to its scholarly antecedents, Russell's comments reiterate the value of comparative and collective inquiry, highlighting what is possible when an exchange among scholars becomes 'more than the sum of its parts'.

Bibliography

Altman, Jon. 'Modern Slavery in Remote Australia?'. *Arena Magazine*, no. 150 (Oct 2017): 12–15.

———. 'What Future for Remote Indigenous Australia? Economic Hybridity and the Neoliberal Turn'. In *Culture Crisis: Anthropology and Politics in Aboriginal Australia*, edited by Jon Altman and Melinda Hinkson, 259–80. Sydney: UNSW Press, 2010.

Altman, Jon and Melinda Hinkson, eds. *Culture Crisis: Anthropology and Politics in Aboriginal Australia*. Sydney: UNSW Press, 2010.

Anderson, Bridget. 'Migration, Immigration Controls and the Fashioning of Precarious Workers'. *Work, Employment & Society* 24, no. 2 (2010): 300–17. doi.org/10.1177/0950017010362141.

Banivanua Mar, Tracey. *Decolonisation and the Pacific: Indigenous Globalisation and the Ends of Empire*. Cambridge: Cambridge University Press, 2016.

———. *Violence and Colonial Dialogue: The Australian-Pacific Indentured Labor Trade*. Honolulu: University of Hawai'i Press, 2007.

Burke, Paul. 'Indigenous Diaspora and the Prospects for Cosmopolitan "Orbiting": The Warlpiri Case'. *The Asia Pacific Journal of Anthropology* 14, no. 4 (2013): 304–22. doi.org/10.1080/14442213.2013.804870.

Carey, Jane and Jane Lydon, eds. *Indigenous Networks: Mobility, Connections and Exchange*. London: Routledge, 2014. doi.org/10.4324/9781315766065.

Curthoys, Ann and Clive Moore. 'Working for the White People: An Historiographic Essay on Aboriginal and Torres Strait Islander Labour'. *Labour History* 69 (1995): 1–29. doi.org/10.2307/27516388.

Davidson, Julia O'Connell. 'Troubling Freedom: Migration, Debt, and Modern Slavery'. *Migration Studies* 1, no. 2 (2013): 176–95. doi.org/10.1093/migration/mns002.

De Costa, Ravindra Noel John. *A Higher Authority: Indigenous Transnationalism and Australia*. Sydney: UNSW Press, 2006.

Evans, Raymond. '"Kings" in Brass Crescents: Defining Aboriginal Labour Patterns in Colonial Queensland'. In *Indentured Labour in the British Empire, 1834–1920*, edited by Kay Saunders, 183–212. London: Croom Helm, 1984.

——. *'A Permanent Precedent': Dispossession, Social Control and the Fraser Island Reserve and Mission, 1897–1904*. St Lucia: University of Queensland Aboriginal and Torres Strait Islanders Unit, 1991.

Evans, Raymond, Kay Saunders and Kathryn Cronin. *Race Relations in Colonial Queensland: A History of Exclusion, Exploitation and Extermination*. St Lucia: University of Queensland Press, 1988.

Faleolo, Ruth (Lute). 'Pasifika Trans-Tasman Migrant Perspectives of Well-Being in Australia and New Zealand'. *Pacific Asia Inquiry* 7, no. 1 (2016): 63–74.

Fijn, Natasha, Ian Keen, Christopher Lloyd and Michael Pickering, eds. *Indigenous Participation in Australian Economies II: Historical Engagements and Current Enterprises*. Canberra: ANU E Press, 2012. doi.org/10.22459/IPAE.07.2012.

Forrest, Andrew. 'The Forrest Review: Creating Parity'. Canberra: Commonwealth of Australia, 2014.

Grainger, Andrew. 'From Immigrant to Overstayer: Samoan Identity, Rugby, and Cultural Politics of Race and Nation in Aotearoa/New Zealand'. *Journal of Sport and Social Issues* 30, no. 1 (2006): 45–61. doi.org/10.1177/0193723505284277.

Hammond, Jeremy, and John Connell. 'The New Blackbirds? Vanuatu Guestworkers in New Zealand'. *New Zealand Geographer* 65, no. 3 (2009): 201–10. doi.org/10.1111/j.1745-7939.2009.01163.x.

Hauʻofa, Epeli. 'Our Sea of Islands'. *The Contemporary Pacific* 6, no. 1 (2004): 147–61.

Hinkson, Melinda. 'Precarious Placemaking'. *Annual Review of Anthropology* 46 (2017): 49–64. doi.org/10.1146/annurev-anthro-102116-041624.

Konishi, Shino. 'Idle Men: the Eighteenth-Century Roots of the Indigenous Indolence Myth'. In *Passionate Histories: Myth, Memory & Indigenous Australia,* edited by Frances Peters-Little, Ann Curthoys and John Docker, 99–122. Canberra: ANU E Press, 2010. doi.org/10.22459/PH.09.2010.05.

Konishi, Shino and Leah Lui-Chivizhe. 'Working for the Railways: Torres Strait Islander Labour and Mobility in the 1960s'. *Journal of Australian Studies* 38, no. 4 (2014): 445–56. doi.org/10.1080/14443058.2014.952766.

Konishi, Shino, Maria Nugent and Tiffany Shellam, eds. *Indigenous Intermediaries: New Perspectives on Exploration Archives.* Canberra: ANU Press and Aboriginal History, 2015. doi.org/10.22459/II.09.2015.

Lan, Pei-Cha. 'Legal Servitude and Free Illegality: Migrant "Guest Workers" in Taiwan'. In *Asian Diasporas: New Conceptions, New Frameworks,* edited by Rhacel S. Parreñas and Lok C. D. Siu, 253–77. Stanford: Stanford University Press, 2007.

Loomis, Terrence. *Pacific Migrant Labour, Class and Racism in New Zealand: Fresh off the Boat.* Aldershot: Avebury, 1990.

Losurdo, Domenico. *Liberalism: A Counter-History.* London: Verso, 2011.

MacDermott, Therese and Brian Opeskin. 'Regulating Pacific Seasonal Labour in Australia'. *Pacific Affairs* 83, no. 2 (2010): 283–305. doi.org/10.5509/2010832283.

Maclellan, Nic and Peter Mares. 'Remittances and Labour Mobility in the Pacific: A Working Paper on Seasonal Work Programs in Australia for Pacific Islanders'. Working Paper, Institute for Social Research, Swinburne University of Technology, 2006.

Macpherson, Cluny, Paul Spoonley and Melani Anae, eds. *Tangata o te Moana Nui: The Evolving Identities of Pacific Peoples in Aotearoa/New Zealand.* Palmerston North: Dunmore Press, 2001.

Mahdavi, Pardis. *Gridlock: Labor, Migration and Human Trafficking in Dubai.* Stanford: Stanford University Press, 2011.

Mares, Peter and Nic Maclellan. 'Pacific Seasonal Workers for Australian Horticulture: A Neat Fit?'. *Asian and Pacific Migration Journal* 16, no. 2 (2007): 271–88. doi.org/10.1177/011719680701600207.

Martínez, Julia and Adrian Vickers. *The Pearl Frontier: Indonesian Labour and Indigenous Encounters in Australia's Northern Trading Network.* Honolulu: University of Hawai'i Press, 2015. doi.org/10.21313/hawaii/9780824840020.001.0001.

Mignolo, Walter D. and Arturo Escobar, eds. *Globalization and the Decolonial Option.* Oxon: Routledge, 2010.

Moore, Clive. *Kanaka: A History of Melanesian Mackay.* Port Moresby: University of Papua New Guinea Press, 1985.

Neale, Timothy. *Wild Articulations: Environmentalism and Indigeneity in Northern Australia.* Honolulu: University of Hawai'i Press, 2017. doi.org/10.21313/hawaii/9780824873110.001.0001.

Nishitani, Makiko and Helen Lee. 'Invisible Islanders? Precarious Work and Pacific Islander Settlers in Rural Australia'. *Pacific Studies* 40, no. 3 (2017): 430–49.

Pearson, Noel. 'The Cape York Partnership Plan'. Brisbane: The Brisbane Institute, 2000.

———. 'Radical Hope: Education and Equality in Australia'. *Quarterly Essay* 35 (2009).

———. *Up from the Mission: Selected Writings.* Melbourne: Black Inc., 2011.

Quijano, Aníbal. 'Coloniality and Modernity/Rationality'. *Cultural Studies* 21, no. 2–3 (2007): 168–78. doi.org/10.1080/09502380601164353.

———. 'Coloniality of Power, Ethnocentrism, and Latin America'. *Nepantla* 1, no. 3 (2000): 533–80.

Reynolds, Henry. *With the White People: The Crucial Role of Aborigines in the Exploration and Development of Australia.* Ringwood: Penguin, 1990.

Scarr, Deryck. 'Recruits and Recruiters: A Portrait of the Pacific Islands Labour Trade'. *The Journal of Pacific History* 2, no. 1 (1967): 5–24. doi.org/10.1080/00223346708572099.

Sharp, Ian and Colin Tatz, eds. *Aborigines in the Economy*. Brisbane: Jacaranda Press, 1966.

Shellam, Tiffany, Maria Nugent, Shino Konishi and Allison Cadzow, eds. *Brokers and Boundaries: Colonial Exploration in Indigenous Territory*. Canberra: ANU Press and Aboriginal History, 2016. doi.org/10.22459/BB.04.2016.

Shlomowitz, Ralph. 'Markets for Indentured and Time-Expired Melanesian Labour in Queensland, 1863–1906: An Economic Analysis'. *The Journal of Pacific History* 16, no. 2 (1981): 70–91. doi.org/10.1080/00223348108572416.

———. 'Time-Expired Melanesian Labor in Queensland: An Investigation of Job Turnover, 1884–1906'. *Pacific Studies* 8, no. 2 (1985): 25–44.

Standfield, Rachel, ed. *Indigenous Mobilities: Across and Beyond the Antipodes*. Canberra: ANU Press and Aboriginal History, 2018. doi.org/10.22459/IM.06.2018.

Stead, Victoria. *Becoming Landowners: Entanglements of Custom and Modernity in Papua New Guinea and Timor-Leste* Honolulu: University of Hawai'i Press, 2017.

———. 'Doing "Social Cohesion": Cultural Policy and Practice in Outer Metropolitan Melbourne'. *Critical Social Policy* 37, no. 3 (2017): 405–24. doi.org/10.1177/0261018316681283.

———. 'Mobility and Emplacement in North Coast Papua New Guinea: Worlding the Pacific Marine Industrial Zone'. *The Australian Journal of Anthropology* 27, no. 1 (2016): 30–48. doi.org/10.1111/taja.12174.

———. 'The Price of Fish: Problematising Discourses of Prosperity at the Pacific Marine Industrial Zone'. In *Securing a Prosperous Future: Papers from the Second Annual Alfred Deakin Research Institute Papua New Guinea Symposium, 2012*, edited by Jonathan Ritchie and Michelle Verso, 197–230. Goolwa: Crawford House Publishing, 2014.

Stevens, Michael J., 'Māori History as Maritime History: A View from The Bluff'. In *New Zealand and the Sea: Historical Perspectives,* edited by Frances Steel, 156–80. Wellington: Bridget Williams Books, 2018. doi.org/10.7810/9780947518707_8.

Taylor, John and Martin Bell, eds. *Population Mobility and Indigenous Peoples in Australasia and North America*. London: Routledge, 2004.

Teaiwa, Teresia and Sean Mallon. 'Ambivalent Kinships? Pacific People in New Zealand'. In New Zealand Identities: Departures and Destinations, edited by James H. Liu, Tim McCreanor, Tracey McIntosh and Teresia Teaiwa, 207–29. Wellington: Victoria University Press, 2005.

Wilson, Rob and Christopher Leigh Connery, eds. The Worlding Project: Doing Cultural Studies in the Era of Globalization. Santa Cruz: New Pacific Press, 2007.

Wolfe, Patrick. Traces of History: Elementary Structures of Race. London: Verso, 2016. doi.org/10.1111/1468-229X.12265.

Newspapers

The Guardian
Northern Territory News

2

Intermediaries, Servants and Captives: Disentangling Indigenous Labour in D. W. Carnegie's Exploration of the Western Australian Desert

Shino Konishi[1]

In the late fifteenth century, Christopher Columbus kidnapped Caribbean people to train and use them as translators who could inform him about potential dangers and desirable commodities. The Dutch East India Company in the early seventeenth century instructed their captains to capture Indigenous peoples whenever possible for the same purpose. Then, in the late eighteenth century maritime explorers like James Cook and Matthew Flinders, on occasion, kidnapped Islander and Aboriginal people in the Pacific and Australia as punishment for perceived thefts, and as a means of asserting their authority over seemingly recalcitrant native peoples.[2] Thus, for centuries European explorers felt at liberty to

1   Acknowledgements: I would like to thank the editors and participants in the Labour Lines Workshop at Deakin University, as well as Ethan Blue, Ann Curthoys, Ned Curthoys, Nicola Froggatt, Andrea Gaynor, Tony Hughes-d'Aeth, Dylan Lino, Jeremy Martens and Tiffany Shellam for feedback on earlier drafts of this paper. This work was supported by the Australian Research Council Grant DP110100931.
2   Konishi, *Aboriginal Male in the Enlightenment World*, 116–17, 97.

capture Indigenous individuals as a strategy for discovering information about local environments and polities, as well as for enforcing discipline and control.

However, this practice changed in the nineteenth century with the rise of international humanitarian networks and a successful abolitionist campaign that saw both the official condemnation of slavery in the British Empire and a new rhetoric of protection. Exploration was increasingly considered as a more noble and scientific pursuit, as evident in the establishment of the Royal Geographical Society (RGS) in 1830, which 'began as a club for travellers and explorers, supported by gentleman, and [was] made intellectually respectable by scientists'.[3] With these changing aims, explorers, now largely overland as opposed to maritime, began to recruit and enlist Indigenous intermediaries to guide them on their expeditions, provide important intelligence about finding necessary resources and mediate with Indigenous groups encountered along the way.[4] Despite this evolution in political ethos and exploration practices, by the end of the century a young British overland explorer revived the use of kidnapping, finding a new purpose for this now reviled practice as he journeyed through the Western Australian desert.

In 1896, the young adventurer David Wynford Carnegie led a privately funded expedition from Coolgardie to Halls Creek and back through the Gibson and the Great Sandy deserts. While Robert Austin (1854), John Forrest (1869 and, with his brother, Alexander Forrest, in 1870 and 1874), Peter Egerton Warburton (1872–74) and Ernest Giles (1873, 1873–74, 1875 and 1876) had all explored Western Australian deserts before him, Carnegie was the first to traverse the desert from south to north and back again. He also travelled further through the desert than any of his predecessors. However, now he is best remembered for kidnapping Aboriginal people as a means of finding water, an extreme practice that none of his predecessors had undertaken.[5] In his study of

---

3   Stoddart, 'The RGS and the "New Geography"', 192.

4   See, for example, Burnett, '"It is Impossible to Make a Step without the Indians"', 3–40; Driver and Jones, *Hidden Histories of Exploration*; Fritsch, '"You Have Everything Confused and Mixed Up"', 87–101; Konishi, Nugent and Shellam, *Indigenous Intermediaries*; Shellam, Nugent, Konishi and Cadzow, *Brokers and Boundaries*.

5   John Forrest later reported that during his expedition he 'found the natives of very little use to him', and that he 'had always with him civilized natives of a high standard of intelligence, who were equally as well versed in the habits and ways of the bush natives as they were in the habits and customs of white men'. 'The Canning Enquiry: Royal Commission's Report', *Kalgoorlie Western Argus*, 25 February 1908, 34.

explorers and Aboriginal guides, Henry Reynolds explained that, 'when prospects became grim', Carnegie resorted to capturing an Aboriginal man and woman—the former being first 'run down and subjected to prolonged thirst'—so that they could lead him to water.[6] Dane Kennedy also discussed Carnegie, who 'repeatedly rode down Aborigines, chained or tied them up, and denied them food and drink until they had guided his party to water', and similarly concluded that to 'kidnap an indigene was an act of desperation'.[7]

Though critical, both Reynolds and Kennedy nonetheless rationalised Carnegie's use of kidnap, suggesting that it was dire emergency that drove him to hold Indigenous people captive. Yet, as David Goodman asserts in regard to gold rush history, historians should not naturalise or unquestioningly take for granted certain behaviours and trajectories such as the so-called 'acquisitive instinct that led so many to rush after gold'. Instead, they should investigate the 'particular way of thinking' that underpinned such actions.[8] Rather than rationalise Carnegie's kidnapping of Indigenous people as exceptional—that is, as 'act[s] of desperation'— we should seek to understand both the particular circumstances and the broader colonial mentality about Aboriginal people and labour that led Carnegie to take what seems like an extreme course of action, both to us today and also to other explorers in the nineteenth century.[9]

This chapter seeks to investigate the 'particular way of thinking' that led Carnegie to use kidnap and captivity to coerce Aboriginal people into finding water for his expedition. Rather than focusing on the singular event, I examine Carnegie's earlier forays prospecting in the Western Australian goldfields and his developing views about Aboriginal people

---

6   Reynolds, 'The Land, the Explorers and the Aborigines', 222.

7   Kennedy, *The Last Blank Spaces*, 165.

8   Goodman argues that historians, unquestioning acceptance of the gold rush mentality is even more problematic because 'many contemporaries were indeed alarmed at the rushing after wealth at the expense of all that made it meaningful—family, community, social order'. Goodman, 'The Gold Rushes of the 1850s', 173.

9   Morison argues that he was 'subsequently criticised severely' for 'captur[ing] Aboriginals'. Morison, 'Carnegie, David Wynford (1871–1900)'. When the Western Australian Department of Lands and Surveys surveyor Alfred Canning used the same strategy in 1906, it sparked the *Royal Commission to Enquire into the Treatment of Aboriginal Natives by the Canning Exploration Party* (1908), which discussed Carnegie's example at length. Although the enquiry found that the 'capturing and chaining of natives under any circumstances is undoubtedly unlawful', they eventually decided that it was 'absolutely necessary' to ensure their survival, especially following the Calvert expedition in which two men perished. 'The Canning Enquiry: Royal Commission's Report', *Kalgoorlie Miner*, 22 February 1908, 8.

and their potential as a labour source. I argue that Carnegie's approach was not just a survival strategy, but also reflected changing colonial ideas about Indigenous labour and the coercive measures that were believed necessary to harness it in Western Australia. Moreover, this chapter considers how the justification for such coercive carceral strategies were exacerbated by the mobile exigencies of exploration. Given that Carnegie moved through Aboriginal country rather than settling in a particular place, his encounters with Indigenous individuals were short-lived. Thus, Indigenous people remained alien and unfamiliar to him, which arguably encouraged his callous attitude towards both them and their precious water.

Indigenous Labour in Colonial Western Australia

Since the 1970s, historians have observed that Aboriginal labour was integral to the development of Western Australia's colonial economy, due to its immense size, sparse population, challenging environmental conditions and the limited availability of convict labour. Convict transportation to the colony did not begin until 1850, and the employment of both convicts and ex-convicts was 'banned north of the Murchison River', which meant that the northern industries—pearling and pastoralism—were dependent on Aboriginal labour in the nineteenth century.[10] As John Host and Jill Milroy among others have observed, another crucial factor in relation to this dependence was the 'colonial mindset that saw the exploitation of Aboriginal labour for little or no reward as a perfectly acceptable practice'.[11] The northern Indigenous labour force was not only largely unpaid, but also largely unfree.

Within capitalist economies, unfree labour refers to labour provided by workers who are 'separated from the means of production and subsistence' and unable to freely 'commodify their labour' for wages. Unfree labour includes categories of slavery, in which workers themselves become commodities to be bought (i.e. not just their labour), and forced or coerced labour, in which the 'labour relationship is either entered into

---

10   Host and Milroy, 'Towards an Aboriginal Labour History', 10.
11   Host and Milroy, 'Towards an Aboriginal Labour History', 10.

under duress' or is 'entered into freely but then becomes coercive'.[12] Sean Winter explains that coerced labour is 'a very specific form of exploitation where workers are controlled within institutional and legal structures that limit their freedom and their labour is extracted through threats of negative sanction'. He adds that the coercion can be 'economic, mental, emotional, social and physical' in nature, but that, 'crucially, the worker is not free to withdraw their labour if they wish'.[13]

The most obvious use of coerced labour in Western Australia was in the early pearling industry that began in the Pilbara in 1867 and was widely known for 'blackbirding', or kidnapping, Aboriginal people from across the north who were then 'alienated from their home country and forced to dive for shell'. Not only was this life-threatening work, with many suffering from the 'bends' or shark attack, but also Aboriginal divers faced being marooned on island camps to prevent them returning to their homelands so that they could be put to work the next season.[14] The terrible abuse suffered by Aboriginal divers was widely known and, in the 1870s, Governor Frederick Weld 'passed a series of Acts ... prohibiting kidnapping ... and the employment of women'. In 1880, a more stringent Act was passed regulating the age of divers and their conditions, and 'requiring they be returned home after six months'. Yet, as Ann Curthoys has shown, pearlers reacted strongly against these new regulations, and so the Acts were amended by Weld's successor Governor William Robinson to allow a return to harsher and more exploitative practices. By 1886, between 600 and 700 Aboriginal people were employed in the industry.[15] Further, many pearlers had connections to the emerging pastoral industry, which also depended on unfree Aboriginal labour; between 1881 and 1901, the number of Aboriginal people working on stations increased fivefold to approximately 12,000.[16]

The exploitation of coerced Aboriginal labour was enabled by the frontier violence that drove people off their lands and made them dependent on rations, and by the punitive legislation that criminalised Indigenous resistance to pastoral expansion, including the spearing of livestock and retaliation for settlers' abuse of Aboriginal women, which created a large workforce of Aboriginal prisoners. These prisoners were either

12 Strauss, 'Coerced, Forced, and Unfree Labour', 3–4.
13 Winter, 'Coerced Labour', 3.
14 Winter, 'Coerced Labour', 8.
15 Curthoys, 'Indigenous Dispossession', 218.
16 Host and Milroy, 'Towards an Aboriginal Labour History', 11.

'warehoused' at Rottnest Island where they could no longer disrupt colonial expansion in their homelands[17] or forced to work in chain gangs 'road-making, quarrying stone, protecting river banks, and reclaiming marshy lands', saving the government thousands of pounds in infrastructure costs.[18] Moreover, Aboriginal prisoners were widely forced to wear neck chains, even while locked up in gaol or labouring in the extreme heat. This practice, though censured, was justified by claims such as Western Australian Chief Protector of Aborigines Henry Princep's statement in 1901 that:

> A native is so lithely made that he can get out of a ring fastened with all reasonable tightness round his waist, and that if put around his ankle he can easily get at it with his hands … that it is not effective.[19]

In spite of metropolitan criticisms from London's and Australia's urban centres, which led to various royal commissions and government inquiries, as well as the colonial government's repeated attempts to reform and regulate the employment of Indigenous people, in the late nineteenth century, Aboriginal people in remote parts of Western Australia became increasingly vulnerable to coercive and carceral labour conditions. As Curthoys has shown, this was because of the entwined economic and political interests of pearlers, pastoralists, government agents and the police that sought to dispossess Aboriginal people of their lands and capture and exploit their labour.[20]

Thus, while humanitarian concerns about the protection of Indigenous peoples circulated throughout metropolitan centres, including in scientific societies like the RGS, which sponsored many nineteenth-century expeditions, in remote Western Australia, local conditions fostered a colonial mentality that Aboriginal labour could only be harnessed under duress, and literally with chains. As the former desert explorer and Western Australian premier Sir John Forrest came to argue in 1907, 'the people in Western Australia "knew more about the matter than the people of England" and that "chaining Aboriginals [sic] by the

---

17   Winter, 'Coerced Labour', 7.
18   'W.A. Prisons, Interesting Report, Prison Labour, Native Prisons', *The Daily News* (Perth, 3 September 1909, 6, cited in Harman and Grant, '"Impossible to Detain without Chains"?', 166–67.
19   Henry Princep, 'Aborigines Department Report for Financial Year Ending 30th June 1901', Perth, W. Alfred Watson, Government Printer, 1901, 5, cited in Harman and Grant, '"Impossible to Detain without Chains"?', 164–65.
20   Curthoys, 'Indigenous Dispossession'.

neck was the only effective way to prevent their escape"'.[21] As we will see, Carnegie was arguably both a product of, and contributor to, this more mercantile and mercenary colonial mentality. In his expedition through the Western Australian desert, Carnegie flouted the new metropolitan ideals of scientific exploration, and returned to an older, more exploitative, practice of violently capturing and incarcerating Indigenous people to force them to act as guides.

Carnegie's Early Expeditions

The honourable David Wynford Carnegie, the fourth son of the Sixth Earl of Southesk, arrived in Western Australia from London, via Melbourne, in September 1892 at the age of 21.[22] With his friend Lord Percy Douglas he was determined to make his own name and fortune. Just as he landed, the news of Arthur Bayley and William Ford's discovery of gold at a still 'unnamed' district reached Albany. Carnegie quickly joined the gold rush and set off towards the newly minted town of Coolgardie.[23] On his journey from King George Sound to Perth, and then on to the goldfields, he noticed that the region was suffering a 'water-famine', and that water was the driving preoccupation of everyone he observed.[24] Carnegie shared the road with camel caravans and horse-drawn wagons transporting water to the fledgling township that, upon arrival, were 'swarm[ed] by men brandishing empty waterbags'. On his journey, he saw both 'men and beasts' driven 'mad with thirst'. He also observed a landscape cleared to allow '"dry-blowing" operations', the local process for separating gold from alluvial soil without the need for water. As Carnegie often repeated, '"Prospecting" is generally taken to mean searching for gold', yet:

> [In] Western Australia in the hot weather it resolves itself into a continual battle for water, with the very unlikely contingency that, in the hunt for a drink, one may fall up against a nugget of gold or a gold-bearing quartz reef.[25]

---

21 'Treatment of Aboriginals: Sir John Forrest's Opinion', *Morning Post* (Cairns), 13 July 1907, 3, cited in Harman and Grant, '"Impossible to Detain without Chains"?', 172.
22 Carnegie had entered the Royal Indian Engineering College where he studied maths and surveying; however, due to his 'high animal spirits', he left before finishing and impulsively travelled to Ceylon to work on a tea plantation, which he immediately found 'uncongenial'. He then sailed to Australia with his friend Lord Percy Douglas, Marquis of Queensbury. H. M. Carnegie, 'Introduction', vii–viii.
23 Carnegie, *Spinifex,* 2; Morison, 'Carnegie, David Wynford (1871–1900)'.
24 Carnegie, *Spinifex,* 8.
25 Carnegie, *Spinifex*, 70.

Carnegie spent his first year or so in Coolgardie working at the Bayley's Reward Mine. In his free time, he 'por[ed] over the map of the Colony, longing and longing to push out into the vast blank spaces of the unknown'.[26]

By March 1894, Carnegie's friend, Douglas, had secured London-based investors to establish a mining exploration company to support Carnegie's prospecting expedition to the Hampton Plains, which lay east and north-east of Coolgardie.[27] This was to be very modest in scope, entailing a single offsider, Gus Luck, a French Alsatian prospector with cameleering experience and a smattering of local Aboriginal words; three camels; and 'scanty facilities for carrying water'.[28] Shortly after setting out, the two men met returning parties who warned them that 'every water was dry'.[29] On 29 April, a month into their journey and a week since they had filled their water supplies, they heard a 'shrill "coo-oo"' and were 'startled to see some half-dozen natives gazing' at them. At that moment, one of the camels bellowed and scared the Aboriginal men who quickly ran off. In the heat of the moment, Carnegie and Luck chased them, and the latter managed 'to stop a man'.[30] The man appeared to be:

> A fine, well made chap, short but thickset, with curious marks cut
> & gashed into the flesh on his ribs[,] a belt of plaited reeds round
> his waist and a 'sporan' [sic] of grass in front.

He did not 'seem frightened' of Carnegie, but was scared of the 'camels which he would not approach'.[31] After giving him some food, which Carnegie first tasted to 'put him more at ease', Luck tried to question the man about water. Finally, he seemed to understand. Repeatedly saying *'ingup'*, he led them to a small granite rock and seemingly pointed to a soak or rock hole. While Carnegie and Luck inspected it, the man 'escaped into the scrub and was soon lost to view'.[32] That night, Carnegie and Luck began digging in the rock hole and, over the next two days, collected five or six gallons of water. Perhaps the Aboriginal man's decision to take the explorers to the water source was an act of reciprocity for the food he had been given; it may also have been a pragmatic effort to give the strangers *ingup* so as to encourage them to quickly pass through his

26   Carnegie, *Spinifex*, 15; Peasley, *In the Hands of Providence*, 8.
27   H. M. Carnegie, 'Introduction', ix; Peasley, *In the Hands of Providence*, 9.
28   Carnegie, *Spinifex*, 41.
29   Carnegie, *Spinifex*, 35.
30   Carnegie, *Spinifex*, 47.
31   Carnegie, *Diaries*, vol. 1, 14.
32   Carnegie, *Spinifex*, 47.

country.[33] Yet, for Carnegie, it planted a seed for his future coercive water-gathering strategies. Carnegie and Luck continued on their explorations and, though they found a gold-bearing quartz reef, it was too remote to be promising. On 22 June, they returned to Coolgardie[34] and Carnegie continued to Perth.

However, Carnegie did not relinquish his gold ambitions. In November 1894, he returned to Coolgardie after receiving financial support from a syndicate for a second expedition. This time his crew included Jim Conley, an American who had field experience in South Africa and on the Yukon, and Paddy Egan, an 'Irish-Victorian' who was experienced in the Western Australian goldfields. Carnegie purchased three new camels and, significantly, portable condensers that could render salt water potable.[35] He hoped the condensers would alleviate his need to find water in the desert. On 10 November the party set out from Coolgardie, travelling initially along the Twenty-Five Mile Road, before heading east to where he had previously seen some promising country.[36] Carnegie soon realised that the condensers were not the saviours he anticipated. Shortly after setting out, the party set up the condensers and discovered how laborious they were to run; the process entailed finding, chopping and carrying wood to fire the boilers, which demanded 'constant attention', stoking the fires and decanting the desalinated water as it 'slowly trickled from the cooling tray'. Between maintaining the condensers and tending to the camels, Carnegie learned that he and his crew had little time left to prospect for gold. He would never use them again on another expedition. When the condensers' boilers finally burned through, the frustrated expedition decided to again return to Coolgardie, arriving on 30 December less than two months after they set out.

After a quick stay to reprovision, the expedition set out on 4 January 1895, heading to Mount Darlôt where gold had just been discovered. This time they were successful in their mission for, on 17 February, Carnegie and Paddy found gold. Ironically, it was while Carnegie was out taking a walk. He mused: 'It seems the simplest thing in the world to find a gold mine—that is … after you have found it!'[37] After marking out the find,

33 Don Baker uses the term 'passing on' to describe Aboriginal people who were anxious to urge explorers through their lands into neighbouring territory as quickly as possible. Baker, 'Wanderers in Eden', 10.
34 Carnegie, *Spinifex*, 65.
35 Carnegie, *Spinifex*, 69–71.
36 Carnegie, *Spinifex*, 70.
37 Carnegie, *Spinifex*, 107.

Carnegie raced alone back to Coolgardie to obtain a mining licence, eventually establishing a mine; however, his investors soon decided to sell it.[38] Carnegie was not too upset by this turn of events, as, having achieved his desire to find gold, he now sought fame as an intrepid explorer. Building on the east–west desert explorations of John Forrest and Peter Egerton Warburton, he planned an expedition journeying from south to north.[39] Significantly, he had learned from his desert experiences that he would stand a greater chance of success if he used Aboriginal people.

Aboriginal Labour in the Goldfields

Many scholars have explained that, during the colonial period, Aboriginal people had few economic options, as they were dispossessed of their lands, which were expropriated and violently defended by settlers and the state, and often despoiled by colonial industries and livestock.[40] Robert Castle and Jim Hagan argue that many Aboriginal people were forced to 'depend on handouts from their conquerors' or 'activities regarded as criminal such as stealing, begging and prostitution', or else make-do by providing labour to colonists.[41] Upon first arriving at the new township of Coolgardie in 1892, Carnegie observed that the local Wongatha people were a visible presence in the town, which comprised little more than a general store and post office run by Mr Benstead, who served as postmaster, butcher and storekeeper.[42] In this nascent town, where drought and the difficulty of finding gold ensured that hardship was widespread among the prospectors, few handouts were given to the Wongatha people, who nonetheless appeared to turn to begging. Carnegie was shocked by the appearance of the 'famine-stricken' Wongatha, observing that in the drought 'not a living thing was to be found in the bush', so 'without begging from the diggers I fail to see how they could have lived'.[43]

---

38   He travelled back to Coolgardie on his own to obtain the licence and, during this journey, contracted typhoid fever. Upon arriving in Coolgardie, he then went to Perth to convalesce at the home of Colonel Fleming. H. M. Carnegie 'Introduction', xi.

39   He drew up a map of his extant journeys for the Western Australian surveyor-general, and then went home to Britain for three months before returning to Western Australia in April 1896. H. M. Carnegie, 'Introduction', xi–xii.

40   Keen, *Indigenous Participation in Australian Economies*; Fijn et al., *Indigenous Participation in Australian Economies II*.

41   Castle and Hagan, 'Settlers and the State', 24.

42   Carnegie, *Spinifex*, 8.

43   Carnegie, *Spinifex*, 10.

Yet, Carnegie's account of begging cannot be taken at face value. For instance, as Lynette Russell reminds us, what Europeans construed as begging was not merely an 'opportunistic strategy for the acquisition of money, food and other goods', but instead served as 'a viable, justifiable form of economic engagement [for Aboriginal people]—a kind of reciprocity for what they had lost'.[44] Further, Fred Cahir, in his study of Koories on the Victorian goldfields, observed that 'soliciting in this period' was not 'primarily driven by poverty alone', since many Koories 'were still largely self-sufficient, and when moments of poverty occurred, implored their white brethren for meaningful paid work and keep, rather than simply begging for food and money'.[45] Similarly, in the Western Australian goldfields, Aboriginal people evidently sought to exchange food for their labours in collecting water; however, Europeans generally dismissed this as begging. Carnegie reported that, in Coolgardie, 'hardly a day passed but what one was visited by these silent, starving shadows' who would implore the miners to '"Gib it damper"', and that 'seldom' were these requests 'made in vain'. Yet, he elaborated that, in 'appreciation no doubt of the kindness shown them, some of the tribe volunteered to find "*gabbi*" [water] for the white-fellow in the roots of a certain gum-tree', most likely red mallee roots, which held water that could be drained into a coolamon or other vessel.[46] To Carnegie, this exchange was essentially one of European charity and Indigenous gratitude, and not a legitimate transaction of goods for services.[47] Nor did he see the Wongatha's laborious collection of mallee roots as a form of work.

This framing of Aboriginal work as begging is part of the larger conceptual discourse defined by Claire Williams and Bill Thorpe as 'colonised labour'. They see this form of labour as a product of imperialism and colonialism in which 'Aboriginal and Islander territory and people' were ensnared 'in a racist social relationship' with colonists.[48] The assumed racial and cultural superiority of the colonists meant that the use of colonised labour was riddled with contradictions, as it was both desired

---

44 Russell, '"Tickpen", "Boro Boro"', 27.

45 Cahir, *Black Gold*, 15.

46 Carnegie, *Spinifex*, 11. Ian Bayly explains that Aboriginal people across Australia could obtain water from the cut tree roots of red mallee, which grows in the alluvial soil of the wheatbelt, as well as the desert kurrajong, needle bush, desert oak and water bush. Bayly, 'Review of How Indigenous People Managed for Water', 22–23.

47 For a discussion of this enduring Western blindness to Aboriginal labour see Jon Altman's chapter in this collection.

48 Williams and Thorpe, *Beyond Industrial Sociology*, 88–107.

and derided. According to Williams and Thorpe, the 'colonised worker is alternately valued as a labour commodity but also devalued, employed and unemployed, paid but mostly unpaid, integrated but mostly marginalised'.[49]

Perhaps the most egregious and troubling form of colonised labour evident on the goldfields was the exploitative use of 'black-boys', as Carnegie referred to them. As Kennedy observes, many explorers throughout Australia and Africa 'picked up indigenous youths to assist them in their endeavours', valuing them for their apparent tractability, which was a consequence of their vulnerability as 'deracinated' individuals. In Australia, Aboriginal youths were 'put to work as stock herders, domestic servants, and more', and 'often physically abused and sometimes sexually exploited'.[50] The employment of Aboriginal children in the nineteenth century was, for the most part, unregulated, and protection boards at that time only kept minimal records that rarely included workers' ages. Consequently, the histories of such children are only known through ad hoc references to individual children employed by colonists as domestic servants and labourers, often described as 'companions' in archival sources and published journals and memoirs. Further, according to Shirleene Robinson, Aboriginal children were particularly vulnerable to exploitation as they were not subject to the admittedly limited mechanisms that protected European children from abuse.[51] In addition to the physical abuses and trauma suffered by Aboriginal child workers in the nineteenth century, their labour as servants was not even acknowledged as work, as evident from the title 'companions'. Even in frontier locations, Carnegie met settlers and itinerants who had Aboriginal child companions; however, like other colonists, he perceived their domestic labour not as employment but as a form of tutelage in the benefits of civilisation.

---

49 Williams and Thorpe, *Beyond Industrial Sociology*, 99. Thorpe elaborated on this in his *Colonial Queensland: Perspectives on a Frontier Society*, maintaining that 'colonised labour' is 'subordinate to all other forms of labour' such as migrant labour and convict labour, which perhaps explains its invisibility to mainstream Australian society. More significantly, this conception of labour is underpinned by the colonists' attempt to 'expropriate as much land as possible' and the twin desires to 'eliminate Aborigines altogether' and to use Indigenous people as a 'source of readily available, exploitable labour'. Thorpe, *Colonial Queensland*, 65–66.
50 Kennedy, *The Last Blank Spaces*, 171–72, 175.
51 Robinson's research in late nineteenth-century Queensland, which bore many similarities to Western Australia in terms of frontier economies and attitudes towards Aboriginal people, reveals widespread anecdotal evidence that Aboriginal children were kidnapped from their families, had been witness to frontier violence, and were subject to physical and sexual abuse, as indicated by reported instances of pregnancy and venereal disease. See Robinson, 'The Unregulated Employment of Aboriginal Children', 1–15.

As soon as Carnegie arrived in Coolgardie he met Sylvester Browne and Gordon Lyon[52] who had with them a 'small black-boy whom they tried in vain to tame'. Carnegie did not explain how they came to have the child in their care, only mentioning that he was a local Wongatha boy who 'stood a good deal of misplaced kindness' and yet still 'ran away to the bush'.[53] When Carnegie returned to Coolgardie in 1896 he stayed with Tom and Gerald Browne, reporting that the latter possessed a boy 'taken away from a tribe' east of Lake Darlôt. Unlike the first boy he met, Carnegie exclaimed that this 'little chap' was 'as spruce and as clever as any white boy of the same size'.[54] On his final expedition in 1896, Carnegie benefited directly from the labour of Aboriginal youths, as the party enlisted Warri, a 16-year-old 'aboriginal boy from the McDonnell Ranges in Central Australia'. Warri was the 'black-boy' of Joe Breardon, an Australian 'born and bred in the bush' who Carnegie recruited for his expedition, and who had ostensibly trained Warri since the age of six to ride and track. Carnegie immediately perceived Warri as a 'distinct acquisition' for the expedition, for he had initially intended on 'getting a discharged prisoner from the native jail at Rotnest [sic]' to serve as a guide, so was happy to substitute Warri because 'prison life is apt to develop all [the Aboriginal prisoners'] native cunning and treachery'.[55] In April 1897, towards the end of the expedition, Carnegie also temporarily *acquired* some young boys from Sturt Creek, one of whom Carnegie named Tiger and used as a translator and labourer until he absconded.[56] Reflecting on the various 'black-boys' he had encountered in Western Australia led Carnegie to muse not on how such children came to be wards of settler men, but on the educability of Aboriginal people:

> Great tact is necessary in the education of the aboriginals. Neglect turns them into lazy, besotted brutes who are of no use to anybody; too kind treatment makes them insolent and cunning; too harsh treatment makes them treacherous; and yet without a certain amount of bullying they lose all respect for their master, and when they deserve a beating and do not get it, misconstrue tender-heartedness into fear. The 'happy medium' is the great thing; the most useful, contented, and best-behaved boys that I have seen are those that receive treatment similar to that a highly valued sporting dog gets from a just master; 'to pet' stands for 'to spoil'.[57]

---

52 Carnegie, *Spinifex*, 9. See also Simpson, 'Bayley, Arthur Wellesley (1865–1896)'.
53 Carnegie, *Spinifex*, 11.
54 Carnegie, *Spinifex*, 153.
55 Carnegie, *Spinifex*, 149.
56 Carnegie, *Spinifex*, 365–75; Carnegie, *Diaries,* vol. 3, 64.
57 Carnegie, *Spinifex*, 153–54.

Carnegie's account conspicuously masks the labour performed by Aboriginal youths. In his eyes, the Aboriginal youths seemed more akin to work animals—who the colonial master was obliged to discipline and train—than employees. In turn, as Angela Woollacott has persuasively argued, the patriarchal control of indentured and Aboriginal labour played a crucial role in colonial conceptions of white settler manhood, defined by status that resulted from the control of bonded labour, be it convict, indentured or Indigenous.[58] Carnegie's account suggests that this form of white, settler, masculine identity was not just the privilege of landholding farmers and pastoralists of British extraction, such as those Woollacott describes, but also could be adopted by men with few *possessions* other than a 'black-boy'.

Carnegie's 1896 Expedition

In 1896, Carnegie organised his most ambitious expedition. To follow the likes of John Forrest, who explored an inland route through the desert from Perth to Adelaide in 1870, and Peter Egerton Warburton who crossed the desert in the other direction in 1872–74, Carnegie planned to travel through the Western Australian desert from south to north, investigating new lands between Forrest's and Warburton's travels for signs of gold and a potential new stock route. For this purpose, he assembled a new crew. In addition to Breardon and Warri, Carnegie employed Godfrey Massie and Charles Stansmore, and purchased eight packing camels and a riding camel.

The expedition set out on 9 July and entered the desert on 23 July. Over the course of the expedition, the party spent 13 months in the desert and travelled more than 3,000 miles,[59] further than any previous European explorer had travelled through the Australian desert. More significantly, Carnegie increasingly turned to capturing Aboriginal people as a means of finding water, employing more systematic and coercive methods of detaining his captives, and eventually giving up any pretence of compensating them for their knowledge, labour or suffering.

---

58   Woollacott, 'Frontier Violence and Settler Manhood', 1–11. For more on the treatment of indentured labourers see Tracey Banivanua Mar's chapter in this collection.
59   Carnegie, *Spinifex*, 430.

Figure 2.1: 'Group of explorers'.
Source: Carnegie, *Spinifex*, 352.

On 7 August 1896, nine days after the explorers had last found water, Warri spotted footprints that the party decided to follow, assuming that there 'must be water at the end of them'. After a few false starts, they eventually spied an Aboriginal man on 9 August and Breardon shouted: 'Catch him.' They gave chase and captured the terrified man. Through gestures, they communicated their desire for water. The man seemed to understand their demand and a 'strange procession started':

> Guarded on one side by Breardon, I on the other, we plied our new friend with salt beef, both to cement our friendship and promote thirst, in order that for his own sake he should not play us false.[60]

---

60   Carnegie, *Spinifex*, 189.

As with the man Luck had captured on the previous expedition, they offered their captive food, albeit deliberately salty food, and did not use any physical restraints. When he finally led them to a rock hole, Carnegie and Breardon ran ahead of him, excited by the prospect of water, giving the man a chance to escape. However, upon discovering that the rock hole was dry, they quickly chased him down, this time tying him up with rope and 'watch[ing] him in turn all through the night'.[61] Distressed by his captivity, the man, who Carnegie 'named' King Billy (possibly after one of his camels), stayed awake all night, trying various strategies to escape:

> He would lie still with closed eyes for a time, and then make a sudden struggle to wrench the rope away from his captor; then stealthily with his foot he tried to push the rope into the fire; then he started rubbing it on the rock on which we lay; and last of all his teeth were brought into use.

The next morning Carnegie 'confess[ed] that I saw with delight the evident feelings of thirst that before long overcame him—the salt beef had done its duty'. Driven to desperation, 'King Billy' led them to an underground cave called 'Murcoolia Ayahteenyah'.[62] Carnegie and his men were overjoyed to discover it was a soakage, which Carnegie renamed Empress Spring after Queen Victoria. With little regard for the Aboriginal people who depended on this water supply, the expedition spent four days in the cave, initially making King Billy 'bal[e] water with a meat tin into a bucket', until they watered their camels and replenished their water supplies.

Carnegie did not admit to himself that they had kidnapped the man. Upon gifting King Billy some clothing and the lid of a meat tin, Carnegie asserted that the man 'seemed to warm towards us & … became quite at home'.[63] However, by the 'second morning he had gone', which Carnegie lamented for King Billy had 'become very useful, carrying wood and so forth with the greatest pleasure'. Even after King Billy escaped, Carnegie still claimed that he treated the man well:

> I fancy that his impressions of a white man's character will be favourable; for never in his life before had he been able to gorge himself without having had the trouble of hunting his food.[64]

---

61   Carnegie, *Spinifex*, 189.
62   Carnegie, *Diaries*, vol. 3, 20. Carnegie removed the Aboriginal name of the cave from his word list in in the published account.
63   Carnegie, *Diaries*, vol. 3, 19.
64   Carnegie, *Spinifex*, 198.

Figure 2.2: 'At work in the cave, Empress Spring'.
Source: Carnegie, *Spinifex*, 195.

In early September they again decided to search for an Aboriginal person who could lead them to water, using Warri as a tracker. Eventually, on 11 September, they 'rode right on to [a] camp without warning', and Carnegie captured an older woman who had stopped to save her dingo pups: 'Sorry as I was to be rude to a lady, I had to make her prisoner.'[65] Clearly distressed, she 'shouted, scratching, biting, spitting, and tearing' his skin, 'clutching at every bush' they passed as he carried her along. Upon realising they wanted water, she pointed to a rock hole her camp had been using. However, after his experience with King Billy, Carnegie did not trust her and so tied her up with rope before inspecting the rock hole. After collecting 12 gallons of water, Carnegie was reluctant to give up his captive. Therefore, he:

> Decided to take the [woman] back with us, as it had been clear to me for some time past that without the aid of the natives we could not hope to find water.[66]

The explorers returned to their camp and found that the well had dried out, so they dug down and, over the course of four days—working night and day—dug 30 feet below the surface, collecting 140 gallons of water. From digging down that far, Carnegie concluded that 'no rain can have fallen in the district for some number of years'.[67] During the next five days, the older woman did not lead them to any new water sources and refused to accept any of their food or water; after repeatedly deeming her 'useless', Carnegie let her loose and was surprised by the 'rapidity' with which she fled.[68]

Carnegie's treatment of the older woman was even more draconian than his treatment of King Billy; even after she had led them to water, he decided to take her with them and, as she 'refus[ed] to walk', he 'roped [her] on to one of the camels [sic] back'.[69] Belying any notion that his capture of Aboriginal people was a desperate survival measure, he came to develop an even more systematic approach, as Aboriginal people, not water, became the primary object of his search. On their next 'hunt', the explorers evidently stalked Aboriginal people before confronting them.

---

65   Mike Smith argues that, for many desert communities, the dingo is regarded as 'very close family (*tjarntu*)', as they were used to 'find and run down game, serve as "camp companions"', and as 'sentinels who warned against real and supernatural dangers'. Smith, *Archaeology of Australia's Deserts*, 208.

66   Carnegie, *Spinifex*, 232.

67   Carnegie in a letter to John Forrest, extracted in 'Western Australian Exploration', *South Australian Register*, 25 March 1897, 5.

68   Carnegie, *Spinifex*, 235.

69   Carnegie, *Diaries*, vol. 3, 39.

After tracking an Aboriginal party, the explorers pulled up short on their camels to observe them before 'advancing slowly from opposite directions'. By such methods, the explorers 'were able to get within a hundred yards of [the Aboriginal party] before our silent approach was noticed'. Carnegie exclaimed: 'No words can describe the look of terror and amazement on the faces of those wild savages.'[70] On another occasion, they rode in on a camp, capturing a man who Carnegie facetiously named Sir John, and '[t]ethered [him] to a ti-tree, with a little fire to cheer him'. When they set out the next day, 28 September, they dragged the reluctant man by his rope to coerce him into action.[71] This initiated a battle of wills, as Carnegie and his men tried to force the man into leading them to water (at some point, they swapped his rope for chain). Sir John led them to two dry wells, an act that the increasingly suspicious Carnegie thought was deliberate, believing the captive appeared to watch their 'disgust with evident satisfaction'.[72] In retaliation, Carnegie 'had to resort to the unfailing argument of allowing him no water at all', as he had learned with King Billy that:

> Thirst is a terrible thing; it is also a great quickener of the wits, and the result of this harsh treatment, which reduced the poor buck to tears (a most uncommon thing amongst natives), was that before very long we were enabled to unload and make camp in one of the most charming little spots I have ever seen.[73]

Carnegie named the oasis 'Helena Springs'. His success seemed to justify captivity as a means of finding water: 'what chance of finding such a place without the help of those natives to whom alone its existence was known?'[74] He intended to keep Sir John for a few more days, 'as this is a less tedious method of finding water than following up smokes'.[75] However, during their five days at Helena Springs, Sir John escaped; he used the sharp end of a meat tin to cut the packing bag to which his chain had been secured. As with King Billy, Carnegie maintained that he had admirably compensated his captives for their torture-induced labours; he lamented that Sir John's premature escape prevented him 'return[ing] to his family laden with presents' that were allegedly set aside for him.

---

70 Carnegie, *Spinifex*, 238.
71 Carnegie, *Spinifex*, 260.
72 Carnegie, *Spinifex*, 267.
73 Carnegie, *Spinifex*, 267.
74 Carnegie, *Spinifex*, 272.
75 Carnegie, *Diaries*, vol. 3, 50.

He later rationalised that the 3-foot length of 'light chain on [Sir John's] ankle' might be 'treasured for many years to come' by his tribe;[76] however, his diary presented a darker account:

> So he departed taking his chain with him, how he will remove it from his ankle I have no idea—he tried to burn thro' [sic] the chain one night but found it rather painful—Poor old buck! it [sic] will be a most uncomfortably anklet but he should have waited.[77]

Finding Helena Springs marked a turning point in Carnegie's strategy, as he became even more mercenary and pre-emptive in kidnapping Aboriginal people. Shortly after the expedition resumed, the explorers saw smoke rising nearby and decided to make towards it. As Carnegie explained:

> Though we were not in great want of water, I considered it always advisable to let no chance of letting some slip by, since one never can tell how long the next may be in coming.[78]

His plan to capture an Aboriginal 'guide' despite having ample water complicates the historiographical argument that kidnapping was an act of desperation. Instead, kidnapping seems to have become the primary imperative of the expedition—they tracked footprints and smoke across the desert and increasingly seemed to see Aboriginal people as hard-won trophies. On one occasion, after crossing Davenport Hills, they heard the 'distant call' of a woman and saw the smoke from a fire. Carnegie 'despatched Godfrey to surprise the camp', and when Carnegie 'arrived on the scene' he found:

> Godfrey standing sentinel beneath a tree, in the branches of which stood at bay a savage of fine proportions. He had a magnificent beard, dark brown piercing eyes, splendid teeth, a distinctly Jewish profile, and no decorations or scars on his chest or body. I shall not forget the colour of his eyes nor their fierce glitter, for I climbed the tree after him, he trying to prevent my ascent by blows from a short, heavy stick which I wrested from him, and then with broken branches of dead mulga, with which he struck my head and hands unmercifully, alternately beating me and prodding me in the face, narrowly missing my eyes. If he suffered any inconvenience by being kept captive afterwards, he well repaid himself beforehand by the unpleasant time he gave me.[79]

---

76 Carnegie, *Spinifex*, 273.
77 Carnegie, *Diaries*, vol. 3, 53.
78 Carnegie, *Spinifex*, 278.
79 Carnegie, *Spinifex*, 399.

Figure 2.3: 'Establishing friendly relations'.
Source: Carnegie, *Spinifex*, 401.

Carnegie's party captured another six Aboriginal people, including women,[80] as they travelled through the desert, forcing their captives to lead them to water. Yet, on several occasions, it was not evident that such coercive measures were necessary.

In November 1896, when they were about 100 miles shy of Halls Creek, Carnegie's expedition came across 'the biggest camp of natives' they had seen, comprising a 'dozen little "wurlies" or branch-shelters'. At the time, the only occupants were an 'oldish' man, who Carnegie referred to as the 'old Jew', ostensibly due to the shape of his nose, several women and numerous children. Carnegie noticed that a young girl had skin sores, which he dressed with 'tar and oil', and a boy had 'sore eyes, literally eaten away at the inner corners into deep holes'. He 'doctored' the boy, applying a lotion he had brought with him while the old man 'nodded his head in approval'. Immediately after ministering to the patient, Carnegie reported that the family 'showed us their well close by' and, while Carnegie started baling out water, Godfrey 'pressed the old man into our service', making him cut 'bushes for a shade'.[81] The next day, they were 'greatly entertained by two small boys' who were interested in everything they did and 'were soon tremendous chums with Warri'. One of the boys even 'volunteered to show [Carnegie] a very large water' and led them to a 'nice little pool under a step in the rocky bed'.[82] While this family 'evidently knew all about a rifle',[83] so may have offered to lead Carnegie to water as a means of maintaining peace, it is more likely that they did it as a mark of reciprocity for Carnegie's tending to the ill children. Four or five months later, when Carnegie was on his return journey from Halls Creek, he met the old man again. While the explorers were camped near Sturt Creek, 'a fresh mob of blacks came in':

> They as soon recognised us, and appeared tremendously pleased. The old Jew patted me, and grinned, and squirmed in a most ludicrous way; I discovered that he was thanking me for having cured his son's eyes—so the lotion had done its work well.[84]

---

80 Carnegie, *Spinifex*, 397, 407.
81 Carnegie, *Spinifex*, 296–97.
82 Carnegie, *Spinifex*, 301.
83 Carnegie, *Spinifex*, 297.
84 Carnegie, *Spinifex*, 373.

Moreover, they also presented Carnegie with a 'highly treasured' 'flat stick carved all over into rough patterns', which was 'carefully wrapped' and 'given as a mark of respect or gratitude for curing the boy's eyes'. In addition, they gave him 'throwing sticks, balls of hair string, a shield and tomahawk'.[85] To reciprocate for these gifts, Carnegie gave them 'numerous costly presents from us—one or two old shirts, strips of coloured handkerchief to make sporrans of, a knife or two, and so forth', and they seemed 'perfectly satisfied'.[86] The Aboriginal man's generous gift should have shown Carnegie that he could elicit Aboriginal knowledge of water through displays of kindness and reciprocal exchanges, and not just through violent, coercive means. Yet, within the same month, despite having ample water, Carnegie again kidnapped Aboriginal people:

> The country ahead looked so bad that I decided to take the two bucks with us for as long as they knew the waters, so secured the one to the other by the neck, with plenty of spare chain between.[87]

Carnegie's expedition eventually returned to Coolgardie in April 1897 safe and sound, except for the unfortunate Stansmore who accidentally shot himself in November 1896. Carnegie concluded that it 'has been my fate, in all my exploration work, to find none but useless country'.[88]

Conclusion

Historians have been appalled by Carnegie's strategy of capturing Aboriginal people and yet have rationalised the practice as a desperate means of surviving desert conditions. Such interpretations have been based on passing mentions of only one or two instances in which Carnegie kidnapped people and have not seriously taken into account the 14 Aboriginal men and women he captured and chained over the course of his desert crossing or the dozens of families no doubt traumatised from being hunted by strangers on camel back. In this chapter, I have

---

85   These gifts perhaps contributed to Carnegie's collection of Aboriginal artefacts, which he later exhibited to a meeting of the Anthropological Institute of Great Britain and Ireland, and seven of which he donated to the British Museum. 'Australia at the Anthropological Institute', *The Daily Telegraph* (Sydney), 7 May 1898, 11; Carnegie, *Spinifex*, 227; British Museum, 'David Wynford Carnegie', accessed 6 December 2018, www.britishmuseum.org/research/collection_online/search. aspx?people=41005&peoA=41005-3-9.

86   Carnegie, *Spinifex*, 373.

87   Carnegie, *Spinifex*, 380.

88   Carnegie, *Spinifex*, 433.

considered his water-finding technique within the context of both his personal experiences (the result of his various forays in the desert) and overarching colonial discourses about Indigenous labour. By his own account, it is clear that Carnegie had other means of obtaining water, be it the frustrating and cumbersome use of condensers or through offering reciprocal exchanges with Aboriginal people for water. Yet, after an unexpected and opportunistic encounter with an Aboriginal man who led the explorers to water, Carnegie developed a more systematic, mercenary and pre-emptive strategy of kidnapping Aboriginal people, subjecting them to increasingly brutal incarceration and forcing them to find water for him. He was evidently proud of his systematic and coercive technique for finding water, which he later detailed in a letter to the Western Australian premier, Sir John Forrest, himself an acclaimed explorer of the arid interior:

> All through this sandridge country we carry out the one plan of finding water, which was as follows:- For hunting purposes the natives burn large patches of spinifex. The smoke from these fires can be easily seen for some considerable distance, and frequently I have counted as many as five in a day. Choosing a smoke, if possible, on our general course we would steer for it, and when it died down, as it would do in the course of a few hours continue in the same direction till the burnt ground was reached. We would then spread out, pick up the tracks and if possible catch a native. This we were usually fortunate to manage, though only at the expense of great patience and much labour. Often as many as four days would elapse between the time of our sighting the smoke and catching a black.[89]

Carnegie's attitude arguably reflects a broader culture of colonised labour in which Aboriginal people's work and efforts are rendered invisible, masked as either begging or gratitude, and that led to the colonial fantasy that Aboriginal people's labour could only be harnessed through coercive and punitive means.

---

89 'Western Australian Exploration', *South Australian Register*, 25 March 1897, 5.

Carnegie's increasingly brutal means of kidnapping—or what he called 'nigger catching'[90] in a letter to a friend—reflects what anthropologist Gannanath Obeyesekere calls the 'Kurtz syndrome'. Discussing Captain James Cook's increasingly violent and draconian treatment of Pacific Islanders during his second and third voyages of discovery, Obeyesekere explains that Kurtz syndrome, named after the megalomaniac colonial overlord in Joseph Conrad's novella *Heart of Darkness*, is a myth model in which Europeans 'take on the characteristics of the savage—[that is] the characteristics imputed to the savage by the civiliser's culture'. It lies in opposition to what Obeyesekere calls the 'Prospero syndrome'—the myth that Europeans are 'harbingers of civilisation who remain immune to savage ways'.[91] Obeyesekere's focus on Cook, a maritime explorer, is significant, since, arguably, the mobile nature of imperial exploration amplifies this Kurtzean mentality: physical isolation and hardship; removal from the ameliorating influence of social and moral protocols; an unpredictability of daily circumstances that exacerbates a desire to assert control; and the presence of 'natives' who can be deemed less than human or, in Carnegie's words, 'more like monkeys than anything else'.[92] For Carnegie, his initial ambitions of finding both gold and a new route through the desert were supplanted by the more immediate drive to capture and control Aboriginal people. Kidnapping Aboriginal people was not just a desperate means to an end, but also became an end in itself, providing the only excitement in a long, arduous journey through the desert. As Carnegie himself exclaimed about the Western Australian interior: 'What heartbreaking country, monotonous, lifeless, without interest, without excitement save when the stern necessity of finding water forced us to seek out the natives in their primitive camps!'[93]

---

90   Letter to Tom Stoddart, a camel trader from the Coolgardie Carrying Company, extracted in 'In Dead Man's Land', *Coolgardie Miner*, 10 August 1897, 6. His choice of terminology here is significant, and seems intended to dehumanise his Aboriginal captives. In *Spinifex and Sand* he only uses the term twice, on both occasions in quotes by others; in one case, during his very first expedition, in which he ironically refuted a miner's mother's fears that her son might participate in '"nigger hunting excursions" that she heard went on in Western Australia', claiming that 'she need not have disturbed herself, for such things never existed'. Carnegie, *Spinifex*, 59. However, in his unpublished diaries, he liberally uses this denigratory term, notably beginning around the same time he first kidnaps an Aboriginal man with Gus Luck: prior to this incident, he usually used the term 'native'.

91   Obeyesekere, *The Apotheosis of Captain Cook*, 11–12.

92   'Through Western Australian Deserts', *Clarence and Richmond Examiner*, 26 March 1898, 6.

93   Carnegie, *Spinifex*, 292.

Carnegie's search for excitement led him away from the Western Australian desert and back to England where he wrote his account of the expedition, *Spinifex and Sand: A Narrative of Five Years' Pioneering and Exploration in Western Australia*, presented a lecture to the esteemed RGS and was awarded its Gill Medal in 1898.[94] In 1899, he moved to northern Nigeria, where he gave up the adventure of exploration for the security of tenured employment to serve as assistant resident under Sir Frederick Lugard. There he practised the lessons in settler manhood that he had learned in Western Australia. While believing he 'treated his black "boys" as friends', Carnegie insisted that 'he was also master'.[95] Unfortunately for Carnegie, the Nigerians did not share this sentiment and, in November 1900, during his excursions between Koton Kerifi and Tawaré in pursuit of the so-called 'brigand' Mama Gana, he was killed by a poison arrow.

Bibliography

Primary Sources

Carnegie, David W. *Diaries, 1894–1897 [manuscript]*, 4 vols, State Library of Western Australia, ACC 2693A.

——. 'Explorations in the Interior of Western Australia: Paper Read to the Society, February 14, 1898', *Geographical Journal* 11, no. 3 (March 1898): 258–86.

——. *Spinifex and Sand: A Narrative of Five Years' Pioneering and Exploration in Western Australia*. London: CA Pearson, 1898.

Carnegie, Helena M. 'Introduction'. In David W. Carnegie. *Letters from Nigeria: Of the Honourable David Wynford Carnegie, F.R.G.S.*, v–xli. Brechin: Black & Johnston, 1902.

Secondary Sources

Baker, Don. 'Wanderers in Eden: Thomas Mitchell Compared with Lewis and Clark'. *Aboriginal History* 19, no. 1/2 (1995): 3–20.

---

94   Morison, 'Carnegie, David Wynford (1871–1900)'; Carnegie, 'Explorations in the Interior of Western Australia'.
95   H. M. Carnegie, 'Introduction', xxxv.

Bayly, I. A. E. 'Review of How Indigenous People Managed for Water in Desert Regions of Australia'. *Journal of the Royal Society of Western Australia* 82 (1999): 17–25.

Burnett, D. Graham. '"It is Impossible to Make a Step without the Indians": Nineteenth-Century Geographical Exploration and the Amerindians of British Guiana'. *Ethnohistory* 49, no. 1 (2002): 3–40. doi.org/10.1215/00141801-49-1-3.

Cahir, Fred. *Black Gold: Aboriginal People on the Goldfields of Victoria, 1850–1870*. Canberra: ANU E Press and Aboriginal History, 2013.

Castle, Robert and Jim Hagan. 'Settlers and the State: The Creation of an Aboriginal Workforce in Australia'. *Aboriginal History* 22 (1998): 24–35.

Curthoys, Ann. 'Indigenous Dispossession and Pastoral Employment in Western Australia during the Nineteenth Century: Implications for Understanding Colonial Forms of Genocide'. In *Genocide on Settler Frontiers: When Hunter-Gatherers and Commercial Stock Farmers Clash*, edited by Mohamed Adhikari, 210–31. New York: Berghahn Books, 2014.

Driver, Felix and Lowri Jones. *Hidden Histories of Exploration: Researching Geographical Collections*. London: Royal Holloway, University of London, and Royal Geographical Society (with IBG), 2002.

Fijn, Natasha, Ian Keen, Christopher Lloyd and Michael Pickering, eds. *Indigenous Participation in Australian Economies II: Historical Engagements and Current Enterprises*. Canberra: ANU E Press, 2012.

Fritsch, Kathrin. '"You Have Everything Confused and Mixed Up...!": Georg Schweinfurth, Knowledge and Cartography Of Africa in the 19th Century'. *History in Africa* 36, no. 1 (2002): 87–101.

Goodman, David. 'The Gold Rushes of the 1850s'. In *Cambridge History of Australia*, edited by Stuart McIntyre and Alison Bashford. 2 Vols, 170–88. Melbourne: Cambridge University Press, 2013. doi.org/10.1017/CHO9781107445758.010.

Harman, Kristyn and Elizabeth Grant. '"Impossible to Detain without Chains"? The Use of Restraints on Aboriginal People in Policing and Prisons'. *History Australia* 11, no. 3 (2014): 157–76. doi.org/10.1080/14490854.2014.1166 8538.

Host John and Jill Milroy. 'Towards an Aboriginal Labour History', *Studies in Western Australian History* 22 (2001): 3–22.

Keen, Ian, ed. *Indigenous Participation in Australian Economies: Historical and Anthropological Perspectives*. Canberra: ANU E Press, 2010. doi.org/10.22459/ IPAE.12.2010.

Kennedy, Dane. *The Last Blank Spaces*. Cambridge: Harvard University Press, 2013. doi.org/10.4159/harvard.9780674074972.

Konishi, Shino. *The Aboriginal Male in the Enlightenment World*. London: Pickering and Chatto, 2012.

Konishi, Shino, Maria Nugent and Tiffany Shellam, eds. *Indigenous Intermediaries: New Perspectives on the Exploration Archives*. Canberra: ANU Press and Aboriginal History, 2015. doi.org/10.22459/II.09.2015.

Morison, Patricia. 'Carnegie, David Wynford (1871–1900)'. *Australian Dictionary of Biography*, National Centre of Biography, Australian National University, 1979, accessed 12 June 2017, adb.anu.edu.au/biography/carnegie-david-wynford-5509/text9377.

Obeyesekere, Gananath. *The Apotheosis of Captain Cook: European Mythmaking in the Pacific*. Princeton: Princeton University Press, 1997.

Peasley, William John. *In the Hands of Providence: The Desert Journeys of David Carnegie*. Carlisle, WA: Hesperian Press, 2013.

Reynolds, Henry. 'The Land, the Explorers and the Aborigines'. *Australian Historical Studies* 19, no. 75 (1980): 213–26.

Robinson, Shirleene. 'The Unregulated Employment of Aboriginal Children in Queensland, 1842–1902'. *Labour History* 82 (2002): 1–15. doi.org/10.2307/ 27516838.

Russell, Lynette. '"Tickpen", "Boro Boro": Aboriginal Economic Engagements in Early Melbourne'. In *Settler Colonial Governance in Nineteenth-Century Victoria*, edited by Lynette Russell and Leigh Boucher, 27–46. Canberra: ANU Press and Aboriginal History, 2015. doi.org/10.22459/SCGNCV.04. 2015.01.

Shellam, Tiffany, Maria Nugent, Shino Konishi and Allison Cadzow, eds. *Brokers and Boundaries: Colonial Exploration in Indigenous Territory*. Canberra: ANU Press and Aboriginal History, 2016. doi.org/10.22459/BB.04.2016.

Simpson, Pat. 'Bayley, Arthur Wellesley (1865–1896)'. *Australian Dictionary of Biography*, National Centre of Biography, Australian National University, 1979, accessed 9 June 2017, adb.anu.edu.au/biography/bayley-arthur-wellesley-88/ text8665.

Smith, Mike. *The Archaeology of Australia's Deserts*. New York: Cambridge University Press, 2013. doi.org/10.1017/CBO9781139023016.

Stoddart, D. R. 'The RGS and the "New Geography": Changing Aims and Changing Roles in Nineteenth Century Science'. *The Geographical Journal* 146, no. 2 (1980): 190–202. doi.org/10.2307/632860.

Strauss, Kendra. 'Coerced, Forced, and Unfree Labour: Geographies of Exploitation in Contemporary Labour Markets'. *Geography Compass* 6, no. 3 (2012): 137–48. doi.org/10.1111/j.1749-8198.2011.00474.x.

Thorpe, Bill. *Colonial Queensland: Perspectives on a Frontier Society*. St Lucia: University of Queensland Press, 1996.

Williams, Claire and Bill Thorpe. *Beyond Industrial Sociology*, North Sydney: Allen and Unwin: 1992.

Winter, Sean. 'Coerced Labour in Western Australia during the Nineteenth Century'. *Australasian Historical Archaeology* 34 (2016): 3–12.

Woollacott, Angela. 'Frontier Violence and Settler Manhood'. *History Australia* 6, no. 1 (2009): 1–11. doi.org/10.2104/ha090011.

Newspapers

Clarence and Richmond Examiner

Coolgardie Miner

The Daily Telegraph (Sydney)

Kalgoorlie Miner

Kalgoorlie Western Argus

South Australian Register

3

'Boyd's Blacks': Labour and the Making of Settler Lands in Australia and the Pacific

Tracey Banivanua Mar

Tracey Banivanua Mar's untimely death on 19 August 2017 meant that she never completed this chapter. The version here is an edited draft of the paper that she circulated in the Labour Lines Workshop held at Deakin University in June 2017. Banivanua Mar wrote in regard to that draft: 'NB as per "Labour Lines" suggestions, this paper is still in draft form for the purpose of workshopping. This paper and research has been funded by the Australian Research Council, and is part of the Discovery Project "Land and Colonial Cultures" (DP 120104928).' Where possible, Tracey's own words have been retained and only minor amendments and additional information gleaned from her notes have been made by Kalissa Alexeyeff, Lucy Davies and Alan Lester. We hope that researchers will be genuinely inspired by the paper's insights into the transnational complexity of the early colonial labour trade, the global and intersecting reach of land, labour and commerce, and, most importantly, Pacific Islander experiences of mobility during the early nineteenth century.

In the early evening of a Tuesday night in October 1847, the settlement of Parramatta on the outskirts of Sydney, New South Wales, was 'thrown into considerable alarm and excitement' as a group of around 20 or 30 men and boys recently arrived from what was then called the New Hebrides briefly took over the streets. These 'blackfellows, with red hair', marched into Parramatta, shouting and gesturing as they ignored fences and passed through doors marking the private property of estate owners. After trying and failing to board a nearby steamer, the *Emu*, they eventually settled together 'under a portico at the rear of the military barracks' covered only by a tarpaulin. The following morning, 'with a hideous shout', they rose and continued to march in the direction of Sydney.[1] The Sydney press was unequivocal in reporting this Parramatta scene as one in which violence and an 'outrage of a most serious nature' would have been inevitable without the presence of an ever-watchful police force. No 'outrage was perpetrated' and the Hunter River press reported that this was due to the police having 'acted legally, wisely and judiciously' in closely watching the men whose 'yellings and hootings and violence of gesture', and whose water bottles suspended on 'formidable' sticks, were a clear threat to 'Parramattonians'. The next day, as the men and boys made their way to Sydney, they were watched, followed and reported on, with the *Maitland Mercury* later observing that such surveillance had undoubtedly preserved 'life and property'.[2]

The New Hebrideans, or Ni-Vanuatu, who marched on Parramatta had probably recently arrived in New South Wales on board either the *Portenia* or *Velocity*; both vessels had docked in Sydney loaded with around 100 men and boys from the New Hebrides who were under contract to work for a period of indenture for local pastoralist Benjamin Boyd.[3] Their arrival in Sydney, and that six months earlier of another 100 men and boys aged between 14 and 25, is a well-told story. They were, historians have reported, the first incarnation of what would eventually be a brutal 40-year trade in indentured labour from the Pacific, one that would found and enrich Queensland's sugar industry from 1868.[4] Fewer have wondered who these men were, what their often fatal experience was, and

---

1   'The New Hebrideans', *The Maitland Mercury and Hunter River General Advertiser*, 16 October 1847, 2.

2   'The New Hebrideans', *The Maitland Mercury and Hunter River General Advertiser*, 16 October 1847, 2.

3   'Shipping Intelligence', *The Australian*, 22 April 1847, 2; 'Shipping Intelligence', *The Australian*, 28 September 1847, 2; 'Shipping Intelligence', *Sydney Chronicle*, 19 October 1847, 2. There is some evidence to suggest that Boyd's recruiters also picked up men from Lifou, Loyalty Islands and other adjacent islands.

4   Banivanua Mar, *Violence and Colonial Dialogue*, 12. See also Saunders, 'The Worker's Paradox'; Saunders, 'The Black Scourge'; Saunders, 'Troublesome Servants'; Corris, '"Blackbirding" in New Guinea'; Corris, *Passage, Port and Plantation*; Corris, '"White Australia" in Action'; Moore, *Kanaka*; Moore, '"Whips and Rum Swizzles"'; Graves, *Cane and Labour*; Graves, 'Colonialism'; Graves, 'Crisis and Change'; Graves, 'Trucks and Gifts'; Shlomowitz, 'Epidemiology'; Shlomowitz, 'Indentured Melanesians'; Shlomowitz, 'Markets for Indentured'; Shlomowitz, 'Mortality'.

what their presence in New South Wales in the 1840s might tell us about historical and even contemporary patterns of labour and colonisation in and around the Pacific.[5]

The presence of Māori, Polynesians and, increasingly, Melanesians was commonplace at cosmopolitan ports from the early nineteenth century. By the 1840s, Port Jackson was a central node in an extensive Pacific maritime world. A growing body of scholarly work explores the global reach of this network. Lynette Russell, most notably, has shown how Indigenous Australian sailors and whalers were highly mobile from the late eighteenth century, working throughout the Pacific and beyond since the turn of that century.[6] Other historians have traced Māori and Pacific journeying and historic connections and its shaping of Aotearoa/New Zealand history; however, the extent of Australia's Pacific history remains to be told in its entirety.[7]

In focusing more closely on the experiences of these men and boys in New South Wales and the Port Phillip Protectorate, I reflect on how their stories, important in their own right as testimonials, are also manifestations of interdependent structures of colonisation. In particular, the event of their arrival and presence in New South Wales brings into focus the contingencies through which 'land'—as a British imperial project through which Indigenous spaces were partitioned, converted into property and brought violently into markets of mass production and consumption—was being made through the harnessing, regulation, extraction and eradication of Indigenous bodies and systems of both ownership and industry.

---

5   Banivanua Mar, *Decolonisation and the Pacific*; Chappell, *Double Ghosts*; Shineberg, *The People Trade;* Shineberg, *They Came for Sandalwood*.

6   Russell, *Roving Mariners*.

7   Banivanua Mar, *Decolonisation and the Pacific*; Banivanua Mar, 'Shadowing'; O'Brien, *The Pacific Muse*; Salesa, *Racial Crossings*; Salmond, *Between Worlds*; Salmond, *Two Worlds*; Somerville, 'Living on New Zealand Street'; Standfield, *Race and Identity*; Standfield, 'The Parramatta Maori'; Standfield, 'Mobility, Reciprocal Relationships'. As Banivanua Mar notes, these maritime networks linked to a wider web of imperial discourse that connected trade and labour, but also efforts to reshape Indigenous bodies and souls. Administrators, such as Samuel Marsden, experimented with imparting literacy, language and religion differentially to both Aboriginal and Maori youth at Parramatta. Banivanua Mar, *Decolonisation and the Pacific*, 52–53.

Boyd's Experiment

The Ni-Vanuatu boys and men who arrived in New South Wales in October 1847 belonged to 'Missa Boyd'.[8] Benjamin Boyd was a merchant banker who was keen to try settler colonial experiments, steeped in the experimental zeal of the day, for transforming wasted 'native' land and bodies into productive capital. Boyd entertained Wakefieldian fantasies of socially and spatially engineered settler colonies. First, in the islands of the Pacific, he sought to establish a minor colony that might 'later become a portion of the southern lands of the British Empire'.[9] Later, in the colony of New South Wales, he envisaged the establishment of self-sufficient villages, comprising:

> One to two hundred cottages—every such cottage having attached
> to it a well-fenced garden—and every such village having a church,
> a school, and houses for a clergyman and schoolmaster.[10]

Fuelled by stories of economic opportunities in the young colony of New South Wales, Boyd on sold prospects of handsome return to investors of the Royal Bank of Australia (formed in London in 1839), and was made the bank's director in the colony. With the bank's capital at his disposal, and his own network of commercial assets, Boyd took the colony by storm, establishing a pastoral empire after his arrival on 15 June 1842. Within two years of his arrival he had acquired a total of 426,000 acres, making him the largest landholder after the Crown.[11] From this vast and well-watered swathe of land along the Riverina and the Monaro plateau in New South Wales, cattle and sheep were funnelled into what was to become a pivotal township and seaport. He set up operations in Twofold Bay, building a hotel, church, vegetable gardens and orchards and dwellings for his staff. Boyd, who owned a fleet of vessels, engaged in freighting to overseas markets and whaling.[12] He founded a port, jetty and a lighthouse and furnaces for rendering cattle and sheep for tallow. He named this settlement Boydtown.

---

8   'Yass', *The Sydney Morning Herald*, 27 October 1847, 3; 'Shipping Intelligence (From *The Sydney Morning Herald*): Yass', *The Maitland Mercury and Hunter River General Advertiser*, 30 October 1847, 2–3.
9   Wellings, *Benjamin Boyd in Australia*, 2–4.
10   Boyd, *A Letter to His Excellency*, 4.
11   Wellings, *Benjamin Boyd in Australia*, 5. During the 1840s, the Royal Bank, or Boyd & Robinson, had more than 160,000 sheep and controlled over 2,500,000 acres (1,011,715 ha) in the Monaro and Riverina. Walsh, 'Boyd, Benjamin'.
12   Wellings, *Benjamin Boyd in Australia*, 5–8.

Boyd's pastoral empire was also an empire of labour, having around 800 men constantly employed as shepherds and stockmen on his estates, and labourers and crew as part of his shipping interests. He recruited labour from across the globe including from Britain, Europe and the Pacific Islands, as well as Aboriginal people and former African-American slaves.[13] As the chairman of the powerful Pastoralists' Association, Boyd lobbied for land and labour reform. Indeed, he saw land and labour as existing in an inseparable bind—the question was not about availability, but affordability in the context of making a profit.[14] He continually badgered government for support with labour costs. When giving evidence on 27 September 1843 to the Select Committee on Immigration, he despaired the fate of the colony 'unless we have cheap labour, and can bring the wages of the shepherd … to [10 pounds] a year with rations' of meat and flour, but not tea or sugar.[15] Boyd then began promoting the idea of importing labour from sister colonies such as Van Diemen's Land or Moreton Bay. In a letter to Sir William Denison, lieutenant-governor of Van Diemen's Land, Boyd argued that transpacific passage was a heavy expense to the colony and offered the solution that convicts with tickets of leave in Van Diemen's Land be granted pardons conditional on them going to New South Wales to work on the 'vast labour-fields'.[16] Unfortunately for Boyd, Dension did not consider this scheme attractive.

In the context of pastoralists coming to terms with the end of their access to cost-neutral transported British and convict labour, Boyd developed his ideas about labour importation by extending his employment of Pacific Islanders already working in his whaling and sandalwood ventures. In 1847, he imported nearly 200 Ni-Vanuatu on periods of indenture. As an expansion of an existing set of relationships in the islands, the people or communities he recruited from would have had a working knowledge of the British and Australian thirst for labour. However, agricultural and indentured labour was on a scale that dwarfed demands for whaling and sandalwood extraction.

The language of 'importation' rather than immigration, as adopted by Boyd, framed the commodification and proprietorship of employment and the reductive placement of Islanders' bodies and extracted labour in a language of economic units, and was a precursor to the Australia–Pacific

13   Walsh, 'Boyd, Benjamin'; 'Legislation in New South Wales (From the *London Telegraph*, March 23rd)', *The Port Phillip Patriot and Morning Advertiser*, 7 August 1848, 4.
14   Boyd, *A Letter to His Excellency*.
15   Walsh, 'Boyd, Benjamin'.
16   Boyd, *A Letter to His Excellency*.

indentured labour trade of 1868–1906. Here we note a stark distinction from the widespread use of forced Aboriginal labour in the pastoral/agricultural industries. In Queensland, the use of Pacific Islander labour would be explicitly legalised, quantified and regulated as an industry, and would stand as an acknowledged symbol of settler expedience and success in neatly and visibly converting 'waste' Indigenous land into productive settler property. By contrast, the use of Indigenous peoples' labour, though widespread and normalised, would remain hidden and ignored, indicative as it was of the dependence of settlers on Indigenous knowledge, skills and labour even as they pursued colonial fantasies of empty landscapes converted by Anglo-Saxon industry into 'productive property'.

Ni-Vanuatu Experience, April–November 1847

On arrival in New South Wales, labourers were conveyed to the hastily constructed and ludicrously grand Boydtown near current-day Eden. Boydtown sat on Twofold Bay, where both deep-sea and onshore whaling industries flourished. The beaches, when Ni-Vanuatu labourers arrived, would have been covered in either whale carcasses or the 'enormous bones of whales bleaching in the weather'.[17] On still days, a thick haze of smoke would have settled over the bay and half-built town as enormous vats and cauldrons simmered over open fires extracting the blubber from stinking whale meat. Thousands of sheep and cattle were boiled down for tallow as a direct result, Boyd frequently claimed, of a paucity of labour to tend to them.[18] For newly arrived New Hebrideans, the smell and sight of this gruesome industry must have been a brutal introduction to the colony. From here they were then expected to walk to stations on the Monaro tablelands and Riverina on Yorta Yorta country. The remoteness of shepherding would have characterised their experience of work in New South Wales. There was also evidence that the new arrivals were assaulted 'in a most savage manner' by local stockmen—treatment that Protectors of Aborigines appointed to the neighbouring Port Phillip District were enjoined to intercede against on behalf of workers.[19]

---

17 Wellings, *Benjamin Boyd in Australia*, 42–43.
18 Boyd, *A Letter to His Excellency*; Wellings, *Benjamin Boyd in Australia*, 16.
19 PROV VPRS 11/PO, Unit 10, 'Unregistered Inward Correspondence to the Chief Protector of Aborigines Regarding South Sea Islanders Imported by Mr. Boyd W. Thomas (Assistant Protector, Westernport District)', contains letter to the Chief Protector from W. Thomas, Melbourne, 30 October 1847; 'Local and Colonial Intelligence: BOYD'S SAVAGES and SOUTH SEA ISLANDERS', *Geelong Advertiser*, 2 November 1847, 1.

Boyd did not wait for government permission to import this 'black' labour and the settler response was predictable. Those in favour of indenture lamented the need for pastoralists to resort to barbarous and non-Anglo-Saxon labour. Colonists, it was said, would never import foreigners 'much less savages and heathens' if they could bring in their own countrymen or draw on former convict labour. It was only out of urgency, they argued, that they had to send to India for 'Coolies' or to the Pacific Islands, which 'literally *swarm* with human beings'.[20] Those against importation described it as incipient slavery. Most responses were deeply racialised, highlighting black savagery signified most clearly by cannibalism.[21] The *Sporting Reviewer* christened Boyd as the 'King of the Cannibal Islands', who, in an accompanying ditty, unsurprisingly met an unfortunate end (see Figure 3.1).[22]

Figure 3.1: Cartoon depiction of Boyd as 'King of the Cannibal Islands'.
Source: *Sydney and Sporting Reviewer*, 1 May 1847, 3.

20 'Immigration From Polynesia', *The Sydney Morning Herald*, 23 April 1847, 2. (Emphasis added.)
21 'Local and Colonial Intelligence: BOYD'S SAVAGES and SOUTH SEA ISLANDERS', *Geelong Advertiser*, 2 November 1847, 1. See also Banivanua Mar, 'Performing Cannibalism'; Banivanua Mar, 'Cannibalism and Colonialism'; Banivanua Mar, 'A Thousand Miles of Cannibal Lands'; Barker, Hulme and Iversen, *Cannibalism*.
22 'Gallery of Commicalities No. II. KING OF THE CANNIBAL ISLANDS', *Bell's Life in Sydney and Sporting Reviewer*, 1 May 1847, 3.

The cannibalism trope persistently framed responses to the Islanders' and Boyd's endeavours:

> A New Hebridean Love Song
>
> Wallaloo! Wallaloo!
>
> Love white man, and eat him too! Stranger white, but that's no matter, Brown man fat, but white man fatter! Put him on hot stone, and bake him,
>
> Crisp and crackling soon we'll make him: Round and round the dainty goes,
>
> Eat his fingers—eat his toes, His body shall our palate tickle,
>
> Then we'll put his head in pickle! CHORUS.
>
> On the white man dine and sup, Whet your teeth and eat him up![23]

Concerns about cannibalistic instincts intersected with concerns about the racial composition of the future population. Fear of miscegenation and being 'overwhelmed' by these swarming hoards underlined much commentary, as the *Maitland Mercury* reported of Boyd's workers:

> As a horde of savage cannibals, we cannot regard them otherwise than with loathing and abhorrence. Yet these are people that must be inevitably poured in upon us, as our demands for labour increase, and those who have raised a clamorous opposition to the introduction of British convicts into this colony once more, must be content hereafter to see our pastures filled, not with European Christians, but with cannibals, from their last disgusting banquet—with the flesh of their fellow-creatures hardly digested within them—and almost carrying about with them the repulsive odour of this unnatural food, which they have recently devoured. Then shall we find our fears excited, not for our properties, nor our morals, but for our lives.[24]

This fear and ridicule was echoed in parliamentary debate following Boyd's first shipment of labourers from the New Hebrides. Concern was raised about the nature of the 'importation', referring to it as 'an incipient slave trade, at variance with the spirit, if not the letter, of the British statute levelled at the traffic'. Questions about consent were also aired: 'those

---

23 'A New Hebridean Song', *Bell's Life in Sydney and Sporting Reviewer*, 6 November 1847, 4.
24 'The Recent Experiment In Immigration', *Maitland Mercury*, 28 April 1847, 2.

who were imported here, under the semblance of contracts were people of the most brutal ignorance, totally incapable of understanding the most ordinary matters of civilized life'.[25] The New South Wales Government refused to create a legal mechanism for the use of indentured labour generally and from the Pacific Islands specifically, amending the *Masters and Servants Act 1847* to include Section 15:

> Nothing in this or the said recited Act contained shall be deemed or construed to apply to any native of any savage or uncivilized tribe inhabiting any Island or Country in the Pacific Ocean or elsewhere.[26]

When a second shipload from the New Hebrides of 54 men and three women arrived at Twofold Bay on 17 October 1847, Boyd refused responsibility for them, as the contracts they had signed in the New Hebrides had been rendered null and void by the Masters and Servants Act. Boyd would go on to blame the New South Wales Government for the failure of his labour experiment and the suffering of Ni-Vanuatu, as these 'children of nature' were too wild and unreliable to undertake 'the more sophisticated prospects' that were opened before them; that is, a legal right to accept and to terminate employment.[27] Many sought alternative work or passage home. The surveillance of these freely moving 'blacks' was reported in detail and concern was raised about their near nakedness and 'formidable sticks' in Parramatta.[28]

At the same time, workers from the first shipment left Boyd's stations and intelligence had them in Yass around 25 October on the way to see the governor and 'Missa Boyd'. The press took great delight in speculating about whether they were going to eat them both.[29] Others, who had been employed along the Murray River, 'bolted' to Melbourne, arriving on

---

25 'Legislative Council. FRIDAY, OCTOBER 1', *Sydney Chronicle*, 2 October 1847, 2.

26 *Masters and Servants Act 1847* (NSW) No 9a. No. IX., 16 August 1847, 'An Act to Amend an Act Intituled "An Act to Amend and Consolidate the Laws between Masters and Servants in New South Wales"', accessed 13 June 2018, classic.austlii.edu.au/au/legis/nsw/num_act/masa1847n9262/, Section 15. See earlier debates about Indian indenture. Cullen, 'Empire, Indian Indentured Labour'; Saunders, *Indentured Labour.*

27 Walsh, 'Boyd, Benjamin'; Boyd, *A Letter to His Excellency*, 16.

28 'The New Hebrideans', *The Maitland Mercury and Hunter River General Advertiser*, 16 October 1847, 2.

29 'Shipping Intelligence', *Sydney Chronicle*, 19 October 1847, 2; 'Yass', *The Sydney Morning Herald*, 27 October 1847, 3; 'Shipping Intelligence (From *The Sydney Morning Herald*): Yass', *The Maitland Mercury and Hunter River General Advertiser*, 30 October 1847, 2–3.

2 November, causing alarm in Geelong as they passed through 'in full march to Melbourne' in protest against their treatment and in pursuit of rides home.[30]

Those stranded in Sydney were reported as working around the harbour on boats transporting goods. 'Boyd's blacks', as they were still known, appeared in the colonial record primarily in coronial inquests, as they were engaged in body retrieval from water accidents and suicides.[31] Their swimming and diving abilities were also noted in their attempts to board vessels thought to be travelling to the Pacific, the most tragic of which was recorded in the press report of an inquest into the discovery of 'the body of a black man, name unknown'. Some of 'Boyd's blacks' had swum out to his brig, which was lying about 2.5 miles from Boyd's premises, including the victim. However, 'the master of the *Portenia* would not allow the men on board, and they swam back', one drowning in the process. The jury stated that Boyd should have attended the inquest to:

> Give evidence of what kind of treatment this man had received since his arrival in the country and that it was not-ill-treatment or starvation that induced this unfortunate savage to act in the way which ultimately led to his death.[32]

The missionary ship *Arch D'Alliance* was reported as landing 'the whole of the natives taken from Sydney (known as Boyd's blacks)' on one of the 'Royalty Islands' (presumably Loyalty Islands, present-day New Caledonia) in October 1848.[33]

30   'Local Intelligence', *The Port Phillip Patriot and Morning Advertiser*, 26 October 1847, 2; 'Local and Colonial Intelligence: BOYD'S SAVAGES and SOUTH SEA ISLANDERS', *Geelong Advertiser*, 2 November 1847, 1; 'Port Phillip', *The Moreton Bay Courier*, 20 November 1847, 4.

31   'Coroner's Inquest', *The Sydney Morning Herald*, 20 December 1847, 2; 'Sydney News', *The Maitland Mercury and Hunter River General Advertiser*, 22 December 1847, 4; 'Labor in the Colonies', *The Australian*, 4 February 1848, 3; 'Local Intelligence', *Bell's Life in Sydney and Sporting Reviewer*, 1 April 1848, 2.

32   'Domestic Intelligence', *Sydney Chronicle*, 2 November 1847, 3.

33   Press reports on Ni-Vanuatu divers and coronial inquests, 1847–48. On the landing of 'the whole of the natives taken from Sydney (known as Boyd's blacks)' by the missionary ship Arch d'Alliance at the 'Royalty Islands', see 'Collision Between a Missionary Ship and the Natives of New Guinea', *Geelong Advertiser*, 4 November 1848, 1. See also Banivanua Mar, *Decolonisation and the Pacific*; Chappell, *Double Ghosts*.

By 1849, Boyd was bankrupt, operations in Twofold Bay had ceased and the 'whole venture so brilliantly launched yet so completely wrecked'.[34] He sailed on his yacht, the *Wanderer*, to the Californian goldfields on 26 October and, upon failing to make his fortune there, returned to his idea of the creation of a miniature republic or confederation upon one of the islands of the Pacific. He arrived in Guadacanal in the Solomon Islands in 1851 but went missing on a duck-shooting trip on his second day. The surviving remnants of his Australian entrepreneurial dreams are the extravagant buildings of Boydtown, including 'Boyd's Folly' a partially constructed and huge tower for whale spotting, the Ben Boyd National Park established in 1971 and a smattering of roads named in his honour. While Boyd's life is commemorated, the lives and deaths of the Ni-Vanuatu labourers are largely invisible in Australian history and national projects of memorialisation.

'Boyd's Blacks', Land and Extraction in Settler Colonies

The stories of the 200 or so Ni-Vanuatu brought to New South Wales and the Port Phillip District in the 1840s are virtually impossible to document beyond the feigned outrage of settlers and pastoralists, whose keen observations were focused less on the experiences of the Ni-Vanuatu men and boys, and more on the longer-term outcomes for a colony desperate for free labour. They remain unnamed and brutalised in the archival record, as they were routinely positioned as tools for an ulterior purpose by the colonial press, parliament and colonial speculators and business interests.

Historians have been accustomed to nationalising the history of indentured and forced labour in the Pacific, partitioning trade between Queensland, Peru, Fiji and France, for example.[35] In some ways, this makes sense, as each national labour trade was governed by distinct legislation that had distinct effects on Islander communities, each country had discrete land

---

34 Wellings, *Benjamin Boyd in Australia*, 4–8.
35 Banivanua Mar, *Violence and Colonial Dialogue*; Corris, 'Blackbirding in New Guinea'; Corris, *Passage, Port and Plantation*; Maude, *Slavers in Paradise*; Moore, 'The Counter Culture of Survival'; Moore, *Kanaka: A History*; Moore, 'Kanakas, Kidnapping and Slavery'; Moore, 'The Mackay Racecourse Riot'; Moore, '"Me Blind Drunk"'; Moore, '"Whips and Rum Swizzles"'; Shineberg, *The People Trade*; Shineberg, *They Came for Sandalwood*.

and labour needs, and each adopted apparently vastly different formal and informal colonial structures. On closer inspection, destination sites throughout the nineteenth century are only clearly colonies of settlement or extraction in hindsight. Pastoralists, settlers and plantation owners shared a common intent, whether driven by greed or ideology, of wanting to convert Indigenous social, economic and spiritual spaces—configured as wild and native wastes—into legally owned, economically productive, spatially contained and 'settled' land.

This segmentation of the Pacific labour trade is underpinned by a deeply imperial perspective, one governed by the constrictions and surveillance that accompanied, organised and legalised this trade. It does not necessarily reflect the lived experiences *in* the islands. Islander communities serviced multiple trades—Queensland, British, French and American—and were delivered for labour in multiple industries ranging from sugar, cotton and copra monocultures to mining or domestic labour. For example, on Tanna in 1847, Islanders would have been approached by sandalwood traders, missionaries, plantation and pastoral interests, and labour vessels 'recruiting' for numerous destination sites ranging from Queensland to Hawai'i. Across the course of a working life, individual labourers could engage in various trades and be subjected to varying levels of violence and coercion.[36]

Viewed in isolation, Boyd's experiment in New South Wales in the 1840s appears as a discrete failure. However, if we view the extraction of labour in the Pacific not in isolation, but instead in terms of a spatial and temporal continuum in which Boyd merely refocused his existing uses of Islander labour from maritime to agricultural pursuits, we gain a number of key insights. First, it points to the need for more nuanced understandings of the relationship between consent and coercion. As the desertion of Boyd's labourers and the choices facing Islanders shows, recruiters such as Boyd were dealing with communities that could be assertive about their own interests, even if the individuals 'recruited' were not necessarily consenting individuals. Second, and despite the faltering nature of Boyd's own entrepreneurialism, we need to be aware of the structural or slow violence that presented him with opportunities for personal gain in the newly colonised Pacific, and that underpinned formal, informal and decolonised imperialism, and its continuity.

36 See, for example, Peter Wien and others in 1906 Royal Commission Minutes of Evidence, cited in Banivanua Mar, *Decolonisation and the Pacific*, 71–73.

Together, these insights offer a deeper understanding of the role that Islanders played as 'imported', rather than immigrant, labour throughout the imperial Pacific basin. As active agents within a new world of differentially racialised opportunity and constraint, they created 'labour lines', interweaving fates and creating entangled relationships of contingency that manifested new Oceanias.

Paying attention to the lived experience of Pacific Islanders caught up in the industrial extraction of labour during the colonial period is significant for its own sake. It partly recuperates histories and genealogies shattered and dispersed by the deeply dehumanising history of labour trading in and around the Pacific. At the same time, tracing the interconnectivity of labour lines in and across the Pacific highlights an interconnectedness and interdependence that partially united Indigenous and Islander histories and experiences of labour mobility and autonomy. It shows that settler colonialism was not a neatly and hermetically sealed, autonomous structure, but one that was entwined with other colonial or imperial structures and reliant on contingencies located in offsite colonial projects. The 'settler complex' was 'transnational', somewhat unbounded and spatially expedient. It was an entire empire of what Patrick Wolfe might have considered pre-accumulated power, in which it was necessary to eradicate and replace not just Indigenous systems of land ownership, but Indigenous social economies more broadly.[37]

Bibliography

Primary Sources

Masters and Servants Act 1847 (NSW) No 9a. No. IX., 16 August 1847, 'An Act to Amend an Act Intituled "An Act to Amend and Consolidate the Laws between Masters and Servants in New South Wales"', accessed 13 June 2018, classic.austlii.edu.au/au/legis/nsw/num_act/masa1847n9262/.

PROV VPRS 11/PO, Unit 10. 'Unregistered Inward Correspondence to the Chief Protector of Aborigines Regarding South Sea Islanders Imported by Mr. Boyd W. Thomas (Assistant Protector, Westernport District)'.

---

37   Wolfe, *Traces of History*; Wolfe, *The Settler Complex*.

Secondary Sources

Banivanua Mar, Tracey. 'Cannibalism and Colonialism: Charting Colonies and Frontiers in Nineteenth-Century Fiji'. *Comparative Studies in Society and History* 52, no. 2 (2010): 255–81. doi.org/10.1017/S0010417510000046.

——. *Decolonisation and the Pacific: Indigenous Globalisation and the Ends of Empire*. Cambridge: Cambridge University Press, 2016.

——. 'Performing Cannibalism in the South Seas'. In *Touring Pacific Cultures*, edited by Kalissa Alexeyeff and John Taylor, 323–32. Canberra: ANU Press, 2016. doi.org/10.22459/TPC.12.2016.21.

——. 'Shadowing Imperial Networks: Indigenous Mobility and Australia's Pacific Past'. *Australian Historical Studies* 46, no. 3 (2015): 340–55. doi.org/10.1080/1031461X.2015.1076012.

——. '"A Thousand Miles of Cannibal Lands": Imagining Away Genocide in the Re-Colonisation of West Papua'. *Journal of Genocide Research* 10, no. 4 (2008): 583–602. doi.org/10.1080/14623520802447743.

——. *Violence and Colonial Dialogue: The Australian-Pacific Indentured Labor Trade*. Honolulu: University of Hawai'i Press, 2007.

Barker, Francis, Peter Hulme and Margaret Iversen, eds. *Cannibalism and the Colonial World*. Cambridge: Cambridge University Press, 1998.

Boyd, Benjamin. *A Letter to His Excellency Sir William Denison, Lieutenant-Governor of Van Diemen's Land, on the Expediency of Transferring the Unemployed Labor of that Colony to New South Wales, Benjamin Boyd*. Sydney: E. Wolfe, 1847.

Chappell, David. *Double Ghosts: Oceanian Voyagers on Euroamerican Ships*. London, England: M. E. Sharpe, c. 1997.

Corris, Peter. '"Blackbirding" in New Guinea Waters, 1883–84'. *Journal of Pacific History* 3 (1968): 85–105. doi.org/10.1080/00223346808572126.

——. *Passage, Port and Plantation: A History of Solomon Islander Labour Migration, 1870–1914*. Melbourne: Melbourne University Press, 1973.

——. '"White Australia" in Action: The Repatriation of Pacific Islanders from Queensland'. *Historical Studies* 15, no. 58 (1972): 237–50. doi.org/10.1080/10314617208595469.

Cullen, Co R. 'Empire, Indian Indentured Labour and the Colony: The Debate Over "Coolie" Labour in New South Wales, 1836–1838'. *History Australia* 9, no. 1 (2012): 84–109. doi.org/10.1080/14490854.2012.11668404.

Graves, Adrian. *Cane and Labour: The Political Economy of the Queensland Sugar Industry, 1862–1906.* Edinburgh: Edinburgh University Press, 1993.

——. 'Colonialism and Indentured Labour Migration in the Western Pacific, 1840–1915'. In *Colonialism and Migration: Indentured Labour before and after Slavery*, edited by P. C. Emmer, 237–59. Dordrecht: Martinus Nijhoff Publishers, 1986. doi.org/10.1007/978-94-009-4354-4_11.

——. 'Crisis and Change in the Queensland Sugar Industry, 1862–1906'. In *Crisis and Change in the International Sugar Economy, 1860–1914*, edited by Bill Albert and Adrian Graves, 261–80. Norwich and Edinburgh: ISC Press, 1984.

——. 'Trucks and Gifts: Melanesian Immigrants and the Trade Box System in Colonial Queensland'. *Past and Present* 101 (1983): 87–106. doi.org/10.1093/past/101.1.87.

Maude, Henry Evans. *Slavers in Paradise: The Peruvian Slave Trade in Polynesia, 1862–1864.* Palo Alto, CA: Stanford University Press, 1981.

Moore, Clive. 'The Counterculture of Survival: Melanesians in the Mackay District of Queensland, 1865–1906'. In *Plantation and Accommodation*, edited by Brij Lal, Doug Munro and D. Beechert, 69–100. Honolulu: University of Hawai'i Press, 1993.

——. *Kanaka: A History of Melanesia Mackay.* Port Moresby, Papua New Guinea: University of Papua New Guinea Press, 1985.

——. 'Kanakas, Kidnapping and Slavery: Myths from the Nineteenth-Century Labour Trade and their Relevance to Australian Melanesians'. *Kabar Serang* 8, no. 9 (1981): 78–92.

——. 'The Mackay Racecourse Riot of 1883'. In *Lectures in North Queensland History: Third Series.* Townsville, Queensland: Department of History, James Cook University (1978): 181–96.

——. '"Me Blind Drunk": Alcohol and Melanesians in the Mackay District, Queensland, 1867–1907'. In *Health and Healing in Tropical Australia and Papua New Guinea*, edited by Ray Macleod and Donald Denoon, 103–22. Townsville: James Cook University Press, 1991.

——. '"Whips and Rum Swizzles"'. In *Lectures in North Queensland History: Second Series*, 119–34. Townsville, Queensland: Department of History, James Cook University, 1975.

O'Brien, Patricia. *The Pacific Muse: Exotic Femininity and the Colonial Pacific.* Seattle, WA: University of Washington Press, 2006.

Russell, Lynette. *Roving Mariners: Australian Aboriginal Whalers and Sealers in the Southern Oceans, 1790–1870.* New York: SUNY Press, 2012.

Salesa, Damon. *Racial Crossings: Race, Intermarriage, and the Victorian British Empire*. Oxford: Oxford University Press, 2011. doi.org/10.1093/acprof:oso/9780199604159.001.0001.

Salmond, Anne. *Between Worlds: Early Exchanges between Maori and Europeans, 1773–1815*. Honolulu, HI: University of Hawai'i Press, 1997.

——. *Two Worlds: First Meetings Between Maori and Europeans, 1642–1772*. Honolulu, HI: University of Hawai'i Press, 1992.

Saunders, Kay. '"The Black Scourge": Racial Responses Towards Melanesians in Colonial Queensland'. In *Race Relations in Colonial Queensland: A History of Exclusion, Exploitation, and Extermination*, edited by Ray Evans, Kay Saunders and Kathryn Cronin, 147–234. St Lucia, Queensland: University of Queensland Press, 1988. [1st ed. 1975.]

——. ed. *Indentured Labour in the British Empire, 1834–1920*. London: Croom Helm, 1984.

——. '"Troublesome Servants": The Strategies of Resistance Employed by Melanesian Indentured Labourers on Plantations in Colonial Queensland'. *Journal of Pacific History* 14, no. 3 (1971): 168–83. doi. org/10.1080/00223347908572374.

——. 'The Workers' Paradox: Indentured Labour in the Queensland Sugar Industry to 1920'. In *Indentured Labour in the British Empire, 1834–1920*, edited by Kay Saunders, 213–59. London: Croom Helm, 1984.

Shineberg, Dorothy. *The People Trade: Pacific Island Laborers and New Caledonia, 1865–1930*. Honolulu: Center for Pacific Island Studies, University of Hawai'i Press, 1999.

——. *They Came for Sandalwood: A Study of the Sandalwood Trade in the South West Pacific, 1830–1865*. Melbourne: University of Melbourne Press, 1967.

Shlomowitz, Ralph. 'Epidemiology and the Pacific Labor Trade'. *Journal of Interdisciplinary History* 19 (1989): 585–610. doi.org/10.2307/203955.

——. 'Indentured Melanesians in Queensland: A Statistical Investigation of Recruiting Voyages, 1871–1903'. *Journal of Pacific History* 16, no. 4 (1981): 203–07. doi.org/10.1080/00223348108572428.

——. 'Markets for Indentured and Time-Expired Melanesian Labour in Queensland, 1863-1906'. *Journal of Pacific History* 11, no. 1 (1981): 66–88. doi.org/10.1080/00223348108572416.

——. 'Mortality and the Pacific Labour Trade'. *Journal of Pacific History* 22, no.1 (1987): 34–55. doi.org/10.1080/00223348708572550.

Somerville, Alice Te Punga. 'Living on New Zealand Street: Maori Presence in Parramatta'. *Ethnohistory* 61, no. 4 (2014): 655–69. doi.org/10.1215/00141801-2717813.

Standfield, Rachel. 'Mobility, Reciprocal Relationships and Early British Encounters in the North of New Zealand'. In *Indigenous Mobilities: Across and Beyond the Antipodes*, edited by Rachel Standfield, 57–77. Canberra: ANU Press and Aboriginal History, 2018. doi.org/10.22459/IM.06.2018.03.

——. 'The Parramatta Maori Seminary and the Education of Indigenous Peoples in Early Colonial New South Wales'. *History of Education Review* 41, no. 2 (2012): 119–28. doi.org/10.1108/08198691311269493.

——. *Race and Identity in the Tasman World, 1769–1840*. London: Pickering and Chatto, 2012.

Walsh, G. P. 'Boyd, Benjamin (Ben), (1801–1851)'. *Australian Dictionary of Biography*, National Centre of Biography, The Australian National University, 1966, accessed 4 June 2018, adb.anu.edu.au/biography/boys-benjamin-ben-1815/text2075.

Wellings, Henry Percival. *Benjamin Boyd in Australia: 1842–1849: Shipping Magnate: Merchant: Banker Pastoralist and Station Owner: Member of the Legislative Council: Town Planner: Whaler*. Sydney: D.S. Ford, 1950.

Wolfe, Patrick, ed. *The Settler Complex: Recuperating Binarism in Colonial Studies*. Berkeley: University of California Press, 2016.

——. *Traces of History: Elementary Structures of Race*. London: Verso, 2016. doi.org/10.1111/1468-229X.12265.

Newspapers

The Australian

Bell's Life in Sydney and Sporting Reviewer

Geelong Advertiser

The Maitland Mercury

The Maitland Mercury and Hunter River General Advertiser

The Moreton Bay Courier

The Port Phillip Patriot and Morning Advertiser

Sydney Chronicle

The Sydney Morning Herald

4

A Regulated Labour Trade across the Torres Strait: Papuan and New Guinean Domestic Workers in Australia, 1901–50

Lucy Davies

In 1927, Beatrice Abel, a missionary at the Kwato Mission in the Territory of Papua, asked Alice Wedega, a young Papuan woman, to travel to Australia with the wife of a business manager from the nearby island of Samarai. The wife was an Australian expatriate and she wanted a Papuan 'girl' to accompany her to Australia to care for her children while she was on leave. Since Wedega had a desire to travel, and the only way for a Papuan woman to leave the country at the time was as a servant, she agreed to go. After one week of travel by ship with her employer and her employer's children, Wedega arrived in Sydney. Initially, Wedega revelled in the excitement of visiting a new city; however, following abuse from her employer, she wished to return to Papua. As Wedega later relayed in her autobiography, *Listen, My Country*, 'my employer didn't treat me as an ordinary girl at all, but as a kind of slave'.[1] Wedega's meals consisted of the leftovers from her employer's meals, which she was given on the verandah or in her room. Wedega told Beatrice Abel's friend, who visited Wedega and took her to church in Sydney, that she was being abused and wished to return home. The friend wrote to Abel who wrote to Wedega's employer demanding that she allow Wedega to return home.

---

1   Wedega, *Listen, My Country*, 27.

Wedega's employer refused to release her until she had fulfilled her three months of employment. When Wedega returned home to Papua at the end of the three months, she relayed her experience to her Papuan friends and warned them not to go to Australia to work.[2]

If experiences of labour mobility provide insight into the nature of Australian coloniality, a focus on Papuan and New Guinean domestic workers like Alice Wedega brings fresh understanding by highlighting the experience of women in twentieth-century Australia.[3] The history of the regulated labour trade in Papuan and New Guinean domestic workers remains largely unrecorded.[4] To date, Alice Wedega's autobiography is the only first-person account of a Papuan woman who worked as a domestic labourer in Australia. Donald Denoon has written about a Papuan woman, Tessie Lavau, who worked in Australia as a domestic in the 1950s, and has explored how her application to travel to Australia triggered a re-evaluation of Australia's governance of Papua New Guinea.[5] These histories are important for drawing attention to Papuan and New Guinean domestic workers' experiences of labour in Australia and how their travels to Australia destabilised colonial rule. However, these were not isolated cases. Drawing out traces of evidence within Australian Government records from the beginning of the twentieth century to the 1950s, I show that Papuan and New Guinean women regularly travelled to Australia to work as servants, nursemaids and domestics.[6]

The collecting of information on Papuan and New Guinean domestic workers—which included surveillance of domestic workers' travels to and from Australia, visitations to domestic workers' places of employment and residence, interviews with domestic workers and their employers, and conversations with neighbours and police about domestic workers— shows how, like Aboriginal domestic workers, their 'very presence in

---

2   Wedega, *Listen, My Country*, 27–29.

3   Throughout this chapter, Papua New Guineans, as they are known today, will be referred to separately as Papuans and New Guineans to accurately reflect the terms used at the time. The south and north of the east of the island of New Guinea were governed separately until after the World War II, when they were combined in an administrative union governed by Australia as the Territory of Papua and New Guinea. It was not until independence in 1975 that the 'and' between Papua and New Guinea was removed.

4   Davies, 'The Movement of Papuan Women'.

5   Denoon, *A Trial Separation*, 7–20; Denoon, 'Miss Tessie Lavau's Request', 136–42.

6   It is important to note here that Papuan and New Guinean men also regularly travelled to Australia to work as domestic labourers. While this chapter focuses on the experiences of Papuan and New Guinean women, for further reading on the complex role of Indigenous men in the private sphere, see Martínez et al., *Colonialism and Male Domestic Service*.

the households of the colonizers was inherently destabilizing'.[7] Scholars have demonstrated how government surveillance of Aboriginal women and girls of mixed descent was 'a method of controlling and regulating Indigenous and non-Indigenous relations'. Government surveillance of Papuan and New Guinean domestics, who were also often of mixed descent, served a similar function.[8] As administrators of Papua and New Guinea, Australian officials were anxious that Papuans' and New Guineans' interactions with Australian citizens on the Australian mainland might have negative repercussions for indigenous and non-indigenous relations back in Papua and New Guinea; hence, Australian officials closely regulated Papuans' and New Guineans' travels to and from Australia.

The subtle ways in which Papuan and New Guinean domestic workers in Australia destabilised colonial relations in Papua and New Guinea have been largely overlooked in histories of labour to date, in part due to the ambiguous nature of their work. As Victoria Haskins and Ann Scrimgeour have convincingly argued, during the first half of the twentieth century, domestic work in Australia was widely regarded as not *real* labour.[9] Histories of Papuan and New Guinean labourers during the Pacific War—a period that has been identified as transformative in weakening Australia's control in Papua and New Guinea—have not considered how Papuan and New Guinean domestics working in Australia might have influenced labour relations in the two territories.[10] Thus, a study of Papuan and New Guinean domestic workers in Australia provides an important avenue for telling the history of women's experiences of Australia's administration of Papua and New Guinea in the first half of the twentieth century, and for rethinking dominant understandings of the process (and timing) of decolonisation.

Anne Dickson-Waiko has recorded her own and other Papua New Guinean women's experiences of colonial rule, focusing especially on the role of women in the decolonisation of Papua New Guinea during the 1960s and 1970s. However, histories of Papua and New Guinea prior to the Pacific War have generally overlooked Papuan and New Guinean

---

7   Haskins, 'From the Centre to the City', 155.
8   Austin, 'Cecil Cook, Scientific Thought', 104–05; McGinn, 'Commonwealth Control', 28.
9   Haskins and Scrimgeour, '"Strike Strike, We Strike"', 89.
10   For a recent analysis of the Australian Government's anxieties about a breakdown in colonial order in Papua and New Guinea as a consequence of Papuans' and New Guineans' interactions during the Pacific War, see Banivanua Mar, *Decolonisation and the Pacific*, 127–28.

women labourers.[11] In her 2016 book, *Decolonisation and the Pacific*, Tracey Banivanua Mar demonstrated how decolonisation in the Pacific consisted of a range of 'subtle expressions … that expanded beyond the territorial confines of colonial and national borders'.[12] This chapter adopts Banivanua Mar's interpretation of decolonisation as a gradual process, propelled by indigenous people, that took place in a range of spaces and over a long period of time and applies it to the private sphere. It argues that what went on in the homes of Australians who employed Papuan and New Guinean domestics, such as sexual liaisons and everyday interactions between domestic workers and their employers, had ramifications for the wider colonial order in Papua and New Guinea. As Ann Laura Stoler has established, interactions between people within these 'intimate sites' were 'critical to the making of colonial categories' and in distinguishing 'between ruler and ruled'.[13] By focusing on how Papuan and New Guinean domestics tested colonial categories when they travelled to Australia to work, this chapter expands our current knowledge of colonialism and decolonisation across borders by recognising Papuan and New Guinean women as important actors in these processes.

'Part of the Family': Papuan and New Guinean Domestic Labourers in Australian Homes

During the late nineteenth century, after employing around 60,000 people from islands in the south-western Pacific in the sugar industry from 1863, the colony of Queensland gradually extended its border north towards the island of New Guinea, annexing the south-eastern corner of that island in 1883.[14] It became a British protectorate the following year. In 1885, Britain and Germany divided the eastern side of the island of New Guinea with Germany in the north (German New Guinea) and Britain in the south (British New Guinea).[15] While Britain and Germany negotiated where to draw boundaries across the island of New Guinea, on the Australian mainland momentum for the federation movement grew and the colony of Queensland became part of the Australian Commonwealth in 1901. The *Immigration Restriction Act 1901* (Cwlth) and the *Pacific*

---

11   Dickson-Waiko, 'Women, Nation and Decolonisation', 177–93.
12   Banivanua Mar, *Decolonisation and the Pacific*, 4.
13   Stoler, *Carnal Knowledge and Imperial Power*, 8.
14   Banivanua Mar, *Violence and Colonial Dialogue*, 1.
15   van der Veur, *Search for New Guinea's Boundaries*, 25.

Island Labourers Act 1901 (Cwlth) were passed through the newly formed Commonwealth Parliament, signalling the new nation's hostility towards non-white peoples, including Aboriginal Australians and people from the Pacific. The Pacific Island Labourers Act placed conditions on Pacific Islanders who lived and worked on the Australian mainland and stipulated that there would be a gradual reduction in the number of Islanders entering Australia up to 31 December 1904 when recruitment would end.[16] With the exception of those born in Australia, crews of ships and those with certificates of exemption under the Immigration Restriction Act, all Islanders in Australia on 31 December 1906 were deported.[17]

While people from the islands in the south-western Pacific were being excluded from the newly formed Commonwealth of Australia, indigenous people from the island of New Guinea were able to travel as domestic labourers to the Australian mainland with certificates of exemption. The Papuan and New Guinean men and women who travelled to Australia as domestic workers at the beginning of the twentieth century made up some of the earliest labourers in a new colonial labour trade between the island of New Guinea and Australia. As Barry Higman has argued, non-white domestic workers were accepted during the 'White Australia' policy era on the basis that 'domestics were employed in the private, feminine sphere rather than the public, male workplace'; 'the labour of housework was not classified as real work or employment'; and 'because domestic servants worked in scattered, small workplaces (households)', which meant that 'they were thought less threatening and less likely to be organized'.[18] These assumptions about domestic labourers and their work, which were prevalent in government reports and correspondence about Papuan and New Guinean domestics, placed workers in an ambiguous position. By not being regarded as real labourers, and as a consequence of the isolation of their workplace, domestics were vulnerable to exploitation and abuse. Conversely, domestic workers often had an intimate knowledge of their employers and were able to build up a rapport with them over many years, leaving them in a better position than other Papuan and New Guinean labourers to negotiate directly with their employers. It was this ambiguous position that made Papuan and New Guinean domestic workers' experiences of labour in Australia unique, and it is with this context in mind that the actions of Papuan and New Guinean domestics

---

16   Tavan, *The Long Slow Death of White Australia*, 8.
17   Mercer, *White Australia Defied*, 76.
18   Higman, 'Testing the Boundaries of White Australia', 16.

are best understood. As Banivanua Mar pointed out in her analysis of the Pacific Island labour trade in Queensland, 'resistance or agency take their meaning only from the oppressive context against which they are being asserted'.[19] Examining how Papuan and New Guinean domestics, such as Paula Wessel (discussed below), expressed 'attenuated agency' during their time in Australia provides a deeper understanding of how colonialism affected their lives.[20]

One of the first domestic workers to arrive in the recently federated Commonwealth of Australia from the island of New Guinea was Kumuessa, an indigenous woman from Rogea Island in British New Guinea. Kumuessa's travel conditions were typical for many Papuan and New Guinean domestic workers seeking to enter Australia. In August 1903, Kumuessa travelled to Sydney as the 'female attendant' of Ellen Turner, wife of the resident magistrate at Samarai in British New Guinea, Charles Owen Turner, who was visiting Australia with her husband.[21] As an indigenous person from British New Guinea, Kumuessa was issued a certificate of exemption to enter Australia; she was required to leave Australia at the end of her work contract, at which point her certificate would be cancelled. Kumuessa accompanied Ellen Turner back to Samarai in January 1904.[22] During the British, German and then Australian administration of the east of the island of New Guinea, it was accepted practice for expatriate officials and their wives to travel to Australia for leave accompanied by a Papuan or New Guinean domestic servant.

Australia's administration over the south-east of the island of New Guinea officially began in 1906 following the *Papua Act 1905* (Cwlth), which transferred authority from Britain to Australia.[23] In keeping with the style of the British administration, Australia governed Papua in a colonial fashion, with expatriate officials and a strict labour hierarchy that included few educational opportunities for Papuans. From 1905 to 1940, mission schools subsidised by Australia provided the only educational

---

19   Banivanua Mar, *Violence and Colonial Dialogue*, 12.

20   Russell employs the term 'attenuated agency' to examine Aboriginal Australians' choices and actions within constrained circumstances. See Russell, *Roving Mariners*, 6.

21   NAA: BP342/1, 9115/327/1903, Immigration Restriction Act 1901 Certificate, particulars of coloured persons leaving the Port of Cooktown, Queensland, for parts within the Commonwealth per 'Wyandra', 14 August 1903.

22   NAA: BP342/1, 9115/327/1903, Burns Philp & Co. Ltd on Board S.S. Airlie at Cooktown, 20 January 1904.

23   *Papua Act 1905*, Federal Register of Legislation, accessed 31 May 2017, www.legislation.gov.au/Details/C1905A00009.

opportunity for Papuans.[24] Australia's control over the east of the island of New Guinea expanded during World War I (WWI) into German New Guinea. The Australian Naval and Military Expeditionary Force governed the region in a notoriously harsh manner and maintained many of the German policies that controlled New Guinean labourers. When WWI ended, the treaty of peace, signed at Versailles in France on 28 June 1919, officially brought Germany's control of New Guinea to an end. A few months before the Treaty of Versaille was signed, on 16 April 1919, Paula Wessel was born on Garowe Island off the coast of New Britain, the largest island in the Bismarck Archipelago.[25] Wessel's father was a German plantation manager at Lama, Witu, and her mother, Nothe, was New Guinean. The couple were not married but lived together for some months until Wessel's father disappeared.[26] By their very existence, Papuan and New Guinean children whose fathers were European and whose mothers were indigenous posed a challenge to racial divisions and hierarchies, and thereby Australia's authority in Papua and New Guinea. As John Dademo Waiko has argued, 'the white men established, protected, and maintained a dominant political and economic position by claiming to be a superior race who regarded New Guineans as inferior'.[27] Australians lived in fear that the majority Papuan and New Guinean population would revolt against them. To create and reinforce racial division and hierarchy, they imposed strict regulations on Papuans and New Guineans that dictated where they could walk, sit and stand, during what hours and for what purpose. In 1933, under native labour regulations, all Papuan employees except domestic servants had to live outside of Port Moresby.[28] Like many of the regulations that governed Papuans' and New Guineans' movements, the master–servant relationship was haunted by Australians' insecurity about their precarious control over Papuans and New Guineans.[29]

---

24 Waiko, *A Short History of Papua New Guinea*, 51.

25 NAA: A367, C72805, John W. Burton, General Secretary, Methodist Overseas Missions, to John L. Froggatt, 2 July 1942; NAA: A435, 1945/4/4736, Alfred R. Gardner, General Secretary, Methodist Overseas Missions, to A. R. Peters, Acting Secretary, Department of Immigration, re 'Paula Wessel', 14 August 1945. Encl. signed J. L. Froggatt.

26 Some reports claim that he died, others that he returned to Germany. See NAA: A12508, 21/4641; NAA: A367, C72805, J. K. McCarthy, Inter-Allied Services Department, to J. L. Froggatt, Esquire, 6 July 1942. Report by Capt. J. K. McCarthy. N.G. 3015. I.S.D., 6 July 1942.

27 Waiko, *A Short History of Papua New Guinea*, 70–71.

28 Wolfers, *Race Relations and Colonial Rule*, 46–55.

29 Waiko, *A Short History of Papua New Guinea*, 71. See also Wolfers, *Race Relations and Colonial Rule*, 55.

In 1921, when Wessel was around two years old, Australia was granted a League of Nations mandate over the north-east region of New Guinea. From then until 1942, the former German colony was known as the Mandated Territory of New Guinea.[30] Once Australia established civil administration there, some improvements were made to New Guineans' working conditions: recruitment was forbidden in specified areas; labourers had to be returned to their home at the end of their contract; and, in 1922, 'disciplinary punishments' were repealed from the *Native Labour Ordinance 1920*.[31] However, labour continued to be prioritised over New Guineans' welfare and New Guineans continued to be relegated to working as menial labourers for colonial officials and expatriates. While the new mandate system brought some change to the old imperial system, the 'guardian-to-ward relationship' between the mandate powers and indigenous people continued.[32] This relationship was replicated in the relationship between female Papuan and New Guinean domestic workers and their employers during Australia's administration. While under German administration, some female New Guinean domestic workers had worked as concubines for their single, male European employers; from 1917, unmarried New Guinean women and children could only be employed by married European women.[33] The relationship between Papuan and New Guinean domestics and their Australian employers was regularly framed as being similar to that of parent and child, with many Australian officials referring to employers as the 'guardians' of domestic labourers. As was sometimes the case on pastoral stations in Australia— where Aboriginal workers were often 'cast as children of motherly white women'—Papuan and New Guinean domestics were nebulously positioned somewhere between child, ward and servant within the homes of white Australians.[34]

In 1923, when Wessel was around three years old, a government official took her away from her mother and placed her at the Raluana School near Rabaul where she was brought up by the Methodist Mission.[35]

---

30   Waiko, *A Short History of Papua New Guinea*, 63.
31   Mair, *Australia in New Guinea*, 180–84.
32   Banivanua Mar, *Decolonisation in the Pacific*, 90.
33   Wolfers, *Race Relations and Colonial Rule*, 80–81.
34   Haskins and Scrimgeour, "'Strike Strike, We Strike'", 92.
35   NAA: A367, C72805, Daisy Coltheart, Girls Training Home, Cootamundra, to Mr. Froggatt, 6 July 1942; NAA: A367, C72805, J. K. McCarthy, Inter-Allied Services Department, to J. L. Froggatt, 6 July 1942. Report by Capt. J. K. McCarthy. N.G. 3015. I.S.D., 6 July 1942.

Wessel never saw her parents again.[36] Missions served a similar purpose in Papua and New Guinea as they did in Australia where young Indigenous girls of mixed descent were trained in domestic skills to work in white Australians' homes.[37] Whereas in Australia, assimilation was the motivation for removing girls from families, in Papua and New Guinea, like in other colonies, 'the mission station became a threshold institution for transforming domesticity rooted in European gender and class roles into domesticity as controlling a colonized people'.[38] The Sacred Heart Mission (MSC), like the Methodist Mission, separated boys and girls; the Daughters of Our Lady of the Sacred Heart, who arrived in New Britain in 1892, taught the girls to read, write and embroider.[39] Also like the Methodist Mission, MSC added to its flock by removing children from their parents. As Stewart Firth has pointed out:

> During the 1890s the authorities progressively permitted the MSC to take abandoned children from labour recruiting vessels, to seek them elsewhere from the Bismarck Archipelago and to use its own boats in the work of collection.[40]

In the first half of the twentieth century, the Australian administration in Papua and New Guinea granted concessions to missionaries to take Papuans and New Guineans abroad for purposes not outlined in the Native Labour Ordinance. For example, when it was discovered that the *Native Labour Ordinance 1906* did not cater to the demands of missionaries, new legislation, the *Removal of Natives Ordinance 1907*, was introduced to allow an expatriate 'to take a native out of the Territory either permanently or temporarily' for a purpose not specified in the Native Labour Ordinance.[41] The Removal of Natives Ordinance was repealed after two missionaries from the London Missionary Society (LMS) took Papuan attendants with them to Europe. According to one official, the Removal of Natives Ordinance had not been intended 'to supply cheap servants for passengers to Europe' and, importantly, its repeal would not 'in any way effect the practice of taking natives to Australia under the Native

---

36   NAA: A435, 1945/4/4736, John L. Froggatt, Port Moresby, to the Hon. E. J. Ward, Department of External Territories, 26 November 1946.

37   Firth, *New Guinea under the Germans*, 141.

38   McClintock, *Imperial Leather*, 35.

39   Venard, *The History of the Daughters of Our Lady of the Sacred Heart in Papua New Guinea* (Port Moresby, 1978), 75–99, cited in Firth, *New Guinea under the Germans*, 142.

40   Firth, *New Guinea under the Germans*, 142.

41   NAA: A1, 1909/13132, Papua. *An Ordinance To Allow in Certain Cases the Removal of Natives from the Territory*. Assented to by the Governor-General, 27 September 1907.

Labour Ordinance'.[42] The repeal of the Removal of Natives Ordinance shows that the Australian Government exercised some regulation over missionaries; however, governance and Christian conversion were closely intertwined colonial processes. Missionaries not only 'civilised' Papuans and New Guineans through education and training, but also expanded their contact with Europeans. As European contact expanded, so did the reach of colonial governance, such as through a head tax and other coercive measures that gradually drew more and more Papuans and New Guineans into labouring for the colonial administration.

The Australian Government treated the missions leniently, exempting them from Papua's *Native Labour Ordinance 1908*.[43] Earlier, missions had been consulted about how they wanted a section of the *Native Labour Ordinance 1906* to be amended.[44] In relation to the ordinance, Papua's acting administrator, John Hubert Plunkett Murray, wrote on 1 August 1908: 'For myself I was further influenced by … the warning contained therein of the dangers of introducing legislation of which the Missions disapprove.'[45] Like a missionary education, labour was regarded as a civilising tool in Papua and New Guinea and the two were the main occasions in which Papuans, New Guineans and expatriates came into contact. It is no coincidence that the areas where the Methodist and Catholic missions were most active were also the most popular recruiting grounds for New Guinean women as labourers. From 1905 to 1907, 457 women were recruited from New Ireland to work in the Gazelle Peninsula and around Madang, and another 150 were recruited to work at other places in the colony and Samoa. In 1911, following a decline in the population, and based on the advice of medical experts, the official government gazette advised that all recruiting of women from southern New Ireland should cease.[46]

From the perspective of government, missionaries and labour recruiters, although often in competition with one another for the souls and/or bodies of Papuans and New Guineans, served a similar purpose in that

---

42   NAA: A1, 1909/13132, Repeal of *The Removal of Natives Ordinance*, 1907.
43   NAA: A1, 1909/13132, 'Papua. Bill to Amend the Native Labour Ordinance', memorandum, Atlee Hunt to Prime Minister, re Native Labour Ordinance, Papua, 10 September 1908.
44   NAA: 1909/13131, 'Papua. Bill to Amend the Native Labour Ordinance', memorandum, J. H. P. Murray to G. S., 25 July 1908.
45   NAA: 1909/13131, 'Papua. Bill to Amend the Native Labour Ordinance', memorandum, J. H. P. Murray, Acting Administrator, Government House, Port Moresby, Papua, to Minister of State for External Affairs, Melbourne, 1 August 1908.
46   Firth, *New Guinea under the Germans*, 125, 127.

the Papuans and New Guineans they recruited were brought under the control, or at least the surveillance, of government. In some parts of New Guinea, indigenous people such as the Tolai utilised the knowledge they acquired through regular contact with Europeans to negotiate and resist European control over their lives.[47] By the 1920s, the education that missions provided to Papuans and New Guineans was regarded by some Australian expatriates as undermining white prestige, for teaching Papuans and New Guineans the tools of the colonisers closed the precarious gap that existed between the rulers and the ruled.[48]

Upon leaving the Methodist Mission where she was raised, Wessel worked as a domestic labourer for various 'prominent Australian people resident in Rabaul'.[49] In 1934, she worked as a domestic in the home of John and Mary Froggatt who lived in Rabaul.[50] John Froggatt worked as an entomologist for the New Guinea administration.[51] In January 1938, Wessel travelled from New Guinea to Sydney with Mary Froggatt for the first time. From then on, she travelled back and forth between the east coast of Australia and the island of New Guinea. On 24 May 1939, Mary Froggatt arrived in Sydney for a six-month holiday and Wessel was permitted to land in Australia 'after the usual undertaking'. This included Mary Froggatt agreeing to be responsible for Wessel's 'maintenance and good behaviour' while in Australia and her assurance that Wessel would depart the country at the end of her stay.[52] A certificate of exemption was issued to Wessel for six months starting on 24 May 1939 and an additional six months was granted starting from 24 November 1939.[53] On 22 January 1940, Wessel departed the port of Brisbane in Queensland for Papua.[54]

---

47   Firth, *New Guinea under the Germans*, 58–61, 63, 65, 80.
48   Wolfers, *Race Relations and Colonial Rule*, 2.
49   NAA: A435, 1945/4/4736, Alfred R. Gardner, General Secretary, Methodist Overseas Missions, to A. R. Peters, Acting Secretary, Department of Immigration, re 'Paula Wessel', 14 August 1945. Encl. signed J. L. Froggatt.
50   NAA: C123, 18325, memorandum, 'M.P.I. Section, Police Headquarters, Sydney'.
51   NAA: A367, C72805, Director to Controller, War Damage Commission, re 'National Security (War Damage to Property) Regulations: Claim by Paula WESSEL', 16 September 1947.
52   NAA: SP42/1, C1940/724, memorandum, Commonwealth of Australia, Customs and Excise Office, NSW, 'SUBJECT: Immigration Act 1901–1935: PAULA WESSEL, New Guinea Native (Half-caste) – Servant accompanying Mrs. Froggatt', signed C. F. Marks, A/g. Detective Inspector, 30 May 1939.
53   NAA: SP42/1, C1940/724, Commonwealth of Australia. Immigration Act 1901–1935. CERTIFICATE OF EXEMPTION. Date of Issue: 7 June 1939; Commonwealth of Australia. Immigration Act 1901–1935. CERTIFICATE OF EXEMPTION. Date of Issue: 21 September 1939.
54   NAA: SP42/1, C1940/724, memorandum, J. J. Barry A/g. Collector of Customs, NSW, to Secretary, Department of the Interior, Canberra, 12 February 1940.

Form No. 2.

COMMONWEALTH OF AUSTRALIA.

Immigration Act 1901–1935.

Number *39/826*

State of NEW SOUTH WALES   Port of **Sydney**

Date of Issue *21st September* 19*39*

CERTIFICATE OF EXEMPTION.

𝔗𝔥𝔦𝔰 𝔦𝔰 𝔱𝔬 ℭ𝔢𝔯𝔱𝔦𝔣𝔶 that *Paula Wessel*

who is described hereunder, is exempted from the provisions of the *Immigration Act* 1901–1935

for a period of *six* months from the *Twenty fourth*

day of *November* 19*39*.

Nationality *British* Birthplace *New Guinea* Age *20 yrs*

Particular Marks —

Occupation *Servant*

Signature of Person exempted *Paula Wessel*

e 39/4495

COLLECTOR OF CUSTOMS
New South Wales

[SEE OTHER SIDE.]

Figure 4.1: Paula Wessel's certificate of exemption.
Source: NAA: SP42/1, C1940/724, Certificate of Exemption.

Government correspondence and Australian newspapers from the 1940s indicate that Wessel was one among many Papuan and New Guinean domestics who travelled to Australia to work during the mid-twentieth century. It had become a common enough practice by the 1940s that Australians on the mainland contacted government officials with requests for Papuan and New Guinean domestic labourers. For example, on 4 November 1943, Reverend Mother Fitzpatrick of the Convent of the Sacred Heart, Stuartholme, South Port, wrote to Francis Michael Forde, minister of the army in Brisbane, requesting assistance with obtaining 'the services of three Fuzzy Wuzzy girls'.[55] The letter was received by Australian officials with little surprise. After making some enquiries, Edward John

---

55   NAA: A518, E840/1/1, M. Fitzpatrick, Convent of the Sacred Heart, to F. M. Forde, Minister for Army, 4 November 1943.

Ward of the Department of External Territories replied that he was unable to find any 'New Guinea native girls' in Australia who were able to work for Fitzpatrick.[56] The casual tone of the letters, and the mutual understanding that 'Fuzzy Wuzzy girls' meant New Guineans, suggests the existence of an established routine in recruiting and employing Papuan and New Guinean domestic labourers. Newspaper reports in Australia about the arrival of a New Guinean domestic worker, Nekiwaia, in December 1948, aroused a moderate level of interest, further indicating that there was widespread community awareness and acceptance of New Guinean domestic labourers in Australia after the Pacific War.[57]

World War II (WWII) represents a significant moment in the history of Papuan and New Guinean domestic workers in Australia. The war, which began in Europe in 1939, reached the Pacific in 1941. In December that year, as Japan's invasion of the island of New Guinea appeared imminent, white women and children were evacuated from Papua and New Guinea. While the evacuation only officially applied to white women and children, some Papuan and New Guinean domestic workers accompanied their employers. Wessel was one of these workers, travelling to Australia with her employer, Mary Froggatt, as part of the evacuation in December 1941.[58] Having a German father, Wessel was registered as an 'enemy alien'. When she arrived in Sydney on 31 December 1941, she was required to sign a 'Personal Statement of Alien Passenger' form.[59] A few months after Wessel's arrival, in March 1942, Wessel's residence at Wentworth Falls was searched by the police for subversive or prohibited possessions. The police questioned Mary Froggatt, who assured them that Wessel was loyally British.[60] While in Rabaul, Mary Froggatt had applied for Wessel to be removed from the list of enemy aliens, but approval had not been given.[61] Four months after the police searched Wessel's premises, John Lewis Froggatt employed a solicitor, Mervyn Finlay, to try and have Wessal's name removed the list of enemy aliens. According to Finlay, his

---

56   NAA: A518, E840/1/1, E. J. Ward to Mother Fitzpatrick, Convent of the Sacred Heart, 11 January 1944; E. J. Ward, Minister for External Territories, to Rev. Mother Fitzpatrick, Convent of the Sacred Heart, 18 January 1944.

57   'SUCH WONDERS TO SEE: Sixteen-Years-Old Nekiwaia, of Ferguson Island, Who Came to Town Today, for the First Time Saw City Buildings, Trams, Modern Cars and Other Adjuncts of Civilisation', *Brisbane Telegraph*, 15 December 1948, 2.

58   NAA: A435, 1945/4/4736, John L. Froggatt, Port Moresby, to E. J. Ward, Department of External Territories, Canberra, 26 November 1946.

59   NAA: A12508, 21/4641, Commonwealth of Australia. Immigration Act 1901–1925. Personal Declaration by Alien Passenger.

60   NAA: C123, 18325, memorandum, 'M.P.I. Section, Police Headquarters, Sydney'.

61   NAA: C123, 18325, Deputy Director of Security for New South Wales to Director General of Security, Canberra, re 'PAULA WESSEL, 13 March 1943.

client felt that it was unfair to Wessel, and embarrassing for him and his wife, to have his servant listed as an enemy alien.[62] John Froggatt also contacted various Australians who had worked in Papua, including John Wear Burton, general secretary of the Methodist Overseas Mission, and Daisy Coltheart, from the girls home at Cootamundra, for their assistance in having Wessel's name removed from the list of enemy aliens.

In 1943, John Froggatt applied on Wessel's behalf for her to travel from Campbelltown, where she lived, to 58 Springfield Road, Killara, Sydney, to visit her friend Johanna Lehman, a New Guinean domestic servant who worked for Mrs Coote.[63] Like Wessel, Lehman was listed as an enemy alien.[64] John Froggatt also requested permission for Wessel to travel to Sydney every fortnight to go shopping and to the picture shows at Campbelltown. Similar applications had been made on behalf of Johanna Lehman and Johanna Lieberang, another New Guinean domestic servant in Sydney. According to the director general of security, all three women were 'illegitimate children of mothers of New Guinea'. They had all been raised in missions and were described as 'definitely pro-British in both their outlook and associations'. Lehmann and Lieberang were free to leave their suburb to go shopping and to church as long as they remained within the bounds of metropolitan Sydney.[65] After John Froggatt's application, Wessel was also exempted from compliance with the provisions of Regulation 17(1) of the National Security (Aliens Control) Regulations, which meant she was no longer required to obtain written permission from an aliens registration officer to visit Killara and Sydney.[66] Wessel was also granted permission to travel freely within her own district, including to visit picture shows.[67]

---

62   NAA: C123, 18325, Mervyn Finlay, Solicitor, Newlands House, to Secretary, Department of the Interior, 17 July 1942.

63   NAA: C123, 18325, memorandum, Director General of Security to Deputy Director of Security, Sydney, 'SUBJECT: PAULA WESSEL', 10 March 1943. See also John L. Froggatt to Rev. J. W. Burton, Methodist Overseas Mission, 5 April 1943.

64   NAA: C123, 18325, memorandum, Director General of Security to Deputy Director of Security, Sydney, 'SUBJECT: PAULA WESSEL', 10 March 1943. See also, memorandum, Deputy Director of Security for New South Wales to Commissioner of Police, Sydney, 'SUBJECT: Paula WESSEL – German – Cooper Research Station, St. Helens Park, Campbelltown. Question of Travel', 27 May 1943.

65   NAA: C123, 18325, memorandum, Director General of Security to Deputy Director of Security, Sydney, 'SUBJECT: PAULA WESSEL', 10 March 1943.

66   NAA: C123, 18325, 'NATIONAL SECURITY ACT 1939-1940. NATIONAL SECURITY (ALIENS CONTROL) REGULATIONS. REGULATION 4A-(2) ORDER', signed, Deputy Director of Security for New South Wales, Sydney, 27 May 1943.

67   NAA: C123, 18325, Director-General of Security to Dr Burton, re 'PAULA WESSEL', 20 March 1943; Deputy Director of Security for New South Wales to Commissioner of Police, Sydney, 25 March 1943.

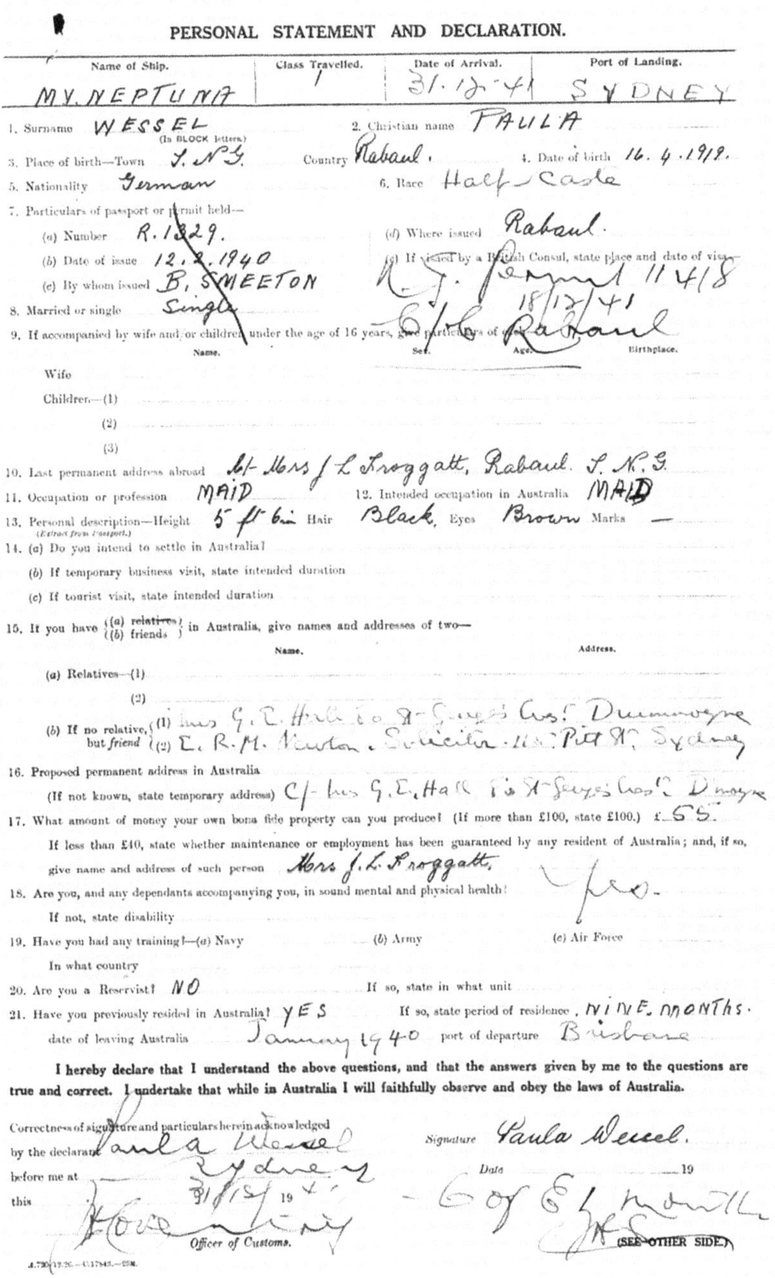

PERSONAL STATEMENT AND DECLARATION.

Name of Ship.	Class Travelled.	Date of Arrival.	Port of Landing.
MV. NEPTUNA	1	31.12.41	SYDNEY

1. Surname WESSEL (In BLOCK letters.) 2. Christian name PAULA
3. Place of birth—Town S. N. G. Country Rabaul. 4. Date of birth 16. 4. 1919.
5. Nationality German 6. Race Half Caste
7. Particulars of passport or permit held—
(a) Number R. 1329. (d) Where issued Rabaul.
(b) Date of issue 12. 2. 1940 (e) If visaed by a British Consul, state place and date of visa—
(c) By whom issued B. SMEETON
8. Married or single Single
9. If accompanied by wife and/or children under the age of 16 years, give particulars of—

Name. Sex. Age. Birthplace.

Wife

Children—(1)

(2)

(3)

10. Last permanent address abroad C/- Mrs J L Froggatt, Rabaul. S. N. G.
11. Occupation or profession MAID 12. Intended occupation in Australia MAID
13. Personal description—Height 5 ft 6 in Hair Black, Eyes Brown Marks —
(Extract from Passport.)
14. (a) Do you intend to settle in Australia?
(b) If temporary business visit, state intended duration
(c) If tourist visit, state intended duration
15. If you have (a) ~~relatives~~ (b) friends in Australia, give names and addresses of two—

Name. Address.

(a) Relatives—(1)
(2)
(b) If no relative, but friend (1) Mrs G. E. Hall c/o St George's Cres. Drummoyne
(2) E. R. M. Newton. Solicitor. Pitt St. Sydney
16. Proposed permanent address in Australia
(If not known, state temporary address) C/- Mrs G. E. Hall St George's Cres. D'moyne
17. What amount of money your own bona fide property can you produce? (If more than £100, state £100.) £ 55.
If less than £40, state whether maintenance or employment has been guaranteed by any resident of Australia; and, if so, give name and address of such person Mrs J. L. Froggatt,
18. Are you, and any dependants accompanying you, in sound mental and physical health? Yes.
If not, state disability
19. Have you had any training?—(a) Navy (b) Army (c) Air Force
In what country
20. Are you a Reservist? NO If so, state in what unit
21. Have you previously resided in Australia? YES If so, state period of residence, NINE MONTHS.
date of leaving Australia January 1940 port of departure Brisbane

I hereby declare that I understand the above questions, and that the answers given by me to the questions are true and correct. I undertake that while in Australia I will faithfully observe and obey the laws of Australia.

Correctness of signature and particulars herein acknowledged by the declarant Paula Wessel
before me at Sydney
this 31/12 1941
Officer of Customs.

Signature Paula Wessel.
Date 19

(SEE OTHER SIDE.)

Figure 4.2: Personal statement by 'Alien Passenger' signed by Paula Wessel.

Source: NAA: A367, C72805, Commonwealth of Australia. Personal Statement by Alien Passenger.

After WWII, the Froggatts applied to have Wessel naturalised. However, in May 1946, the Department of Immigration concluded that, since it was 'contrary to existing policy to naturalize persons of coloured race', and 'as Paula Wessel is a coloured person', she was not eligible.[68] On 26 November 1946, John Froggatt made a direct appeal to Ward regarding Wessel's case. He explained that his wife 'has had this half-caste girl companion with her for nearly thirteen years, and we treat her as one of our family', but to no avail.[69] In January 1947, Wessel's application for naturalisation was again rejected.[70] On 2 June 1948, at the Salvation Army Headquarters, Sydney, Wessel married Arthur C. Thompson of Campbelltown. The couple were expecting a baby in July. Two days after the marriage, John Froggatt notified the Sydney office of the Department of External Territories of the marriage. A little over a fortnight later, Froggatt received a letter from the Department of Immigration informing him that Wessel's certificate of exemption would not be extended, and that Wessel was required to depart Australia 'by the first available vessel'.[71] After almost a decade of travelling to and from Australia, this was the first time that Wessel had been denied a certificate of exemption.

Wessel's employers regularly described her as a member of their family. When Wessel's residence was searched in March 1942, Mary Froggatt described her 'as a friend and companion rather than as an employee'.[72] At other times, Wessel was depicted by the Froggatts as their child; the Froggatts claimed that they could represent her desires and opinions as they knew her so well. For example, John Froggatt, when applying for British naturalisation on Wessel's behalf, wrote that:

> We have seen her grow up in our home, and have thus been able to understand and appreciate her outlook and feelings, and therefore know how keenly she desires to obtain her British Naturalisation.[73]

68 NAA: A435, 1945/4/4736, memorandum, 'Paula WESSEL – Half-Caste – German father and New Guinea Native Mother', Department of Immigration, 23 May 1946.
69 NAA: A435, 1945/4/4736, John L. Froggatt, Port Moresby, Papua, to E. J. Ward, Department of External Territories, Canberra, 26 November 1946.
70 NAA: A435, 1945/4/4736, memorandum, T. H. E. Heyes, Secretary, to Secretary, Department of External Territories, Canberra, re 'Paula Wessel – Naturalization', 13 January 1947.
71 NAA: A435, 1945/4/4736, C. F. Marks, Commonwealth Migration Officer, Department of Immigration, Sydney, to L. J. Froggatt, The Cooper Research Station St. Helens Park, Campbelltown, re 'PAULA WESSEL', 15 June 1948.
72 NAA: C123, 18325, memorandum, 'M.P.I. Section, Police Headquarters, Sydney'.
73 NAA: A435, 1945/4/4736, John L. Froggatt, Port Moresby, Papua, to E. J. Ward, Department of External Territories, Canberra, 26 November 1946.

While Papuan and New Guinean domestics worker did, at times, build amicable relationships with their employers, as histories of Aboriginal domestic workers and their white female employers have shown, 'a fundamental inequality prevailed'.[74] This underlying inequality was evident in the language the Froggatts used to describe Wessel. Mary Froggatt, writing to an Australian official about Wessel, commented: 'a half-caste's life is a sad thing in the Territory'.[75] Thus, Papuan and New Guinean domestic workers, even when they were described as part of the family by employers, could just as easily be represented as racialised subjects and thereby excluded from the family group. Compounding this, all the correspondence about Wessel's travel to Australia, including applications for extension of her stay, were conducted on her behalf by her employers, making her entirely dependent on their support.

It seems that Wessel had limited capacity to express her own opinions and needs. There are no letters from her among the correspondence between the Froggatts and Australian officials. However, her signature at the bottom of one form, and reports on her actions, provide glimpses into the subtle, yet creative, ways she negotiated her situation, as well as the structural constraints she encountered in doing so. During her time in Australia, Wessel developed relative autonomy and increasingly expressed her opinions, even when they differed from her employers. For example, at the beginning of 1946, the Froggatts decided to return to Port Moresby and leave Wessel in Australia, as they believed this would aid her application for British naturalisation; the Froggatts had been told that Wessel needed to be a resident in Australia for five years for her application to be successful. The Froggatts arranged alternative employment for Wessel at the Infants Home, Henry Street, Ashfield. She began working there on 21 February 1946. At the Infants Home, she had 'a delightful room to herself' and was on a wage of 30/- per week plus keep. As part of the nursing staff, she wore a uniform and cap, was not required to undertake any domestic duties and had two days off per week.[76] Prior to starting work, Wessel 'seemed enthusiastic about going to Ashfield'; however, when she was interviewed by a government official, Mr Downing, on 19 March, she explained that, while she was being well treated, she would prefer to move to the Campbelltown Cripple Home,

74   Tonkinson, 'Sisterhood or Aboriginal Servitude?', 29.
75   NAA: A518, E840/1/1, P. Froggatt, Macquarie Club, to Mr Downing, n.d.
76   NAA: A518, E840/1/1, P. Froggatt, Campbelltown, to Downing, 4 February 1946; P. Froggatt, Macquarie Club, to Downing, n.d.

where there was 'less work, and more freedom'. She was adamant that she did not wish to return to New Guinea. Subsequently, Australian officials decided that Wessel had 'been getting a little too much attention' and was 'in need of some control'. Therefore, it was recommended that she remain at Ashfield.[77] This response to Wessel's request to change employment shows that the government prioritised control over the wishes of Papua and New Guinean domestics.[78]

Mary and John Froggatt's actions in seeking naturalisation for Wessel indicate that they cared for Wessel and her wellbeing. John Froggatt cited other actions, such as arranging an apartment, alternative employment and taking out an annuity for Wessel, as evidence that his and his wife's concern for Wessel was sincere. However, the relationship between the Froggatts and Wessel, like that between all employers and domestics, was dependent on the will of the employer.

While the ambiguous position of Papuan and New Guinean domestic labourers in Australians' homes was often precarious, this section has explored through the story of Paula Wessel how this ambiguity was utilised by some domestics to their advantage. The following section, which examines the experiences of other Papuan and New Guinean domestic labourers, such as Susan Hari, Pouna and Lavu, Annie Lundin, Celestine Blanco, Blanche Burfitt and Cecilia Phlug (or Pflug), reveals the vulnerability of domestic workers in Australia and some of the complex ways they negotiated government surveillance and control.

'Certainly the Girl's Work Is Not Arduous': Government Surveillance and Control

The case of a Papuan domestic worker in Australia in the 1940s shows how the position of a domestic could change based on the will of their employer. Susan Hari was born in 1924 in Isuleilei along the south coast of Papua's Fyfe Bay. A teenager when she disembarked in Australia on 2 December 1941, Hari arrived under the 'guardianship' of 'Mrs Fisher' who had four children aged between six and ten. Mrs Fisher's husband

---

77   NAA: A518, E840/1/1, memorandum, C. E. Leake, Officer in Charge, Department of External Territories, Sydney, to Secretary, Canberra, re 'PAULA WESSEL', 2 April 1946.

78   New Zealand officials also sought to control Cook Islander domestic workers' increasing autonomy in New Zealand under the guise of welfare. See Anderson, 'Distant Daughters', 285.

was in the forces in New Guinea. A government report from an inspection of Hari's workplace noted that she 'enjoyed the same privileges as the family'; this was despite Hari not being allowed to leave her employer's house unaccompanied, not having set working hours and having her pay withheld while her contract was finalised.[79] While working in Australia, Hari became pregnant and gave birth to a son, James, at the Salvation Army Home, Marrickville, in July 1944. James's paternity was recorded as 'unknown'.[80] Fisher attempted to have the baby cared for by the Sydney Rescue Work Society or a similar LMS affiliate. She also applied for a maternity bonus and child endowment for Hari; however, since Hari had been in Australia for less than five years and was a 'full native', she was not eligible.[81] In January 1945, Hari was still at Marrickville due to Fisher having 'lost interest in the girl'.[82] By August that year, Hari and James were living with Fisher; however, at the government's recommendation, they departed Sydney on 31 August 1945.[83] Henry Leonard Hurst, a representative from the LMS, confirmed that Hari would be returned to Papua 'in the charge of some woman missionary' and that she would be cared for by the LMS once she was back in Papua.[84] Hari's experience is testament to the vulnerability of Papuan and New Guinean domestic workers in Australia. Often, such women were not only without parents or family in Papua and New Guinea, but also lacked the support of community, and their experience of work in Australia left them vulnerable to physical abuse. As labourers on the Australian mainland, Papuan and New Guinean domestics were reliant on Australian officials' arbitrary protection.

On 9 March 1943, C. E. Leake, the officer in charge of the Department of External Territories, Sydney, wrote to the assistant secretary of the same department in Canberra about Papuan and New Guinean 'half caste and native girls in New South Wales who have been brought south

---

79 NAA: A518, E840/1/1, 'REPORT ON NEW GUINEA (MAIDS) IN AUSTRALIA, HARI, Susan, Papuan Native Girl', Department of External Territories, Sydney, Report No. 1, 14 June 1943.
80 NAA: A518, 822/2/603, memorandum, J. R. Halligan, Secretary, Department of External Territories, Canberra, to Director of Research & Civil Affairs, Headquarters, Victoria Barracks, Melbourne, 9 August 1945 (including attachments).
81 NAA: A518, 822/2/603, extract from Department of External Territories Sydney Office memorandum, 1 August 1945.
82 NAA: A518, 822/2/603, 'HARI, Susan', 7 August 1945.
83 NAA: A518, E840/1/1, memorandum, J. R. Halligan, Secretary, Department of External Territories, to Acting Secretary, Department of Immigration, Canberra, 30 August 1945.
84 NAA: A518, E840/1/1, Hurst London Missionary Society, Sydney, to Mr Halligan, Department of External Territories, Canberra, 7 March 1944.

… concerning whom we have no official knowledge'. Leake's letter had been prompted by 'several indirect complaints by these domestics' and he wished to know whether there were any conditions 'for their keep, wages, hours of recreation, etc'.[85] A list of seven Papuan and New Guinean women's names was attached to the letter.[86] In reply, J. Brack requested that the women be visited by an official from the Sydney branch as soon as possible, and then 'at quarterly intervals' to obtain information on their working conditions, wages and welfare. He also requested that 'complaints should be carefully investigated'. As far as Brack knew, there were no specific conditions of employment for Papuan and New Guinean women in Australia; instead, the women worked under conditions agreed upon with their employers before arriving in Australia.[87] Although this response has the appearance of being motivated by concern for the welfare of Papuan and New Guinean domestic workers, closer scrutiny reveals that Australian officials employed surveillance to control these women.

The process of investigating the complaints included conducting interviews with the Papuan and New Guinean women in front of their employers, which meant that they had limited opportunity to express their complaints without fear of reprisal. Two Papuan and New Guinean domestic workers, Pouna and Lavu, who were visited and interviewed by Downing in front of their employer later walked to Downing's office to voice their discontent in private.[88] Such complaints were often dismissed by Australian officials or retracted by the domestic worker. For example, a report on domestic worker Annie Lundin explained that she:

> Was restless and wanted to go to other employment where she could earn more money but is now contented again, and realises that she is really well off, and among good people.[89]

Celestine Blanco made numerous attempts to leave her place of employment, Prince Henry Hospital, and seek work at a factory near Glebe Point, but the hospital authorities refused to release her. The officer

85   NAA: A518, E840/1/1, memorandum, C. E. Leake, Officer-in-Charge, Department of External Territories, Sydney, to Assistant Secretary, Department of External Territories, Canberra, 9 March 1943.
86   The Papuan and New Guinean women listed included Emma Lehmann, Cecilia Phlug, Johanna Lieverens (or Lieverang), Paula Wessel, Annie Lundin, Luise Taligatus and Susan Hari.
87   NAA: A518, E840/1/1, memorandum, J. Brack, for Assistant Secretary, Canberra, to Officer-in-Charge, Sydney Office, re 'New Guinea and Papuan Half-castes in Australia', 6 May 1943.
88   See: NAA: A518, HH112/1 PART 2; NAA: A518, HH112/1 PART 3.
89   NAA: A518, E840/1/1, memorandum, Department of External Territories, Sydney, to Secretary, Canberra, re 'HALF CASTE AND NATIVE NEW GUINEA GIRLS IN AUSTRALIA', 17 January 1945.

who conducted the report on Blanco did not consider her situation detrimental to her wellbeing and advised her to remain at the hospital.[90] The department's response to these Papuan and New Guinean domestic workers' complaints, when placed alongside the reports of another domestic worker, Cecilia Phlug, illuminate the creative and calculated ways such women both survived and escaped difficult working conditions in Australia.

New Guinean Cecilia Phlug (or Pflug) arrived in Sydney at the end of December 1941 in the company of her employer H. G. Woolcott.[91] Subsequently, Phlug was 'handed over' to Woolcott's sister, Edna McLean, with the approval of T. McAdam of Rabaul Customs.[92] From 30 December 1941 to 23 November 1943, Phlug was employed by Edna McLean in Warrawee, a suburb on Sydney's affluent upper north shore.[93] On 24 November 1943, after almost two years of working in the McLean household, Edna McLean telephoned the Department of External Territories and reported that she had had 'further trouble' with her employee, Phlug. McLean then sent Phlug to her mother-in-law's house at Manly. Phlug remained there for several weeks until McLean's mother-in-law asked for her to be removed following 'further disobedience'. In the wake of these complaints, a department official interviewed Phlug, who requested to leave her current position. The department heeded Phlug's request and found her a job at the Prince Henry Hospital. Thereafter, her behaviour and movements were closely monitored by Australian officials until she was eventually repatriated.[94]

---

90 NAA: A518, E840/1/1, memorandum, C. E. Leake, Officer-in-Charge, Department of External Territories, Sydney, to Assistant Secretary, Canberra, re 'Miss Celestine BLANCO – Report No. 2', 22 November 1943.

91 NAA: A518, E840/1/1, memorandum, Acting Secretary, Department of Immigration, Canberra, to Secretary, Department of External Territories, Canberra, re 'Cecilia Phlug (or Pflug) – Half-Caste New Guinea Native of German Nationality under exemption', 4 February 1946.

92 NAA: A518, E 840/1/1, 'List of Papuan and New Guinean Female Natives & Half … Officially Recorded by this Officer'.

93 NAA: A518, E840/1/1, memorandum, J. R. Halligan, Secretary, to Officer-in-Charge, Sydney, re 'Cecelia Pflugg: Half-caste (New Guinea)', 29 August 1946.

94 NAA: A518, E840/1/1, memorandum, Acting Secretary, Department of Immigration, Canberra, to Secretary, Department of External Territories, Canberra, re 'Cecilia Phlug (or Pflug) – Half-Caste New Guinea Native of German Nationality under exemption', 4 February 1946; 'List of Papuan & New Guinean Female Natives & Half … Officially Recorded by this Officer'; memorandum, J. R. Halligan, Secretary, to Officer-in-Charge, Sydney, re 'Cecelia Pflugg: Half-caste (New Guinea)', 29 August 1946; memorandum, J. Brack, Acting Officer in Charge, Department of External Territories, Sydney, to Assistant Secretary, Canberra, re 'CECILIA PHLUGG', 15 December 1943; memorandum, C. E. Leake, Officer-in-Charge, Department of External Territories, Sydney, to Assistant Secretary, Canberra, re 'Cecilia Phlug – New Guinea Half Caste', 10 January 1944.

As a result of her 'disobedience'—or, rather, the complaints of her white employers—Phlug was subject to government surveillance. By contrast, the complaints of Papuan and New Guinean domestic labourers, like those of Pouna, Lavu, Lundin and Blanco, were largely dismissed. This was in part due to Australian officials not regarding Papuan and New Guinean domestics' labour as real work. Papuan and New Guinean domestics' wages were often described by employers and Australian officials as 'pocket money' and many employers were described as 'guardians'.[95] As Leake wrote on 25 June 1943:

> There is some differences in the pocket money being paid to these maids by their guardians, but this is not great, and as all express contentment, and are being well cared for, the reports may be considered as very satisfactory.[96]

Australian officials' disregard for domestic labour contributed to the already vulnerable position of domestic workers and increased the likelihood of exploitation, as employers were not held to account by Australian officials or given any guidelines on working hours, wages and tasks. For example, Papuan domestic worker Blanche Burfitt was paid £1 per month in Papua; however, in Australia her employer was unable to afford the cost of her wages and instead gave her 'pocket money' and paid for her expenses.

Domestic workers' working tasks and hours were loosely described by employers and officials as 'general household duties' and 'an ordinary household day'.[97] Domestic worker Annie Lundin's employer, Mrs Hawnt, described Lundin's jobs as looking after her daughter and her daughter's three children and 'helping generally', leading one government official to conclude that: 'Certainly the girl's work is not arduous.'[98] This is in stark contrast to other descriptions of domestic work in Australia.

---

95 NAA: A518, E840/1/1, memorandum, C. E. Leake, Officer-in-Charge, Department of External Territories, Sydney, to Assistant Secretary, Canberra, re 'New Guinea & Papuan Half Castes in Australia', 25 June 1943.

96 NAA: A518, E840/1/1, memorandum, C. E. Leake, Officer-in-Charge, Department of External Territories, Sydney, to Assistant Secretary, Canberra, re 'New Guinea & Papuan Half Castes in Australia', 25 June 1943.

97 For example, NAA: A518, E840/1/1, 'REPORT ON NEW GUINEA FEMALES (MAIDS) IN AUSTRALIA. LIEVRANG, Johanna Half Caste German (Single)', Department of External Territories, Sydney Office, Report No. 1 17/6/43.

98 NAA A518, E840/1/1, memorandum, A. J. Gaskin, Department of External Territories, Sydney, to Secretary, Department of External Territories, Canberra, re 'HALF CASTES AND NATIVE GIRLS IN AUSTRALIA', 28 July 1944.

Historian Shirleene Robinson has described the work of Aboriginal child domestics in Queensland as 'physically laborious, emotionally exhausting and low paying'.[99] Further, as Alice Wedega's personal account of working in Australia attests, Papuan and New Guinean domestic workers were also regularly subject to abuse by their employers.

Papuan and New Guinean domestic workers who expressed discontent and demanded improvements in their conditions of work caught the attention of Australian officials; these women came under close government supervision and their stories have made it into the archives. In other cases, the mere presence of Papuan and New Guinean domestics in Australia was enough to attract surveillance. The regulation of Papuan and New Guinean domestic workers was extensive; however, there is evidence that not all Papuan and New Guinean domestic workers were watched by government. For example, a death notice in *The Sydney Morning Herald* in 1946 reported that Nati, a 'native of New Britain, loved and faithful friend of the family for over 50 years', had passed away at Wollstonecraft. Nati had travelled to Australia 'many years ago' with the Reverend Rickard, a former member of the Methodist Missionary Society, but she was unknown to government.[100] The stories told in this chapter have only scratched the surface of the history of Papuan and New Guinean domestic workers in Australia in the first half of the twentieth century. The regulations catering to the travel of Papuan and New Guinean domestic workers to Australia, and evidence that this was a widely accepted practice, indicates that a more extensive labour trade in Papuan and New Guinean domestics to Australia existed than has previously been imagined.

Conclusion

This chapter opened with the story of Alice Wedega who, as a young woman, travelled to Australia to work as a domestic labourer. Her story, like the stories of other Papuan and New Guinean domestic workers, illustrates how intersecting forces of coloniality, such as having a mission education and government regulation, affected her experience of working

---

99   Robinson, *Something Like Slavery?*, 162, 163.
100 NAA: A518, E840/1/1, memorandum, Major for DA&QMG (ANGAU), HQ Eight Military, District Rabaul CA70/6 Australian Military Forces, to Secretary, Department of External Territories, Canberra, re 'NEW GUINEA NATIVES IN AUSTRALIA, NATI (Deceased)', 26 March 1946.

abroad. When Wedega returned to Papua and relayed her experience to her friends, she influenced how other Papuans viewed work and life in Australia. Wedega's criticism of Australians, based on her newly acquired knowledge of them, may not have been transformative for Australia's administration in Papua, but her criticisms nevertheless had the effect of subtly undermining Australian authority.

The stories of Papuan and New Guinean domestic workers outlined in this chapter were accessed through the lens of the government officials who tracked their travels to and from Australia, movements around Australia, and everyday working and personal lives. The extent of Australia's surveillance of Papuan and New Guinean domestics, and official view that such workers needed to be controlled and disciplined through surveillance, regulation and even repatriation, point to the ways in which these women, through their mere presence in the homes of Australian citizens, unsettled Australian officials.

By placing the stories of individual Papuan and New Guinean domestic workers in the foreground, this chapter has provided a glimpse of Papuan and New Guinean women's experiences of labour in Australia during the first half of the twentieth century. Their stories show that the relationship between employers and domestics was undefined and exploitative, as workers were left vulnerable to the will of employers and without the protection of officials. Yet, despite these circumstances, some Papuan and New Guinean domestics, like Paula Wessel, exercised autonomy. Wessel and other domestic labourers' actions do not appear significant unless they are properly considered in terms of their colonial context—they were simply women working as domestic labourers who visited friends, went shopping and attended the cinema on their days off. However, placed within the context of Papua and New Guinea, their everyday actions were exceptional. Not only did these non-white women travel to Australia and work in white Australian citizens' homes during the era of 'White Australia', they travelled around the suburbs of Sydney, married Australian citizens and had children. Even more extraordinary is the fact that they did this while regarded as 'enemy aliens'. Although they were required to obtain a permit to visit Sydney, their ability to do so and subsequent exercise of autonomy and freedom of mobility made them vastly different to their peers in Papua and New Guinea. The strict segregation between Papuans and New Guineans and Australian expatriates in the towns of Port Moresby and Rabaul continued long after the Pacific War. Australia did not repeal its curfew laws in Papua and New Guinea until 1959.[101] This makes the stories of Papuan and New Guinean domestic workers valuable in their own right (as little-known historical subjects) and vital in terms of their collective role as important actors in colonial relations between Australia and Papua and New Guinea.

Bibliography

Primary Sources

NAA: BP342/1, 9115/327/1903.

NAA: A367, C72805.

NAA: A435, 1945/4/4736.

NAA: A12508, 21/4641.

NAA: 1909/13131.

NAA: A1, 1909/13132.

NAA: SP42/1, C1940/724.

NAA: C123, 18325.

NAA: A518, E840/1/1.

NAA: A518, HH112/1 PART 2.

NAA: A518, HH112/1 PART 3.

NAA: A518, 822/2/603.

Papua Act 1905, Federal Register of Legislation, accessed 31 May 2017, www.legislation.gov.au/Details/C1905A00009.

Secondary Sources

Anderson, Rosemary. 'Distant Daughters'. *The Journal of Pacific History* 48, no. 3 (2013), 267–85. doi.org/10.1080/00223344.2013.823008.

Austin, Tony. 'Cecil Cook, Scientific Thought and 'Half-Castes' in the Northern Territory 1927–1939'. *Aboriginal History* 14, no. 1 (1990): 104–22.

Banivanua Mar, Tracey. *Decolonisation and the Pacific: Indigenous Globalisation and the Ends of Empire*. Cambridge, United Kingdom: Cambridge University Press, 2016.

---

101 Wolfers, *Race Relations and Colonial Rule*, 45.

———. *Violence and Colonial Dialogue: The Australian-Pacific Indentured Labor Trade*. Honolulu: University of Hawai'i Press, 2007.

Davies, Lucy. 'The Movement of Papuan Women into Australia as Domestic Servants during the 1940s and 1950s'. Honours Thesis, La Trobe University, 2011.

Denoon, Donald. 'Miss Tessie Lavau's Request'. *Meanjin* 62, no. 3 (2003): 136–43.

———. *A Trial Separation: Australia and the Decolonisation of Papua New Guinea*. Canberra: ANU E Press, 2012. doi.org/10.22459/TS.05.2012.

Dickson-Waiko, Anne. 'Women, Nation and Decolonisation in Papua New Guinea'. *The Journal of Pacific History* 48, no. 2 (2013): 177–93. doi.org/10.1080/00223344.2013.802844.

Firth, Stewart. *New Guinea under the Germans*. Carlton: Melbourne University Press, 1983.

Haskins, Victoria. 'From the Centre to the City: Modernity, Mobility and Mixed-Descent Aboriginal Domestic Workers from Central Australia'. *Women's History Review* 18, no. 1 (2009): 155–75. doi.org/10.1080/09612020802608108.

Haskins, Victoria and Anne Scrimgeour. '"Strike Strike, We Strike": Making Aboriginal Domestic Labor Visible in the Pilbara Pastoral Workers' Strike, Western Australia, 1946–1952'. *International Labor and Working-Class History*, 88 (2015): 87–108. doi.org/10.1017/S0147547915000228.

Higman, B.W. 'Testing the Boundaries of White Australia: Domestic Servants and Immigration Policy, 1901–45'. *Immigrants and Minorities* 22, no. 1 (2003): 1–21. doi.org/10.1080/02619288.2003.9975051.

Mair, Lucy Philip. *Australia in New Guinea*. Carlton, Victoria: Melbourne University Press, 1970.

Martínez, Julia, Claire Lowrie, Frances Steel and Victoria Haskins. *Colonialism and Male Domestic Service across the Asia Pacific*. eBook: Bloomsbury Academic, 2019.

McClintock, Anne. *Imperial Leather: Race, Gender and Sexuality in the Colonial Contest*. New York: Routledge, 1995.

McGinn, Ian. 'Commonwealth Control of Non-Indigenous and Indigenous Relations and Mixed-Descent People in the Northern Territory, 1911–1939'. *Journal of Northern Territory History* 23 (2012): 25–41.

Mercer, Patricia. *White Australia Defied: Pacific Islander Settlement in North Queensland*. Townsville: James Cook University, 1995.

Robinson, Shirleene. *Something Like Slavery? Queensland's Aboriginal Child Workers, 1842–1945*. North Melbourne: Australian Scholarly Publishing, 2008.

Russell, Lynette. *Roving Mariners: Australian Aboriginal Whalers and Sealers in the Southern Oceans, 1790–1870*. Ithaca: State University of New York Press, 2012.

Stoler, Ann Laura. *Carnal Knowledge and Imperial Power: Race and the Intimate in Colonial Rule*. Berkeley: University of California Press, 2010.

Tavan, Gwenda. *The Long, Slow Death of White Australia*. Carlton North, Victoria: Scribe, 2005.

Tonkinson, Myrna. 'Sisterhood or Aboriginal Servitude? Black Women and White Women on the Australia Frontier'. *Aboriginal History* 12 (1988): 27–39.

van der Veur, Paul W. *Search for New Guinea's Boundaries: From Torres Strait to the Pacific*. Canberra: Australian National University Press, 1966. doi.org/10.1007/978-94-015-3620-2.

Waiko, John Dademo. *A Short History of Papua New Guinea*. South Melbourne, Victoria: Oxford University Press, 2007, 2013. [2nd edition.]

Wedega, Alice. *Listen, My Country*. Sydney, NSW: Pacific Publications, 1981.

Wolfers, Edward. *Race Relations and Colonial Rule in Papua New Guinea*. New South Wales: Australian and New Zealand Book Company, 1975.

Newspapers

Brisbane Telegraph

5

New Histories but Old Patterns: Kāi Tahu in Australia

Rachel Standfield and Michael J. Stevens

Kāi Tahu (also known as Ngāi Tahu) is the predominant Māori tribe from the South Island of New Zealand.[1] As with Ngāpuhi in the northern North Island, Kāi Tahu, especially in the southern South Island, were pulled into the expanding maritime frontier of New South Wales in the first decade of the nineteenth century. In this chapter, we examine some of the initial travels of Kāi Tahu people to Australia, focusing on the earliest periods of encounter with Europeans and Euro-Americans—collectively known as *tākata pora* (ship men or boat people). We do this to explore how this travel reflected Kāi Tahu worldviews, social structures and economic priorities. Shedding light on features of Kāi Tahu epistemologies of movement, we highlight how cultures of mobility and strategic responses to the historical circumstances they were operating within shaped Kāi Tahu decisions to travel to the Australian continent. We focus on Kāi Tahu people 'Jacky Snapper' and Tokitoki, and their *tākata pora* companion, James Caddell, who first ventured to Sydney in 1822 from Foveaux Strait, as well as two young men, 'Chief Attay' and 'Quolla', believed to have been taken as hostages to Sydney in 1834. These young chiefs from Ōtākou are believed to have arrived in Sydney after having been kidnapped by the Sydney owners of an Ōtākou-based whaling station after increasing tensions with local Kāi Tahu. We also outline the longer history of travel to New South

---

1   We use the spelling Kāi Tahu rather than Ngāi Tahu in accordance with the southern dialect of *te reo Māori* in which a k is used in place of ng.

Wales of the Kāi Tahu chief Karetai, whose travel to Australia was shaped by hostilities between Kāi Tahu and Ngāti Toa, a tribe based in the southern North Island. For these two tribes, and several others, the consequences of travel to and connection with Australia were violent conflict, shifting tribal boundaries, forced migration and population decline.

From the beginning of British colonisation in Australia to the signing of the Treaty of Waitangi in 1840, which signalled the formal colonisation of New Zealand, British relationships with the archipelago and with *iwi* (tribes, people, nations) were centred on economic relationships. Māori connections with Australian-based British colonists were founded on labour and trade, as Māori engaged with British extractive industries that looked to New Zealand resources for profit. As Standfield has noted elsewhere:

> From the outset … the New South Wales colony … sought to exploit resources from New Zealand to defray the costs of the penal settlement and contribute important commodities to the empire at the same time as they colonized Aboriginal land.[2]

James Belich has explained how:

> Sydney has long been one of New Zealand's most important cities, and for a century New Zealand was one of Sydney's most important hinterlands. Much European influence on New Zealand was strained through Sydney first. Most Europeans living in New Zealand before 1840 had done time in New South Wales; it was also the most popular overseas destination for Maori.[3]

New Zealand thus held significant interest for Australian Government and private commercial interests as a source of profit to support the colony. In this sense, Australian colonisation and its economic prosperity prior to the Treaty of Waitangi was engaged with Māori (and other Pacific peoples') labour at the same time as it was dispossessing Aboriginal peoples of their lands. These varied relationships, drawn out of different aspects of Australian coloniality but all having, at their foundation, the buttressing and extension of British colonial power and presence in the region, grew out of, and in turn further extended, different forms of recognition and rights. As Mark Hickford has argued, Māori 'propensity and capacity to

---

2   Standfield, *Race and Identity*, 5.
3   Belich, *Making Peoples*, 134.

engage in transactional conduct',[4] as well as trade and labour relations, were vital aspects of this, as were European notions of Māori relations to land. As Standfield has argued elsewhere, these varied but related colonial projects in the region shaped racial discourses and created and reiterated racial hierarchies.[5] In summary, Māori labour and trade was a key plank of the British colonisation of Australia *and* New Zealand.

Within this broader framework of colonial history, we argue that travel and movement to Australia operated as an extension of Kāi Tahu life and culture that was deeply shaped by cycles of movement and histories of travel into and within Te Waipounamu, the South Island of New Zealand. We outline our approach to tracing Kāi Tahu travel and our methodologies in engaging with archives but aim to do more than this by bringing these into conversation with Kāi Tahu community understandings; we wish to construct a history that affirms the connections between and across generations that have journeyed across the Tasman in 'pursuit of *mana*' (power, authority, prestige).[6]

This chapter comes out of a nascent research project being undertaken by Rachel Standfield from the Monash Indigenous Studies Centre and Michael Stevens from Te Rūnanga o Ngāi Tahu, the Kāi Tahu tribal council.[7] The project looks to explore long histories of travel and migration to Australia by Kāi Tahu *whānau* (family groups). This westward movement, which began for Kāi Tahu in the 1820s, brought diverse travellers to Kāi Tahu territory, some as sojourners and some to stay, from as early as 1810. It also meant that Kāi Tahu moved beyond their own borders, both within the New Zealand archipelago and beyond it. Within this history of Kāi Tahu mobility, Australia looms large as a destination.

Māori travel goes almost entirely unrecognised in Australian histories of early colonisation. As Cassandra Pybus in *Black Founders* has shown, Australian history is overwhelmingly structured by narratives of the entanglement of Aboriginal and non-Aboriginal people, in which racial signifiers are read as 'non-Aboriginal'/white and 'Aboriginal'/black.[8] Pybus complicates this reading with careful historical research of the 'black founders' who left the United States, Britain and Europe before

4   Hickford, 'Vague Native Rights to Land', 177.
5   Standfield, *Race and Identity.*
6   Parsonson, 'The Pursuit of Mana'.
7   Formed by private statute in 1996 to replace the Ngāi Tahu Maori Trust Board.
8   Pybus, *Black Founders.*

heading to Australia. She argues that silence around these stories is framed by twentieth-century histories of the operation of the 'White Australia' policy. It also shows the central importance of relations between Aboriginal people and British settlers at the heart of Australian colonialism. Yet, Māori presence in the Australian colonies still struggles to find a place in early colonial histories; likewise, discussions of imperial relationships with New Zealand are absent or obscured. As Grace Karskens pointed out in her significant work *The Colony*, Australian historians are still breaking out of the 'Great Australian Silence'. She states that if readers are 'surprised' by the fact that half her book is devoted to the Aboriginal people of the Sydney region, and think 'this is out of proportion. I assure you it is not: it reflects historical reality'.[9] Historians of Australia, then, are still attempting to make the nation recognise and respect the place of Aboriginal people as active agents in Australian history.

We further argue that a history of Australian colonisation without Māori, including Kāi Tahu from the 1820s, is incomplete. Māori histories in Australia complicate the bifurcated narrative of Aboriginal and European. They demonstrate how British hunger for Aboriginal land lay at the very foundation of relationships with Aboriginal people from the initiation of European invasion. Māori and other visiting peoples to New South Wales were treated differently by colonial authorities, were courted for their resources, and were drawn into relationships with colonial authorities in Australia as workers and as owners of valuable resources. We agree with Fred Cahir and Ian Clarke who, in beginning to uncover Māori presence in Victoria, emphasise the importance of comparison in establishing assumptions about race, as eighteenth- and nineteenth-century racialised discourses used comparison between racialised 'others' to develop the hierarchies that underpinned colonial power relationships.[10] As Mackay and Guinness point out in this volume, Australian historiography reflects a broader strand of Australian thought that does not easily recognise its relationship to its Pacific neighbours and role in labour relations in the region. Like Mackay and Guinness, we want to trace a long history of labour relations between peoples of the region and interrogate the ways these relations were underpinned by, and helped to create, racialised hierarchies that continue to shape the colonial present. To understand this is to further destabilise ideas about race, emphasise just how constructed

---

9   Karskens, *The Colony*, 12.
10   Cahir and Clark, 'The Maori Presence in Victoria', 109–26.

racialised thinking is, unpack the relationship between racial ideas and European desires for land or natural resources, and complicate racialised representations of labour and supposed indigenous capacity or interest in work.

We hope that our project will begin to redress this gap in the Australian scholarship while also complicating New Zealand historical scholarship of Māori travel. A number of significant Ngāpuhi leaders, their travels and their time in Australia have become well-known names and moments in New Zealand history. Thanks to the work of scholars such as Judith Binney and Anne Salmond, these travellers are relatively well-known, at least historiographically.[11] Binney and Salmond's work, which drew on narratives of specific Māori travel, have been woven more broadly into histories of early New Zealand. This reaffirms New Zealand historical scholarship's strong focus on Māori in the north of the North Island and, specifically, Ngāpuhi experiences in New Zealand's pre-colonial period. In so doing, it under-appreciates the experiences of other *iwi*.[12] After the 'firsts' that Binney and Salmond focus on, wider Māori mobility, which took place a number of years later, tends to fade into the background. For example, initial Kāi Tahu engagements with Sydney are rarely recounted outside of the tribe itself. Instead of offering a generic history of Māori travel, in which the experiences of people from the more populous North Island, especially the Bay of Islands region, stand in for the whole of Māori experience, our project is a specifically Kāi Tahu–centred history. It traces Kāi Tahu individuals through public, private and tribal archives.

Central to this work is recognition of the place that Australia plays within Kāi Tahu experience and identities. Te Rūnanga o Ngāi Tahu has its core focus on the tribe's traditional heartland villages, but is also invested in Kāi Tahu households located outside its tribal catchment—in other parts of New Zealand and, increasingly, Australia. In other words, the Australian continent looms large in the Kāi Tahu past, but also the Kāi Tahu present and future. Since the 1960s, Australia has become a major destination for Māori immigration. This more recent movement is the subject of scholarly interest for the significant effect it has on Māori communities

---

11   Salmond, *Between Worlds*; Judith Binney, 'Tuki's Universe', 215–32.
12   See, for example, O'Malley, *The Meeting Place*. Quite recently, for example, Vincent O'Malley's monograph has been published, which, despite a statement that the work will engage with the history of the South, has an overwhelming focus on the history of the North, accounting for approximately 250 pages compared to 2.5 pages. This continues a trajectory whereby the specific history of the north of the North Island comes to stand for all.

and economic life, as well on New Zealand society and economics more generally.[13] Scholarship has examined the effect of this immigration on aspects of contemporary culture and also language.[14]

However, this phenomenon has a long history. Indeed, Kāi Tahu *kaumātua* (elder) Sir Tipene O'Regan states that, for Kāi Tahu, 'the voyage west has always been more attractive … than the journey north'. He explains:

> Since the early nineteenth century when we first learnt about muskets, potatoes and whaleboats and that fabled place Poi Hakena—Port Jackson—Ngai Tahu have been crossing the Tasman to trade, to settle and to marry.[15]

O'Regan's emphasis on the voyage is no accident; it reflects the centrality of the sea voyage to the identity and life of the people concerned. Kāi Tahu are, and have always been, a sea people, and it is this relationship between Kāi Tahu and the sea that has shaped engagement with Australia.[16] While most now travel to Australia by plane, the relationship and strength of the connection continues. As O'Regan outlined 15 years ago: 'There are now some 5,000 Ngai Tahu living in Australia from a total census population of some 30,000. The old pattern continues stronger than ever.'[17]

There are now almost 60,000 registered members of the Kāi Tahu *iwi* and 10 per cent live in Australia. However, this is a smaller proportion of registered *iwi* members living in Australia than for other *iwi*. Significant numbers of Kāi Tahu people attended Australian roadshows organised by Te Rūnanga to mark the twentieth anniversary of the tribe's constitutional property settlement, negotiated with the New Zealand Government in 1998, and this has produced an upswing of enrolment. These points suggest that the 10 per cent figure may under-represent the actual number of Australian Kāi Tahu. Indeed, the fact that Te Rūnanga has been holding roadshows on both sides of the Tasman Sea is further evidence of the importance of Australia in Kāi Tahu life. Hence, our project is working to trace a long history and to engage with contemporary concerns vis-à-vis

---

13   Hamer, *Māori in Australia*; Kukutai and Pawar, *A Socio-Demographic Profile of Māori Living in Australia*; Hamer, 'Measuring Māori in Australia', 77–81; Hamer, 'One in Six?', 153–76.
14   Hamer, *The Impact on Te Reo Māori of Trans-Tasman Migration*; Hamer, 'The Split Totara', 45–69; Bergin, 'Maori Sport and Cultural Identity in Australia', 257–69.
15   O'Regan, 'The Dimension of Kinship', 36.
16   Stevens, 'Māori History as Maritime History: A View from The Bluff'.
17   O'Regan, 'The Dimension of Kinship', 37.

the way that people in Australia identify as Kāi Tahu, how they express their Kāi Tahu identity in Australia and the important role played by Australian Kāi Tahu in being Kāi Tahu as a whole.

Kāi Tahu Mobilities, Māori Histories and Aboriginal Sovereignty

Our approach reflects a broader methodology for those who write Māori histories to engage with Māori approaches to organising the past. As Danny Keenan argues in his introduction to the edited collection *Ngā Tāhuhu Kōrero—Huia Histories of Māori*, there is considerable work now among Māori researchers, scholars and historians to bring the 'silences and invisibilities' of the Māori past to light. This involves 'utilising differing narrative styles, shaped by a range of customary or theoretical frameworks, to unravel essential Māori stories'.[18] We agree with Guerin, Nikora and Rua who argue in their research on contemporary Tūhoe regional mobility that, with increasing interest in the geographic mobility of indigenous peoples generally, and Māori in particular, 'has … come an awareness of the need for iwi-specific research because of the diversity within and between Māori and iwi'.[19]

Histories that are *iwi* specific and explore the diversity of particular communities align with the historical narratives of Māori kin groups, who tell their stories for the purposes of their own people, as Te Maire Tau argues. Discussing Māori and specifically Kāi Tahu epistemology, Tau, a senior Kāi Tahu scholar, contemplated whether Māori historical narratives are 'history' in the Western sense:

> The past is recalled and retained by the community because it matters to the community. The truisms of the community will remain if judged authentic by the standards of that community.[20]

Within this style of historical narrative there is an emphasis on histories told to meet the needs of a community itself. This accepts—in fact, it assumes—that there will be more than one story; indeed, that there will be a multiplicity of perspectives. Each of these foregrounds and highlights

---

18   Keenan, 'Land, Culture and History Interwoven', xvii–xi.
19   Guerin, Nikora and Rua, 'Tūhoe on the Move', 65–90.
20   Tau, 'Matauranga Maori as an Epistemology', 64.

the deeds, events or places that are important to that community or particular families within it.[21] Being informed by Māori historical narratives means utilising *whakapapa* (genealogy) as a central organising principle of Māori life, as we set out later in this chapter. We are also cognisant of the role that histories play in contemporary identity-making. Some Kāi Tahu have long family histories in Australia, but newer migrants can undertake border crossings earlier conducted by their ancestors. Our aim is to open up access to these experiences in a way that contributes to historical scholarship, but also supports Kāi Tahu people to know that their travel, or that of their ancestors, has its own specifically Kāi Tahu aspect, which is part of a wider epistemology of movement.

Kāi Tahu people who have a long history in Australia, or indeed in any place out of their tribal territory, remain Kāi Tahu. Melissa Williams, in her exploration of Te Rarawa migration from and between Panguru and Auckland in the post–World War II period, makes this point beautifully:

> The people who migrated out of Panguru did not migrate out of their whakapapa and, by extension, their connection to the whenua [land]. Tribal connections were not cut by geographical space, state policy or academic theory. You remain part of a tribal story regardless of where you live or the degree of knowledge or interaction you may have with your whanaunga [kin] and tribal homeland.[22]

In tracing histories of Kāi Tahu engagement with Australia, and sitting alongside histories of Aboriginal and other Pacific Islander mobilities for labour, it is important to engage with the complex place of Māori generally and Kāi Tahu specifically—as peoples neither indigenous to Australia nor, as popularly imagined, as 'Pacific peoples'.

As mobile peoples encountering Australia and, for some people, long-term migrants making their home in Australia, Kāi Tahu are living on Aboriginal land. Although they are *tāngata whenua* (people of the land) in their own tribal territory, they are not this in Australia. Kāi Tahu and other Māori people's experiences in Australia are facilitated by colonisation and dispossession, like every other person who is not Aboriginal or Torres Strait Islander who lives in or visits Australia. For the authors, this creates another area of investigation, one that may or may

---

21   Tau, 'Matauranga Maori as an Epistemology', 64.
22   Williams, *Panguru and the City*, 28.

not be able to be adequately answered or understood, but which remains conceptually vital: how to understand the experiences of one distinct indigenous community travelling to and living on other indigenous peoples' land/territories. When thinking about Kāi Tahu specifically or Māori experience more generally in Australia, it is vital to examine the relationship between Māori experiences and Aboriginal or Torres Strait Islander sovereignties and experiences of colonisation, and the varied imperial and colonial projects pursued by colonists in the region and their local geographical variations and how these have changed over time. Did Kāi Tahu recognise Aboriginal sovereignty when travelling to or within early colonial New South Wales? Did Kāi Tahu people who met or worked with Aboriginal people recognise them as *tāngata whenua* in their own territories? What sort of recognition might there have been of shared experience by indigenous peoples in the region? While archival evidence for these sorts of discussions appears slight at best, there are moments when these shared recognitions seem to have been captured in the archive. For example, in 1814, on the eve of Samuel Marsden's trip to establish the first New Zealand mission, Judith Binney argues that Ngāpuhi chief Ruatara displayed 'sullenness' and 'ambivalence' towards the mission after being warned by a 'gentleman' in Sydney who:

> Bid him look at the conduct of our countrymen in New South Wales, where, on their first arrival, they despoiled the inhabitants of all their possessions, and shot the greater number of them.[23]

On 12 February 1840, during a meeting to discuss signing the Treaty of Waitangi, Te Taonui, chief of the Ngāpui hapū Te Popoto, stated:

> We are glad to see the Govr let him come to be a Govr to the Pakias [now rendered as Pākehā, meaning fair-skinned, or in contemporary New Zealand, a New Zealander of European descent], as for us we want no Govr, we will be our own Govr. How do the Pakias behave to the black Fellows at Port Jackson? They treat them like Dogs … We are not willing to give up our land.[24]

Certainly, in common with Indigenous nations in Australia, Māori generally, and Kāi Tahu in particular, have been subjected to processes of dispossession, economic marginalisation and erosion of their sovereignty. In a New Zealand context, colonial processes are ones that have worked to disconnect people from connection with other Pacific peoples. As with

---

23   Binney, 'Tuki's Universe', 220.
24   Binney, 'Tuki's Universe', 230.

Māori generally, Kāi Tahu are not viewed as 'Pacific' people, despite their East Polynesian origins. As such, Māori are denied the associations that entails—of movement, encounter and perceiving the sea as 'home'. Having settled the largest landmass in Polynesia, and then having been colonised by a settler colonial state, Māori are primarily seen as land-based and land-bound. Moreover, as peoples indigenous in a settler colonial state, *iwi* have been positioned, and, of course, have had to position themselves, to retain or regain some rights to land. Māori are literally *tāngata whenu*: 'people of the land'. Consequently, as Alice Te Punga Somerville has argued, Māori are not readily viewed as being '*tangata o le moana* (people of the ocean)', which their origins would otherwise suggest. However, if the Māori relationship with Oceania and all the peoples who inhabit that vast space is prioritised, the racist logic of the settler colonial nation state can, to some extent, be bypassed.[25]

As with indigenous peoples in other settler societies, there is a general assumption in national histories that Māori were principally fixed and static: that the people were and are bound to the land. While home places are important—and *tūrangawaewae* (place to stand) and *hau-kainga* (home, home people) are key Māori concepts—the sense of fixity framed by settler culture barely aligns with how Māori communities and individuals live their everyday lives. The insights afforded by Pacific studies, and the seminal work of Pacific scholars and theorists such as Epeli Hau'ofa, are important for interrogating these assumptions of fixity, yet they are rarely applied to New Zealand and Māori histories.[26] This is despite the fact that, in terms of cultures, longer-term and contemporary patterns of migration and the creation of diasporic communities, Māori and other Pacific Islander populations have much in common. Hau'ofa's work places mobility at the heart of Pacific cultural and community life, speaking back to the limiting Eurocentric views of Pacific Islands as 'tiny' by calling for a return to embracing the Pacific as a 'sea of islands'. Movement is not an exceptional occurrence, but an everyday outcome of culture, economics and social organisation.[27] Hau'ofa states that the '"world enlargement"'

---

25 Somerville, *Once Were Pacific,* 91–96.
26 Hau'ofa, 'Our Sea of Islands', 2–16. It is not surprising that Damon Salesa is an exception to the lack of application of Pacific methodologies to New Zealand histories, as he is a scholar whose work and life crosses the boundary between Pacific and New Zealand viewpoints. His call to place New Zealand histories within the Pacific has yet to be incorporated into the general trajectory of national histories. See, for example, Salesa, 'New Zealand's Pacific', 149–72. See also Stevens, 'A Defining Characteristic of the Southern People'.
27 Hau'ofa, 'Our Sea of Islands'.

carried out by tens of thousands of ordinary Pacific Islanders, which is an amplification of traditional patterns, makes 'nonsense of all national and economic boundaries'.[28] In drawing attention to the effect of these traditional patterns and specific meanings shaping Kāi Tahu travel, we agree with Ruth Faleolo's arguments in her chapter in this volume that Pasifika mobility for labour is shaped by specifically Pacific cultural and social concepts, and that these concepts shape and support mobility even in precarious situations. Since 2001, New Zealand citizens, while they continue to have unrestricted access to travel and life in Australia, must apply for, and meet, the requirements for permanent residency if they wish to access social welfare provisions, including social welfare payments and support with tertiary fees (see Faleolo's chapter in this volume for details of the treatment of New Zealand citizens migrating to Australia). Māori continue to travel to Australia despite this vulnerability and precarity. This migration to Australia, as Stevens' previous work shows, is shaped by the position of Māori generally and Kāi Tahu specifically in relation to the New Zealand settler colonial state. Kāi Tahu and members of other *iwi* travel for labour in ways that are fundamentally shaped by their position as indigenous people in New Zealand, including long histories of dispossession from their tribal territories and racialised marginalisation within the New Zealand's labour market.[29]

Economics and Mobility in Epistemology

Our research is not simply designed to uncover Kāi Tahu experience for its own sake but is informed by the specific epistemological, ontological and, indeed, axiological basis for Kāi Tahu identity in which mobility is central to life. Movement is often critical to resource exploitation and mobility was intrinsic to Kāi Tahu economic life and, within this, to labour histories. Living in an environment too cold for kumara cultivation south of Kaiapoi, mobility was (and is) central to economic life for Kāi Tahu; which is to say that much of Kāi Tahu territory was traditionally used in an exclusively hunter-gatherer way. Kāi Tahu are also primarily coastal people and have long used the sea as a vital mode of travel. Kāi Tahu movement thus occurred—and still occurs—over both relatively short and long distances, and in land- and sea-based contexts. While occupying

---

28   Hauʻofa, 'Our Sea of Islands', 6.
29   Husband, 'Brian Easton'.

a 'huge territory', Kāi Tahu 'settlements were mainly concentrated along the east coast'. Resource rights were 'exploited largely through continual mobility. People travelled constantly, accessing widely scattered resources and attending to the complex requirements of marriage, social networks and tribal politics'. The longest seasonal migration for many people was travel for the annual *tītī* or mutton-bird harvest in autumn, conducted on the islands of the Foveaux Strait, which for Kāi Tahu from Kaikōura, meant a round trip of 1,500 kilometres by sea.[30] Resources also travelled constantly, and trade over time and place was central to Māori life. Two of the most important resources in the entire New Zealand archipelago were Kāi Tahu–owned: *pounamu* (nephrite jade) and preserved *tītī* (juvenile sooty shearwaters/'muttonbirds'). Tribal communities were connected throughout the islands of New Zealand to trade for these commodities and still very much are.

Movement is central to Māori histories of first discovery of Aotearoa and Te Waipounamu through the *waka* (canoe) traditions by which all *iwi* trace their migration to those islands from Hawaiiki.[31] Migration is also central to the particular Kāi Tahu experience of successive waves of southern migration and adaptation to cooler Te Waipounamu. Strategies for managing the *tākata pora* who came to Kāi Tahu shores in the early nineteenth century, and subsequent travel of Kāi Tahu people to Australia, were thus arguably extensions of ways that Kāi Tahu communities had been formed in earlier generations. Stevens sums up the histories of the three peoples who came together to form Kāi Tahu:

> Ngāi Tahu whānui is the collective of individuals who descend from Waitaha, Ngāti Māmoe and Ngāi Tahu. These three tribal ascriptions broadly represent the successive groups of people who migrated to Te Waipounamu and became genealogically and politically interwoven.

> Waitaha is used as a collective label for all pre-Ngāi Tahu and Ngāti Māmoe tribes, as well as more specifically for the descendants of Rākaihautū. Waitaha are said to have arrived in Te Waipounamu on the waka *Uruao*. Waitaha whakapapa, place names and creation stories are still with us.[32]

---

30   Anderson, 'Introduction 2: A Migration History', 34–35. Stevens' work on the *tītī* harvest is important for understanding the phenomenon, and derives from his lived experience of *tītī* harvesting, a form of work that is central to Kai Tahu experience and life.

31   Taonui, 'Ngā Waewae Tapu'.

32   Stevens, 'Ngāi Tahu Whānui', 12.

The community that is now known as Kāi Tahu had long histories of movement, migration and the subsequent drawing together of communities. Kāti Māmoe and Kāi Tahu travelled south from their territories in the North Island, using 'warfare, diplomacy and marriage' to establish themselves in the South Island.[33] Kāti Māmoe undertook the initial wave of migration from the North Island being 'closely succeeded' by Kāi Tahu groups, repeating the pattern as they moved further south within the South Island. The nature of this migration, and the combining of the communities means that the Waitaha *whakapapa* continues in the South Island. Thus Te Maire Tau describes how Kāi Tahu *whānau* at Temuka and Moeraki are 'strongholds of Waitaha whakapapa'.[34] The migration process, then, is not a straightforward one of transplanting or replacing an original group of people but one of warfare combined with alliances and strategic marriage, in which hostility coexists with connection in the formation of new communities.

These marriages allow the joining together of *whakapapa* from different groups to increase *mana* and cement relationships between new groups and property rights. As Tau outlines:

> For Māori, the preferred custom in claiming land was always through descent lines from the original occupants. Consequently, even though subsequent tribes would base their claim on conquest, the leading chiefs always married into the earlier tribes so that their descendants could claim descent from them as well.[35]

Tau provides a Waitaha/Ngāi Tahu *whakapapa*, which is:

> Important because it illustrates the preference for claiming a right to land in the South Island through ancestral links that could be traced to Waitaha. Among the conquering tribes that followed, the leading chiefs always took wives who could claim Waitaha ancestry.[36]

---

33 Stevens, 'Ngāi Tahu Whānui', 12.
34 Tau and Anderson, *Ngai Tahu: A Migration History,* 45.
35 Tau and Anderson, *Ngai Tahu: A Migration History*, 48.
36 Tau and Anderson, *Ngai Tahu: A Migration History*, 48.

Marriage and diplomacy are deliberately used to combine peoples and, at key moments, to bring about an end of hostilities and cement a lasting peace. As tensions between Kāti Māmoe and Kāi Tahu continued into the late eighteenth century, 'key figures brokered a peace agreement and a series of high-ranking marriages'.[37]

Atholl Anderson, a pre-eminent archaeologist and demographer of Māori, himself Kāi Tahu, suggests that these waves of migration from the North Island may have occurred more recently than is generally understood. Anderson's analysis suggests that 'the entire migration sequence' culminating in the truce between Kāti Māmoe and Kāi Tahu in about 1790 may have occurred within 'two adult lifetimes' or, depending on the overlapping of generations of people, 'might even have been slightly shorter than that'.[38] While this view is not uncontested, it nonetheless has, in Anderson's words, 'important historical implications' for documented Kāi Tahu histories shared with Pākehā historians in the nineteenth century. In exploring Kāi Tahu engagement with Australia, it is possible that Kāi Tahu people who made the first journeys across the Tasman Sea may have been the immediate descendants of those who settled in the lower South Island.

To understand Kāi Tahu (and, more generally, Māori) motivations for travel and for crossing the sea to Australia, one needs to understand the notion and operation of *mana* as a driving force within Māori culture, and the ways that this is connected to both mobility and economics. When Europeans began to arrive on the northern shores of the North Island and southern shores of the South Island, especially from the early 1820s, the *tāngata whenua/moana* in each region were presented with an opportunity to pursue *mana*, at both individual and community levels. The 'pursuit of *mana*' is central to Māori life and leadership, and an important aspect of this was achieved through economic life—the ability to provide for the community as a whole and to demonstrate the affluence of the community through the provision of food as gifts and during feasts.[39] Indeed, in setting out the requirements of Māori leaders, the Ngāti Rangiwewehi leader and scholar Te Rangikaheke—who is particularly known for teaching Māori culture to New Zealand Governor Sir George Grey in the late 1840s and 1850s—emphasised skill

---

37   Stevens, 'Ngāi Tahu Whānui', 12.
38   Anderson, 'Introduction 2: A Migration History', 29.
39   See Parsonson, 'The Pursuit of Mana', 140–67.

in warfare, economic security and hospitality.[40] In 1850, Te Rangikaheke wrote 'Te Tikanga o Tenei Mea te Rangatiratanga o te Tangata Maori' ('The Principles of Chieftainship of Maori Society') to educate Grey.[41] This document set out the 'eight talents or pumanawa', and emphasised the twin requirements of prowess in war and the ability to procure food for the community as central to Māori leaders, as well as three talents that encompass hospitality to visitors: 'restraining the departure of visiting parties', the ability to 'welcome guests' and 'looking after visitors small or large'.[42] Raymond Firth, in his classic work of Māori anthropology, noted that leaders and 'people of no particular rank' all worked.[43] Firth described how 'work had a distinct social value' and 'was regarded as honourable':

> Even a chief lost no prestige by carrying on such a manual task as the hewing-out of a canoe … [or] working side by side with his people in the cultivations, and took a prominent part in the labours of fishing or the snaring of birds. Competent participation in economic pursuits was in fact a distinct asset in increasing his influence and authority with his people.[44]

It is no surprise then that *manaaki* (support, hospitality), mobility, migration and offers of labour characterise the ways that Kāi Tahu leaders systematically engaged with *tākata pora*.[45] To be clear, the *rakatira* described in our examples below were not simply travelling for the sake of travel. They were using mobility, the labour of their communities, and tribal resources and trade goods, to shape kin wealth, bolster personal *mana* and consolidate Kāi Tahu power in relation to other tribal communities. Honekai is believed to be the chief who moved his people to Ruapuke Island in the far south of Te Waipounamu by 1820 to connect with 'sealers and sailors from all corners of the world', the majority coming from Sydney or Hobart. Honekai's son, Te Whakataupuka:

> Extended his father's work by enabling sealers and Ngāi Tahu women to establish a community at Whenua Hou, an island west of Rakiura. Many present-day Ngāi Tahu people descend from at least one of [these unions].[46]

---

40   Curnow, 'Te Rangikaheke, Wiremu Maihi'.
41   Mead et al., *Maori Leadership in Governance*, 7.
42   Mead et al., *Maori Leadership in Governance*, 8.
43   Firth, *Economics of the New Zealand Maori*, 177.
44   Firth, *Economics of the New Zealand Maori*, 176.
45   Stevens, 'Ngāi Tahu Whānui', 13.
46   Stevens, 'Ngāi Tahu Whānui', 13.

Thus, intermarriage has been a key aspect of the Kāi Tahu experience of engaging with newcomers, and has created *whānau* that were, over the longer period of Australian and New Zealand imperial and colonial histories, very likely to have connections with Australia. The Kāi Tahu practice of strategic intermarriage with Europeans to formalise, through kinship, the sharing of experiences and resources, meant that communities of mixed-descent peoples were, and are, central to Kāi Tahu *whakapapa*. As O'Regan explains:

> It was from Sydney and Hobart that many of our first Pakeha came as whalers, sealers and traders—our first agents of globalisation. Particularly in the far south—my mother's home—many of our Ngai Tahu families root back to that early contact period with Australia.[47]

Stevens also outlines how this intermarriage influences the shape of the contemporary Kāi Tahu community:

> These interracial unions, which were a feature of whaling stations throughout southern New Zealand, led to the surnames of Pākehā whalers becoming identifiably Kāi Tahu names and many of them now function like hapū names. I refer here to names like Stirling, Spencer, Anglem, Palmer, Brown, Bragg, Newton, Joss, Haberfield, Acker, Wixon, Ashwell, Gilroy, Goomes, Ryan, Howell, Bates and Wybrow, which sit alongside tūturu names like Topi, Whaitiri, Karetai, Taiaroa, Te Au, Kini and Te Koeti.[48]

The role of intermarriage and the place it plays in engagement with Australia is exemplified by an early example of Kāi Tahu travel to Australia, that of Tokitoki to Sydney, who accompanied her 'Pākehā-Māori' partner, James Caddell. In late 1822, the New South Wales Government contracted Captain Edwardson to take the *Snapper*, a 29-ton colonial sloop, to southern New Zealand and secure samples of dressed *harakeke* (New Zealand 'flax') or 'hemp' and gather information about it.[49] Arriving in the far south of New Zealand, Edwardson managed to get 300 pounds of this product and also 'shipped a large quantity of potatoes for Sydney', all produced by Kāi Tahu. He also visited Awarua/Bluff where he met with the chief Te Wera. As a result of their cordial meeting, Edwardson took one of the chief's 'relatives' back to Port Jackson. It is likely that this person, referred to as 'Jacky Snapper', was Tūhawaiki—the

47 O'Regan, 'The Dimension of Kinship', 36.
48 Stevens, 'Māori History as Maritime History'.
49 McNab, *Murihiku,* 309–10.

pre-eminent Kāi Tahu *rakatira* from the mid-1830s until his untimely drowning in 1844.[50] The *Snapper* also carried Caddell and his Kāi Tahu wife Tokitoki on board. The vessel arrived in Sydney on 28 March 1823 after five months absence. The *Sydney Gazette* reported that it brought 'about a ton of prepared flax from New Zealand, which is supposed to surpass any in the known world, for its amazing strength'.[51] Of more interest, though, were its passengers: 'Jacky Snapper', Tokitoki and her husband, James Caddell. The party were described as 'two chiefs, one of whom is accompanied by his wife'; the chiefs were said to be aged about 16 and 30. James Cadell, 'an Englishman by birth', had been living with southern Kāi Tahu for about a decade, after violence between the crew of his sealing vessel and Kāi Tahu left his crewmates dead. Having been 'allied' to a chief's daughter, Tokitoki, whose brother was also a chief, for nine years, Caddell was described as 'a prince of no small influence'.[52] Tokitoki was also an important visitor in her own right, not only because of her social status but also for her knowledge of flax preparation, the vital commodity that had initiated the journey in the first place.[53] This was not the end of the association that these three Kāi Tahu people had with Australia. Kāi Tahu narratives assert that Tokitoki returned to Australia with Caddell and her brother. The ethnographer, Herries Beattie, who collected a rich archive of oral history from Kāi Tahu in the late nineteenth century, was told that Tokitoki 'married Jimmy, and went over to Sydney with her husband. Te Pahi [i.e. her brother Te Pai or Te Pae] went over later, and both died in Parramatta, and thus ended that branch'.[54] Caddell appears to have travelled between Sydney and Foveaux Strait a number of times, making a subsequent trip with a group of Kāi Tahu, mostly women, to demonstrate flax dressing. Caddell returns to the archival record when interviewed by the first New Zealand Company agricultural superintendent in 1826, after which he 'fades from view'.[55]

50   Boultbee, *Journal of a Rambler*, 78–79.
51   'Ship News', *The Sydney Gazette and New South Wales Advertiser*, 3 April 1823, 2(b).
52   McNab, *Murihiku*, 316.
53   The first Māori captured by Australian colonists, Tuki and Huru, had been kidnapped from the north of the North Island in 1793 for their assumed knowledge of flax preparation. When taken to Norfolk Island to teach convicts to dress flax, they declared they could not assist as flax preparation was women's work. See Binney, 'Tuki's Universe', 215–32; Standfield, *Race and Identity*.
54   Beattie, 'Traditions and Legends Collected from the Natives of Murihiku', 158–59. O'Regan describes Beattie's 'extraordinary industry' in collecting Kai Tahu narratives as 'one of our great taoka, one of our great treasures'. O'Regan, *New Myths and Old Politics*, 25.
55   Hall-Jones, 'Caddell, James'. See McDonnell, 'The Rosanna Settlers', 45–47.

Perhaps Caddell, Tokitoki and Te Pai went back to Sydney sometime after 1826 and never returned, which would explain the information provided to Beattie by later Kāi Tahu narrators.

If Jacky Snapper was Tūhawaiki, then he also continued to have a close association with Australia, making 'several trips to Sydney from the 1820s'. For Tūhawaiki, this was a logical extension of his maritime life in which he:

> Led armed flotilla against Ngāti Toa in the 1830s, signed a copy of the Treaty of Waitangi on board HMS *Herald* at Ruapuke in June 1840 and used his own vessel, the *Perseverance*, to ferry Bishop George Selwyn around southern New Zealand in 1843.[56]

Mobility, sea travel and leadership were deeply connected in his life, in the defence of the *iwi*, in his actions to sign the treaty and in his travel to Australia. For Tūhawaiki and other Kāi Tahu leaders, extending their maritime lives helped them to secure a much sought-after new commodity: muskets. The desire for muskets, indeed the need for muskets, was an important driver of mobility and labour to ensure the survival of the various *hapū* that, at this time, were consolidating into the *iwi* of Kāi Tahu. The introduction of muskets through engagement with Europeans and travel to Australia and further afield is central to general Māori experience in this period of history. Ngāpuhi, through their engagement and trade with European missionaries, and their desire to seek revenge for previous tensions between and within communities, began a series of battles with neighbouring peoples.[57] The resulting wars began a chain of dislocation that resulted in people throughout New Zealand being moved and displaced. This conflict also rewrote several tribal boundaries. There was an intensification of 'warfare-induced mobility' throughout the country as muskets were introduced and began to be deliberately sought out.[58] Manahuria Barcham has concluded that:

> The period of the early nineteenth century was … characterized by extremely high levels of mobility for Māori as large numbers of people were displaced as they attempted to escape the various conflicts that raged over the country during this period.[59]

---

56   Stevens, 'Māori History as Maritime History'. See also Anderson, 'Tuhawaiki, Hone'.
57   Mikaere, 'Musket Wars, Migrations, New Tribal Alignments'; Crosby, *The Musket Wars*; Ballara, *Taua;* Vayda, 'Maoris and Muskets in New Zealand', 560–84.
58   Barcham, 'The Politics of Maori Mobility', 163.
59   Barcham 'The Politics of Maori Mobility', 163–64.

Ngāti Toa *rakatira* under Te Rauparaha, themselves pushed off tribal land in the Kawhia region, launched musket attacks into the south from their new Kapiti Island base from 1828–29. Ngāti Toa's 'first mover advantage' in terms of muskets had serious consequences for Kāi Tahu. Ngāti Toa travelling to Australia and arming themselves with muskets for their southern raids seriously threatened the survival of Kāi Tahu, and shaped the trajectory of its history in the lead-up to large-scale European settlement. Ngāti Toa could only be held off if Kāi Tahu also acquired muskets and more boats. Hence, Kāi Tahu leaders engaged, we surmise, in more travel to Australia, and chose greater entanglement with Europeans visiting and staying on Kāi Tahu land, for trade to acquire muskets and other objects that would secure their position against Ngāti Toa.

Kāi Tahu were thus attempting to take control of journeying, and their economic relationship with early colonial Australia, to secure the future of the tribe. An example of this might be seen in the activities undertaken by Karetai, a senior Ōtākou *rakatira*, whose life and chieftainship coincide with the first arrivals of *tākata pora*. The nature of his interaction shows the continuation of Kāi Tahu cultures of mobility, the centrality of economics and work for chiefs intent on maintaining their *mana*. Harry Evison's biography of Karetai pays respect to Karetai as a leader and his decision to negotiate the new influences he confronted, including his 'astute' dealings with Europeans. Evison notes that large boats or sealing boats were an 'integral part' of the land deals Karetai conducted with Europeans, 'as they were popular with Ngāi Tahu who wished to continue coastal trade'.[60] Large boats were also becoming vital to warfare with other *iwi*, and 'Karetai commanded four of the twenty boats in the final expedition of Tūhawaiki against Te Rauparaha'.[61] Boats, highly prized when Kāi Tahu engaged with Europeans, met multiple needs of the community: to confront and engage with Ngāti Toa, to engage with Europeans and to secure food for the community. Anderson has described how, in the immediate pre-treaty period, the importance of the sea for Kāi Tahu travel seemed to intensify. New boat technologies meant that, by the 1840s, 'parts of the main east coast trail were overgrown' as sea travel dominated Kāi Tahu movement.[62] The desire for sealing boats may show an intensification of maritime lifeways as well as the association of sea travel with the *mana* of chiefs. Sealing boats, like muskets, had vital

---

60 Evison, 'Karetai', 99.
61 Evison, 'Karetai', 100.
62 Anderson, 'Introduction 2: A Migration History', 36.

practical purposes in terms of warfare and food procurement, which, as noted previously, was an important basis of chiefly *mana*. For a leader to secure and command large boats was a visible symbol of *mana* and, in this respect, continued the deep association between Kāi Tahu leaders and canoes, in which a canoe would be cut and placed upright in the ground as a memorial marking where a *rakatira* was buried. This made boats significant and highly desired objects, important for travel, warfare, economic pursuits and as symbols of the wealth of the community.

However, this is not to suggest that Kāi Tahu were always mobile of their own volition or able to entirely control the terms of trade with Europeans. We have recently uncovered copies of images of two young Kāi Tahu chiefs, one of whom may be Karetai,[63] in the Mitchell Library, State Library of New South Wales.[64] These young people were drawn by the Sydney-based, ex-convict artist Charles Rodius, and included in an album among images of Aboriginal chiefs of the Sydney region.[65] It is possible that they are young men from Ōtākou who arrived in Sydney after seemingly having been kidnapped by Captain Anglem of the *Lucy Ann*.[66] Captain Anglem gave his version of events to the *Sydney Herald*, describing how 'a very large body of natives, about five hundred' had arrived from Cloudy Bay where they had been engaged in battles with Ngāti Toa:

> They treated the residents with much insolence, and struck Mr. Weller repeatedly, and assaulted Captain Hayward, and most of the gentlemen there. They took the pipes out of the mouths of the servants, and went into the houses and broke open the boxes, taking whatever they thought proper from them.

63   Peter Entwisle suggests that one of the men kidnapped was Karetai. He bases this conclusion on a letter that George Weller penned to his brother the following year. Entwisle, *Behold the Moon*, footnote 480. However, Harry Evison in *Tāngata Ngāi Tahu* identifies that Karetai had been invited to Sydney to stay with Samuel Marsden and was given Christian instruction. Evison, 'Karetai', 99. Certainly Karetai was being detained in Sydney at this time, see Church, *Gaining a Foothold*, 200.

64   Rodius, [Copies of Charcoal Drawings of NSW Aborigines]. Image 17 is described in the catalogue as '[?] Chief of Otargo New Zealand by Chs Rodius 12 Decem 1834 Sydney' (the name of the person is unable to be deciphered) and Number 18 is 'qualla from Otargo'. The Mitchell Library holds copies of the original album, which is held at the British Library.

65   Just weeks after we uncovered these images, the Hocken Library in Dunedin purchased another image, this one marked more clearly 'Chief Attay' on the drawing, which is another version of Image 17, Roduis, [Copies of Charcoal Drawings of NSW Aborigines]. The Hocken image is dated a few months later and is also drawn by Charles Rodius. The subjects and pose of the portraits are the same, suggesting that Rodius may have made another version of his first portrait. It may well be that the young man identified as 'Chief Attay' is Karetai.

66   'Ship News', *The Sydney Herald*, 18 August 1834, 3. Frequently spelt 'Anglim' in archival sources. However, its current form within the *iwi*, and also in placenames, is 'Anglem'. For example, Mount Anglem/Hananui the tallest mountain on Rakiura.

When the child of a chief died 'which, under some superstitious impression, they attributed to the visit of the *Lucy Ann*', the Kāi Tahu group decided to take the boat and, Anglem stated, kill all the Europeans. Alerted to the plan 'by one of the native boys', Anglem prepared the ship for 'defence'. The group realised they would not be able to take the ship, Anglem wrote, and when he 'persuaded' two *rakatira* to come on board, he 'set sail for Sydney in the most secret manner, and kept the natives as hostages for the good conduct of their tribe during the absence of the *Lucy Ann*'.[67] Rodius's images of the (possibly kidnapped) men highlight the ways that violence, coercion and the increasing European desire for control over resources and, soon to be, territory in southern New Zealand, was beginning to affect Kāi Tahu communities.

In this early period, Kāi Tahu labour at home was also increasingly connected to European Australia. Kāi Tahu women and men laboured to supply visiting ships with potatoes and flax, and, later, seal skins and whale bone, and their labour connected them to shipping and trade interests in Australia and the wider world. This labour was part of a regional imperialism and colonialism that drew Māori into trading relationships with Europeans who were working to consolidate and expand their colonisation of Aboriginal lands in Australia and to secure Aboriginal dispossession. Kāi Tahu people also joined sealing crews, whaling stations and whaling ships, labouring in maritime environments as their families had before them and would after; many Kāi Tahu continue such practices through deep-sea fishing and oil and gas exploration.[68] These processes also brought Kāi Tahu, and Māori more generally, into connection with Aboriginal people, including Aboriginal people who travelled to southern New Zealand. The most well-known of these is Tommy Chaseland, whose parents were an Aboriginal woman from the Hawkesbury and a European convict.[69] Chaseland became a sailor from 1817, working with people from many different ethnic backgrounds including Pacific and Māori people. Later, as a sealer, he travelled to Tonga and New Caledonia before settling in the southern South Island from 1824.[70] He went on to become a central figure in southern Kāi Tahu life as a whaler of renown and a husband of Puna, a Kāi Tahu woman of chiefly status, until his death in 1869.

---

67 'New Zealand', *The Sydney Herald*, 21 August 1834, 2.
68 See, for example, Mike Stevens' discussion of his family's relationship to the maritime environment and labour in maritime industries: Stevens, 'Māori History as Maritime History'.
69 His name is also rendered as Chasling and Chasland.
70 Russell, '"A New Holland Half-Caste"', 08.1–08.15.

As Kāi Tahu engaged more with Europeans and their labour turned increasingly to maritime or at least coastal pursuits, people began to live more permanently in coastal settlements, facing the sea both literally and in terms of identities and perspective on the world. As colonisation progressed and wholesale dispossession began for Kāi Tahu, communities clung to coastal settlements, which are the contemporary tribe's heartland villages and the basis of its governance structures.[71]

Archives and Methodologies

The nature of Kāi Tahu interaction with Australia was somewhat different in form to the earliest Māori travel to Australia, and this has shaped the way it is imprinted in the archival record. As foreshadowed earlier, the first Māori travellers to Australia—those people whose stories are more often recognised (at least in New Zealand historiography)—hailed from the northern North Island, and their travel sparked intense interest from Australian colonial authorities as well as missionaries. This travel consolidated both trading and missionary interest in this region, and initiated relationships with mission and evangelical figures, of which significant archival records remain.[72] Thus, it is relatively easy to access descriptions of travel and the meanings attributed to it by Europeans, though these do not necessarily reflect the motivations of the travellers themselves.

Early Kāi Tahu travel, which began a little later, but was also closely connected to commercial interests and labour, has not been captured in the archival record in the same way or to the same extent as the 'archetypal' early travels most often referred to in academic histories. By the time Kāi Tahu were venturing to Port Jackson, Māori were relatively well-known in the developing colonial town. Kāi Tahu travelled with Europeans who were less likely to leave detailed written records, such as ships' captains, sealers and whalers. Hence, their stories are not captured to the same extent as other travellers who journeyed with missionaries or encountered

---

71 'Governance', Te Rūnanga o Ngāi Tahu, accessed 14 March 2019, ngaitahu.iwi.nz/te-runanga-o-ngai-tahu/ngai-tahu-governance/.
72 See, for example, Jones and Jenkins, *He Kōrero*; Salmond, *Between Worlds*; O'Malley, *The Meeting Place*.

colonial authorities.[73] Stevens has described his 'tākata-pora forebears …
like their Kāi Tahu wives … [as] little more than ghosts in the colonial
archive'.[74] Our nascent project thus also takes seriously the call issued
by Robert Warrior for indigenous studies to engage with theories of the
subaltern, 'because there's just so much subalternity in the Native world
that needs somehow to be addressed'.[75]

This creates a particular style of methodology for us. Uncovering Kāi
Tahu experience in the archives effectively needs to be a *whakapapa*-
based project. Individuals must be traced, if they can be traced at all,
through their names and knowledge of their connection to their kin and
communities. In doing this, we are using the process that Te Rūnanga
employs as part of its everyday work to connect Australian Kāi Tahu back
to their communities in Te Waipounamu. These people may have been
disconnected from their families and *whakapapa* for entire lifetimes, even
multiple generations. We hope we can support this work by offering
insights from our archival work.

This methodology is not simply expedient. It is also of real importance
for writing histories that are meaningful to Māori communities and
respectful of Māori forms of history. As O'Regan writes, *whakapapa* is
central to Māori history-making:

> Whakapapa can be stated to demonstrate a direct line of descent
> from an ancestor … [and also illustrate] the network of lateral
> relationships involved … an understanding of whakapapa can
> illuminate, or become, the vehicle of history. It is the relationships
> between people and the way in which the whakapapa links them
> and stores that information that is the critical element in the study
> of traditional history. The point is that in Māori tradition one
> requires the skeletal framework of whakapapa to authenticate the
> historical tradition.[76]

In the documentation of Tokitoki, James Caddell and Jacky Snapper
provided in *The Sydney Gazette*, it is the story of the *tākata pora* man that
dominates the newspaper account. However, with Kāi Tahu *whakapapa*

---

73   See, for example, the type of information included in 'Ship News', *The Sydney Gazette*, 21 August
1823, 2, on the return of the ship *Mermaid* from southern New Zealand: 'Friday last returned from
a three months' cruize to New Zealand, His Majesty's cutter Mermaid, Mr. Wm. Kent commander.
Four of the natives are visitors by this trip.'
74   Stevens, '"The Ocean is Our Only Highway"', 157.
75   Warrior, 'The Subaltern Can Dance', 90.
76   O'Regan, *New Myths and Old Politics*, 24.

and narratives, it is women like Tokitoki and the other Kāi Tahu women who married sealers, and later whalers, who are central. The relationships between these Kāi Tahu women and *tākata pora* men often drew those men into broader Kāi Tahu social formations allowing children to maintain Kāi Tahu culture and lifeways. While Tokitoki may hardly figure in the archival sources that historians rely on, she has a prominent place in the tribe's genealogical tapestry. Other Kāi Tahu women like her, especially those with descendants, are deeply respected and remembered with love for their role in creating the Kāi Tahu community as it is today. For example, on Te Rau Aroha Marae in Bluff, striking carvings of the ancestors adorn the *marae* and watch over the people. These display large depictions of women proudly in the foreground, with much smaller figures of the sealing and whaling *tākata pora* men sitting behind, flanking and supporting the women.

Kāi Tahu perspectives such as these complicate and should cause us to interrogate the nature of our archival sources, in which the 'European' man (although it is debatable whether James Caddell was culturally European or Kāi Tahu at this point in his life) is almost always accorded the central role within the archival depiction. By contrast, indigenous people play only minor roles in the European documentary evidence; Jacky Snapper and Tokitoki are represented as simply 'accompanying' Caddell. If we are to recognise Kāi Tahu *whakapapa* and narrative, it is the mobility of all members of the travelling group—Cadell, Tokitoki and Jacky Snapper together—that should be traced in the archive, no matter how small or subtle the fragments that remain.

At the symposium on which this edited collection is based, Tracey Banivanua Mar offered an important methodological strategy for recognising and respecting subaltern subjects barely noticed in archives. She suggested that, while the voices of Indigenous Australian or Pacific Islander people, including Māori, tend not to be recorded in written documents, their actions often are recorded. Thus, it is important that we recognise Kāi Tahu ancestors, by birth or through marriage, in the archive wherever we can find them. We can highlight their actions and try to fill in their stories, and attempt to explain their lives within the context of the historical circumstances they faced and within the framework of their own epistemologies. We can think through the importance of their stories for their descendants, and the ways that their actions reverberate through the actions of Kāi Tahu people who walk in their footsteps in the present-day.

Bibliography

Primary Sources

Rodius, Charles. [Copies of Charcoal Drawings of NSW. Aborigines by Charles Rodius], 1982. [Original charcoal drawings date c. 1834.] State Library of New South Wales.

Secondary Sources

Anderson, Atholl. 'Introduction 2: A Migration History'. In *Ngāi Tahu: A Migration History: The Carrington Text*, edited by Te Maire Tau and Atholl Anderson, 20–37. Wellington: Bridget Williams Books, 2008.

——. 'Tuhawaiki, Hone'. Dictionary of New Zealand Biography, first published in 1990. *Te Ara—the Encyclopedia of New Zealand*, teara.govt.nz/en/biographies/1t110/tuhawaiki-hone.

Ballara, Angela. *Taua: 'Musket Wars', 'Land Wars' or Tikanga?: Warfare in Māori Society in the Early Nineteenth Century*. Auckland: Penguin Books, 2003.

Barcham, Manahuia. 'The Politics of Maori Mobility'. In *Population Mobility and Indigenous Peoples in Australasia and North America*, edited by John Taylor and Martin Bell, 163–83. London and New York: Routledge, 2004.

Beattie, James Herries. 'Traditions and Legends Collected from the Natives of Murihiku. (Southland, New Zealand)'. *Journal of the Polynesian Society* 28 (1919): 158–59.

Belich, James. *Making Peoples: A History of the New Zealanders: From Polynesian Settlement to the End of the 19th Century*. Auckland: Penguin, 1996.

Bergin, Paul. 'Maori Sport and Cultural Identity in Australia'. *Australian Journal of Anthropology* 13, no. 3 (December 2002): 257–69. doi.org/10.1111/j.1835-9310.2002.tb00208.x.

Binney, Judith. 'Tuki's Universe'. *New Zealand Journal of History* 38, no. 2 (2004): 215–32.

Boultbee, John. *Journal of a Rambler—The Journal of John Boultbee*, edited by June Starke. Auckland: Oxford University Press, 1986.

Cahir, Fred and Ian D. Clark. 'The Maori Presence in Victoria, Australia, 1830–1900: A Preliminary Analysis of Australian Sources'. *New Zealand Journal of History* 48, no. 1 (2014): 109–26.

Church, Ian. *Gaining a Foothold: Historical Records of Otago's Eastern Coast, 1770–1839*. Dunedin: Friends of the Hocken Collections, 2008.

Crosby, Ron D. *The Musket Wars: A History of Inter-Iwi Conflict, 1806–45*. Auckland: Reed, 2001 (2nd ed.).

Curnow, Jenifer. 'Te Rangikaheke, Wiremu Maihi'. Dictionary of New Zealand Biography, first published in 1990. *Te Ara—the Encyclopedia of New Zealand*, teara.govt.nz/en/biographies/1t66/te-rangikaheke-wiremu-maihi.

Entwisle, Peter. *Behold the Moon: The European Occupation of the Dunedin District, 1770–1848*. Dunedin: Port Daniel Press, 2010.

Evison, Harry. 'Karetai (1781?–1860), Ngāi Tahu, Ngāi Tahu leader'. In *Tāngata Ngāi Tahu: People of Ngāi Tahu, Volume 1,* edited by Helen Brown and Takerei Norton, 99–102. Christchurch: Te Runanga o Ngai Tahu and Bridget Williams Books, 2017.

Firth, Raymond. *Economics of the New Zealand Maori*. Wellington: R. E. Owen, Government Printer, 1959. [1st ed. 1929.]

Guerin, Pauline, Linda Waimarie Nikora and Mohi Rua. 'Tūhoe on the Move: Regional Mobility'. *New Zealand Population Review* 32, no. 2 (2006): 65–90.

Hall-Jones, John. 'Caddell, James'. Dictionary of New Zealand Biography, first published in 1990. *Te Ara—the Encyclopedia of New Zealand*, teara.govt.nz/en/biographies/1c1/caddell-james.

Hamer, Paul. *The Impact on Te Reo Māori of Trans-Tasman Migration*. Wellington: Institute of Policy Studies, 2010.

——. *Māori in Australia: Ngā Māori i Te Ao Moemoeā*. Wellington: Te Puni Kokiri, 2007.

——. 'Measuring Māori in Australia: Insights and Obstacles'. *Social Policy Journal of New Zealand* 36 (2009): 77–81.

——. 'One in Six? The Rapid Growth of the Māori Population in Australia'. *New Zealand Population Review* 33 and 34 (2008): 153–76.

——. 'The Split Totara: Te Reo Māori and Trans-Tasman Migration'. *Te Reo* 54 (2011): 45–69.

Hau'ofa, Epeli. 'Our Sea of Islands'. In *A New Oceania: Rediscovering Our Sea of Islands*, edited by Eric Waddell, Vijay Naidu and Epeli Hau'ofa, 2–16. Suva: School of Social and Economic Development, University of the South Pacific, and Bleake House, 1993.

Hickford, Mark. '"Vague Native Rights to Land": British Imperial Policy on Native Title and Custom in New Zealand, 1837–53'. *The Journal of Imperial and Commonwealth History* 38, no. 2 (2010): 175–206. doi.org/10.1080/03086531003746802.

Husband, Dale. 'Brian Easton: Māori Have Been Trapped in a Poverty Cycle'. *E-Tangata,* 13 May 2018, e-tangata.co.nz/korero/brian-easton-maori-have-been-trapped-in-a-poverty-cycle/.

Jones, Alison and Kuni Jenkins. *He Kōrero—Words Between Us: First Māori-Pākehā Conversations on Paper.* Auckland: Huia, 2011.

Karskens, Grace. *The Colony: A History of Early Sydney.* Crows Nest: Allen and Unwin, 2010.

Keenan, Danny. 'Introduction: Land, Culture and History Interwoven'. In *Huia Histories of Māori: Ngā Tāhuhu Kōrero,* edited by Danny Keenan, xvii–xi. Wellington: Huia, 2012.

Kukutai, Tahu and Shefali Pawar. *A Socio-Demographic Profile of Māori Living in Australia.* NIDEA Working Papers, No. 3. Hamilton: National Institute of Demographic and Economic Analysis, June 2013.

McDonnell, Hilda, ed. *The Rosanna Settlers: With Captain Herd on the Coast of New Zealand 1826–7: Including Thomas Shepherd's Journal and his Coastal Views.* Wellington: Wellington City Library, 2002.

McNab, Robert. *Murihiku: A History of the South Island of New Zealand and the Islands Adjacent and Lying to the South, from 1642 to 1835.* Wellington: Whitcombe & Tombs, 1909.

Mead, Hirini, Shaan Stevens, John Third, B. Jackson and D. Pfeifer. *Maori Leadership in Governance: Scoping Paper.* Wellington: Centre for the Study of Leadership, Victoria University, 2006.

Mikaere, Buddy. 'Musket Wars, Migrations, New Tribal Alignments'. In *Huia Histories of Maori: Nga Tahuhu Korero*, edited by Danny Keenan, 109–30. Wellington, Huia, 2012.

O'Malley, Vincent. *The Meeting Place: Māori and Pākehā Encounters, 1642–1840.* Auckland: Auckland University Press, 2012.

O'Regan, Tīpene. 'The Dimension of Kinship'. In *States of Mind: Australia and New Zealand 1901–2001,* edited by Arthur Grimes, Lydia Wevers and Ginny Sullivan, 35–38. Wellington: Institute of Policy Studies, Victoria University of Wellington, 2002.

——. *New Myths and Old Politics: The Waitangi Tribunal and the Challenge of Tradition.* Wellington: Bridget Williams Books, 2014.

Parsonson, Ann. 'The Pursuit of Mana'. In *Oxford History of New Zealand*, edited by W. H. Oliver and B. R. Williams, 140–67. Auckland: Oxford University Press, 1981.

Pybus, Cassandra. *Black Founders: The Unknown Story of Australia's First Black Settlers.* Sydney: UNSW Press, 2006.

Russell, Lynette. '"A New Holland Half-Caste": Sealer and Whaler Tommy Chaseland'. *History Australia* 5, no. 1 (2008): 08.1–08.15.

Salesa, Damon. 'New Zealand's Pacific'. In *The New Oxford History of New Zealand,* edited by Giselle Byrnes, 149–72. South Melbourne: Oxford University Press, 2009.

Salmond, Anne. *Between Worlds: Early Exchanges between Maori and Europeans, 1773–1815.* Auckland: Viking Press, 1997.

Somerville, Alice Te Punga. *Once Were Pacific: Māori Connections to Oceania.* Minneapolis and London: University of Minnesota Press, 2012. doi.org/10.5749/minnesota/9780816677566.001.0001.

Standfield, Rachel. *Race and Identity in the Tasman World, 1769–1840.* London: Pickering and Chatto, 2012.

Stevens, Michael J. '"A Defining Characteristic of the Southern People": Southern Māori Mobility and the Tasman World'. In *Indigenous Mobilities: Across and beyond the Antipodes*, edited by Rachel Standfield, 79–114. Canberra: ANU Press and Aboriginal History, 2018. doi.org/10.22459/IM.06.2018.04.

——. 'Māori History as Maritime History: A View from The Bluff'. In *New Zealand and the Sea: Historical Perspectives*, edited by Frances Steel, 156–80. Wellington: Bridget Williams Books, 2018. doi.org/10.7810/9780947518707_8.

——. 'Ngāi Tahu Whānui'. In *Tāngata Ngāi Tahu: People of Ngai Tahu*, edited by Helen Brown and Takerei Norton, 79–114. Wellington: Te Rūnanga o Ngāi Tahu and Bridget Williams Books, 2017.

——. '"The Ocean is Our Only Highway and Means of Communication": Maritime Culture in Colonial Southern New Zealand'. *Journal of New Zealand Studies* 12 (2011): 155–70.

Taonui, Rāwiri. 'Ngā Waewae Tapu—Māori Exploration'. Dictionary of New Zealand Biography, first published in 1990. *Te Ara—the Encyclopedia of New Zealand*, teAra.govt.nz/en/nga-waewae-tapu-maori-exploration/page-7.

Te Maire Tau. 'Matauranga Maori as an Epistemology'. In *Histories, Power and Loss: Uses of the Past—A New Zealand Commentary*, edited by Andrew Sharp and Paul McHugh, 61–73. Wellington: Bridget Williams Books, 2001. doi.org/10.7810/9781877242205_3.

Te Maire Tau and Atholl Anderson, eds. *Ngāi Tahu: A Migration History: The Carrington Text*. Wellington: Bridget Williams Books, 2008.

Vayda, Andrew P. 'Maoris and Muskets in New Zealand: Disruption of a War System'. *Political Science Quarterly* 85, no. 4 (1970): 560–84. doi.org/10.2307/2147596.

Warrior, Robert. 'The Subaltern Can Dance, and So Sometimes Can the Intellectual'. *Interventions* 13, no. 1 (2011): 85–94. doi.org/10.1080/1369801X.2011.545579.

Williams, Melissa Matutina. *Panguru and the City: Kāinga Tahi, Kāinga Rua: An Urban Migration History*. Wellington: Bridget Williams Books, 2015.

Newspapers

The Sydney Herald
The Sydney Gazette and New South Wales Advertiser

6

Money Trees, Development Dreams and Colonial Legacies in Contemporary Pasifika Horticultural Labour

Victoria Stead

Rosemary and I are sitting at a round plastic table, out the front of the small cabin she shares with four other Ni-Vanuatu women in a caravan park in north-central Victoria. It is about six o'clock in the evening and they, and another 14 Ni-Vanuatu living in the surrounding cabins, have not long gotten back from their shifts sorting and packing boxes of apples and pears at a local packing shed. As we sit drinking mugs of tea, some of the older women inside the cabin are preparing dinner in a small, portable convection oven perched on a bench in the cramped kitchen space. Outside, others are making their way to or from the shower block at the other end of the caravan park, carrying with them the work clothes that they wash daily in the showers to save the two dollars required to use the park's washing machines. Rows of work clothes, imprinted with the logo of the packing shed where the group work, hang from clothes lines strung up between the caravans. The group arrived four months ago as part of the Seasonal Worker Programme (SWP) that brings Pacific Islander workers to labour in the Australian horticultural industry on a seasonal basis; they will be here for another two months before they return to Vanuatu. This is Rosemary's third trip, and she will return again in subsequent years if she is able. Her experience at the packing shed has been positive by many measures; however, other Ni-Vanuatu workers have had negative experiences and, in any case, even those aspects she finds positive are never quite straightforwardly so. We drink our tea slowly and our conversation turns to the experiences of another group of Ni-Vanuatu workers, mostly male, who are also resident at the same caravan park and working picking tomatoes on a nearby farm. It has been a poor season for tomatoes and, with the men paid on a piece rate basis, the poor size and quality of the crop makes for tough work and very low pay. Rosemary is narrating a conversation she had with another Pacific Islander, not a temporary labour migrant but a resident in the area. In discussing the workers' conditions, particularly on the tomato farm, the man had said to her, 'you know what, this is what we call modern-day slavery'. I mention the allusion to the nineteenth-century blackbirding of Melanesians, many of them Ni-Vanuatu, to the sugar cane plantations of Queensland and northern New South Wales. Rosemary pauses, sips her tea, and replies: 'Yes, that was us'.

Pacific Islanders have long formed a significant component of the workforce within Australian horticulture (fruit and vegetable production). The labours of contemporary Pacific Islanders who travel to rural Australia as temporary workers, as well as the labours of settled Pacific Islanders who form a significant part of the workforce in many rural areas, take place within complex ecologies and histories of colonial encounter. Most notably, the contemporary horticultural labour of Pacific Islanders takes place against the historical backdrop of the nineteenth-century Pacific labour trade, which saw thousands of Pacific Islanders 'blackbirded'—transported through coercion, kidnapping or trickery— from their Melanesian homes, or else recruited in legal but nevertheless exploitative conditions, to labour on the cane fields of north-eastern Australia.[1] This is a period of Australian and Pacific history that has been written about powerfully by Tracey Banivanua Mar and others.[2] It is invoked by contemporary Australian South Sea Islander activists, who are the descendants of those blackbirded workers and who are campaigning for recognition of the Pacific labour trade and the harms done to their ancestors. It is also a history that is sometimes invoked by contemporary Pacific Islanders in response to their own labour experiences, or those of their kin or community. These references to the blackbirding past

1   Connell, 'From Blackbirds to Guestworkers'.
2   Banivanua Mar, *Violence and Colonial Dialogue*; Banivanua Mar, *Decolonisation and the Pacific*. See also, Munro, 'The Pacific Islands Labour Trade'; Saunders, 'Masters and Servants'; Graves, *Cane and Labour*.

are often made to draw parallels between historical and contemporary labour experiences, and often invoke the language of 'slavery' in doing so. This language appears in descriptions of Pacific Islander workers— past and present—as 'slaves', as well as through references to the 'slave-like' conditions of some contemporary Pacific Islander labour, and in descriptions of contemporary Pacific Islander labour migrations, as in the vignette above, as 'modern-day slavery'. These references, and invocations of the past, have also found expression in a stream of news reports about exploitation in the scheme and the industry more widely, including reports commenting on concerns raised within the context of the Australian Government's parliamentary inquiry into modern slavery, and local arenas such as the 2017 community forum on modern slavery held at Mildura in northern Victoria.[3] At the same time, though, some contemporary Pacific Islander workers *also* describe the fruit trees they labour on as 'money trees', and large numbers of Pacific Islanders, like Rosemary, desire and actively seek out opportunities for horticultural work in rural Australia, including through the SWP, which is actively promoted (and often pursued) as a path to 'development'.[4]

'Money trees', development dreams and colonial legacies thus converge, and sometimes collide, in the orchards, caravan parks, churches and community spaces of rural Australia. In this chapter, I explore the complex, charged discourses and affects that accompany these convergences, focusing particularly on the experiences of Pacific Islanders who prune, thin and harvest the fruit trees of the Greater Shepparton Region in north-central Victoria. Placing contemporary Pasifika labour in conversation with its historical antecedents, I map out some of the key contours of debates among historians about the nature of the nineteenth-century labour trade, and the proper relationship between recognising Pacific Islander agency and the coercive force of the state and labour recruiters. I also engage with more contemporary discussions about 'modern-day slavery', race and

---

3   For example, Emma Field, 'Seasonal Worker Program Exploitation Claims Raised at Mildura Forum', *Weekly Times*, 31 October 2017, www.weeklytimesnow.com.au/news/national/seasonal-worker-program-exploitation-claims-raised-at-mildura-forum/news-story/6e49e03051905d7204f bb35753e0bd64; Locke, Buchanan and Graue, 'Seasonal Worker Program'; Ben Doherty, 'Hungry, Poor, Exploited: Alarm over Australia's Import of Farm Workers', *The Guardian*, 3 August 2017, www.theguardian.com/global-development/2017/aug/03/hungry-poor-exploited-alarm-over-australias-import-of-farm-workers; Nick McKenzie, 'Slavery Claims as Seasonal Workers from Vanuatu Paid Nothing for Months' Work', *The Sydney Morning Herald*, 27 March 2017, www.smh.com.au/national/slavery-claims-as-seasonal-workers-from-vanuatu-paid-nothing-for-months-work-20170327-gv7k99.html. On the Australian Government's parliamentary inquiry, see Joint Standing Committee on Foreign Affairs, *Hidden in Plain Sight*, particularly Chapter 9.

4   Doyle and Sharma, 'Maximizing the Development Impacts from Temporary Migration'.

migration. However, in doing so, I am not so much interested in wading into debates about whether or not Pacific horticultural labour *is* or *was* 'slavery' as I am in charting some of the different ways in which slavery has been imagined and discursively mobilised. For all the scholarly merit of debates around whether the Pacific labour trade constituted slavery,[5] the danger in these debates is that they slip into a particular mode of legalistic technicality, and of contestation around terminology and definitional criteria, that can miss the lived substance and experience of what people are talking about when they invoke the language of slavery. Likewise, with debates over the definitional scope and parameters of 'contemporary' or 'modern slavery'.[6] What I seek to do in the following pages, then, is to interrogate discourses both of 'slavery' and of 'development' as two intersecting strands of narrative and meaning-making that circulate in relation to Pacific Islander horticultural labour, and through which contemporary Pacific Islanders locate themselves in relation to contested colonial pasts. These discourses articulate with one another in the messy terrain of everyday encounter and affect and, in doing so, tell us something about the kinds of precarity experienced by Pacific Islander horticultural workers, the continuities and colonial legacies that inform contemporary Pacific Islander lives, and the interplays of structural forces and Pasifika agency.

Blackbirds, Slaves and Willing Workers

From 1863 until Federation in 1901, some 60,000 men, women and children were transported to the cane fields in north-eastern Australia from what are now the countries of the Solomon Islands, Vanuatu, Papua New Guinea, Fiji and Kanaky/New Caledonia. Debates about how best to characterise and understand the migrations of these Pacific Islanders have occupied historians over the last 60 or so years, hinging particularly on the question of the relationship between coercion and agency. There is broad agreement that the early years of the trade, particularly, were characterised by incidences of coercion, trickery, deceit and, sometimes, outright kidnapping of workers by recruiters—those practices captured in

5   For example, Graves, *Cane and Labour*; Munro, 'Revisionism and Its Enemies'; Munro, 'The Pacific Islands Labour Trade'; Scarr, 'Recruits and Recruiters'; Shlomowitz, 'Markets for Indentured'; Shlomowitz, 'Time Expired Melanesian Labor in Queensland'.
6   For example, Weitzer, 'Human Trafficking and Contemporary Slavery'; Quirk, 'The Anti-Slavery Project'.

the descriptor 'blackbirding'.[7] Commencing after the abolition of slavery in Britain in 1833, blackbirding was never formally part of the slave trade, and commentators have disagreed, often vehemently, over the extent to which it might be compared to, or indeed classified as, slavery. Indeed, as Reid Mortensen has shown in his analysis of trials in Australian courts of recruiters charged with abuses in this early period, the question of whether the labour trade constituted slavery was very much alive at the time of the trade itself, with attempts made in 1869–71 to use post-abolition anti-slavery legislation as a basis for prosecution. Ultimately, while some recruiters were found guilty of kidnapping, the effect of the cases was to draw a legal distinction between that offence and slavery proper.[8] The cases nevertheless draw attention to the definitional debates and subjective, contested uses to which both 'slavery', and the murky descriptor 'slavery-like', have been and continue to be put.

By the mid-1870s, the Pacific labour scheme was largely regulated, and outright forcible recruitment had largely given way to at least nominally voluntary enlistment, mediated through the legal mechanism of indenture. It was this shift, in particular, that was highlighted in a body of revisionist scholarship, commencing in the late 1960s, that aimed to draw attention to the agency and active, consensual participation of Pacific Islanders within the labour trade. As Deryck Scarr put it in an early and influential voluntarist account, the Pacific labour trade was, from the mid-1870s, a 'business'—brutal and sometimes backed up by force, to be sure, but a business nonetheless, and one that operated with the consent of those involved.[9] Other revisionists emphasised the role of Pacific Islander agents and facilitators of the trade, with Clive Moore, for example, re-evaluating the role of 'beach payments' given by recruiters to the relatives of Malaitans recruited from Solomon Islands, not as payments indicative of human purchase (and thus of slavery) but rather as gifts in the spirit of reciprocal relations.[10] Others pointed to the high prevalence of so-called 'time-expired' workers, namely those who signed up for a second period of service after their initial period of indenture was completed, as evidence of the voluntary nature of the trade.[11]

---

7   Banivanua Mar, *Violence and Colonial Dialogue*; Munro, 'The Pacific Islands Labour Trade'; Shlomowitz, 'Markets for Indentured'; Shlomowitz, 'Time Expired Melanesian Labor'.
8   Mortensen, 'Slaving in Australian Courts'.
9   Scarr, *Fragments of Empire*, 139. See also Scarr, 'Recruits and Recruiters'.
10   Moore, *Kanaka: A History of Melanesian Mackay*.
11   For example, Shlomowitz, 'Markets for Indentured'; Shlomowitz, 'Time Expired Melanesian Labor in Queensland'.

Figure 6.1: South Sea Islanders on a Queensland sugar plantation at the end of the nineteenth century.
Source: Photograph by Henry King, 'Sugarcane', c. 1880–1900, Museum of Applied Arts & Sciences, Object 85/1285-1138, accessed 14 March 2019, ma.as/30615.

In emphasising the voluntary nature of participation, the revisionists were, in part, motivated by the push towards 'island-oriented' histories being championed through the late 1960s into the early 1990s, particularly within The Australian National University. To this extent, they were interested in highlighting the agency of Pacific Islanders, both in their recruitment and in their control over their own working lives. The rush to credit agency, though, often came at a cost of minimising the coercive conditions within which (and against which) agency was enacted; these are not always neatly counter-posed forces. As Tracey Banivanua Mar argued in her groundbreaking book, *Violence and Colonial Dialogue*:

> For all the exercise of agency on the part of Islanders, the labor trade was not, as many have written, a benign labor migration. It was a trade in labor. Searching for signs of historical agency should not preclude the ongoing recognition that the labor trade was premised on a determination to be profitable, which ultimately rendered negligible (unless profitable) the existence of agency. In other words, and in relation to current debates over the appropriateness of slavery as a description for the labor trade,

resistance or agency take their meaning from the oppressive context against which they are asserted. In the end, surely some measure of the 'damage' inflicted can derive from the number of times we feel we must assert that people were resisting agents.[12]

In place of a zero-sum consideration of Islander agency and colonial force, Banivanua Mar called instead for attention to the 'dialogue' between the 'vertical' structures of colonial power and communication, and the 'horizontal' rhythms of Islanders' own exchanges, decisions, actions and interrelations. This approach—also evident in her chapter in this volume—is one in which 'Islanders' agency, resistance, and consciousness can be celebrated, but not at the expense of minimizing scrutiny to the violent capabilities of colonization'.[13] It is an approach, as well, that acknowledges and holds space for the multiple modalities of violence through which colonialism was conceived, enacted, reasoned and rationalised in the labour frontiers of the Pacific Islands as well as on the plantations of north-eastern Australia. Colonial violence, Banivanua Mar showed, was physical, discursive and economic, and bound up in racialised stereotypes that legitimated gross inequalities and mistreatment. It was also, often, a 'regulated standard', wielded through systematised and legal standards of indenture, accommodation, diet and care that resulted in sometimes extraordinarily high mortality rates, as well as through extra-legal modalities of brute force and terror.[14] This 'regulated standard' has echoes in the restrictive and racialised nature of regulation in the labour migrations of Papuan and New Guinean domestics, some 50 to 70 years later, described by Lucy Davies in this volume.

The bifurcation of coercion and voluntarism both echoes and emerges out of the positioning of 'slavery' and 'freedom' as counter-posed values within the structures of Enlightenment thought.[15] It is a bifurcation that struggles to accommodate the lived complexities of power and agency, whether they be within the context of the formal slave trade, nineteenth-century indenture, or indeed the increasingly broad and amorphous range of labour relations that are included within a growing scholarship on so-called 'new' or 'modern slavery'.[16] Encompassing wage exploitation,

---

12   Banivanua Mar, *Violence and Colonial Dialogue*, 12.
13   Banivanua Mar, *Violence and Colonial Dialogue*, 7.
14   Banivanua Mar, *Violence and Colonial Dialogue*, 13.
15   Davidson, 'Troubling Freedom'.
16   On 'modern slavery' see, for example, Weitzer, 'Human Trafficking and Contemporary Slavery'; Quirk, 'The Anti-Slavery Project'; Bales, *Disposable People*.

involuntary servitude, debt bondage, human trafficking, forced marriage and other 'slavery-like' conditions as diverse as honour killings, genital mutilation, child soldiers and the sale of organs, scholarly and policy treatments of modern slavery are spectacularly broad, inherently subjective and often political.[17] Many of the types of labour relations that fall under the banner of modern slavery are elsewhere captured by the descriptor of 'unfree labour', a phrase that has, in recent years, been used to describe various guestworker schemes, as well as a host of other conditions that fall uncomfortably outside the counter-posed extremes of coercion and voluntarism.[18]

Focusing on contemporary debt-financed migration as particularly 'troubling' of the forced/voluntary dyad, Julia O'Connell Davidson argues that migrants may well voluntarily enter debt relationships that entail severe restrictions on their freedom, both because they are enacting agency in contexts of limited or unequal choice, and also because their migration is oriented towards temporal, as well as spatial, horizons. That is to say, we need to consider the future-oriented aspirations that can compel migrants to accept present conditions, even unfree or exploitative ones, as well as the past experiences or conditions that inform their decision-making.

In highlighting the constrained conditions within which choice is exercised by contemporary debt-financed migrants, Davidson echoes points made in relation to the nineteenth-century Pacific labour trade. For example, Adrian Graves argued that Pacific Islanders often signed up to the trade because of a lack of alternatives in the face of drought and capitalist disruption of local economies.[19] Doug Munro has subsequently raised questions about Graves' argument, pointing out that extensive out-migration often occurred in places where there had been less penetration by European capitalism; however, he nevertheless concurs with the need to consider the options and alternatives available. 'Melanesians', Munro writes, 'often recruited only in the absence of better alternative means to obtaining European goods'.[20] Similarly, Moore argues that there was little recruiting from areas beyond the 'labour frontier' in Solomon Islands, where communities already had access to Western goods from traders,

---

17   Altman, 'Modern Slavery in Remote Australia?'; Bales, *Disposable People*; Davidson, 'Troubling Freedom'; Weitzer; Quirk, 'The Anti-Slavery Project'.
18   Basok, 'Free to Be Unfree'; Miles, *Capitalism and Unfree Labour*; Lewis et al., 'Hyper-Precarious Lives'.
19   Graves, 'The Nature and Origins of Pacific Islands Labour'.
20   Munro, 'Revisionism and Its Enemies: Debating the Queensland Labour Trade', 242.

and the option of cash cropping as an alternate pathway to development.[21] Attending to the temporal horizons of people's choices, as well to the cultural and imaginative dimensions through which coercion was (and is) produced, we also need to ask *why* European goods were so sought after, and how it was that developmentalism's future orientations were produced through colonial encounters. This is to attend both historically and *anthropologically* to the intersection of coloniality and Pasifika agency.

Doing so calls attention to race as a structure of power underpinning the collisions of development dreams, agency and colonial force on the beachfront labour frontiers of the nineteenth century as well as in the orchards and packing sheds where contemporary Ni-Vanuatu labour. To draw on the late Patrick Wolfe, practices of racialisation are the means through which groups of colonised peoples have been (and continue to be) marked, coopted into unequal relationships, governed and assigned their place within colonial orders.[22] The violence of the nineteenth labour trade was made possible, as Banivanua Mar documented, by racialised stereotypes of savagery that produced Melanesians as 'colonizable, oppressable, and exploitable'.[23] Agricultural labour in tropical north-eastern Australia was popularly understood as fatal to white workers, but 'constitutionally suited' to the 'lower races'.[24] It was also understood as having civilising benefits. As the lawyer defending the recruiter John Coath, charged with kidnapping nine men from Vanuatu's Epi Island, declared in 1871: 'It is no offence to go to islands inhabited by a savage and barbarous people, and to bring these people into the protection of English law.'[25] In fact, the use of indenture as a mechanism for organising Pacific labour involved a substantial reconfiguration of race and plantation labour. Globally, prior to abolition, indentured servitude had been primarily used for securing white labour, sourced from temperate Europe for the similarly temperate plantations of the Caribbean and the Americas, in contrast to the non-white labour mobilised through the slave trade for tropical or semitropical plantation economies. In the wake of slavery's abolition, white servitude gradually gave way to voluntary forms of labour migration, while servitude, through indenture, was recast as the mechanism through which to organise non-white labour. Indenture

21   Moore, *Kanaka: A History of Melanesian Mackay.*
22   Wolfe, *Traces of History.*
23   Banivanua Mar, *Violence and Colonial Dialogue*, 3.
24   Saunders, 'Masters and Servants', 98.
25   Quoted in Mortensen, 'Slaving in Australian Courts'.

became, then, 'a racial category as well as a legal formula'.[26] It was this racialisation that made indenture, as Hugh Tinker put it in relation to the indenture of Indian workers, 'a new system of slavery', differing only in that it was temporary rather than permanent bondage.[27] This racialisation was critical to the lived experience and enactment of indenture. Further, as Ann Curthoys and Clive Moore argue in their historiographic essay on Aboriginal and Torres Strait Islander labour, this racialisation has made 'ex-slave status' an intrinsic part of the self-understanding and historical consciousness of Aboriginal peoples and Melanesians alike.

Work and Place in North-Central Victoria

In Shepparton, the horticultural work that Ni-Vanuatu workers do today is predominantly seasonal labour, which is to say labour that is tied to particular stages of production and harvest—fruit picking, pruning, thinning—and that generally involves working on farms owned by others. This work is done on the pear and apple orchards that cover large sections of the landscape, on the other fruit and vegetable farms that make up a secondary part of the local industry, and in the packing sheds where fruit is sorted for quality and packaged prior to transportation to supermarkets or to the local SPC Ardmona cannery. Seasonal labour is usually paid on a piece rate basis, although the Ni-Vanuatu workers in the packing shed received a much-desired hourly rate, and packing shed work is often available on a year-round basis, thanks to developments in refrigeration technologies that allow fruit to be stored for long periods of time after its harvest.

In packing sheds and on farms, Ni-Vanuatu labour alongside other Pacific Islanders—particularly Tongans and Samoans—from a small but growing local Pacific Islander population that has been resident in the region for about 30 years, with many of its members now permanent residents or citizens. They also work alongside recently arrived refugees from Afghanistan and the Horn of Africa, as well as Chinese, Malaysian, Albanian and other migrants, both settled and temporary. Additional to these are the large numbers of, predominantly European, backpackers who travel to the region to work for periods of 88 days as a pathway to

---

26   Munro, 'The Pacific Islands Labour Trade', 89.
27   Tinker, *A New System of Slavery.*

receiving a second year-long extension of their Working Holiday Maker visas. Dominant narratives in the region—including those of council and local business groups—celebrate its cultural diversity and history of migration, although these narratives also belie experiences of racism and marginalisation among migrants, as well as among the region's Indigenous people, the Yorta Yorta.[28] The extensive role of Yorta Yorta labour in the early years of the industry's formation is largely obscured within popular accounts of the region's history. Meanwhile, pervasive narratives that 'locals don't do fruit picking work anymore' leave unrecognised the work of the many local workers, including resident Pacific Islanders and asylum seekers, who *do* make up a significant section of the industry's workforce. These narratives function to code 'local' as 'white' in ways that discursively and epistemically exclude others from belonging.

The establishment of the fruit-growing industry in the region dates back to the mid-1800s, beginning with the arrival in the area of white settlers in 1838. These were followed by squatters who 'opened up' huge tracts of land and, later, surveyors who parcelled it up for sale to 'men of means' in the 1850s–70s. This was, of course, a process of colonial settlement and Indigenous dispossession. Seasonal labour in the early years of the industry was done by settlers and Yorta Yorta. From the early twentieth century through to the 1980s, it was largely done by itinerant male workers known as canecutters. These men, usually European and single, would migrate on an annual labour circuit, beginning in the cane fields of Queensland and northern New South Wales, moving down to pick apples and pears in north-central Victoria, and then up towards Robinvale and Mildura in the state's north-west. Pacific Islander labour was never used within the north-central Victorian area during the period of the Pacific labour trade, but blackbirding was certainly implicated in the wider patterns of labour and race relations that affected the area. The labour circuits of canecutters, in particular, followed from an economic restructuring of the Queensland sugar industry following the cessation of the labour trade in the early twentieth century.

This restructuring, which was accompanied by the deportation of many Melanesians back to the Pacific, required a shift from the use of indentured Pacific Islander labour towards the use of white labour. The 'bitterly fought' debates that accompanied this transition reveal

---

28 Moran and Mallman, 'Understanding Social Cohesion'.

themes that continue to animate contemporary debates over the SWP. The shift required a change in the racialised narratives that had positioned agricultural labour as precisely unsuited to such workers who, at any rate (it was argued), would have been degraded by the experience of doing '"niggers" work'.[29] This was a reconfiguring that nevertheless continued to invoke starkly racialised hierarchies. Thus, a growing union presence in the Queensland sugar industry began to campaign against the use of 'Kanaka' labour on the basis that it denied employment to white Australians and posed a threat to community safety and moral integrity. Asserting the superiority of white workers, union campaigns demanded that they receive superior conditions to those of non-white workers, and argued vehemently when they did not. Kay Saunders quotes from an article in the union newspaper *The Worker* in 1911, which angrily decried the treatment of a group of white mill workers who had been housed in the same accommodation previously used for indentured Melanesian workers, and who were 'herded together, without privacy or convenience and with the smell of the kanakas in their nostrils all the time'.[30]

This was the context in which the canecutters emerged as a prominent source of plantation labour, and subsequently of harvest labour, in the south-east horticultural regions. They remained the key source of harvest labour in the Victorian industry until around the 1980s, when the numbers of canecutters began to decline as socio-economic shifts encouraged a reduction in this kind of domestic itinerant labour. In Shepparton, the shift away from canecutters also reflected shifts in the local industry, including a decline in the proportion of fruit being sold for the canneries, and a concomitant increase in the proportion being produced for the fresh fruit market. With this came a shift away from 'strip-picking'—in which all the crop on a tree is removed in one go— towards forms of selective picking on the basis of size, colour and quality, and a lower tolerance for bruising or damage to the fruit (which are less consequential when fruit is being peeled and preserved in the canning process). Farmers in the region describe the unsuitability of the 'rough' and 'tough' canecutters to this more selective form of harvesting.

---

29   Saunders, 'Masters and Servants', 99.
30   Saunders, 'Masters and Servants', 100.

In lieu of canecutters, farmers turned increasingly to backpacker labour, with the introduction of the first working holiday visa in 1975, available in the first instance to young people from the United Kingdom and Canada, but subsequently expanded between 1980 and 2006 to include other countries. Since 2005, young people on one-year Working Holiday Maker visas (subclasses 462 and 417) have had the option of securing a second year-long visa upon completion of 88 days of 'specified work' in a rural industry, most commonly fruit picking. Backpackers have thus become a significant component of harvest workforces, but the industry has continued to experience difficulties in securing what it considers adequately reliable and sufficiently plentiful labour. At the same time, Pacific Island countries have long lobbied for temporary labour access for Pacific Islander workers. The push from Pacific Island countries, lobbying from the Australian Farmers Federation and the success of New Zealand's seasonal worker scheme for Pacific workers (the Recognised Seasonal Employer scheme) were among the factors that led to the introduction of the Pacific Seasonal Worker Pilot Scheme in 2009, with the SWP proper commencing in 2012.[31] Nationally, including in Shepparton, the take up of the SWP was slower than initially anticipated, but is growing. Pacific Islander workers are promoted to farmers (through labour hire company and government marketing) as well-suited to horticultural labour (not unlike their nineteenth-century forebears). While the administrative and bureaucratic requirements of recruiting workers through the SWP are off-putting for many farmers, what appeals about the scheme is that the workers' mobility (and thus agency) is controllable in ways that the mobility of backpackers is not. Whereas backpackers can, and do, leave or change employers if conditions are poor, the visa conditions that tie SWP workers to specific employers mean that they lack that critical negotiating chip. For employers, this is a key benefit of the scheme. As one of the managers of the packing shed put it, describing their decision to use workers through the SWP, 'we can get a group of staff and know that they can't actually go and work anywhere else'. In key ways, what the scheme represents is a new form of indenture.

---

31   MacDermott and Opeskin, 'Regulating Pacific Seasonal Labour in Australia'; Maclellan and Mares, 'Remittances and Labour Mobility in the Pacific'; Mares and Maclellan, 'Pacific Seasonal Workers for Australian Horticulture'.

Discourses of Slavery Today

The Ni-Vanuatu workers assigned to the packing shed arrived in Australia with two other groups of Ni-Vanuatu whose migration and recruitment was managed by the same labour hire agency. The packing shed workers and the group assigned to the tomato farm—those whose labour conditions prompted the allusion to 'modern-day slavery'—stayed at the same caravan park in one of the region's small towns. The third group, assigned to pick apples and pears, were accommodated on the orchard of the farmer for whom they worked. While the packing shed workers were predominantly female, ranging in age from early 20s to mid-50s, the other two groups were primarily male (as, indeed, most SWP workers have been).

The seasonal nature of horticultural work makes it, by its nature, precarious—farmers often need to pull together workforces at short notice, and dissolve them again just as quickly. Unexpected weather events and a host of other factors can have sudden and dramatic effects on the availability of work. The payment of piece rates (e.g. per bin of fruit picked) enables the flexibility that farmers seek, and is also widely understood (by farmers) to motivate workers to work faster. However, the variability of horticultural production means that piece rates can also be highly variable. This is what played out with the group of Ni-Vanuatu workers allocated to the tomato farm. Like other SWP workers, the group had guaranteed minimum hours; however, the crop at the tomato farm had been particularly poor that season. Small tomatoes, and fewer fruit on plants, meant that it took longer and was harder work to fill the bins, and, with piece rates, fewer bins equated to lower pay. This was coupled with regular deductions from workers' pay, which are a major source of grievance for many SWP workers, including those working at the packing shed who were otherwise pleased to enjoy hourly rates. SWP workers have their accommodation, transport, mandatory health insurance (because they are not entitled to public health care) and other aspects of their living conditions while in Australia organised for them by their employers or by the labour hire companies managing their employment. This is packaged as part of the pastoral care dimension of the scheme—bound up in its developmentalism—but also functions as a control on the movement of workers, amid a context of Australian governmental anxiety about Pacific workers 'absconding' and overstaying their visas. Thus, expenses are set outside of the control of workers themselves, with deductions taken from their pay to cover their repayment. Many workers must also make repayments to cover part of the cost of their travel to and from Australia, and the effect of all of these deductions, when coupled with low pay from piece work, is that workers, like the Ni-Vanuatu picking on the tomato farm, can be left making little more than a pittance. Crucially, whereas backpackers who found themselves picking a poor-sized and poor-quality crop could—and generally would—leave in search of better conditions, SWP workers do not have this option available to them. As Makiko Nishitani and Helen Lee explain in this volume, this is a critical factor in the preference of many of their informants in the north-west Victorian region of Mildura to work informally rather than through the SWP. It is this constrained mobility, and the experience of it as racialised and unequal (in relation to other groups of workers), that fuels discourses of slavery.

Beyond the packing sheds, caravan parks, orchards and community spaces of Australia's horticultural regions, these discourses also, increasingly, circulate via social media networks that extend transnationally across Australia and the Pacific, and provide important forums for sharing stories and experiences about the SWP, as well as about New Zealand's equivalent Recognised Seasonal Employer (RSE) scheme, and life more generally across the Pasifika diaspora. In July 2017, a post on the popular Facebook group Café Koko Samoa prompted an extensive discussion, garnering thousands of comments over a period of a few months. The post that launched this particular discussion featured a short exposé-style video about Pacific Islanders reportedly being paid $9 or less a week while working on a South Australian farm, because of the kinds of factors described above related to piece rate pay and deductions. Among the pages of comments, slavery was a persistent theme, invoked in ways that explicitly referenced the labour trade and blackbirding past. For example:

> 'Get out of [there]. We aint slaves. Fuck tht [sic] shit.'
>
> 'modern day slavery'
>
> 'this is slave labour'
>
> 'Slave labor. wake up Australia'
>
> 'We are People of the Pacific that had a lot of respect towards any other human race when they come to our land of pride but saddly [sic] that we are treated like slaves because of our colour or our way of living.'
>
> 'Racism and modern day slavery'
>
> 'Blackbirders'
>
> 'This is slavery'
>
> 'Hey look out! … I thought slave days were long gone.'

References to slavery were intertwined with a wider discussion of colonial histories and colonial continuities across the region. At one point, the discussion deviated into a debate between Samoans and Māori about whether New Zealand or England was responsible for Samoa's colonisation. Other commenters invoked Australia's settler colonial history and its treatment of Aboriginal people. Still others picked up on the South African accent of the farmer featured in the expose, with one declaring: '[he] thinks he's got black African slaves like back in his country!' Some United States–based Pasifika drew in references to the mistreatment of Mexican workers, and to the enslavement and indenture of African Americans. Another commented, in response to the sprawling and wideranging discussion: 'We calling out ALL colonizers.' Thus situated, slavery was produced as a referent that invoked specific pasts, such as the blackbirding of Pacific Islanders to Australia, as well as much wider complexes of race, inequality and exploitation extending across both the past and the present. It became a powerful motif through which people's affective responses to those specific and generalised structures of power—anger, outrage, sadness—could be articulated.

Development Dreams

Yet, even as discourses of slavery proliferate—as one commentator on the Café Koko Samoa post put it, 'these stories just keep coming'—Pacific Islander participation in the SWP continues to be actively sought. Pacific Island countries lobbied hard for labour mobility schemes to Australia and continue to advocate for their expansion. Within the 10 participating countries, there are high levels of demand for SWP places. Like many of the trans-Tasman migrants described by Ruth Faleolo in this volume, Pacific Islanders seeking access to the scheme pursue Australia as a 'land of milk and honey'—a land considered to offer possibilities not attainable in the islands or in New Zealand. However, unlike trans-Tasman migrants, those seeking places in the SWP do not enjoy freedom of entry into Australia and face onerous migration and labour regimes. In Shepparton, the group of Ni-Vanuatu workers—all of whom had willingly, often enthusiastically, pursued employment through the SWP—had negotiated long and complex processes to secure their places. These processes required prospective migrants finding agents back in Vanuatu that would put their names forward, and leveraging personal connections to ensure that their inclusion on various lists translated into actual possibilities for work. The packing shed workers had then needed police and medical clearances and to pass selection tests and interviews conducted in Port Vila by representatives of the packing house company before their positions were finally confirmed.

Many of the packing shed workers pointed to positive aspects of their labour migration experiences. As one woman put it: 'We are lucky, so lucky to come.' Grace, one of the workers on her third SWP placement in Australia, used the income from her first year to purchase a large freezer and a portable ice box and establish a small business with her husband, buying fish from their home island that they freeze, transport to the Vanuatu capital, Port Vila, and sell for a profit in the urban market. She used her earnings from the second year to purchase a car that she runs as an informal transport business. Anne, another of the returning workers, described her joy the year before when, mid-way through her placement, she heard from her husband that the money she had been sending back had finally paid off the loan that they had taken out to purchase land and a house in Port Vila, on the country's largest island Efate:

> I feel excited and tears running down my face, my cheeks because I, like, never expected … So that's why I am come here from three years now … I've got two things that I came here for: the school fees for my children and my land.

Several other women were similarly hoping to use the money they earned to purchase land for a house in Vila or elsewhere on Efate. As Rachel Smith notes in relation to Ni-Vanuatu participating in the New Zealand RSE scheme, 'the affective value of place (*ples*) is crucial to social identity' within Vanuatu, and the attainment of a 'good house' has become a key indicator of the moral and material achievement through overseas horticultural work.[32] Others among the group of packing shed workers were paying school fees for their children; several were also using their income and their location in Australia to purchase cooking equipment that they intended to use for informal entrepreneurial activity back in Vanuatu, or mobile phone handsets, bluetooth speakers and other goods that they hoped to be able to resell for a profit. Many of the women also valued their trip as an 'experience' or an 'adventure'. All said they would like to return again in following seasons.

---

32   Smith, 'Changing Standards of Living', 45.

Figure 6.2: Money trees.
Source: Photograph by Victoria Stead.

The development dreams that coalesce around horticultural labour also extend to Pacific Islander communities that are permanently resident in Shepparton. At the start of a recent harvest season, Sina, a Samoan woman whose family has been resident in the region for over 30 years, posted a photo of rows of apple trees on her social media account. She captioned the photo: 'Been a long time—getting that $$$ for Christmas. Can always count on the trees to give when in need lol. #oldschoolskills #moneytrees.' Her friend commented in reply: 'Money does grow on trees.' Indeed, horticultural work is a large part of what has drawn Pacific Islanders to the region. It remains a primary occupation for much of the local Pasifika community, and most of those resident in the region—including Sina's own family—also commit time and resources to facilitating and supporting the migrations, both temporary and permanent, of their kin in New Zealand, Samoa and Tonga, who also want to come and work on the money trees.

Work and Dreams Beyond the Forced/Free Dyad

How do we make sense of these tensions and competing narratives about Pacific Islander horticultural labour? One explanation, of course, is simply that different Pacific Islander workers have different experiences. Some have a positive time and experience benefits, others have a negative time and experience exploitation. Certainly, Pacific Islanders working in the horticultural industry today are not a homogeneous or undifferentiated group. For example, the Ni-Vanuatu women working in the packing shed had, on the whole, a much more favourable experience than the workers at the tomato farm. As an explanatory framework, though, this fails to account for the intersections of different imaginaries—of development dreams and blackbirding legacies—or for the ambivalences and multiplicities of Pacific Islander experiences of horticultural work, both past and present.

Writing in a blog post for a development policy website, the economist Stephen Howes highlighted findings from a 2015 survey, conducted by the World Bank, of close to 400 Pacific seasonal workers. The survey found that 98 per cent would refer the SWP scheme to a friend, and that workers, on average, rated their satisfaction with the scheme at 8.6 out of 10. Howes, having long opposed media reports making the link between contemporary seasonal labour and slavery, concluded triumphantly:

> Overwhelmingly, seasonal workers have a great time here in Australia; they want their friends to come and work here; and they are returning themselves for more of the same. It is nothing like blackbirding.[33]

There are a number of questions that could be asked of the World Bank survey's methodology, not least related to the intense anxieties that many SWP workers—including those in Shepparton—feel about the possibility of any negative feedback by them about the scheme getting back to employers who have the power to determine whether or not they are able to come back in subsequent years. More fundamentally, the question that needs to be asked is about the capacity for statistics like 98 per cent, or 8.6 out of 10, to tell a full and human story of Pacific Islanders' experiences of horticultural labour.

---

33 Howes, 'Satisfied Seasonal Workers'.

Thus, Sina, my Samoan friend in Shepparton who describes the fruit trees her family picks, prunes and thins as 'money trees', also narrates her father's three decades of horticultural labour in the region through reference to his aching back, chronic respiratory problems and a gruelling weight of obligation to kin back in Samoa who cannot secure Australian visas. She describes her frustration with the persistent lack of recognition of the contributions her father and other Pasifika workers in Shepparton make to the industry. She recounts how the farmer for whom her father and uncle have worked, for years, enthusiastically welcomes back each season the white workers who travel down from Queensland for harvest, sidelining her father and uncle who work day in, day out, keeping the farm ticking over.

Grace and Anne, two of the Ni-Vanuatu women who highlighted positive aspects of their work, also describe the work as 'difficult' and 'hard'. They talk about being hyper-scrutinised by farmers who stand behind them as they work the line at the packing shed, watching how they pack the fruit, correcting them and pushing them to work faster. They describe feeling unappreciated, and they struggle with not knowing from year to year whether they will be invited back again. They talk about being beholden to labour hire agents who mediate their employment and wield enormous power, often unscrupulously. They recount with sadness their isolation in the tiny rural town where they are accommodated, and their almost complete lack of interaction with local residents there.

Mary, who, in her early 20s, is one of the younger women in the group of packing shed workers, is also planning to use the money she earns through the SWP to buy land to build a house in Port Vila. She estimates that she can earn four times in Australia what she can back home. She, like the others, and like the survey respondents Howes invokes, would readily come back in subsequent years. However, she is also a single mother, and has had to leave her seven-year-old son behind with extended family while she is here for six months. She aches for him, as do others in the group who have left behind young children. One night, while sharing a meal in the caravan park where the workers stay, one of the male Ni-Vanuatu workers assigned to the tomato farm asks me, gently, if he can pick up and cuddle my then two-year-old son who is there with me. He tells me he is the same age as his twins, and as he sits with my son snuggled on his lap he shows me their picture on his phone. He has not seen them in five months.

These ambivalences find little expression in the World Bank's '98 per cent' and '8.6 out of 10' ratings. Nor, and this is perhaps the more significant point, do these figures capture the structural, racialised and historical conditions that inform both the contemporary conditions and experiences of seasonal labour, and the choices that SWP workers are able to make. When Mary leaves behind her son to work in the SWP so she can make money to build a home for the two of them, she does so in large part because foreign demand for beachside land in Efate has massively increased land pressures for Ni-Vanuatu, and made land all but unattainable for Ni-Vanuatu working for local wages.[34] This foreign demand for land includes demand by Australians keen for their own piece of tropical Vanuatu 'paradise'. Not unlike the choices of Pacific Islanders who voluntarily boarded the ships of nineteenth-century recruiters, the choices that contemporary Ni-Vanuatu make are made in contexts in which their alternatives are limited (and structurally so), and in which forces of race and coloniality serve to position particular forms of life and goods as valuable and desirable. As post-development critics and anthropologists of development have argued forcefully, 'development' is at once ideological, material and affective; it acts on the subjectivities of those who are deemed in need of it, and is experienced in ways that can be at once profound and deeply ambivalent.[35]

Thus, when local Samoan and Tongan workers experience their own labour being devalued and unrecognised, they do so in the context of long-running, known and felt histories of racialised inequalities that render particular types of people and bodies as 'constitutionally suited' for tough, agricultural labour, and simultaneously diminish their contributions. These are the structural conditions within which both development dreams and discourses of modern-day slavery are entangled with one another and made meaningful. Participation in the SWP can thus be sought after, valued, even enjoyed in part, and *also* be experienced as reflective, and indeed constitutive, of deeply entrenched inequalities that run through and characterise Australian coloniality in relation to the Pacific region.

---

34 McDonnell, 'Urban Land Grabbing by Political Elites'.
35 Stead, 'The Price of Fish'; Stead, *Becoming Landowners*; Bulloch, *In Pursuit of Progress*; Shrestha, 'Becoming a Development Category'.

Contemporary horticultural labour is not a simple revamping of nineteenth-century blackbirding, but nor are these two disconnected phenomena; the Pacific labour trade forms part of the colonial lineage through which the Pacific and Australia are produced in relation to one another, and within which contemporary subjectivities, developmentalist paradigms and racialised inequalities are ultimately embedded, known and felt.

Bibliography

Altman, Jon. 'Modern Slavery in Remote Australia?'. *Arena Magazine,* no. 150 (Oct 2017): 12–15.

Bales, Kevin. *Disposable People: New Slavery in the Global Economy.* Los Angeles: University of California Press, 2012 (3rd ed.).

Banivanua Mar, Tracey. *Decolonisation and the Pacific: Indigenous Globalisation and the Ends of Empire.* Cambridge: Cambridge University Press, 2016.

——. *Violence and Colonial Dialogue: The Australian-Pacific Indentured Labor Trade.* Honolulu: University of Hawai'i Press, 2007.

Basok, Tanya. 'Free to Be Unfree: Mexican Guest Workers in Canada'. *Labour, Capital and Society* 32, no. 2 (1999): 191–21.

Bulloch, Hannah. *In Pursuit of Progress: Narratives of Development on a Philippine Island.* Honolulu: University of Hawai'i Press, 2017. doi.org/10.21313/hawaii/9780824858865.001.0001.

Connell, John. 'From Blackbirds to Guestworkers in the South Pacific. *Plus Ça Change…?'*. *The Economic and Labour Relations Review* 20, no. 2 (2010): 111–22. doi.org/10.1177/103530461002000208.

Davidson, Julia O'Connell. 'Troubling Freedom: Migration, Debt, and Modern Slavery'. *Migration Studies* 1, no. 2 (2013): 176–95. doi.org/10.1093/migration/mns002.

Doyle, Jesse and Manohar Sharma. 'Maximizing the Development Impacts from Temporary Migration: Recommendations for Australia's Seasonal Worker Program'. Washington DC: World Bank Group, 2017.

Graves, Adrian. *Cane and Labour: The Political Economy of the Queensland Sugar Industry, 1862–1906.* Edinburgh: University of Edinburgh Press, 1993.

———. 'The Nature and Origins of Pacific Islands Labour Migration to Queensland, 1863–1906'. In *International Labour Migration: Historical Perspectives*, edited by Shula Marks and Peter Richardson, 112–39. London: Maurice Temple Smith, 1984.

Howes, Stephen. 'Satisfied Seasonal Workers'. *DevPolicyBlog*, 3 April 2018, www.devpolicy.org/satisfied-seasonal-workers-20180403/.

Joint Standing Committee on Foreign Affairs, Defence and Trade. *Hidden in Plain Sight: An Inquiry into Establishing a Modern Slavery Act in Australia.* Canberra: Parliament of the Commonwealth of Australia, 2017.

Lewis, Hannah, Peter Dwyer, Stuart Hogkinson and Louise Waite. 'Hyper-Precarious Lives: Migrants, Work and Forced Labour in the Global North'. *Progress in Human Geography* 39, no. 5 (2015): 580–600. doi.org/10.1177/0309132514548303.

Locke, Sarina, Kallee Buchanan and Catherine Graue. 'Seasonal Worker Program in Australia Gets Backing from Farmers but with Concerns about Rogue Operators'. *ABC News*, 21 December 2017, www.abc.net.au/news/rural/2017-12-21/seasonal-worker-program-supported-by-farmers/9276672.

MacDermott, Therese and Brian Opeskin. 'Regulating Pacific Seasonal Labour in Australia'. *Pacific Affairs* 83, no. 2 (2010): 283–305. doi.org/10.5509/2010832283.

Maclellan, Nic and Peter Mares. 'Remittances and Labour Mobility in the Pacific: A Working Paper on Seasonal Work Programs in Australia for Pacific Islanders'. Working Paper, Institute for Social Research, Swinburne University of Technology, 2006.

Mares, Peter and Nic Maclellan. 'Pacific Seasonal Workers for Australian Horticulture: A Neat Fit?'. *Asian and Pacific Migration Journal* 16, no. 2 (2007): 271–88. doi.org/10.1177/011719680701600207.

McDonnell, Siobhan. 'Urban Land Grabbing by Political Elites: Exploring the Political Economy of Land and the Challenges of Regulation'. In *Kastom, Property and Ideology*, edited by Siobhan McDonnell, Matthew G. Allen and Colin Filer, 283–304. Canberra: ANU Press, 2017. doi.org/10.22459/KPI.03.2017.09.

Miles, Robert. *Capitalism and Unfree Labour: Anomaly or Necessity?* London: Tavistock, 1987.

Moore, Clive. *Kanaka: A History of Melanesian Mackay*. Port Moresby: University of Papua New Guinea Press 1985.

Moran, Anthony and Mark Mallman. 'Understanding Social Cohesion in Shepparton and Mildura: Literature Review'. Bundoora: La Trobe University and Victorian Multicultural Commission, 2015.

Mortensen, Reid. 'Slaving in Australian Courts: Blackbirding Cases, 1869-1871'. *Journal of South Pacific Law* 4 (2000), accessed 14 March 2019, www.usp.ac.fj/index.php?id=13200.

Munro, Doug. 'The Pacific Islands Labour Trade: Approaches, Methodologies, Debates'. *Slavery and Abolition* 14, no. 2 (1993): 87–108. doi.org/10.1080/01440399308575099.

———. 'Revisionism and Its Enemies: Debating the Queensland Labour Trade'. *The Journal of Pacific History* 30, no. 2 (1995): 240–49. doi.org/10.1080/00223349508572798.

Quirk, Joel. 'The Anti-Slavery Project: Linking the Historical and Contemporary'. *Human Rights Quarterly* 28, no. 3 (2006): 565–98. doi.org/10.1353/hrq.2006.0036.

Saunders, Kay. 'Masters and Servants'. *Labour History* 35 (1978): 96–111. doi.org/10.2307/27508338.

Scarr, Deryck. *Fragments of Empire: A History of the Western Pacific High Commission, 1877–1914*. Canberra: Australian National University Press, 1967.

———. 'Recruits and Recruiters: A Portrait of the Pacific Islands Labour Trade'. *The Journal of Pacific History* 2, no. 1 (1967): 5–24. doi.org/10.1080/00223346708572099.

Shlomowitz, Ralph. 'Markets for Indentured and Time-Expired Melanesian Labour in Queensland, 1863–1906: An Economic Analysis'. *The Journal of Pacific History* 16, no. 2 (1981): 70–91. doi.org/10.1080/00223348108572416.

———. 'Time-Expired Melanesian Labor in Queensland: An Investigation of Job Turnover, 1884–1906'. *Pacific Studies* 8, no. 2 (1985): 25–44.

Shrestha, Nanda. 'Becoming a Development Category'. In *Power of Development*, edited by Jonathan Crush, 266–77. London: Routledge, 1995.

Smith, Rachel E. 'Changing Standards of Living: The Paradoxes of Building a Good Life in Rural Vanuatu'. In *The Quest for the Good Life in Precarious Times: Ethnographic Perspectives on the Domestic Moral Economy*, edited by Chris Gregory and Jon Altman, 33–55. Canberra: ANU Press, 2018. doi.org/10.22459/QGLPT.03.2018.03.

Stead, Victoria. *Becoming Landowners: Entanglements of Custom and Modernity in Papua New Guinea and Timor-Leste*. Honolulu: University of Hawai'i Press, 2017.

——. 'The Price of Fish: Problematising Discourses of Prosperity at the Pacific Marine Industrial Zone'. In *Securing a Prosperous Future: Papers from the Second Annual Alfred Deakin Research Institute Papua New Guinea Symposium, 2012*, edited by Jonathan Ritchie and Michelle Verso, 197–230. Goolwa: Crawford House Publishing, 2014.

Tinker, Hugh. *A New System of Slavery: The Export of Indian Labour Overseas, 1830–1920*. London: Oxford University Press, 1974.

Weitzer, Ronald. 'Human Trafficking and Contemporary Slavery'. *Annual Review of Sociology* 41 (2015): 223–42. doi.org/10.1146/annurev-soc-073014-112506.

Wolfe, Patrick. *Traces of History: Elementary Structures of Race*. London: Verso, 2016.

Newspapers

The Guardian
The Sydney Morning Herald
The Weekly Times

7

Becoming 'Overstayers': The Coloniality of Citizenship and the Resilience of Pacific Farm Workers

Makiko Nishitani and Helen Lee

The Australian Government once described Pacific people as too 'unsophisticated' and 'unsuited' to settle in Australia and as a likely source of social problems.[1] Ironically, this statement was made in a Cabinet submission in 1971, when the government was making progress towards abolishing the 'White Australia' policy in an attempt to signify Australia's departure from racist immigration policies. This contradiction vividly illustrates Australia's ambivalent attitude towards migrants from the Pacific. More than four decades later, the Australian Government's view of Pacific people as permanent migrants has scarcely changed, although, in recent years, it has introduced the Seasonal Worker Programme (SWP), which encourages temporary labour migration from Pacific countries. This chapter explores the complex ways Australia's immigration regime has influenced Pacific people's mobility through forms of inclusion and exclusion, and their equally complex responses. In particular, we focus on the irregular migrants often referred to as 'overstayers' both by Australian authorities and within Pacific migrant communities.

---

1   Hamer, '"Unsophisticated and Unsuited"', 104.

Pacific people's worldview tends to emphasise a borderless world shaped by connections with kin and kin-like relationships.[2] Nevertheless, national borders and immigration laws inevitably shape people's opportunities for migration in various ways, determining whether migration is permanent or temporary, as well as assigning different rights and benefits according to their immigration status. Most of the Pacific people in Australia who are 'overstayers' have entered the country legally using a visitor visa, but then remained after the expiration of their visa, making their immigration status 'unlawful'.

Pacific overstayers have been present in Australia for many years and the dominant narrative about them has long been one of 'illegal immigrants' stealing jobs and costing taxpayers, as reflected in this newspaper report from 1989:

> [Name], 39, an illegal immigrant from Fiji, used his real name to take a job and then four aliases to milk the welfare system of $84,000 in dole payments. The Victorian judge who later jailed [Name] condemned the case as an outrageous rip-off of Australian taxpayers … A Tongan immigrant and his wife, who entered Australia illegally, cost the Australian Legal Aid office $1 million in their successful appeal against deportation orders … Illegal immigrants are costing taxpayers more than $400 million a year. Because the illegals are on the run from the moment they arrive here, they are much more likely than legitimate citizens to engage in systematic fraud of welfare, financial and tax systems.[3]

To challenge that narrative, we apply the lens of the 'coloniality of power',[4] arguing that the category of 'overstayers' is socially and politically produced by Australia's immigration system. Drawing on field work conducted since 2014, we also focus on Pacific overstayers' voices, which reveal their concerted efforts to legalise their status and their resilience despite the precariousness of their everyday lives in Australia.[5] Our research participants are mainly

2   Hau'ofa, 'Our Sea of Islands'; Ka'ili, *Marking Indigeneity*.
3   Bob Bottom, 'Illegal Migrants: How They Cost Us $400M', *The Sydney Morning Herald*, 28 August 1989, 1.
4   Quijano, 'Coloniality of Power'.
5   This research has been funded by an Australian Research Council Linkage Project grant and a La Trobe University Research Focus Area (Transforming Human Societies) grant. Our partner organisations are the Sunraysia Mallee Ethnic Communities Council (its EO Dean Wickham is our partner investigator) and the Mallee Sports Assembly. Participants include over 100 Pacific people, including Tongans, Cook Islanders, Fijians, Solomon Islanders and Ni-Vanuatu, who completed questionnaires and in-depth interviews and participated in focus group discussions. In addition, interviews were conducted with key stakeholders such as farmers and service providers in the area.

farm workers who live in north-west Victoria in the towns of Mildura and Robinvale.[6] Although many are, or were, overstayers, they have made a significant but often unacknowledged contribution to the economy of the region, known as Sunraysia, for many years.[7]

Figure 7.1: 'Welcome to Sunraysia', north-west Victoria.

Signs like these present an idealised view that obscures the work done by Pacific Islanders and others to sustain the local horticultural industry. Still, for some informal workers, Sunraysia is an 'oasis' of sorts, offering relative protection from surveillance and migration regimes.

Source: Photograph by Makiko Nishitani.

According to the 2016 census, Mildura has a population of 32,738, including various Pacific groups, whereas Robinvale has a population of only 3,088 and its Pacific population is predominantly Tongan.[8] Sunraysia is a highly productive horticultural region and Pacific farm workers are employed in citrus orchards and in the many vineyards, which

6   Nishitani and Lee, 'Invisible Islanders?'
7   We believe naming the towns will not have negative implications for our research participants. The presence of overstayers and other 'illegal' migrants is shared knowledge in the towns as well as among stakeholders, and it was openly discussed by many witnesses, including our partner investigator, Dean Wickham, at the parliamentary public hearing, 'Inquiry into Establishing a Modern Slavery Act', in October 2017. The Hansard is publicly available.
8   '2016 Census Quickstats: Mildura', Australian Bureau of Statistics, released 23 October 2017, accessed 14 March 2019, www.censusdata.abs.gov.au/census_services/getproduct/census/2016/quick stat/SSC21671?opendocument; '2016 Census Quickstats: Robinvale', Australian Bureau of Statistics, released 23 October 2017, accessed 14 March 2019, www.censusdata.abs.gov.au/census_services/get product/census/2016/quickstat/SSC22171?opendocument.

produce table grapes and wine, surrounding the towns. In addition, due to growing demand within Australia, almond farms are expanding in the Robinvale area, where some of the Tongan settlers are employed to operate machinery for harvesting and processing. Although the emergence of corporate farming, or 'agribusiness', is rapidly changing the horticultural landscape and associated industries, relatively small farming 'blocks' are still predominant. Many Italian and Greek migrants, who moved into the area in the nineteenth century and during the two world wars, established these blocks. They arrived in search of opportunities that were unavailable in the cities under the 'White Australia' policy. These early migrants:

> Experienced constraints on employment and economic opportunities, being restricted to poorly paid, low status, low skilled jobs, often with poor working conditions, in the service sector and as 'factory fodder' in the cities. Fruit picking and seasonal work in intensive horticultural areas such as the Goulburn Valley and Sunraysia often gave an introduction to the district and also some horticultural skills such as picking and pruning. Purchasing small-scale farms presented opportunities for economic advancement for immigrants and others with limited opportunities for social mobility in other sectors of the economy.[9]

These Southern European farmers have now become the main employers of the many Pacific people who have moved to the region since the 1980s. Tongans were the first to arrive in the area, also in search of job opportunities. Many were already overstayers and had been living in Melbourne or Sydney but had been unable to find work due to their immigration status. They were attracted by the relative lack of surveillance in regional communities and ready availability of farm work. Other Tongans initially went to the area on visitor visas and decided to overstay for various reasons: primarily, the ease of finding work without being questioned about their immigration status. Over time, some were caught by immigration officers and deported, or had their visa applications rejected and left Australia, but others were able to get permanent residency or Australian citizenship and many continue to live in the area today. It was not unusual for it to take more than 10 years and several migration review tribunals for overstayers to 'win' permanent residency status, while others gained it through amnesties.[10] There were three amnesty periods in Australia in the 1970s and 1980, which aimed to 'regularise the status

---

9   Missingham, Dibden and Cocklin, 'A Multicultural Countryside', 136.
10   As of July 2015, the Migration Review Tribunal is called the Administrative Appeals Tribunal.

of people who had overstayed their visas'.[11] After the last amnesty in 1980, special legislation was enacted that was 'designed to block government from declaring amnesties in the future',[12] and was supported by the main political parties.[13]

Since the last amnesty, 'the Department tightened border controls, instructing officers to be more stringent and look more closely at the bona fides of people applying for visitor visas'.[14] Meanwhile, Tongans and other Pacific migrants, including Cook Islanders, Solomon Islanders and Fijians, have continued to move into regional Victoria. Cook Islanders are eligible for New Zealand passports by birth and are thus entitled to work rights and unlimited residence in Australia, although New Zealand citizens' rights to welfare benefits have been restricted since 2001. Other Pacific people have arrived in the region with a range of immigration statuses and their communities now include irregular migrants (much like other regional areas, as discussed by Mackay and Guinness, this volume). Many of our research participants shared the view that issues associated with immigration status are among the most serious problems facing these communities. As scholarship on national borders shows, immigration status and citizenship are not only legal concepts but also historically and socially constructed.[15] Thus, each immigration status should not be treated as a 'transparent and self-evident fact'.[16] Instead, it is necessary to consider the role of changing immigration policies and their allocation of rights.

Australia's Immigration Policies and the Coloniality of Citizenship

Within the boundaries of nation-states, citizenship has levelling effects that ideally provide equal rights to the members of those states. However, on a global level, each nation-state's citizenship provides different opportunities. In this sense, citizenship is a crucial 'opportunity-allocating

11   Mence, Gangell and Tebb, *A History of the Department of Immigration*, 58.
12   David Solomon, 'Australia's "Last" Amnesty for Illegal Aliens Gets Mixed Results', *The Christian Science Monitor*, 7 January 1981, www.csmonitor.com/1981/0107/010758.html.
13   Bob Bottom, 'Illegal Migrants: How They Cost Us $400M', *The Sydney Morning Herald*, 28 August 1989.
14   Mence, Gangell, and Tebb, *A History of the Department of Immigration*, 58.
15   De Genova, 'Migrant "Illegality" and Deportability in Everyday Life'; Gonzales and Sigona, 'Mapping the Soft Borders of Citizenship'.
16   De Genova, 'Migrant "Illegality" and Deportability in Everyday Life', 432.

institution of the modern era'.[17] Although citizenship can be acquired when the requisite conditions are met, for most people, citizenship is ascribed at birth. As Boatcă and Roth argue, this 'birthright transmission of citizenship' and resultant unequal 'allocation of life chances' is 'the very proof of its coloniality'.[18] They claim that 'the institution of citizenship has developed in the West through the legal (and physical) exclusion of non-European, non-White and non-Western populations from civic, political, social and cultural rights'.[19]

Tracing Australia's immigration policies, Claudia Tazreiter states that 'Australia has developed a proactive approach to immigration—actively recruiting and selecting prospective newcomers', while excluding the negatively defined 'Other' since white settlement.[20] This exclusion of non-Europeans was enforced in two ways. Aboriginal people were excluded 'by the denial of citizenship' and acts of violence and segregation, and non-European migrants were barred entry through legislation, most significantly the *Immigration Restriction Act 1901* that aimed to 'preserve the social and political fabric of a settler society'.[21] Sanjugta Vas Dev argues that:

> Within this historical trajectory of White settlement and its emphasis on control of 'the other', constructions of asylum-seeker identity as 'illegal', 'burdensome' and 'threatening' have been thus viewed as a continued form of racism traced back to British colonisation, in an attempt to unite the predominantly white community first against indigenous people and then against all non-Anglo outsiders.[22]

Immigration and citizenship laws are intricately related to projects of state building.[23] As mentioned at the start of this chapter, the Australian Government once described Pacific Islanders as 'unsuited' to settle in the country and regarded them as a potential source of problems. Australia's strong preference for skilled migration continues to prevent many Pacific Islanders from permanently migrating to the country and they have been admitted only on particular terms, such as through the SWP. However, Pacific people have continued to resist the restrictions and conditions

---

17 Shachar, 'The Birthright Lottery: Response to Interlocutors', 1.
18 Boatcă and Roth, 'Unequal and Gendered', 205.
19 Boatcă and Roth, 'Unequal and Gendered', 191.
20 Tazreiter, *Asylum Seekers and the State*, 126.
21 Tazreiter, *Asylum Seekers and the State*, 126–27.
22 Vas Dev, 'Accounting for State Approaches', 38.
23 Kipnis, 'Anthropology and the Theorisation of Citizenship', 265.

that attempt to control their mobility and have sought alternative ways to be able to live and work in Australia, often taking the risk of becoming overstayers to achieve their goals.

Using quantitative data on patterns of inequality in more than 96 countries, Korzeniewicz and Moran demonstrated that international migration is the 'single most immediate and effective means of global social mobility for populations in most countries of the world'.[24] This motivates many people to be 'able and willing to risk illegal, undocumented or non-citizen status in a rich state'.[25] Pacific overstayers exemplify this pattern; however, they have always been a minority in relation to the overall number of people similarly attempting to improve their life chances by overstaying their visas in Australia. For example, in 2012, there were 1,090 Tongan passport holders with visitor visas who had not returned to Tonga before their visa expiry date. By contrast, 7,800 overstayers held Chinese passports.[26] If non-return rate is used as the measurement, Tongans' rate of 5.6 per cent was the highest of all countries, whereas the Chinese non-return rate was only 0.32 per cent. Focusing on rates rather than numbers has enabled the Australian Government to justify instituting, since the 1990s, 'strict requirements for visitors from Fiji, Tonga and other Pacific countries because of people overstaying in the past'.[27] This has included family members living in Australia often being required to pay security bonds, usually between AU$5,000 and AU$15,000 per person if they want to sponsor relatives from their home country via the Visitor Visa – Sponsored Family stream.[28]

A 'Closed' Path to Citizenship and Permanent Migration

Australia's strong preference for skilled migration, particularly in relation to permanent migration, limits the options for Pacific people who want to live in Australia but do not have access as New Zealand citizens through Australia's travel agreement with New Zealand (see Faleolo,

---

24   Korzeniewicz and Moran, *Unveiling Inequality*, 107.

25   Boatcă and Roth, 'Unequal and Gendered', 199.

26   'Population Flows: Immigration Aspects (2010–11 ed.)', Department of Immigration and Citizenship, accessed 16 December 2013, www.immi.gov.au/media/publications/statistics/popflows 2010-11/pop-flows.pdf (site discontinued).

27   Maclellan and Mares, 'Remittances and Labour Mobility in the Pacific', 46.

28   'Fact Sheet –Sponsored Family Stream', Department of Home Affairs, accessed 20 April 2018, archive.homeaffairs.gov.au/about/corporate/information/fact-sheets/54sponsored.

this volume). Having a passport from one of the Pacific nations places people in a disadvantaged position when seeking to live and work in Australia and the almost closed path to permanent residency is one of the factors that produces overstayers. One of the limited options available to people is to apply for a protection visa, which is common for Fijians due to the political situation in their country, although the success rate is low. Another option is family reunification visas, including carer visas or partner visas. However, carer visas are capped each year and are difficult to obtain. For example, in Mildura, one Tongan couple with four children had been caring for aged parents (Australian citizens) for more than four years without themselves having legal immigration status. They had originally intended to stay in Australia for a holiday, but when the aged parents became unwell they felt they could not leave them. Although they were intending to apply for the carer visa, they could not afford the high application fees. As of October 2017, onshore applications for carer visas cost AU$1,625 and a child visa cost AU$2,415 per applicant.

Compared to carer visas, partner visas do not have any caps and are usually granted if a couple can show evidence of a genuine relationship. As one Tongan female overstayer observed, 'the luckiest people are those who are married to a [Australian] citizen'. It is not unusual for Australian-born Pacific women to find partners from among those without work permits; sometimes they fall in love but in other cases family members of overstayers ask second-generation women's family members to agree to the marriage. Since 2011, the application fee for partner visas has dramatically increased. Whereas in 2007 it cost AU$2,060, as of July 2017, the fee was AU$7,000,[29] which is extremely difficult for farm workers to save, leading many to remain without legal rights to live in Australia even if they are eligible for this visa. In addition, while the United States and New Zealand have avenues for Pacific people without specified skills to obtain permanent residency through their lotteries (the Pacific Access Category Resident Visa in New Zealand and the Diversity Visa Lottery in the United States), Australia does not have a similar system.

---

29 'Charges – July 2007', Department of Home Affairs, accessed 9 April 2018, www.homeaffairs. gov.au/FormsAndDocuments/Documents/990i/990i0707.pdf (site discontinued); 'Partner Visa (subclasses 820 and 801)', Department of Home Affairs, accessed 9 April 2018, www.homeaffairs. gov.au/trav/visa-1/801- (site discontinued).

The Seasonal Worker Programme and the Emergence of 'Absconders'

As MacDermott and Opeskin have observed: 'Over a sustained period, the Australian government resisted pressure to give preferential treatment to Pacific Islanders through a temporary work scheme.'[30] Potential problems with such a scheme were debated, most prominently that:

> A key concern with temporary labor programs is that workers will overstay their visas and fail to return home when seasonal work ends. Australian immigration officials warn that without 'very strong enforcement', the non-return of seasonal workers would incur significant expenses for government.[31]

However, the government was under pressure from both Australian farmers, who were desperately short of labour,[32] and the governments of Pacific countries, which were eager to see Australia increase labour opportunities for their people, even if these were only temporary. Eventually, the Pacific Seasonal Worker Pilot Scheme was trialled in 2008–12, then, in July 2012, the SWP commenced.

Although it serves Australia's need for 'unskilled' farm labourers, the SWP has been promoted as a form of development aid, enabling temporary migrants to send remittances to their families in the islands.[33] An analysis by Andrew Kipnis of the relationship between aid and immigration in the Australian context is relevant here:

> Why does the Australian government … supply aid to some of the same countries from which it severely limits immigration? … The lens of citizenship provides a harsh answer to this query. The provision of foreign aid outside Australia and the production of illegality within Australia can be seen as linked carrot-and-stick strategies to prevent immigration … From the perspective of a would-be immigrant, the objectives of 'foreign' 'aid' could be seen as intended to identify those 'foreigners' who should be prevented from immigrating and 'aid' them by offering just enough help to induce them not to immigrate.[34]

30 MacDermott and Opeskin, 'Regulating Pacific Seasonal Labour in Australia', 286.
31 Mares and Maclellan, 'Pacific Seasonal Workers for Australian Horticulture', 279.
32 Mares and Maclellan, 'Pacific Seasonal Workers for Australian Horticulture', 273.
33 Mares and Maclellan, 'Pacific Seasonal Workers for Australian Horticulture', 280.
34 Kipnis, 'Anthropology and the Theorisation of Citizenship', 266–67.

One can observe the coloniality of power in the relationships between Australia and Pacific countries in the SWP, which has parallels with the nineteenth-century 'blackbirding' of Pacific labourers.[35] The scheme provides no means for workers to permanently migrate to Australia and imposes tighter regulations on them than it does on the non-Pacific workers eligible for other temporary labour schemes. As with other visa categories, Australia has the power to limit eligibility, the number of people admitted from each country and to control how the scheme operates. In addition, Pacific countries are keen to increase the number of seasonal workers they can send, so they are careful to select 'ideal' workers. For example, the Fijian and Samoan governments include fitness tests in the process of recruitment. In its explanation of the implementation of the fitness test, the Samoan Government stated: 'if Samoa is to increase the number of people participating it is essential they send the best possible people who are physically and mentally fit'.[36] Similarly, Minister for Employment, Productivity and Industrial Relations Jone Usamate stated that the Fijian Government is recruiting more people from rural areas because 'people living in rural settings were loyal to their employers whilst in New Zealand or Australia'.[37] The SWP accepts men and women aged over 21 who fit the eligibility criteria, although, between 2012 and 2015, the majority of participants were males between 21 and 45 years old.[38]

With the SWP now in place, the Australian Government's concerns about the scheme leading to overstaying have intensified, with a notable shift in language from 'overstayers' to 'absconders'. Whereas New Zealand 'emphasizes the lack of overstaying' in regard to the 'success' of the Recognised Seasonal Employer (RSE) scheme,[39] the Australian Government is clearly worried that this is not the case for the SWP. The Labour Mobility Assistance Program (LMAP), established by the government to assist countries participating in the SWP, put out a call for research in 2016 and identified a study into Tongan 'absconding' as

---

35   Connell, 'From Blackbirds to Guestworkers'; Maclellan and Mares, 'Remittances and Labour Mobility in the Pacific'. See also, Stead, this volume.
36   'Fitness Test for Samoan RSE Workers Introduced', *Radio New Zealand*, 1 May 2017, www.radionz.co.nz/international/pacific-news/329797/fitness-test-for-samoan-rse-workers-introduced.
37   Arieta Vakasukawaqa, 'Nineteen Fijian Seasonal Workers Still on Run in Australia', *Fiji Sun*, 7 October 2017, fijisun.com.fj/2017/10/07/nineteen-fijian-seasonal-workers-still-on-run-in-aust/.
38   Joint Standing Committee on Migration, *Seasonal Change*.
39   Rockell, 'Pacific Island Labour Programmes in New Zealand', 246.

the first priority. This call for research also listed other areas of research priority, including 'issues contributing to SWP workers absconding while in Australia … and approaches to reducing the number of absconders'.[40]

The LMAP call for research noted that 'various unofficial reports on the drivers for absconding' have identified 'poor working conditions' as one factor.[41] These poor conditions, including the exploitation and ill-treatment of SWP employees, have now been well documented and have received considerable media and scholarly attention.[42] There is some recognition by the Australian Government of these problems, as indicated by the inclusion of testimony on the SWP within the inquiry into establishing a Modern Slavery Act in Australia, conducted in 2017 by the Joint Standing Committee of the Department for Foreign Affairs, Defence and Trade. Yet, the government's focus remains mainly on the illegal status of those who breach their contracts. SWP contracts tie workers to specific farms, so if they leave those farms and do not return immediately to their homeland, they not only breach the terms of their employment but also risk overstaying their visas. This shift in government discourse is telling, as the label 'absconders' indicates intentional illegality, denotes an abandonment of contracted responsibilities and assumes that the workers will become overstayers. This resonates with the broader shift in political discourse around border control and criminalisation of irregular migrants, as evident in the *Australian Border Force Act 2015* and raids on farms in recent years, including in Sunraysia, by Border Force officers.

Given the unequal relationship between Australia and Pacific countries mentioned earlier, incidents of absconding from the SWP give the Australian Government bargaining power with Pacific nations. For example, after confirming that 19 Fijians from the 2015 intake of the SWP were 'still on the run' in 2017, Usamate commented that:

40　Labour Mobility Assistance Program, Call for Expressions of Interest, Research Panel Providing Socio-Economic Research Design and Implementation related to the Seasonal Worker Programme, July 2016, 9 (in author's possession).

41　Labour Mobility Assistance Program, Call for Expressions of Interest, Research Panel Providing Socio-Economic Research Design and Implementation related to the Seasonal Worker Programme, July 2016, 10 (in author's possession).

42　Forsyth, *Victorian Inquiry*; Segrave, *Exploited and Illegal*; Nick Toscano, 'Fruit Pickers Paid Pittance, Forced to Work for Weeks', *The Age*, 25 August 2016, 23, www.smh.com.au/business/work place/fruit-pickers-paid-a-pittance-forced-to-work-five-weeks-straight-20160824-gqzrz3.html.

Employers from Australia and New Zealand have started to lose interest on recruiting Fijians because they ended up breaching their work contracts. 'The recruitment from Australia and New Zealand employers under the programme is now stagnant, it neither increased nor decreased'.[43]

Fears of losing access to the SWP leads island governments to blame the workers, rather than raising concerns about the conditions they face in Australia.[44]

Pacific Settlers' Views of 'Absconders'

Within Pacific populations in Australia there are ambivalent views towards SWP workers who leave the scheme and attempt to overstay. A study in Tonga by Lupe Moala-Tupou found that families feared workers would leave the scheme in Australia, abandon their children and stop sending money.[45] Rather than the Australian Government's term 'absconder', Tongans use the term *hola* (literally 'run away'). While Moala-Tupou's research found that those who *hola* were mainly considered negatively by Tongans in Tonga, our research found that settled Tongans in Mildura and Robinvale judge them according to context. For example, when a Tongan man left a group of seasonal workers as soon as they arrived at Sydney airport, this was seen negatively, and Tongan women who were exchanging this news talked about how 'stupid' he was, expressing concern about Tonga's reputation in the SWP. However, the exploitation of seasonal workers is well-known in settled communities and those who *hola* because of poor working conditions receive sympathy; their decisions to leave the program are considered valid. Fijian participants had similar views, and were also sympathetic to SWP workers who left their workplace due to poor conditions. The strong association between the SWP and exploitation is reinforced by the experiences of these workers who breach their contracts. A second-generation Tongan woman whose family had offered refuge to two 'absconders' described visa and immigration issues as among the largest problems for the Tongan community in Mildura.

43   Arieta Vakasukawaqa, 'Nineteen Fijian Seasonal Workers Still on Run in Australia', *Fiji Sun*, 7 October 2017, fijisun.com.fj/2017/10/07/nineteen-fijian-seasonal-workers-still-on-run-in-aust/.
44   Hermant, 'Seasonal Farm Workers'.
45   Moala-Tupou, 'The Social Impacts of Seasonal Migration'.

She explained: 'There is a lot of overstayers here, [it] is because [of these] stupid programs that contractors bringing people from Tonga … they [contractors] cheat them, then they [workers] take off.'

Overstayers can be paid directly by farmers and have more freedom of movement; consequently, most of our research participants argued that overstaying is preferable to participating in the SWP. Indeed, those who were overstayers expressed sympathy towards SWP workers, whom they regarded as poorly paid, tied to one workplace and often exploited by the contractors. An interview with a Tongan 'absconder' revealed strong pressure from his family in Tonga, which made it impossible to return empty handed. As he was only paid AU$150 a week in the SWP, he decided to leave the program and overstay in Australia so he could remit more money. He acknowledged that being an overstayer presents serious problems and was keen to find a way to change his immigration status to stay legally in Australia. However, as with other overstayers, 'absconders' are able to continue to find work as many farmers are more concerned with getting their crops harvested and other farm work done than with identifying which workers are legal. Indeed, a service provider in Mildura reported that farmers do not like to have immigration raids before the harvest season because there will be a significant lack of available labour if overstayers are caught and detained.

The Predicaments of Everyday Life and the Agency of Pacific People

Pacific people continue to stay and work illegally in regional communities in Australia, using their agency to seek a better life both for themselves and for their families at home by becoming breadwinners. Some of them work within the period of their visitor visas and go home with their savings, but others overstay their visas and send remittances over a long period. As with the majority of other Pacific people in the region, overstayers in Sunraysia typically do seasonal work on farms. Although the stereotype of Pacific horticultural workers is that they are uneducated and unskilled, people's previous occupations are actually diverse. Many were professionals or office workers in their home country, and some had no experience of working on a farm before moving to the area. It is difficult for Pacific people with permanent residence or Australian citizenship to find employment other than farm work due to their stigmatisation as 'fruit pickers'. Those who are overstayers have even less choice in their occupation, as they are unable to use their prior skills and qualifications; therefore, they remain in farm work where their visa status is rarely questioned.

Susan, a 57-year-old Fijian woman, had been overstaying in Robinvale for three years at the time of her interview. She was a civil servant in Fiji but, when she retired at age 55, she decided to come to Australia to work.[46] Her husband was in the army before his retirement, her son is a school teacher and her daughter is a research officer in a government department in Fiji. Although she and her family members are well educated, she perceived her life in Fiji as hard, especially because she still had to pay her mortgage despite being retired. Working in Australia, she explained, she now earned AU$600–700 a week and sent AU$400 of that to family in Fiji towards the mortgage. She referred to paying the mortgage as her 'project', saying that once she achieved her goal she intended to go home. Susan explained what it was like working on a farm on her first day:

> When I first started working, like I find it very hard … First day … it was very hot because that day it was 42 degrees. Then we were running out of water when we worked there and the place where we work was very far from our cabin. We couldn't walk back to get water … I just make a few boxes then I sit. I couldn't work anymore because I find it very hard because sitting in the office and come and work in the farm is very different. Yeah, two different things, but then I tried to cope. Next day I take a lot of water and I tried to work more harder. Now I find that it's getting easier.

Moving from being a clerical officer in Fiji to a farm worker in Australia increased her income:

> Here it's better. For me I earned $140 net a week [back home], but then I had to pay for my house $100 a week so I'm just left with $40. I know that life is very hard back at home … Not enough money because cost of living is very high and as I said, what we earn is very less. Even if you just get your money, pay for the bills, buy for the food, buy the petrol for the car so, it's not enough.

---

46   Most of the Fijian research participants aged in their 50s and 60s refer to the change in retirement age in 2006 from 60 to 55 as their reason for migration.

Figure 7.2: An aerial shot of the region, showing the 'blocks' where Pacific Islander migrants work.

Source: Photograph by Helen Lee.

While Susan has a clear goal of paying her mortgage, other people come to Australia to support their family at home. Una, a 72-year-old Fijian woman who entered Australia with a visitor visa in 2000, came here to work because her husband was negligent in supporting her family. She explained:

> I was thinking … who's going to care for my kids, who's going to feed us? Because the way he's drinking too much and sometimes come home and you know, husband like that, so I was planning to come … I'm the breadwinner of my family, yeah. My own family, my two daughters and my son, and my brother's son, whatever they need I will always support them … My grandchildren, they're going to school … so I help them for their school fees and whatever they need. I am the only one in the family [that has an income source].

She proudly reported that she had paid for the renovation of the house in Fiji. Una said her daughter 'always calls me [to say] "mum, this part of the house is finished", and I did that'. She continued:

173

Now they said they wanted to repainting the house and I said 'oh, just, because I'll send the money for your food and just take me slowly' … I did it myself. Even my brother they need the help and who helps? It's only me. The Fijian ways of living is like that but I can't leave them, I have to be there for them. Without me; so hard. One of my eldest daughter's daughter she went to New Zealand for two weeks for education or something and they need fare to go.

Overstayers such as Susan and Una become breadwinners but they face financial instability due to the seasonal nature of their work. Such work does not provide security to anyone, and even Australian citizenship holders also struggle financially.[47] However, those with citizenship and permanent residency can get Medicare and are eligible to apply for welfare payments (with certain restrictions for New Zealand citizens). Overstayers cannot get any benefits, and thus many experience more severe financial insecurity, especially during winter when there are fewer jobs. A Fijian man with a wife and three children, all of whom are overstayers, explained his annual income:

Three months [in summer], I can earn a thousand dollars [a week]. That's only go for three months. After that we slow down … We do a bit by bit. $400 a week, $500 a week.

Mele is a Tongan woman in her 40s who was an overstayer for 12 years until she received her permanent residency in 2008. When asked what kind of difficulties she experienced while overstaying Mele said:

The money. Because we had to pay for every single thing that we get. Not like these days, that the government can help us when we have the paper [permanent residency] … Before, we got nothing from no-one. We only depend on what we are doing in the block [i.e. on the farm]. When it's rain, there's no money … I was looking forward to go back to school and get something more easier [once her visa was sorted]. Not only easier, but something that you can get the bread and the milk on the table from January to December, because here, it's seasonal work. There is nothing in this country that is seasonal except the work. You can't say to the government, 'Okay, now the grape is finished, I can't pay my house'. No, you still have to pay it. Not only that, but you can't

47   Nishitani and Lee, 'Invisible Islanders'.

tell your kids, 'Okay we're going to fast this week because there's no job'. No. You have to get something that you can work all the way through to feed your family.

Interviewees who were overstayers described the many difficulties of everyday life. For example, Besi, a Tongan woman who was a former teacher, was overstaying as was her husband and their children:

> We don't have Medicare for our medical stuff. We have to pay the full fee of like visiting the doctors. This one [her child] was born here, we have to pay for my blood tests. It's free for the citizen, but us we have to pay 600 plus for one blood test. I find it very difficult because we pay a lot. All the medical things, especially the medical stuff, but the other stuff, it's okay and the school fees too. There's a fee paid by the government for the citizens, but us we have to pay the whole fee. Education fee, trip fees and other fees from curriculum fees.

While some of the irregular migrants live with family members who have citizenship or permanent residency, others live in a farmhouse or a cabin on a farm. Such accommodation typically costs them around $40 a week and their living conditions are usually very poor. A Fijian woman on a visitor visa claimed: 'if the Ministry of Health goes to the farmers and checked the farm, I think all the farmhouses are closed. It's no hygiene; there is no hygiene'. Another Fijian woman who lives on a farm complained that she has been worried for three years the roof of the house in which she lives is going to collapse. She and the other Fijians with whom she shares the home have repeatedly asked the owner to fix it without success.

Despite their difficult living conditions, research participants often tried to be positive about their circumstances. When asked for a more detailed description of her poor living conditions, a Fijian female overstayer in her 30s replied instead:

> Yeah, maybe, but I'm just, sometimes I'm going to look at it my way, that we don't have working visa, [we are] living here illegally, and the farmers have really, really helped us. Providing us with accommodations. Like if we don't work, if there's no work in the farm, we stay there and don't pay nothing. They don't charge us for rent when there's no work, so we get free rent, free electricity, everything, free gas provided by the farmers.

Some people also described positive aspects of their work, particularly the camaraderie with fellow Pacific workers. However, overstayers are inevitably in an unequal relationship with their employers, even more than other employees. A Fijian female tourist visa holder, who planned to stay in Australia for only three months while working illegally, observed of overstayers:

> The problem is you cannot complain, because you don't have the paper. You're not a resident. I think that's why farmers are still not happy with people with papers [because] they can complain. They can report the matters. Because the farmers, whatever they say that's it. You have to follow. Otherwise, go find other place. You don't wanna lose job, you want to work. See? Even though the box is $2, you cannot say anything, just work.[48] Otherwise, you ask for a raise [and] you're fired.

In addition to financial exploitation, the treatment of overstayers can be far more dangerous and problematic:

> Sometimes we never have our lunch, even when it's very hot they keep pushing us to do this, do that ... You know when you stay there they [contractor] know that we are illegal in here, that's why ... Sometimes when it's hot, when it's sometimes 40, 35, 39 degrees and it's hot, and you want to go home and they say just keep going on picking ... Don't let us go home ... We are keeping doing the work because we picking, it's very hard to do that in the hot. (Fijian overstayer, female aged in her 60s)

Although they are aware of their illegal status and are prepared to endure exploitative relationships and harsh conditions, Pacific people also know they are contributing to the economy:

> We helping the farmer. Because Australians, they don't want to work. They're very grateful with us Fijians and even Asians ... They want to get the work done. They don't want to get lost of a million things, what they've been planting and growing ... We help them, the farmers ... When you're good to people, your manager or the working place, they see you're a good worker. (Fijian overstayer, female aged in her late 50s)

---

48   The piece rate for picking table grapes ranges from AU$2 to AU$3.50 per box, weighing around 8–10 kg, with rates depending on the quality and kind of grapes and their destination (e.g. exported overseas or sold by domestic supermarkets).

Pacific overstayers also contribute to their local communities, particularly through the churches. Some of them take leadership roles at church or contribute to choir groups. Others contribute to local sports teams as players, or participate in multicultural festivals as performers. As Gonzales and Sigona observe:

> On a daily basis, one's immigration status may be less or more salient to most of their activities. They may be regular in one sense and irregular in another; they may be fully excluded from the legal-political system but able to carry out a range of social interactions and activities. Migrants who have little or no formal rights interact every day with a multitude of state agencies, community institutions, and individuals. These conditions make it possible for both citizens and migrants to sometime operate 'as if the boundaries did not exist'.[49]

The Shifting Status of Overstayers

For overstayers, national boundaries are hard to forget, as is the fear of possible deportation and the probability that their lives will suddenly and irrevocably change if they are caught. A Fijian female overstayer in her 60s explained:

> When I see the police now [I'm] scared because I knew I'm illegal. When the others say that the immigration is in town, nobody will come to town, we just stay in the bush, and just let the people in town buy the food and bring it back to us.

Susan, the ex–civil servant from Fiji, had just received a bridging visa, having applied for a protection visa a week before her interview. She explained why she applied:

> Because as we stay like this it's sometimes the immigration come, they [are] trying to get all illegal stayers in the country and every time people have to run away to the bush and hide. That's why I've decided to do something at least to protect me while I'm staying here … I was just thinking that we can't be running away all the time like that.

---

49   Gonzales and Sigona, 'Mapping the Soft Borders of Citizenship', 6.

Before she applied for the visa she was worried:

> Because you're not sure, anything can happen at any time …
> Interaction is not easy at first … People might ask you why you
> come to Australia or what visa you are on … so I didn't [socialise]
> … If you get into an accident then you go to the hospital, then the
> hospital ask for Medicare and [you get] medical bills … Every day
> you just live in uncertainty. You just think if something happen
> how you going to handle it? … Sometimes you don't walk freely,
> you scared to talk to other people and sometimes at night don't
> really have a comfortable sleep. You're worried and you thinking
> a lot. Night and day you think a lot … Always stay frightened all
> the time and, like, when we hear rumours that they [immigration
> officers] are around, we don't feel like going anywhere. Just stay
> lock in your room. It's not safe. Maybe we are like prisoners in
> our room.

However, this has changed since she submitted her application. She said:
'I feel better now. I'm not really worried like before.' Acquiring a bridging
visa is merely a temporary remedy because there is no guarantee that
Susan will get the protection visa she applied for, and even then it could
be temporary or permanent. Immigration decision-making often seems
arbitrary to applicants, and while some successfully get a visa and remain
in Australia lawfully, others are rejected. Some of these may try to stay as
long as possible by going through an Administrative Appeals Tribunal;
among those whose appeals are rejected, some may be apprehended by
immigration officers and deported but others will try to stay in Australia.

For overstayers, the pathways to permanent residence are confusing and
require English skills, knowledge of the complex immigration system
and understanding of categories such as 'refugee'. Una, the 72-year-old
woman discussed previously, extended her visitor visa for six months on
the advice of her relatives in Australia and then applied for a refugee visa.
Her application was rejected and she explained: 'Well they said I am not
a refugee then, because I was applying for that and they said no.' When
asked why she had applied for a refugee visa, she replied:

> Because I just … [I was] with my friend who fill the form, my
> friend too we do the same thing. We thought that it might accept
> us but after all they said 'no Fiji is … not a refugee country'.

While some irregular migrants rely on the advice of friends and relatives, others become victims of scams by unregistered 'immigration agents' who take their money, or pay expensive lawyers without achieving a successful outcome.

The term 'overstayers' masks the fact that many people do make contact with immigration officials and try to correct their immigration status. Many irregular migrants make concerted efforts over a long period to be legal, despite the confusing processes and repeated rejections of their applications. Over time, some people successfully acquire permanent residency, but others shift between the categories of illegal and legal, often without fully understanding the reasons for their current status. This is illustrated in the experience of a Fijian woman in her 30s who came to Australia in 2009. Before her visitor visa expired, she applied for a protection visa and immediately was offered a bridging visa with work rights; she received a tax file number within two weeks. Although this bureaucratic process made her status legal, her application was rejected and subsequently rejected again when it went through the Migration Review Tribunal in October 2010, making her 'illegal'. In 2013, immigration officers visited Robinvale to encourage people to reapply for their visas. Together with other irregular migrants, she went to see them and received another bridging visa. She reported: 'We were made legal.' However, the immigration officer told her the only option she had left was to apply for a ministerial intervention. She wrote a letter and then undertook interviews that involved several trips to Melbourne but eventually was rejected again, returning her status to illegal.

Gonzales and Sigona write: 'illegality is a legally and routinely produced status [and] there is a need for a critical examination of the social and political conditions under which people are constructed as "illegal"'.[50] The situation for overstayers in Australia is thus similar to 'unauthorized immigrants' in the United States, who:

> are viewed as criminals who break the law, precisely because the law does not provide sufficient mechanisms for those who need and want to live and work in the United States to do so legally.[51]

---

50 Gonzales and Sigona, 'Mapping the Soft Borders of Citizenship', 6–7.
51 Dreby, *Everyday Illegal*, xii.

Limited and expensive visa options and confusing processes for seeking legal residence, combined with factors such as economic pressures in the home country and familial obligations, create a situation in which people become overstayers while still desperately attempting to find ways to regularise their status. In this sense, Australia can be seen as 'producing' illegal workers.

Discussion

Despite the long processes of decolonisation-led independence of previously colonised countries, including many Pacific Islands,[52] 'durable', 'stable' and long-lasting elements of colonialism remain, and the 'coloniality of power' still shapes global inequality and affects people's everyday lives.[53] Viewed through the lens of the coloniality of citizenship, the term 'overstayers' appears far from neutral; instead, it masks the unequal opportunities allocated among people within that category. The meaning of 'overstaying' for working holiday makers from wealthy nations like Britain or Japan needs to be understood differently than for Pacific Islanders overstaying entry on a visitor visa or through the SWP. Pacific people's decision to overstay is a demonstration of their agency as they attempt to make their families lives better in the context of ongoing inequalities between their homelands and Australia. Their 'illegal' status is 'produced' because the logic of Australia's immigration regime generally excludes them from permanent migration, only allocating limited 'opportunities' to temporarily provide their labour as seasonal workers. Yet, for some Pacific people, the temporary work offered through the SWP holds a greater risk of exploitation than becoming overstayers, and provides less freedom of movement. They choose to be 'illegal' in the hope of converting that status over time.

Overstaying can entail a range of problems including poor living conditions, precarious employment and fear of deportation, yet almost all research participants who had overstayed their visas claimed to have made a good decision to remain in Australia. For them, the ability to work and support their family in the islands is of paramount importance. They can earn far more money working on a farm in Australia than by remaining

---

52   Banivanua Mar, *Decolonisation and the Pacific*.
53   Quijano, 'Coloniality of Power', 533.

in their Pacific homeland and they are prepared to endure risks, as well as physically challenging labour and often poor working conditions, to do so.

Longer-term options for labour mobility are now being considered for some Pacific nations, but it is unlikely Australia will move away from highly regulated and restrictive schemes that centre on labour migration as a form of development aid. The Pacific Labour Scheme introduced in July 2018, initially for people from Kiribati, Nauru, Samoa, Solomon Islands, Tuvalu and Vanuatu, involves 'low and semi-skilled work opportunities in rural and regional Australia for up to three years'.[54] The new scheme will not permit workers to bring their families, causing even longer family disruptions than the SWP. Given the government's focus on the problem of 'absconders' from the SWP, it will not be surprising if this scheme has even tighter regulations and controls over the freedoms of the workers involved.

Pacific people continue to be perceived as potential overstayers or 'absconders' from the regulated system who need to be controlled and policed, despite the historically small numbers of Pacific overstayers relative to the overall number of overseas visitors and other temporary immigrants who have remained in Australia beyond their visa's expiry date. The governments of Pacific countries appear to be more concerned with ensuring ongoing access to labour migration opportunities than with the conditions in which their people are working in Australia. In a sense, they are contributing to the ongoing coloniality of power by surrendering to Australia's governance of Pacific people's labour.

Yet, some Pacific people continue to resist that coloniality by seeking ways to live and work in Australia despite immigration restrictions. People's lived experiences of moving between legal and illegal statuses demonstrate how (il)legality is a product of the bureaucratic system, not a static definition. Nevertheless, the implications of being labelled 'illegal'—or, in the case of the SWP, as 'absconders'—are significant. The labels stigmatise and dehumanise overstayers, for whom daily life is marked by insecurity both in the seasonal work undertaken and in the constant threat of being caught and deported. As a result, people remain vulnerable to exploitative employers and labour contractors, and to immigration scams and expensive

---

54   'Australia's Pacific Engagement', Department of Foreign Affairs and Trade, accessed 27 April 2018, dfat.gov.au/geo/pacific/engagement/Pages/stepping-up-australias-pacific-engagement.aspx.

lawyers. Our research participants have varied reasons for overstaying that typically centre on family responsibilities, including a desire to care for elderly parents, obligations to support their families in the islands, or women's need to support themselves and their children. They, like other Pacific people in rural Australia, have amply demonstrated their resilient agency both through their engagement in arduous horticultural work and in their tenacious attempts to regularise their immigration status.

Bibliography

Banivanua Mar, Tracey. *Decolonisation and the Pacific: Indigenous Globalisation and the Ends of Empire*. Cambridge: Cambridge University Press, 2016.

Boatcă, Manuela and Julia Roth. 'Unequal and Gendered: Notes on the Coloniality of Citizenship'. *Current Sociology Monograph* 64, no. 2 (2016): 191–212. doi.org/10.1177/0011392115614781.

Connell, John. 'From Blackbirds to Guestworkers in the South Pacific. *Plus Ça Change…?'*. *The Economic and Labour Relations Review* 20, no. 2 (2010): 111–22. doi.org/10.1177/103530461002000208.

De Genova, Nicholas. 'Migrant "Illegality" and Deportability in Everyday Life'. *Annual Review of Anthropology* 31 (2002): 319–37. doi.org/10.1146/annurev.anthro.31.040402.085432.

Dreby, Joanna. *Everyday Illegal: When Policies Undermine Immigrant Families*. Oakland: University of California Press, 2015.

Forsyth, Anthony. *Victorian Inquiry into the Labour Hire Industry and Insecure Work Final Report*. Melbourne: Department of Economic Development, Jobs, Transport & Resources, 2016.

Gonzales, Roberto and Nando Sigona. 'Mapping the Soft Borders of Citizenship: An Introduction'. In *Within and Beyond Citizenship: Borders, Membership and Belonging*, edited by Roberto Gonzales and Nando Sigona, 1–16. Abingdon: Routledge, 2017. doi.org/10.4324/9781315268910.

Hamer, Paul. '"Unsophisticated and Unsuited": Australian Barriers to Pacific Islander Immigration from New Zealand'. *Political Science* 66, no. 2 (2014): 93–118. doi.org/10.1177/0032318714554495.

Hau'ofa, Epeli. 'Our Sea of Islands'. *The Contemporary Pacific* 6, no. 1 (2004): 147–61.

Hermant, Norman. 'Seasonal Farm Workers Receiving Less than $10 a Week after Deductions, Investigation Reveals'. *ABC News*, 26 February 2016, www. abc.net.au/news/2016-02-25/seasonal-farm-workers-receiving-as-little-as-$9-a-week/7196844.

Joint Standing Committee on Migration. *Seasonal Change: Inquiry into the Seasonal Worker Programme*. Canberra: The Parliament of the Commonwealth of Australia, 2016.

Ka'ili, Tēvita. *Marking Indigeneity: The Tongan Art of Sociospatial Relations*. Arizona: The University of Arizona Press, 2017. doi.org/10.2307/j.ctt1t89kr9.

Kipnis, Andrew. 'Anthropology and the Theorisation of Citizenship'. *The Asia Pacific Journal of Anthropology* 5, no. 3 (2004): 257–78. doi.org/10.1080/1444221042000299592.

Korzeniwicz, Roberto Patricio and Timothy Patrick Moran. *Unveiling Inequality: A World-Historical Perspective*. New York: Russell Sage Foundation, 2009.

Maclellan, Nic and Peter Mares. 'Remittances and Labour Mobility in the Pacific: A Working Paper on Seasonal Work Programs in Australia for Pacific Islanders'. Melbourne: Institute for Social Research, Swinburne University of Technology, 2006.

MacDermott, Therese and Brian Opeskin. 'Regulating Pacific Seasonal Labour in Australia'. *Pacific Affairs* 83, no. 2 (2010): 283–305. doi.org/10.5509/2010832283.

Mares, Peter and Nic Maclellan. 'Pacific Seasonal Workers for Australian Horticulture: A Neat Fit?'. *Asian and Pacific Migration Journal* 16, no. 2 (2007): 271–88. doi.org/10.1177/011719680701600207.

Mence, Victoria, Simone Gangell and Ryan Tebb. *A History of the Department of Immigration: Managing Migration to Australia*. Belconnen: Department of Immigration and Border Protection, 2017.

Missingham, Bruce, Jacqui Dibden and Chris Cocklin. 'A Multicultural Countryside? Ethnic Minorities in Rural Australia'. *Rural Society* 16, no. 2 (2006): 131–50. doi.org/10.5172/rsj.351.16.2.131.

Moala-Tupou, Lupe. 'The Social Impacts of Seasonal Migration on Left behind Children: An Exploratory Study from Lifuka, Tonga'. MA thesis, University of Waikato, 2016.

Nishitani, Makiko and Helen Lee. 'Invisible Islanders? Precarious Work and Pacific Settlers in Rural Australia'. *Pacific Studies* 40, no. 3 (2017): 430–49.

Quijano, Anibal. 'Coloniality of Power, Ethnocentrism, and Latin America'. *Nepantla* 1, no. 3 (2000): 533–80.

Rockell, Dennis. 'Pacific Island Labour Programmes in New Zealand: An Aid to Pacific Island Development? A Critical Lens on the Recognised Seasonal Employer Policy'. PhD thesis, Massey University, 2015.

Segrave, Marie. *Exploited and Illegal: Unlawful Migrant Workers in Australia.* Melbourne: The Border Crossing Observatory and the School of Social Sciences, Monash University, 2017.

Shachar, Ayelet. 'The Birthright Lottery: Response to Interlocutors'. *Issues in Legal Scholarships* 9, no. 1, Article 13 (2011): 1–25. doi.org/10.2202/1539-8323.1133.

Tazreiter, Claudia. *Asylum Seekers and the State: Approaches to Protection in a Security-Conscious World.* London: Ashgate, 2004.

Vas Dev, Sanjugta. 'Accounting for State Approaches to Asylum Seekers in Australia and Malaysia: The Significance of "National" Identity and "Exclusive" Citizenship in the Struggle against "Irregular" Mobility'. *Identities: Global Studies in Culture and Power* 16, no. 1 (2009): 33–60. doi.org/10.1080/10702890802605679.

Newspapers

The Age
The Christian Science Monitor
Fiji Sun
The Sydney Morning Herald

8

Wellbeing Perspectives, Conceptualisations of Work and Labour Mobility Experiences of Pasifika Trans-Tasman Migrants in Brisbane

Ruth (Lute) Faleolo

> *Moʻui ʻoku lelei* … the way I see it, as I compare it to [New Zealand] our quality of life as a family is affected by our income. Our income here is good with only my husband working … You know what makes a 'good and happy life'? It is when a person makes a decision to take a chance. When I go and look for my life goals and I achieve it; this is what makes my life good because I made the move to go and look for it. (Interview/*Talanoa* with Safaia, 16 July 2015)

Pasifika trans-Tasman migrations include processes of labour mobility that reflect Pasifika agency in the pursuit of wellbeing. This chapter draws on the preliminary findings of wider ongoing research that has examined the wellbeing of Pasifika trans-Tasman migrants moving from New Zealand to Australia. The narratives of Samoan and Tongan trans-Tasman migrants reveal a holistic, Pasifika notion of wellbeing that influences migrants' decision-making in relation to migration and employment. This notion, articulated in Samoan as *ola manuia* and in Tongan as *moʻui ʻoku lelei*—literally, 'a good and happy life'[1]—in turn influences the labour

---

1 Faleolo, 'Pasifika Trans-Tasman Migrant Perspectives'.

mobility experiences of Pasifika trans-Tasman migrants, including their negotiations of immigration and social security policies, and sometimes restrictive regulatory regimes.

The term 'Pasifika' denotes a pan-Pacific Islander collective identity.[2] It is used by many Pacific Islanders themselves, including the Samoan and Tongan trans-Tasman migrant groups whose experiences are the focus of this chapter. An increasing number of Pasifika migrants, particularly New Zealand–born Pasifika, are moving from New Zealand to settle long-term in Australia.[3] While much existing research has emphasised the political-economic factors underlying this migration, including higher wages and accessible standards of living in Australia,[4] little research has been conducted into the thoughts and experiences of trans-Tasman Pasifika migrants themselves. We can gain insight into trans-Tasman Pasifika labour mobility, and better understand the motivations and experiences of these migrants,[5] by hearing their migration narratives and accurately capturing their voices as Pasifika migrants.[6] The wellbeing perspectives of Pasifika trans-Tasman migrants influence their decisions on where and how they will participate in the labour market, whether in New Zealand or Australia. The narratives documented in this discussion reveal the advantages and disadvantages experienced in Auckland[7] and Brisbane[8] that have encouraged the relocation of Pasifika to Australia since the 1990s. More importantly, this discussion delves into the most recent (often unrecorded) experiences of labour mobility in Australia, highlighting Pasifika narratives and voices to contribute to an indigenous account of Pasifika labour mobility.

In exploring this intersection of regulatory regimes and Pasifika conceptualisations of wellbeing, this chapter draws on 40 interviews carried out in 2015–17 with Samoan and Tongan communities in both Brisbane and Auckland. The research is informed by my own positions

2   McGavin, 'Being Nesian'; Mila-Schaaf, 'Polycultural Capital'.
3   Both Bedford and Ravulo detail the growing trend of New Zealanders, particularly New Zealand–born Pasifika, moving to Australia. Bedford, '*Pasifika* Migration'; Ravulo, *Pacific Communities in Australia*.
4   For example, Brown and Walker, *Migrants and their Remittances*; Hamer, '"Unsophisticated and Unsuited"'; Ho, Hugo and Bedford, 'Trans-Tasman Migration in Context'.
5   Hamer acknowledges that there is an evident silence in the diaspora literature of *Pasifika* migrant voices about their migration from New Zealand to Australia. Hamer, '"Unsophisticated and Unsuited"'.
6   Smith, *Decolonizing Methodologies*.
7   Salesa, 'Damon Salesa: Our Pacific'.
8   Ravulo, *Pacific Communities*.

as a Tongan researcher who is married to a Samoan. Importantly, my inquiry and participant-observation work have embraced both a Samoan and Tongan framework of cultural knowledge and protocols, *tauhi vā*[9] and *teu le vā*,[10] both of which are important in nurturing and maintaining mutually respectful relationships and spaces, or *vā*, within Pasifika contexts.[11] In upholding *vā* in my research practice, I have used a culturally responsive interviewing methodology based on the Tongan concept of *talanoa*[12]—that is, a reciprocal 'two-way' interviewing process. *Talanoa* is a 'conversation, a talk, an exchange of ideas or thinking, whether formal or informal … and interacting without a rigid framework'.[13] It is promoted by Pasifika scholars as a way of opening up dialogue about traditional values and in-depth understanding that is within the hearts and minds of Pasifika.[14] Standfield and Stevens, in this volume, promote the importance of indigenous methodology based on conversational narratives that illuminate the connected migration histories between New Zealand and Australia. The traditional method of face-to-face *talanoa* was supplemented in this research by a novel use of online forums for *talanoa*, which I term e-*talanoa*. The development of this method was 'in direct response to the request of Pasifika informants'[15] to communicate via online forums. As a method, e-*talanoa* is more suited to contemporary ways of communicating (i.e. by email or Facebook private messenger); it gave informants more time to contemplate their responses to questions and was also responsive to the pressures of time experienced by many of these Pasifika migrants. The discussion that follows focuses predominantly on the experiences of Pasifika migrants in Brisbane, but also draws on relevant material from Auckland-based interviews, as the relationship between the two sites casts particular light on trans-Tasman labour mobility.

---

9   Ka'ili, *Marking Indigeneity*, 31–33; Mahina, 'Tā, Vā, and Moana', 169.

10   Anae, 'Teu Le Va', 222.

11   Developing good relations with Pasifika rests on *vā*, a reciprocal relationship that upholds the moral, ethical, spiritual dimensions of social relationships as Pasifika. Anae, 'Teu Le Va', 222–23. The term *vā* is used by both Samoan and Tongan groups.

12   *Talanoa* has been widely accepted as a qualitative approach within several Pasifika Melanesian and Polynesian academic circles. Fa'avae, Jones and Manu'atu, 'Talanoa'i 'a e Talanoa'; Halapua, 'Talanoa-Talking from the Heart'; Latu, *Talanoa: A Contribution*; Otsuka, Talanoa Research; Prescott, 'Using Talanoa'; Vaioleti, 'Talanoa Research Methodology'; Vaka'uta, 'Tālanga: Theorizing a Tongan Mode'.

13   Vaioleti, 'Talanoa Research Methodology', 16.

14   Havea, *Talanoa Ripples*; Latu, *Talanoa: A Contribution*.

15   Faleolo, 'Pasifika Trans-Tasman Migrant Perspectives'.

In focusing on the lived experiences, wellbeing perspectives and motivations of Pasifika labour migrants, this account also contributes to important 'indigenous narratives of decolonisation'[16] by detailing Pasifika migrants' own narratives of the limitations and regulations that they have experienced living in Australia, particularly since the 1990s, as well as their own agency and meaning-making in the context of their transnational lives.

Holistic Wellbeing—Mo'ui 'Oku Lelei— Ola Manuia

In narrating their migration experiences, Pasifika trans-Tasman migrants articulated understandings of 'wellbeing' that went beyond tangible outcomes or improvements in the life of an individual.[17] The Tongan concept *mo'ui 'oku lelei* and Samoan concept *ola manuia* ('a good and happy life') embrace many dimensions of life that are integral to how Pasifika people live on a daily basis. Pasifika trans-Tasman migrants defined wellbeing beyond just a state of physical or emotional health, including important familial and spiritual dimensions. Other Pasifika studies have found a similar holistic notion of wellbeing.[18]

Sione,[19] a 38-year-old, second-generation Pasifika migrant of Tongan descent,[20] was based in Perth at the time of our initial e-*talanoa*. By the time of a follow-up, face-to-face *talanoa* a year later, Sione had successfully migrated to Brisbane after purchasing a family home in Ipswich. Although Sione continued to fly out to the mines for work, he had plans to leave this form of employment in exchange for a family business that would build on his existing community networks across Tonga, Auckland, Sydney, Perth and Brisbane. He explained his understanding of *mo'ui 'oku lelei*:

---

16   Banivanua Mar, *Decolonisation and the Pacific*, 179; See also Sailiata, 'The Samoan Cause'.

17   Faleolo, 'Pasifika Trans-Tasman Migrant Perspectives'; Faleolo, 'Understanding Pasifika Migrant Behaviour'.

18   Manuela and Sibley, 'The Pacific Identity'; Meo-Sewabu and Walsh-Tapiata, 'Global Declaration'.

19   Pseudonyms are used for all interviewees/informants mentioned in this discussion.

20   First-generation Pasifika migrants were either born in Samoa or Tonga prior to migrating. Second-generation Pasifika migrants were born to first-generation Pasifika migrants in either Australia or New Zealand, and third-generation Pasifika migrants were born to second-generation Pasifika migrant parents in either New Zealand or Australia.

> Being physically and mentally healthy … being able to have quality time and being content with [a] lifestyle that is healthy … happy with family life. Spending time with my family. Staying true to God and my family. Being able to spend my time doing what really matters to me. To be around to meet my grandchildren and to be able to retire from working full-time before I turn 50.

'Ina, a 35-year-old Samoan, second-generation migrant, had moved to Brisbane from Auckland in 2015 after receiving spiritual confirmation that it was the right time for her to leave the sales industry and take up a new career in social work. She shared her understanding of *ola manuia*:

> Having the simple necessities in life to at least be comfortable. Healthy family relationships, being well connected to family. Being physically healthy, able to still do physical activity to feel good and eating well. Being spiritually healthy too, having that intimate relationship with God. Mentally stable too, which I guess ties in with the other three. If one area is lacking, it can affect the others.

These two narratives reveal the holistic notions of wellbeing valued by all the Pasifika migrants interviewed in the study. Particularly significant are the familial and spiritual spheres. For instance, the underlying motivation for Sione's decision to move to Brisbane was for his children to grow up in close proximity to his sister's family who was already living in Brisbane at the time. 'Ina's decision to move to Brisbane from Auckland was inspired by her faith in God and a belief that she was 'called' by God to change her location and career. She believed that this trans-Tasman migration would help to strengthen her relationship with God as well as her relationships with others, especially family. References to spiritual and familial influences recurred throughout the 40 migration narratives captured in the study.

Importance of Familial Wellbeing in Pasifika Decision-Making

Both Gershon and Lilomaiava-Doktor highlight the importance of Pasifika familial connections in the process of migration.[21] When making decisions to live and work in Brisbane, Pasifika prioritise their familial sphere of wellbeing—*fāmili* (Tongan) and *'āiga* (Samoan).

---

21 Gershon, 'Viewing Diasporas from the Pacific'; Lilomaiava-Doktor, 'Beyond "Migration"'.

The progress of *fāmili* and *'āiga* are important considerations that sit at the core of Pasifika trans-Tasman migrants' decisions to transfer between employment opportunities in Auckland to Brisbane. These anticipated mobility 'benefits' exceed the temporal, emotional, financial or cultural 'costs' of leaving family members and familiar ways of life that are in New Zealand.[22] Within Pasifika conceptualisations of wellbeing, aims such as 'getting better pay' or securing 'better job opportunities', although seemingly individualistic wellbeing aims for migration, are conceived primarily as means of providing for and maintaining 'familial' connections or *vā* (good, positive and strong relationships within Pasifika families). Within Pasifika conceptualisations and lives, familial connections and obligations extend far beyond nuclear families; for many, they also extend across expansive transnational spaces.

'Alisi, a 48-year-old Tongan woman and first-generation trans-Tasman migrant to Brisbane, had just started up a family-run courier franchise at the time of her *talanoa*. She was also studying part-time towards a business diploma. 'Alisi shared her desire to maintain *fāmili* wellbeing in Brisbane:

> We moved here because I wanted to be closer to my parents who live in Inala [a Brisbane suburb], and the lifestyle here is better for my children … plus, when I go to send money to my [extended] family back in Tonga, the exchange rate is better here than in New Zealand.

Sharing her hopes for an improved *mo'ui 'oku lelei* for herself and her family, 'Alisi continued:

> My goal is to carry on with my education here in Brisbane. I believe that a better education will help me to reach my goals for a good life here with my family … I've been in the factory all my life, and I have to struggle with it … when I reach a higher education, I will achieve higher goals, because the higher I go, the better it will be for my family and a happy life for us, *mo'ui 'oku lelei* … yeah, I've been working in the factory all my life, but when I get to a level 3 certificate in my business studies, I can get a better job, so I know that if I keep on studying I will get a better job.

---

22 Ehrenberg and Smith, *Modern Labor Economics*, 362–63.

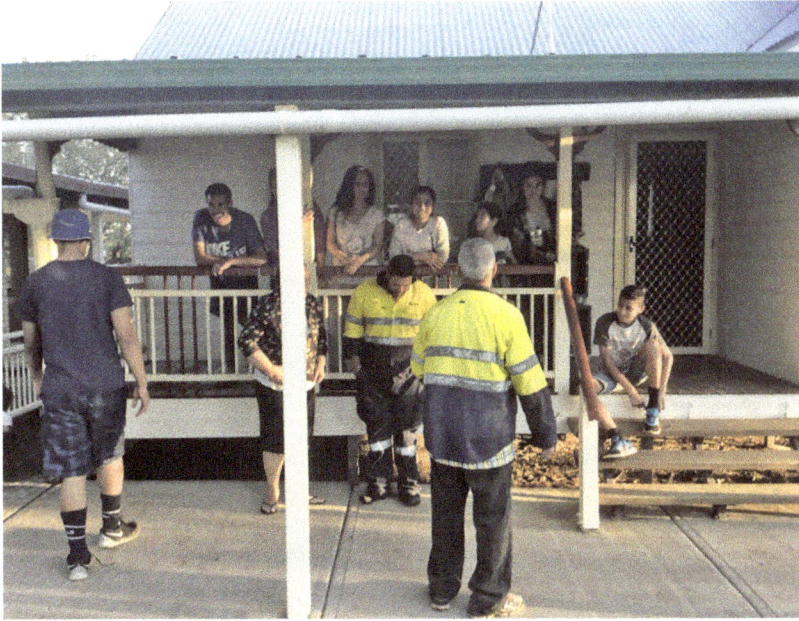

Figure 8.1: A Brisbane-based Tongan/Māori family relaxing after work on their rural property, 2016.

Source: Photograph by Ruth (Lute) Faleolo.

Sinamoni, a Tongan, second-generation trans-Tasman migrant, had migrated from New Zealand in 2011 to develop her career and to pursue a higher education degree. Now 31 years old, she described her and her husband's experiences of an improved *mo'ui 'oku lelei* in Brisbane:

> I like my life here in Brisbane, I wanted to be in Brisbane for education and work experience because it is a great stepping stone to the global places like America … I like that you can make out of life what you want here in Brisbane, it's like a blank piece of paper, it's a freedom that I get being in a place of opportunities, just make what you want of it. Money is good here, better than in Auckland … and there is a greater margin of savings here … I think that people are more fulfilled here because they've come here and they are being creative. It makes me and my husband feel alive to set financial goals, achieve them and then plan the next goal, it builds our self-esteem as a family. There is a faith we have here in this country that 'you can do it', we have a greater chance of achieving our goals here as a family.

Pasifika in Australia

Pasifika migration across the Tasman Sea from New Zealand to Australia, and particularly to Brisbane, is part of a general trans-Tasman migration flow of New Zealanders. There has been a consistent increase in this flow since the late 1960s, due mainly to the two countries' close proximity, as well as their cultural connections.[23] Pasifika trans-Tasman migration is also often facilitated by the preferential migration access accorded to New Zealanders under Australia's migration policy; this is particularly so for those Pasifika who are born in New Zealand and, thus, have New Zealand citizenship or permanent residency rights, or who otherwise obtain these rights because of New Zealand's visa and citizenship regimes that accord rights to people from many Pacific Island nations on the basis of New Zealand's colonial history in the region (something, incidentally, that Australia does not do). Green, Power and Jang explain that New Zealanders sometimes become permanent migrants 'by default' when they continue living in Australia after a temporary move.[24] This is often the case for New Zealand–born Pasifika, or Pasifika who have obtained New Zealand citizenship, who often become permanent migrants after travelling to Australia to visit family.

Since the mid-1990s, the number of New Zealand–born Pasifika arriving in Australia has exceeded the arrival numbers of Pasifika born in the Pacific Islands.[25] Currently, Queensland is home to the largest cluster of Pasifika in Australia, with more than 102,000 Pasifika living there, particularly in Brisbane.[26] As a New Zealand documentary series, *Tagata Pasifika*, described it in 2015, Australia has become the new 'land of milk and honey' for New Zealand Pasifika seeking improved lifestyles.[27] Indeed, since the 1960s, migration flows between Australia and New Zealand have moved strongly in Australia's favour, with relative economic conditions between the two countries being the main cause of high net migration loss to Australia.[28] There has also been a broadening of Australia's immigration

---

23   Green, Power and Jang, 'Trans-Tasman Migration', 34; Poot, 'Trans-Tasman Migration'.
24   Green, Power and Jang, 'Trans-Tasman Migration', 35.
25   Based on Australian census figures available for 2011, Hamer reported that New Zealand–born Samoans outnumbered those born in Samoa for each year of arrival since 1995. Similarly, New Zealand–born Tongans outnumbered those born in Tonga. Hamer, '"Unsophisticated and Unsuited"', 113.
26   Ravulo, *Pacific Communities*, 4.
27   Tagata Pasifika. *Second Migration*.
28   Haig, *New Zealand Department of Labour Report*.

policies since the mid-1970s that allowed for new groups of migrants arriving from all parts of the world to enter Australia. However, the usual migration procedures that other migrants have to comply with do not always apply to New Zealand citizens under the trans-Tasman agreement that exists between the two nations. This freedom of entry, together with New Zealand and Australia's close proximity and the strong pull of employment opportunities, encourages New Zealand–born Pasifika and those with New Zealand citizenship to live and work in Australia. Although the increase of Pasifika arriving in Australia has been recorded as a migration trend occurring since the 1990s, this contemporary trans-Tasman migration by Pasifika forms part of a centuries-old tradition of Pasifika migrating away from their homelands, in search of new opportunities and resources.[29]

Wellbeing Possibilities and Regulated Inequalities for Pasifika Trans-Tasman Migrants

Since the 1920s, the Australian and New Zealand governments have had arrangements in place that have allowed their citizens ease of movement between the two countries; Australian and New Zealand citizens are allowed to migrate between Australia and New Zealand without the need to obtain visas, and have the ability to live and work within these two countries without qualifying on skills-based or humanitarian grounds.[30] The 1973 Trans-Tasman Travel Arrangement (TTTA) formalised this long-standing understanding.[31] As a result of this arrangement, an estimated 640,770 New Zealand citizens were present in Australia by 2013 with work and residence rights.[32] The preferential migration arrangements that New Zealand have with many Polynesian countries (including Samoa and Tonga) mean that Pasifika with New Zealand citizenship are able to access Australian residence and work opportunities by virtue of the TTTA. A consequence of this is a much higher rate of migration to Australia (and Australian labour market participation) by

29   Banivanua Mar, 'Shadowing Imperial Networks'; Hau'ofa, 'Our Sea of Islands'; Keck and Schieder, 'Contradictions and Complexities'; Mallon, Māhina-Tuai and Salesa, *Tangata o le Moana*.
30   Green, Power and Jang, 'Trans-Tasman Migration', 35.
31   Walrond, 'Kiwis Overseas'.
32   'Fact Sheet – New Zealanders in Australia', Department of Home Affairs, accessed 14 March 2019, archive.homeaffairs.gov.au/about/corporate/information/fact-sheets/17nz.

Polynesian people in contrast to Melanesians entering the country via New Zealand. This implication of the TTTA is discussed by Mackay and Guinness in this volume in relation to Fijian migrants who have experienced more difficulty in obtaining residency in either Australia or New Zealand. However, since 1994, policy changes announced by the Australian Government have meant residency status changes and decreased benefits for migrants, including Pasifika, arriving from New Zealand. As of 1 September 1994, all non-citizens in Australia were expected to hold a visa to remain in the country. The Special Category Visa (SCV), introduced for New Zealand citizens as a temporary visa, was automatically issued upon arrival in Australia. It controls the benefits and opportunities received by New Zealand citizens in Australia, such as social welfare assistance, medical benefits and tertiary fees support. These policy changes reveal the ambivalent role that government visa schemes and social welfare policies play in controlling the level of access to socio-economic benefits.[33] As discussed by Mackay and Guinness in this volume, Australia has gradually withdrawn benefits and rights to New Zealand citizens. This ultimately creates an un-level playing field of challenging social and economic circumstances that contemporary Pasifika trans-Tasman migrants find themselves in on arrival to Brisbane. The recent changes to Centrelink access have created socio-economic differences across the community with benefits changing over time and affecting people's circumstances across several generations.

In 2001, the Australian Government introduced changes to the *Social Security Act 1991*. After 26 February 2001, a New Zealand citizen arriving for the first time in Australia was classified as a non-protected SCV holder and was required to apply for an Australian permanent visa to access particular social security assistance. In short, this meant that a New Zealander could enter Australia to settle and work, but could not have any benefits or rights as Australian citizens or permanent residents. For example, New Zealand citizens, on turning 18 or after leaving high school, although considered 'domestic' fee-paying students on enrolment to an Australian tertiary institution, are required to pay full fees up-front at the beginning of each semester. They are not eligible for student loans or allowances and do not qualify for Australian scholarships unless they have completed their final year of high school in Australia. Some Pasifika

---

33   Note: Some Australian Government policies (e.g. 2017 changes to Centrelink children's education bonuses) affect both New Zealand citizens and Australian citizens alike.

trans-Tasman migrants who want a tertiary qualification will have to choose between returning to New Zealand for a student loan supported degree and entering the Australian workforce as an unskilled or untrained worker. Pasifika migrant narratives highlight the ripple effect of the 2001 policy changes on the level of education and employment opportunities accessible to them and their New Zealand–born children in Brisbane.

'Onika, a 37-year-old, first-generation Tongan woman living in Brisbane, shared during *talanoa* her experience of paying her New Zealand–born children's university fees up-front at the beginning of each semester. In the face of significant challenges, she had successfully set up a trans-Tasman business in Brisbane and Auckland with the help of her father and siblings in Auckland. This strategy of utilising family connections had enabled her to provide important financial support while her children completed their studies in Brisbane. 'Onika is committed to working long hours, flying constantly between Auckland and Brisbane to build a successful business that will ensure her family's future wellbeing.

During participant observation at a Brisbane-based Pasifika cultural event in 2016, three second-generation New Zealand–born Pasifika youth, all in their early 20s, shared their concerns about being 'stuck in the factory' as picker packers[34] because they were unable to afford the course fees to attend TAFE or university in Australia. The effects of the 2001 policy changes are part of the coloniality evident in Pasifika experiences of labour mobility (i.e. the engrained way that Australia looks to Pasifika as a source of 'unsophisticated and unsuited' labour[35]) whereby policies reinforce colonial labour relations and socio-economic inequality.

Pasifika Wellbeing: Housing, Work and Family in Brisbane

For a Pasifika worker, the familial sphere of wellbeing is maintained through the act of giving and sharing their work outcomes through their extended, often transnational, family networks. These outcomes (such as resources, time, talents, skills and money) are given by Pasifika to help the

---

34   The 'picker packer' role in a warehouse or factory usually involves an individual or team of individuals 'picking' up shelved or stored items, as listed in an order sheet, and 'packing' these items ready for despatch and delivery.
35   Hamer, '"Unsophisticated and Unsuited"', 93.

progress of their family livelihood and wellbeing. Despite the challenges affecting Pasifika trans-Tasman migrants, particularly in relation to access to Australian benefits, Pasifika rated their improved wellbeing experiences more highly in Brisbane compared to Auckland. Pasifika migrants in Brisbane were more satisfied with their ability to provide a better lifestyle and home for their nuclear family, as well as to help their extended family, in comparison to Pasifika satisfaction to do likewise in Auckland. What Auckland provides in family and Pasifika community support cannot be matched in Brisbane. However, what Brisbane provides is the fulfilment of trans-Tasman migration aims for better job opportunities, more money to improve living standards for the family (both nuclear and extended) and a lifestyle that provides more quality time with the family. There is a higher level of Pasifika satisfaction in job security, career prospects, income and home ownership in Brisbane compared to Auckland. An interesting finding in the Brisbane-based interviews with informants who had moved to Brisbane in the last five to 10 years was their ownership of a home. There is greater opportunity for Pasifika to own a home in Brisbane, reflecting the greater margin of savings that is possible in Brisbane as a result of higher incomes and lower living expenses. In most cases, this meant a short time of shared sacrifices—staying with relatives who owned a home and sharing the costs of living to maximise their collective incomes while saving for a home deposit. For these informants, owning a home and having the income to afford this asset, as well as a better lifestyle, has helped them to achieve wellbeing for their whole family, not just themselves. Here, again, family is conceived in expansive and transnational terms. For example, a family home will not only provide accommodation and support for immediate family, but also for extended family members visiting or relocating to Brisbane from New Zealand, Samoa, Tonga or elsewhere. Home ownership thus forms part of the familial support systems[36] through which Pasifika enact agency and sustain relationships in the context of regulated inequalities, governmental coercion and socio-economic pressures.

36　Gershon, 'Viewing Diasporas from the Pacific'.

Figure 8.2: A Tongan family home used for weekly Pasifika community meetings in Brisbane, 2015.

Source: Photograph by Ruth (Lute) Faleolo.

'Amelika, a 42-year-old, first-generation migrant from Tonga, shared her story of labour mobility in Auckland and Brisbane. 'Amelika and her husband had each worked two full-time jobs in Auckland just to keep up with their living expenses and mortgage payments. After visiting relatives in Brisbane during 2008 and seeing the possibilities of a better lifestyle for their family, they decided to sell their family home in Auckland and move to Brisbane. In Brisbane, with the support of their extended family and church community, they purchased a better quality home at a more affordable price. 'Amelika set up a family day care centre that allowed her to spend time with her children while working from home. She took advantage of government-funded night courses for family day care educators and inspired other Pasifika women in her networks to do the same. Further, by sharing her family's progressive experiences in Brisbane on her Facebook page, she inspired other family members in Auckland to join them.

Pasifika understandings of the value of work relate to improved wellbeing. In many ways, this is similar to notions of work within the non-migrant mainstream.[37] Pasifika understandings of work and wellbeing departs from mainstream notions at the point of motivation. There was general consensus among the Pasifika informants of this study that work and participation in the labour force is, first and foremost, about helping family to progress. According to all 40 narratives, going to work and having a job is something that Pasifika take great pride in because they are able to contribute to the wellbeing of their family, which, in turn, nurtures their individual wellbeing. Dominant notions of work suggest that an individual's participation in labour is mainly driven by the desire for personal gain (i.e. more money to buy goods and services) and more leisure.[38] When an understanding of Pasifika wellbeing (i.e. holistic progress in all spheres, particularly for the family) is applied to the daily work life of a Pasifika migrant, we begin to understand that the desire for 'work' for Pasifika is not about their individual benefit but, rather, their capacity to share the benefits of their labour with others. Indeed, for some Pasifika trans-Tasman migrants, it has been more important to take up a job based in Brisbane that paid better wages than to stay in higher ranking or more professional occupational roles in Auckland that did not provide the same opportunities for meeting familial obligations.

Pasifika trans-Tasman migrants use these understandings and draw on family networks to mitigate negative experiences of labour mobility in Brisbane. Dialogue with Brisbane-based informants about their experiences of Australia's 2001 policy changes highlighted the importance of Pasifika trans-Tasman support networks that helped to sustain migrants and their families on first arrival to Brisbane from Auckland. Thus, as well as providing accommodation for arriving family, as discussed above, these forms of transnational familial support also extend to employment. It is common practice among Pasifika migrants living in Brisbane to 'hook up a job' or 'put in a good word' for their relatives who are planning to join them. This networking of *fāmili* or *'āiga* is a result of the Pasifika understanding that their employment in a company is not just about their own livelihood but is also, if possible, and where possible, an avenue for them to extend the job opportunity to others.

---

37   Arenofsky, *Work-Life Balance*; Gray et al., 'Post-Fordist Reconfigurations of Gender'.
38   Ehrenberg and Smith, *Modern Labor Economics*; Fleming, Kifle and Kler, 'Immigrant Occupational Mobility'.

Tavake's story illustrates the significance of this concept of a shared labour mobility. In 2003, Tavake, a trans-Tasman migrant, was being forced to work extra days and for longer hours in his work as a labourer in Auckland. This began to take a toll on his health and it was not long before his relatives in Brisbane heard about his situation. Tavake's cousin in Brisbane helped him to find a job in his workplace and Tavake was able to start there as a labourer in 2004. Although he was doing similar labour-intensive work as he had been in Auckland, he was getting a higher pay rate in Brisbane. A year later, he had saved enough funds to bring his wife and children from Auckland to Brisbane. The following year, Tavake saved enough money from his job to make a deposit on a home for his family in Brisbane. During the *talanoa* with Tavake's family, they explained how grateful they were for the opportunities they had received through their cousin in 2004. In exchange for his kindness, they were helping another family who had just migrated to Brisbane with provision of a job at Tavake's workplace as well as shared accommodation in their family home.

There is a shared understanding among the informants that the outcome of their labour not only contributes to the wellbeing of their nuclear and extended family, but also to a wider community. Pasifika migrant narratives make reference to this wider community that has provided a support network in Brisbane extending beyond *fāmili* or *'āiga*. For most of the 40 informants, this wider community included church families and local connect groups[39] that they met with on a regular basis and other local associations (such as their children's sports club, school or work community). These social networks help Pasifika migrants to find their place within diaspora contexts like Brisbane. 'Alisi, the Tongan trans-Tasman migrant running a courier franchise while studying for a business diploma, explained that, apart from providing for her *fāmili* based in Brisbane and in Tonga, she wants 'to be a good citizen in Australia, someone that is useful to her country'. For 'Alisi, building a successful business in Brisbane has a greater purpose of serving the wider community, and this gives her a sense of improved wellbeing. Similarly, La'ei, a 29-year-old Samoan first-generation migrant, shared her hopes of helping struggling youth through her performing arts career in Brisbane.

---

39 Connect groups (home groups) are based on social connections within the church community that informants belonged to.

Many other informants shared similar stories of proactively supporting other Pasifika migrants in Australia. Stead, in this volume, describes the supportive role Tongans and Samoans who have lived in Victoria for decades play in facilitating the migration and settlement of other Pasifika. These support systems have been formed through family and church networks and maintained by regular events such as family celebrations, reunions or annual church conferences. According to Pasifika migrant narratives, these networks often span across more than one state (the most frequently mentioned interstate support systems were family and church connections existing across New South Wales and Queensland) and often include New Zealand, their Pacific homelands of Samoa and/or Tonga, and sometimes the United States. Pasifika migrant families who are established in Brisbane often become fundamental support networks for family members planning to migrate from Auckland, and this is an accepted form of contribution to the collective good. Therefore, the Pasifika conceptualisation of work is essentially of a meaningful process through which an individual can produce good outcomes that flow into social progress for the family and community, including their country. These notions of work and wellbeing motivate Pasifika participation in economic opportunities and encourage positive responses to challenges met during their migration to Australia.

However, the labour mobility experiences of Pasifika trans-Tasman migrants are not always positive, and migration to Brisbane does not always yield the improvements to wellbeing that are hoped for. Depending on the date of their migration to, and settlement in, Brisbane, different Pasifika trans-Tasman migrants have varying levels of access to financial assistance. As discussed previously, there are differences in the levels of access to benefits and support based on the date of arrival to Australia from New Zealand. One effect of these different regulations is the inconsistent spread of benefits available to any given family. For example, a family with first-, second- and third-generation migrants will experience differing levels of access to education and, therefore, unequal opportunities to develop their career pathways based on their age cohort, place of birth and citizenship rights as Australians, New Zealanders or Pasifika.

For some families, the disparity caused by social security regulatory changes in Queensland have led to a separation of parents from their children. Australian-born Pasifika children have been left with their Brisbane-based extended family members (acting as legal caregivers) when New Zealand–born Pasifika parents, who have struggled to find permanent employment in Brisbane and received no access to social security to support their children, are forced to return to Auckland for work. Loto, a 45-year-old Samoan woman, shared her story of migration from Auckland to Brisbane in 2013 and her return to Auckland in 2014. After several months of struggling to transfer her academic qualifications and skills into meaningful employment in Brisbane, Loto returned to Auckland, leaving her children in Brisbane in the care of her parents. It is an acceptable and common practice among Pasifika extended family networks to share the responsibilities of looking after children when parental support is required. To this extent, Loto's story emphasises the role of extended family as a safety net in the process of Pasifika labour mobility and wellbeing fulfilment. However, it is also the case that Loto experienced great sadness, both in her inability to secure employment, and in her separation from her children.

Shared Labour Mobility, Pasifika Agency and Regulatory Constraint

The ability to network across the Tasman and remain connected across families (nuclear and extended) through church and wider community support systems is what sustains Pasifika trans-Tasman migrants in Brisbane. In articulating a vision of a good and happy life, the concepts of *ola manuia* and as *mo'ui 'oku lelei* facilitate a positive mindset among Pasifika, encouraging them to seek opportunities, including employment and business, through migration. This positive mindset is built on two important outlooks. First, the anticipation of migration and labour mobility benefits for the *fāmili* or *'āiga*. Second, a progressive outlook for the flow-on effect of migration and labour mobility on others (the wider community that a migrant strongly identifies with including the church, community, city, region or country). At the same time, the forms of relationship that these concepts engender underpin support networks that better enable Pasifika migrants to migrate and to settle with relative ease in Brisbane. The creation and maintenance of these networks, and the active seeking out of *ola manuia* and *mo'ui 'oku lelei*, are forms of restorative Pasifika agency that allow trans-Tasman migrants to negotiate the labour mobility challenges posed by Australian regulatory regimes. Similarly, in this volume, Stead discusses the 'development dreams' that maintain the numbers of Pasifika horticulture workers in Victoria, while Mackay and Guinness discuss the 'economies of hope' that drive Fijian rugby players to Australia. These forms of Pasifika agency are fuelled by shared future aspirations and supported by transnational familial connections that also share the sacrifice of labour mobility and migration. The act of giving support to fellow Pasifika trans-Tasman migrants enriches relationships or *vā* between new arrivals, *'āiga* or *fāmili* remaining in the homelands, and host Pasifika families that provide support.

In a sense, contemporary Pasifika migrants have contributed (and are contributing) to an ongoing indigenous globalisation[40] that works to overcome coloniality—reflected here in the ongoing, racialised and hierarchical structures of power that Pasifika migrants encounter in Australia and New Zealand's current labour market—determining their own indigenous mobility outcomes through mobilising culturally rich understandings and values, and strong local and global *fāmili* or *'āiga* connections. This indigenous globalisation does not simply negate or ameliorate the effects of colonial histories and ongoing racialised hierarchies, but it does highlight the role and capacity of Pasifika people as agents in their own labour mobility experiences, and the importance of Pasifika worldviews and transnational networks. These are considerations that dominant theories of diaspora negate in their analyses of Pasifika migrants.

Centering an indigenous perspective on Pasifika labour mobility also challenges the prevailing emphasis within much migration and diaspora literature on financial remittances as the primary measure of Pacific Islander labour migrations and networks. As shown here, the narratives recounted by Pasifika trans-Tasman migrants in Brisbane emphasise complex and multidimensional flows across transnational spaces, not only of people and money, but also of immaterial resources like skills, support, encouragement, care and community. The extended networks that underpin Pasifika notions of *fāmili* and *'āiga* highlight transnational labour mobility as a shared experience, incorporating individual, adult labour migrants, together with the family members who move with them, and extended families and communities in New Zealand, Tonga, Samoa and elsewhere. These extended family relations motivate and facilitate Pasifika labour mobility, and are at the heart of the 'good and happy life' that Pasifika seek.

---

40   Banivanua Mar, *Decolonisation and the Pacific.*

Bibliography

Anae, M. 'Teu Le Va: Toward a Native Anthropology'. *Pacific Studies* 33, no. 2 & 3 (August/December 2010): 222–40.

Arenofsky, J. *Work-Life Balance: Health and Medical Issues Today.* California: Greenwood Publishing Group Inc., 2017.

Banivanua Mar, Tracey. *Decolonisation and the Pacific: Indigenous Globalisation and the Ends of Empire.* New York: Cambridge University Press, 2016.

——. 'Shadowing Imperial Networks: Indigenous Mobility and Australia's Pacific Past'. *Australian Historical Studies* 46, no. 3 (2015): 340–55. doi.org/10.1080/1031461X.2015.1076012.

Bedford, R. '*Pasifika* Migration: The New Zealand Story'. *Around the Globe* 6, no. 1 (2009): 37–44.

Brown, R. P. C. and A. M. Walker. *Migrants and Their Remittances: Results of a Household Survey of Tongans and Western Samoans in Sydney.* Sydney: Centre for South Pacific Studies, University of New South Wales, 1995.

Ehrenberg, Ronald G. and Robert Stewart Smith. *Modern Labor Economics: Theory and Public Policy* (13th ed.). New York: Routledge, 2018.

Fa'avae, David, Alison Jones and Linitā Manu'atu. 'Talanoa'i 'a e Talanoa: Talking about Talanoa'. *AlterNative* 12, no. 2 (2016): 138–50. doi.org/10.20507/AlterNative.2016.12.2.3.

Faleolo, Ruth (Lute). 'Pasifika Trans-Tasman Migrant Perspectives of Well-Being in Australia and New Zealand'. *Pacific Asia Inquiry* 7, no. 1 (2016): 63–74.

——. 'Understanding Pasifika Migrant Behaviour and Perspectives of Well-Being in Brisbane through Material Cultural Adaptations'. 8th State of Australian Cities National Conference, 28–30 November 2017, Adelaide, South Australia. Australian Cities Research Network, 2018.

Fleming, Christopher M., Kifle Temesgen and Parvinder Kler. 'Immigrant Occupational Mobility in Australia'. *Work, Employment and Society* 30, no. 5 (2016): 876–89. doi.org/10.1177/0950017016631446.

Gershon, Ilana. 2007. 'Viewing Diasporas from the Pacific: What Pacific Ethnographies Offer Pacific Diaspora Studies'. *The Contemporary Pacific* 19, no. 2 (Fall 2007): 474–502. doi.org/10.1353/cp.2007.0050.

Gray, Breda, Luigina Ciolfi, Aparecido Fabiano Pinatti de Carvalho, Anthony D'Andrea and Lisa Wixted. 'Post-Fordist Reconfigurations of Gender, Work and Life: Theory and Practice'. *The British Journal of Sociology* 68, no. 4 (2017): 620–42. doi.org/10.1111/1468-4446.12267.

Green, Alison E., Mary R. Power and Deannah M. Jang. 'Trans-Tasman Migration: New Zealanders' Explanations for Their Move'. *New Zealand Geographer* 64 (2008): 34–45. doi.org/10.1111/j.1745-7939.2008.00125.x.

Haig, R. *New Zealand Department of Labour Report: Working across the Ditch – New Zealanders Working in Australia.* Department of Labour, New Zealand Government, 2010.

Halapua, S. 'Talanoa – Talking from the Heart'. *SGI Quarterly* 47 (2007): 9–10.

Hamer, Paul. '"Unsophisticated and Unsuited": Australian Barriers to Pacific Islander Immigration from New Zealand'. *Political Science* 66, no. 2 (2014): 93–118. doi.org/10.1177/0032318714554495.

Hauʻofa, Epeli. 'Our Sea of Islands'. In *A New Oceania: Rediscovering Our Sea of Islands* edited by Epeli Hauʻofa, V. Naidu, and E. Waddell, 2–17. Suva: USP, Beake House, 1993.

Havea, Jione. *Talanoa Ripples: Across Borders, Cultures, Disciplines.* Albany, New Zealand: Massey University, 2010.

Ho, Elise, Graeme Hugo and Richard Bedford. 'Trans-Tasman Migration in Context: Recent Flows of New Zealanders Revisited'. *People and Place* 11, no. 4 (2003): 53–62.

Kaʻili, Tēvita O. *Marking Indigeneity: The Tongan Art of Sociospatial Relations.* Tuscon, AZ: The University of Arizona Press, 2017. doi.org/10.2307/j.ctt1t89kr9.

Keck, Verena and Dominik Schieder. 'Contradictions and Complexities: Current Perspectives on Pacific Islander Mobilities'. *Anthropological Forum*, 25, no. 2 (2015), 115–30. doi.org/10.1080/00664677.2014.999644.

Latu, M. *Talanoa: A Contribution to the Teaching and Learning of Tongan Primary School Children in New Zealand.* MA thesis, Auckland University of Technology, Auckland, New Zealand, 2009.

Lilomaiava-Doktor, Saʻiliemanu. 'Beyond "Migration": Samoan Population Movement (Malaga) and the Geography of Social Space (Vā)'. *The Contemporary Pacific* 21, no. 1 (2009): 1–32. doi.org/10.1353/cp.0.0035.

Māhina, H. O. 'Tā, Vā, and Moana: Temporality, Spatiality, and Indigeneity'. *Pacific Studies*, 33, no. 2 (2010): 168–202.

Mallon, Sean, Kolokesa Māhina-Tuai and Damon Salesa, eds. *Tangata o le Moana: New Zealand and the People of the Pacific.* Wellington: Te Papa Press, 2012.

Manuela, Sam and Chris G. Sibley. 'The Pacific Identity and Wellbeing Scale Revised (PIWBS-R)'. *Cultural Diversity and Ethnic Minority Psychology* 21, no. 1 (2015): 146–55. doi.org/10.1037/a0037536.

McGavin, Kirsten. 'Being Nesian: Pacific Islander Identity in Australia'. *The Contemporary Pacific* 26, no. 1 (Spring 2014): 95–154.

Meo-Sewabu, Litea and Wheturangi Walsh-Tapiata. 'Global Declaration and Village Discourses: Social Policy and Indigenous Well-Being'. *AlterNative: An International Journal of Indigenous Peoples* 8, no. 1 (2012): 305–17. doi.org/10.1177/117718011200800306.

Mila-Schaaf, K. 'Polycultural Capital and the Pasifika Second Generation: Negotiating Identities in Diasporic Spaces'. PhD thesis, Massey University, New Zealand, 2010.

Otsuka, S. *Talanoa Research: Culturally Appropriate Research Design in Fiji.* Proceedings of the Australian Association for Research in Education (AARE) 2005 International Education Research Conference, Melbourne, 2006. Accessed 14 March 2019, www.aare.edu.au/data/publications/2005/ots05506.pdf.

Poot, Jacques. 'Trans-Tasman Migration, Transnationalism and Economic Development in Australasia'. *Asian & Pacific Migration Journal* 19, no. 3 (2010): 319–42. doi.org/10.1177/011719681001900302.

Prescott, S. M. 'Using Talanoa in Pacific Business Research in New Zealand Experience with Tongan Entrepreneurs'. *AlterNative: An International Journal of Indigenous Peoples* 4, no. 1 (2008): 127–48. doi.org/10.1177/117718010800400111.

Ravulo, J. *Pacific Communities in Australia.* Sydney: University of Western Sydney, 2015.

Sailiata, K. G. 'The Samoan Cause: Colonialism, Culture, and the Rule Of Law'. PhD thesis, University of Michigan, 2014.

Salesa, Damon. 'Damon Salesa: Our Pacific Future Is Already Here'. *E-Tangata*, 10 December 2017, e-tangata.co.nz/news/damon-salesa-our-pacific-future-is-already-here.

Smith, Linda Tuhiwai. *Decolonizing Methodologies: Research and Indigenous Peoples* (2nd ed.). London: Zed Books, 2012.

Tagata Pasifika. *Second Migration of Pacific People*. 3 part documentary series (presented by Sandra Kailahi). New Zealand: Tagata Pasifika, 2015.

Vaioleti, Timote. '*Talanoa* Research Methodology: A Developing Position on Pacific Research'. Paper presented at the *Pasifika Symposium on Pacific Research in Education*, Hamilton, 2003.

Vakaʻuta, Nasili. 'Tālanga: Theorizing a Tongan Mode of Interpretation'. *AlterNative: An International Journal of Indigenous Peoples* 5, no. 1 (2009): 126–39. doi.org/10.1177/117718010900500109.

Walrond, C. 'Kiwis Overseas'. *Te Ara—the Encyclopedia of New Zealand, 2014,* teara.govt.nz/en/kiwis-overseas.

9

Coloniality of Power and the Contours of Contemporary Sport Industries: Fijians in Australian Rugby

Scott Mackay and Daniel Guinness

Over several days in 2016, conditions became so bad in the Rugby Futures' dormitory in Sydney that the young Fijian men who resided there needed to ask local leaders in the Fijian community for food and other essentials.[1] Some of the men had previously experienced periods of hunger while looking for work or training for rugby in one of Fiji's regional centres. However, in Australia, things had become worse. The Fijians had moved to Australia under the promise of a clear pathway into professional rugby. Yet, one man reported to us that, instead, they found themselves with a strict curfew, performing manual labour for salaries (75 per cent of which were confiscated by the Rugby Futures' program head for what he called 'board and services'), and unable to control their careers or even their passports. Occasionally, the program head would leave for the weekend, temporarily locking the men out of their only kitchen and food supplies.

---

1   All names are pseudonyms and certain identifying features of individuals and organisations have been altered to preserve anonymity.

Without food or resources to buy food, the men contacted Seva and Va, two members of a previous generation of *itaukei* (indigenous) migrants. Seva, who had arrived as an aspiring young rugby player 20 years earlier, had learned how to negotiate the labour lines in and out of the rugby industry from another Fijian, Isei. Isei had migrated to Australia in the 1970s—during the first years of Fijian independence, when the nation was beginning to break out of the British colonial social order and was struggling to form relationships with the regional power. In Australia, Seva met and started a family with Va, who had moved from Fiji as a teenager for high school, staying with an Anglo-Australian couple she had met in Fiji. Now, Seva and Va form a prominent part of the Fijian diaspora in Australia, supporting new arrivals and providing a safety net of basic material needs, home-cooked food, a hub for social relations and a place for sharing experiences across generations. They regularly advise new arrivals on how to manage finances and carry out day-to-day chores, find formal and informal work, and balance the demands from family in Fiji with the task of building a new life in Australia. Through locations like Seva and Va's house, collective migration histories, forged over two centuries of relations and migration between Fiji and Australia, shape the experiences of today's migrant workers. However, there is also a formal, institutional aspect of this history.

The contours of rugby-specific contemporary migration from Fiji to Australia are built on historical connections and lines between the two nations. Both nations experienced a colonial system of governance that worked to produce and discipline people to be particular kinds of subjects for labour, while establishing differentiated categories of citizenship based on two different ideas of ethnicity and indigeneity, each originating in colonial thought. As has been shown elsewhere in this volume, the legacy of colonialism persists in current migration and labour regimes— in the 'coloniality of power'[2] of present-day Australia. This approach to coloniality unpacks the intersections between race, gender and other hierarchies that have historically occurred in systems of migration and labour. Further, it shows how aspects of these systems continue to exist, structuring access to labour markets in ways that ensure the subordination of some for the benefit of others. In this case, the historical hierarchies between the two countries were dominated by ethnicised divisions of labour, the exclusion of Fijians from Australia (and its labour force) and the extraction of resources from Fiji by Australian corporations.

---

2   Quijano, 'Coloniality of Power'; Quijano, 'Coloniality and Modernity/Rationality'.

In other ways, the struggles of Fijian rugby players are products of very contemporary dynamics. Australian policies of labour governance are heavily influenced by neoliberal forms of governance as the state pursues privatisation and deregulation,[3] and, as distinct from late capitalism, implements changes to regulate more aspects of life by the market, such as education, healthcare and the environment.[4] Neoliberal styles of governmentality position individual workers/migrants as responsible for their own position, and as being capable of negotiating fair and equitable contracts from an equal position as employers (including large multinationals and government-backed organisations),[5] ultimately creating insecurity and precarity for individual subjects.[6] These logics pervade not only the Australian labour market but also immigration policies. Australian employers are imagined as operating in a global market place, with Australia competing with other countries for the best educated, wealthiest and most highly skilled migrants. Would-be migrants with skills identified by the government as valuable can gain work permits easily, while others are excluded or confined to visa classes with highly restricted rights. In line with neoliberal ideologies, migrants/workers are cast as being responsible for their own ability to compete on the migration labour market. This rhetoric helps to obscure the perpetuation of colonial hierarchy obvious in the preferential passage through Australia's migration and labour regimes granted to migrants from selected countries. This coloniality, while it helps some Fijian migrants, leverages the positive outcomes experienced by the few to coerce the many to accept their position as cheap labour.

Would-be rugby players epitomise the ambivalence of the system, as the men oscillate between very high paying jobs that offer easy pathways to residency and citizenship rights and precarious labour that is entirely 'uncoupled from any possibility of citizenship'.[7] In Australia, professional rugby union has emerged as a new employer of Fijians, and one that, uncharacteristically, offers high-paying contracts to some new migrants. The professional Australian rugby union clubs, located in Brisbane, Sydney, Canberra and Melbourne, now offer 30 full-time contracts

---

3   Harvey, *Brief History of Neoliberalism*, 3.
4   Mirowski, 'Defining Neoliberalism', 434–35; Besnier et al., 'Rethinking Masculinity'.
5   Gershon, 'Neoliberal Agency'; Gershon and Alexy, 'Ethics of Disconnection'; McGuigan, 'Neoliberal Self'; Rose and Miller, *Governing the Present*.
6   Bourdieu, *Firing Back*.
7   Stead and Altman, 'Labour Lines and Colonial Power', this volume.

to rugby players, with starting salaries of around AU$70,000, and are actively recruiting *itaukei* Fijian rugby athletes for their athleticism and skills.[8] These prospects are alluring to many young indigenous men and some women, who see rugby as the most natural and lucrative possibility for migration and employment.[9]

The economies of hope that motivate young *itaukei* men have resulted in a rapid increase in the number of Fijians entering Australian clubs, including, although in smaller numbers, Australia's National Rugby League, a professional competition of a different code of rugby. However, the majority of Fijian athletes play for amateur clubs. Without high-paying contracts, they find themselves working outside of sport—sometimes exploited or left to fend for themselves on the margins of Australia's labour markets and migration regimes—as seasonal workers, manual labourers or religious workers.

Individual and collective mobility aspirations are intertwined with understandings and histories of what it is to be Fijian in a postcolonial nation and global world. Numerous periods of multi-sited field work in Fiji and Australia with Fijian rugby players and their families demonstrate the important role that Australian rugby plays as a site of hope for young Fijian men today. Once they arrive in Australia, these men encounter the legacy of past connections between Australia and Fiji—the symbolic, political and cultural contours that continue to shape the lives of young migrants. These contours have been formed in relation to those that structure the working opportunities of Indigenous Australians. The experiences of Fijian athletes highlight the intertwining of Australian and Fijian migration regimes, labour markets and social worlds, exposing the contours of global and domestic labour markets.

8   During the field work period there were five professional rugby franchises in Australia. However, at the end of the 2017 season, one of the five, the Perth-based Western Force, was disbanded.
9   In the last five years, small numbers of Fijian women have migrated to Australia in pursuit of professional rugby careers, including some in Rugby Futures. There are significantly fewer opportunities in Australian rugby for women than men, with only the national 7s squad receiving a salary from the Australia Rugby Union, as compared to a 7s squad and four Super Rugby franchises, each with 30 full-time professional athletes.

The Historical Lines between Australia and Fiji

Australia and Fiji share long histories of engagement framed by their respective, yet very different, colonisation by the British. Defined by an ambivalence reflective of Australia's broader kinship with its Pacific neighbours (borrowing from Teaiwa and Mallon in a New Zealand context[10]), Australia–Fiji histories have often been erased or relegated to the footnotes of Australian history. This is symptomatic of an Australian historiography that 'has been reluctant to acknowledge [its] constitutive imperial ambition and the long history of exploitation of labour and land that has marked Australian relations with the Pacific'.[11] When Australia–Pacific histories are illuminated, they often neglect the concurrent Australian violence towards, and dispossession of, Indigenous Australians (an exception being the work of Tracey Banivanua Mar[12]), an 'academic division of labour' that reflects governmental tendencies to 'treat "white-Aboriginal" and "Anglo-ethnic" relations as mutually exclusive spheres'.[13]

Formed via the reliance of the newly established British colony of New South Wales on Fijian and broader Pacific resources and labour, the earliest Australian–Fiji kinships stretch back over 200 years. In 1809, New South Wales informally declared Fiji's islands as lying within its political jurisdiction for economic and geopolitical reasons.[14] Not officially annexed, Fiji eventually became a separate British colony in 1874. The lure of economic opportunities brought many white Australian people and businesses to Fiji. In fact, such was the connection between Australia and Fiji in the late nineteenth century that, in the two decades leading up to Australian Federation in 1901, dialogue was entered into between Australia's colonies and Fiji on its possible inclusion within the soon-to-be Commonwealth of Australia; however, this union did not eventuate.

---

10   Teaiwa and Mallon, 'Ambivalent Kinships?'.
11   Lake, 'Island Empire', 411.
12   Banivanua Mar, *Violence and Colonial Dialogue*; Banivanua Mar, 'Shadowing Imperial Networks'.
13   Stephenson, 'Beyond Black and White', 5; Hage, *White Nation*.
14   Gammage, 'Early Boundaries'.

Both Australia and Fiji developed systems of labour governance that were clearly structured around imagined racial divisions. The British-Fijian colony built its future on large-scale sugar industries in the second half of the nineteenth and early part of the twentieth century, utilising cheap, imported, indentured coloured labour to maximise economic profit. While the British-Australian colony of Queensland (established in 1859) pursued similar projects by acquiring labour predominantly from the Melanesian islands of New Caledonia, Papua New Guinea, Solomon Islands and Vanuatu (collectively known as South Sea Islanders[15]), Fiji sought its labour for the most part from India.[16] Descendants of Indian indentured labourers and those who migrated to Fiji as merchants during the first half of the twentieth century identify as Indo-Fijian and represent the second-largest ethnic group in Fiji. Arguments against the use of white labour in Fiji and Queensland shared similarities in that they were based on price, availability and the 'conventional wisdom' that positioned plantation labour in tropical climates as fatal to European workers. However, the rationale for the omission of indigenous labour differed. A paid and regulated Aboriginal Australian workforce was not considered in Queensland, as Aboriginal Australians were viewed as 'uncivilisable' and a 'dying race'. By contrast, indigenous Fijians were prevented from working as plantation labour on the grounds that it would be 'detrimental to [the] traditional Fijian way of life'.[17] The colonial–indigenous engagement in Fiji was based on the (partial) recognition of *itaukei* sovereignty, which contrasted markedly with the concurrent definition of Indigenous Australians' land and resources as *terra nullius* and, thus, justifiably claimable without negotiation and/or a treaty.

Australia significantly influenced the economic and social dynamics of early and mid-twentieth-century Fiji, establishing the unilateral dynamics that have predominantly defined Australia and Fiji's relationship. In 1907, the Australian Government forcibly deported 427 South Sea Islanders (half of whom were from the island of Malaita in the Solomon Islands) to Fiji under the *Pacific Island Labourers Act 1901*, part of a broader

---

15   Less than 1 per cent of the 60,000 South Sea Islanders brought to Queensland between 1863 and 1904 came from Polynesian islands—Samoa, Niue, Kiribati, Tuvalu and Rotuma (today a Fijian dependency).

16   Pacific Island labour—predominantly from Solomon Islands and New Hebrides (Vanuatu)—extensively used in the preceding cotton industry, was also employed.

17   Lawson, 'Military Versus Democracy', 138.

bipartisan policy decision to construct a 'White Australia'.[18] After World War II, Australia, in collaboration with the British and New Zealand governments, also forcibly resettled the indigenous population from the Kiribati island of Banaba to the Fijian island of Rabi, following the catastrophic environmental degradation caused on the island by decades of phosphate rock extraction and exportation for agricultural purposes by the three nations.[19] The movement of people was in part facilitated by the dominance that Australian companies had asserted over Fiji's sugar, gold, banking and fledgling tourism industries.

Under the Australian Government's *Immigration Restriction Act 1901*, non-white Fijians were restricted from entering Australia until 1958 when it was repealed by the Migration Act. This established a universal visa and entry permit system yet did not promote non-white visitation or residency. Australian census figures documented an indigenous Fijian presence of only 45 in 1911 and 99 in 1954.[20] Most of these were granted temporary access for family reunion (mostly by way of marriage to Australian citizens), religious and sporting purposes (by way of acquiring a certificate of exemption from the Immigration Restriction Act). Entry for religious purposes included *itaukei* missionaries who were brought over by the Methodist Overseas Missions of Australasia to Arnhem Land in the Northern Territory from 1928 through to the mid-1970s to convert and 'civilise' Aboriginal Australians. This replicated a broader 'missiological method' previously utilised in other parts of the Pacific that substituted European missionaries in favour of Pacific Island missionaries to more effectively Christianise indigenous peoples.[21] Instances of *itaukei* and Indo-Fijian's overstaying their temporary residency in Australia often resulted in their swift deportation by Australian immigration officials.

---

18 Māori exclusion was implicated in continued Australian efforts post-Federation to entice New Zealand to join its Commonwealth (see Hamer, '"Unsophisticated and Unsuited"'). See also, Moore, *Making Mala*.

19 Teaiwa, *Consuming Ocean Island*.

20 'Census of the Commonwealth of Australia, 1911: Part VIII. Non-European Races', Melbourne: Commonwealth Bureau of Census and Statistics, 1911. Accessed 14 March 2019, www.ausstats. abs.gov.au/ausstats/free.nsf/0/F8A631CD75497EA6CA25783900132215/$File/1911%20Census %20-%20Volume%20II%20-%20Part%20VIII%20Non-European%20Races.pdf; 'Census of the Commonwealth of Australia, 1954: Supplement to Part I. Cross Classifications of the Characteristics of the Population: Race', Canberra, 1954. Accessed 14 March 2019, www.ausstats.abs.gov.au/ ausstats/free.nsf/0/D26840459C2A2338CA25787200212D27/$File/1954%20Census%20-%20 Volume%20VIII%20-%20Part%20I%20SUPPLEMENT%20AUSTRALIA%20Characteristics %20of%20Population%20-%20Race.pdf.

21 Kadiba, 'Methodist Mission', 103.

The policing was so stringent that, in 1965, Nancy Prasad, a six-year-old Indo-Fijian girl, was taken from family members who were legally allowed to reside in Australia and deported to Fiji due to the expiration of her travel permit. This highly publicised event demonstrated to the world the longevity and severity of Australia's racialist immigration policies, evoking national and global outcry that helped to expedite the dismantlement of seven decades of explicit race-based political discourse and policy.

Contemporary Links between Australia and Fiji

Despite Australia's official transition from an explicitly 'white' to a 'multicultural' nation under the Whitlam Labor Government (1973–75), its immigration policies post-1973 targeted highly skilled, non-white migrants, a position that hardened in the wake of John Howard's election as prime minister in 1996. From a Fijian perspective, contemporary Australian immigration policies are contoured by the coloniality of power, as they restrict migration in ways that continue to be correlated with colonial-era divisions of labour.

Australian immigration pathways for highly skilled migrants have favoured Indo-Fijians over indigenous Fijians, as a consequence of their higher educational attainment brought about by colonial policies that divided education and labour in Fiji on ethnic grounds.[22] Australian population statistics reflect this; out of 56,979 Fijian-born people in Australia in 2011, 35,411 identified as Fijian-Indian or of Indian ancestry. By contrast, only 12,485 identified as being of Fijian ancestry—loosely assumed to be those who identify as indigenous.[23]

Four indigenous-led military coups have taken place since the British granted Fiji independence in 1970 (two in 1987 and one each in 2000 and 2006). These have motivated Indo-Fijian migration to Australia and other parts of the world (i.e. New Zealand, Canada and the United States). Commonly framed in simplistic terms as the result of interethnic tensions between *itaukei* (54 per cent of the population) and Indo-Fijian's,[24] these undertakings have had significant effects on Fiji's political

---

22   Sharma et al., 'Fiji: Evolution of Education'.
23   'Community Information Summary: Fiji-Born'.
24   This simplistic framing elides the more intricate dynamics at play. See Lal, *Broken Waves*.

and economic landscape, as well as emigration. Indo-Fijians, notably in the post-coup years, have witnessed the diminishing of their economic and political rights, resulting in large rates of emigration. They have gone from making up over half the total population of Fiji in the mid-1980s to comprising just 38 per cent.[25] Simultaneously, there has been a rise in youth unemployment rates for all groups as a result of a combination of post-coup economic sanctions from trading partners, including Australia; the failure of 1990s structural adjustment to stimulate economic growth in Fiji as it entered global markets; and significant rural to urban migration.

Migration routes for indigenous Fijians to Australia post-1973 have, for the most part, built upon pre-existing pathways of temporary visas connected to family reunion, education (Australian Government–sponsored scholarships), religion and sport. Since the 1990s, a migratory disposition has developed among many indigenous Fijians in which 'the future is synonymous with exile and emigrating'.[26] However, Fiji's lack of postcolonial migration alliances, such as the Cook Islands, Niue, Tokelau and Samoa have with their respective current or former colonial administrator, New Zealand, inhibits *itaukei* mobility. Many Cook Islanders, Niueans, Tokelauans and Samoans have New Zealand citizenship status, granted either by birth or the uptake of immigration schemes, which allows them to enter Australia under the bilateral Trans-Tasman Travel Arrangement (TTTA) signed by Australia and New Zealand in 1973. The TTTA affords citizens of each country the right to free travel, work and indefinite residence in both nations. By contrast, Fijian migrants find it difficult to obtain citizenship or permanent residency in either Australia or New Zealand, which significantly limits their possibilities in the labour market and their access to state-provided social security services.

A small number of *itaukei* (and Indo-Fijians) have been able to follow the TTTA route to Australia. This is reflected in statistics that show that 2,858 of Australia's Fiji-born population in 2008 held New Zealand citizenship.[27] Yet, this path produces its own insecurities. Initially, when the TTTA was signed in 1973, a host of bilateral agreements accompanied

---

25   Connell and Voigt-Graf, 'Towards Autonomy'; Trnka, *State of Suffering*.
26   Guinness and Besnier, 'Nation, Nationalism, and Sport', 1131; Macpherson and Macpherson, *The Warm Winds*. The migratory disposition resembles the ideas of 'a good and happy life', 'development dreams', and the operation of mana, which motivate and steer migration of other Pasifika people, as described by Faleolo, Stead, and Standfield and Stevens elsewhere in this volume.
27   Bedford and Hugo, 'Population Movement', 57.

it, ensuring that citizens from both countries enjoyed access to social security services and voting rights in Australia and New Zealand. However, Australia has unilaterally withdrawn most of these rights to New Zealand citizens over time. Simultaneously, it has made it extremely difficult for New Zealand citizens to acquire Australian permanent residency and, thus, Australian citizenship (while still according them free access and the right to work and reside indefinitely in Australia). New Zealand citizens in Australia are denied access to unemployment and sickness benefits, youth allowances, emergency public housing and student and trade support loans, and are prevented from voting (as discussed in detail by Faleolo in this volume).

Rather than as a response to economic concerns (i.e. the cost of New Zealand citizens on Australia), some commentators frame Australia's policy changes in terms of race, arguing that Australia's concerns are not about the number of New Zealanders entering the country, but the type (i.e. Pacific Island people).[28] This is an example of how the historical legacy of 'White Australia' continues to reproduce itself. Pacific Islanders who enter Australia via New Zealand have been defined as 'queue jumpers'; that is, 'inauthentic' New Zealanders who possess few of the skills (social and economic) required by other immigrants, but instead take advantage of what is sometimes described as New Zealand's 'race-privileging' immigration policies. Australia's legislative changes seek to deter New Zealand citizens of low socio-economic status—a population that includes a disproportionately high number of Pacific people—from migrating to Australia. However, to comply with Australia's *Racial Discrimination Act 1975,* the policy changes apply to all New Zealanders.

An important new emigration pathway for *itaukei* was established in 2015 when Australia allowed Fijians to apply for non-skilled seasonal work visas as part of its broader Seasonal Worker Programme (SWP) established in 2012.[29] Fiji and other Pacific Island nations had long called for a partnership of sorts with Australia; as early as 1971, Fiji's first prime minister, Ratu Sir Kamisese Mara, had labelled Australia's continued opposition to migration from Pacific Island nations as racist.[30] However, Fijians arriving as part of the SWP have no chance of transitioning to

---

28   Hamer, "'Unsophisticated and Unsuited'"; Mackay, 'Australia in the Pacific'.
29   See Stead, and Nishitani and Lee (this volume), for more detailed analyses of the seasonal worker programs from a broader Pacific perspective.
30   Mara quoted in Connell, 'Emigration from the South Pacific'.

permanent residency visa status, which raises questions about reciprocity and the power imbalance that defines Australian–Fiji kinship. For some Fijians, exploitation has come to define their seasonal work experience in Australia. On 25 February 2016, the Australian Broadcasting Commission aired a report on *7.30*, its flagship current affairs program, claiming that a Fijian worker brought to Australia as part of the SWP received AU$58.80 for one week of full-time work from a government-approved employer. Subsequently, 13 out of 20 workers employed by that employer walked off the job.[31]

Regardless of their pathways into Australia, the country is home to a large population of *itaukei* migrants who exist as part of a precarious workforce. Rural towns such as Griffith in New South Wales have been home to groups of Fijians (*itaukei* and Indo-Fijians) seeking to build a new life for at least 20 years.[32] Such places have agricultural-based economies and high demands for 'low' or 'unskilled' workers, and, importantly, are geographically isolated from Department of Immigration and Border Protection offices, allowing Fijians who overstay their visas to find work and form a local community. Fijian communities also exist in low socio-economic neighbourhoods in some major cities (especially Sydney, Melbourne and Brisbane), where undocumented Fijian workers can find refuge and anonymity in a large population. Fijians who overstay their visas reside and work in Australia under conditions that allow for exploitation in the labour market and necessitate the contravention of migration regulations—both products of the ongoing coloniality of power. It is likely that some of the seasonal workers will end up in communities such as these. On 13 October 2016, an article in the *Fiji Times* reported that 18 out of 137 seasonal workers had not returned to Fiji upon expiry of their visas.[33] It is against this backdrop that rugby offers greater promise to would-be Fijian migrants.

---

31   Australian Broadcasting Corporation, *7.30*, 25 February 2016.
32   Schubert, 'Griffith's Transnational Fijians', 135.
33   Litia Cava, '18 Seasonal Workers From Fiji Didn't Return From Australia', *Fiji Times*, 13 October 2016, www.pireport.org/articles/2016/10/12/18-seasonal-workers-fiji-didnt-return-australia.

Historical Contours of Fijian and Australian Rugby

Rugby has played a significant role in pre- and post-independence nation building in Fiji. British colonial agents—military officers, police commanders and schoolmasters—introduced rugby to Fiji in the late nineteenth century, utilising it to promote the doctrine of muscular Christianity, thereby supporting broader colonial attempts to control indigenous masculinities throughout the British-Pacific.[34] More recently, rugby has become an important way of building a Fijian sense of themselves as a nation in the world. Success at an international level in both the 7-a-side and 15-a-side formats of the sport has served as 'a medium of symbolic resistance against post-colonial marginality' and as a way 'of asserting an alternative collective self-definition',[35] albeit in a context in which many indigenous Fijians see their experience of colonialism in a favourable light.

In many respects, the contours of Fijian rugby mirror and sometimes reinforce the shape of post-independence Fiji. Rugby articulates with militarism as a dual site for the reflection and facilitation of a contemporary Fijian nationalism that is intensely gendered and indigenised (as well as Christianised).[36] Through the overwhelming predominance of indigenous men playing rugby at all levels of the game, to the exclusion of women and Indo-Fijian men,[37] the sport emphasises a *bati* (warrior) form of the nation, clearly associated with indigenous men.[38] Casual games of rugby played in villages and urban public spaces, and more formal rugby in schools and clubs, are crucial sites for the socialisation of a masculinity that emphasises a strong, fast and powerful athletic body, coupled with a Christian discipline and respect for indigenous social order. Through the national team, which is wildly popular and watched fanatically by a broad range of Fijians, this form of indigenous masculinity is promoted as being the essence of Fiji, both internally and to the increasing global audience for the sport. Playing the sport becomes a more meaningful activity because of its associations with ethnic, gender and national identities.

---

34 Besnier, 'Sports, Bodies, and Futures'.
35 Kanemasu and Molnar, 'Negotiating Gender and Sexuality'.
36 Teaiwa, 'Articulated Cultures'.
37 Besnier and Brownell, 'The Untold Story'; Kanemasu and Molnar, 'Negotiating Gender and Sexuality'.
38 Presterudstuen, 'The Mimicry of Men'.

Rugby in Australia has taken a different trajectory and has acquired a different set of meanings. Unable to solidify itself as the pre-eminent sport of the Australian nation, or even one of its six states and two territories, rugby has long been associated with the small confines of Sydney's wealthy north-eastern suburbs, although this is changing. Within the main rugby-playing states (New South Wales and Queensland), rugby's biggest and more popular rival is rugby league. Distinguishable by rules and skillsets, the two sports have historically also been differentiated socially, with player and fan bases split loosely on issues of 'national loyalty, political affiliation, class, sectarianism, parochialism, sporting ethos and amateurism'.[39] Rugby is situated as the footballing code of middle- to upper-class, private school–educated, Liberal voters; this British form is influenced by an ideal of amateurism that emphasises both a player's technical ability and attributes as a 'gentleman'.[40] By contrast, rugby league is cast as the sport of working-class, state school–educated, anti-establishment Labor voters; rather than amateurism, it supports financial remuneration for players— that is, professionalism. This dichotomy has never represented the reality of there being a significant overlap of players and spectators.

Also dissimilar to the Fijian context was rugby's exclusion of Aboriginal Australian participation. Rugby in Australia was never used as a tool for colonial control of indigenous masculinity. Australia's experience of colonisation—overt violence towards, and segregation and confinement of, an Indigenous people who were deemed 'uncivilisable' and soon to be 'extinct'—justified their omission from the game. Despite changes in racial discourse and the dismantling of race-based policies over time, the continued lack of Indigenous participation reflects their ongoing, systemic exclusion. Of the 917 rugby players who have represented Australia in test rugby since 1899, only 13 have been Aboriginal (not including Wendell Sailor who is a Torres Strait Islander); the first was Lloyd McDermott in 1962.[41]

---

39   Horton, 'Land of the Wallabies', 1620.
40   Blackledge, 'Rationalist Capitalist Concerns'.
41   This figure was correct in 2017. Lloyd McDermott's time in the Wallaby team was not without difficulty in an era of overt racism. In 1963, he refused to tour apartheid South Africa as an 'honorary white'.

Fijian involvement in Australian rugby has its roots in the national team's first tour of Australia in 1952, and subsequent tours in 1954 and 1961.[42] The 1954 Fijian rugby tour of Australia had a significant, yet inadvertent, effect on Fijian participation in Australian rugby league. During the British rugby league team's tour of Australia, Arthur Walker, manager of the British team and chairman of the Rochdale Rugby League Club in Britain, watched the Fijian rugby team beat Australia in Sydney in the second and final test match. Subsequently, Walker began conversing with a number of Fijian rugby players, encouraging them to move to Britain, convert to rugby league—a sport not played in Fiji at that time[43]— and take up professional contracts with his Rochdale club. One player to do so was Apisai Toga, who signed with Rochdale in 1965.[44] After playing for two years in Britain, Toga moved to Sydney, signing with the St George Dragons, known as the most inclusive club in the New South Wales' Rugby League, in 1968. Toga was joined at the club by his brother, Inosi, a year later. The Toga brothers were the first of what today is a swell of professional Fijian players excelling at the sport in Australia.[45] Their arrival in 1968 and 1969 occurred only a few years after the deportation of Nancy Prasad in 1965. The fact that the brothers were able to play in Australia during the era of 'White Australia' indicates that they enjoyed a special status, arguably due to their position as athletes or having links to a well-established club.

42   The touring rugby teams were not the first Fijian sporting teams to enter Australia. That took place in the summer of 1907–08, when the Fijian national cricket team visited. Comprising only one non-*itaukei* player, the team attracted crowds upward of 9,000 people with interest centering on a paradoxical curiosity in the 'savage', and cricket's ability as a colonial tool to 'tame' the 'native' (see Anae, '"Very Scanty Covering"'). Illustrating a mastery of the sport while infusing indigenised elements to their performance, the team proved to be tough competition for Australian state, university, and district teams. Special permission to enter under the 'White Australia policy' was granted by the Australian Government as a result of the team's sponsorship by the governor of Fiji at the time, Sir Everard im Thurn (who was also the high commissioner of the Western Pacific).

43   Until the early 1990s, rugby union was the only code played in Fiji. Rugby league was founded in Fiji as a solution to a power struggle between the chiefly elite and the military leadership that had gained significant control of national politics after the 1987 coup led by Sitiveni Rabuka. Specifically, the formation of the Fiji Bati as the national rugby league team allowed Rabuka to be appointed to the symbolically important position of president of a rugby organisation without directly challenging the authority of Ratu Sir Kamisese Mara, who was president of Fiji and of the Fijian Rugby Union, and had been Fijian prime minister from independence in 1970 until 1987 (see Teaiwa, 'Articulated Cultures').

44   Other Fijians to sign for Rochdale in this period were Jo Levula and Orisi Dawai in 1961, Voate Drui and Liatia Ravouvou in 1962, and Litai Burogolevu and Gideon Dolo between 1965 and 1967.

45   In 1973, Apisai died suddenly at a team training session, the tragic result of tetanus poisoning from an unattended coral injury acquired while home in Fiji during the off-season. Apisai Toga played 103 games for St George (65 in first grade) over five seasons. Inosi Toga continued to play for St George through to 1974.

Figure 9.1: Apisai Toga in action.
Source: Unknown; photograph courtesy of Rochdale Hornets Heritage Committee.

Fijians in the Australian Rugby Industry

In the past 25 years, rugby has taken on extra significance for *itaukei* men as a rare means to access geographical and social mobility. With the professionalisation of rugby union in 1995, full-time professional teams in prominent rugby-playing countries, such as France, the United Kingdom, New Zealand, Japan and Australia, have grown to the point where they can now offer some Fijians contracts worth as much as AU$80,000 a month, greater than the collective incomes of some extended families living in Fijian villages, and certainly far higher than the salaries available in Fiji. Further, rugby players who have success overseas remain in the spotlight in Fiji, where their achievements are well-known to many, bringing acclaim and respect to their parents, extended families and villages, all of which are partially credited for the individual success of young men. This respect continues even when the athlete decides, for financial and/or career reasons, to represent other nations—a sign of the 'globalised nationalism' that is emerging as the postcolonial norm for the island nation.[46] Consequently, several hundred Fijians have moved to different corners of the globe to apply their trade, 'adapting to and being adopted into the very different cultures of their host clubs' and countries.[47]

Australia is a significant site on the global rugby circuit. Across all levels (professional and amateur), and including its national side, the Wallabies, an increasingly visible Fijian presence is evident in the men's game. Surnames such as Naivalu, Kuridrani, Kerevi and Koroibete have become common, albeit awkwardly pronounced, household names among Australia's predominantly white, middle- to upper-class rugby-supporter base. Twelve *itaukei* men have been selected since Acura Niuqila became the first Fijian to represent the Wallabies in 1988. However, the bulk of the elite Fijian players have been recruited during the professional era.

The professionalisation of rugby union in Australia has featured processes of mediatisation, corporatisation and commoditisation, which have been common in global sport industries since the 1980s, and which arise from neoliberal ideologies of deregulation and free enterprise.[48] These processes have greatly increased the possibilities for a career as a rugby athlete. Simultaneously, new demands have been introduced on athletes within the newly corporatised professional sporting teams to meet the standards of 'professionalism', an emic term that encompasses the behaviours and dispositions believed to be required of a professional player.[49] Lucrative pay packages have been able to not only motivate migration from Fiji, but also attract rugby league stars to switch codes, including the signing of Fijian-born Lote Tequiri in 2003 at the peak of his rugby league career with the Brisbane Broncos.

---

46   Guinness and Besnier, 'Nation, Nationalism, and Sport'.
47   Guinness, 'The Battle for Talent'; Schieder, 'Fiji Islander Rugby Union Players'.
48   Andrews and Silk, *Sport and Neoliberalism*; Miller et al., 'Modifying the Sign'; Scherer and Jackson, *Globalization, Sport and Corporate Nationalism*.
49   Besnier et al., 'Rethinking Masculinity'.

While some well-known Fijians have been recruited directly to professional sides from Fijian teams, other Fijian men, and now women, travel more circuitous routes to careers. Some Fijian boys migrate independently of their families during high school to take up scholarships offered by major rugby-playing schools in New Zealand and Australia (e.g. Kinross Walaroi School). These schools often have links to the professional rugby clubs, acting as part of the feeder system that identifies and trains talented players, some of whom are later recruited into academies where they are joined by other Fijians who have migrated to play for amateur club teams. The academies provide specialist training to improve rugby skills, enhance athletic potential and teach the requirements of 'professionalism'. This amounts to a significant form of disciplining of young men to perform certain types of labour—in this case, as highly valuable athletes.

In several Australian cities, rugby union is making special efforts to engage and recruit young Fijians and other Pacific Islanders into their rugby development systems. Many coaches, managers and player agents believe that Pacific people have rugby in their 'blood'.[50] In ways that mirror what occurred previously in New Zealand,[51] there has been significant growth in Pacific participation in Australian rugby. Their increased presence is frequently discussed in the mainstream media in New South Wales and Queensland,[52] and is normally explained in terms of their physical attributes and 'warrior element', as encapsulated by journalist Spiro Zavos in his article 'The Browning of the Wallabies'.[53] Some recruiters, such as former New South Wales Rugby League Development Officer Frank Barrett, believe that Pacific Islanders' physical attributes are complemented by their upbringing in a 'tough, hard culture … that has bred them for a physical game like rugby league'.[54] Fijians are widely sought after for their large size, speed, power and skills with the ball. The best are regarded as extremely valuable assets to any team.

---

50   McDonald, Belanji and Derham, 'It's in the Blood'; McDonald, 'Developing "Home-Grown" Talent'.

51   Teaiwa and Mallon, 'Ambivalent Kinships'; Grainger, 'Browning of the All Blacks'; Grainger, Falcous, and Newman, 'Postcolonial Anxieties'.

52   Daniel Lane, 'Islanders in Junior Leagues, It's a Really Big Issue', *The Sydney Morning Herald*, 16 July 2006, www.smh.com.au/news/league/islanders-in-junior-leagues-its-a-really-big-issue/2006/07/15/1152637922188.html.

53   Zavos, 'The Browning of the Wallabies'.

54   Barrett quoted in Daniel Lane, 'Islanders in Junior Leagues, It's a Really Big Issue', *The Sydney Morning Herald*, 16 July 2006, www.smh.com.au/news/league/islanders-in-junior-leagues-its-a-really-big-issue/2006/07/15/1152637922188.html.

However, coaches are wary when hiring players from the Pacific Islands who have not been through training pathways that teach professionalism, either in Australia or New Zealand. Pacific players are ascribed with physical and cognitive shortcomings attributed to their biology and culture that are not applicable to non-Pacific (Anglo-Australia) players, leading to positional segregation within the labour market. Within rugby league and rugby union hierarchies, some observers view Pacific rugby players as only able to play a 'jungle ball' game—athletically impressive, but ill-disciplined.[55] Stories circulate about star recruits who could not fit in with team cultures or were not able to learn the complicated strategies that elite teams use. These stories partly derive from the experiences of a few high-profile migrants from Fiji in the early 2000s, but also feed into stereotypes about exotic, hyper-masculine men that linger from the colonial era.[56] Positive and negative judgements are not attached equally to all Fijians, and rugby migrants fall into two distinct classes of worker— those who have been through professional rugby pathways and those who have not.

Today, the professional system is also establishing itself directly in Fiji, with the formation of three formal academies at Nadi, Suva and Sigatoka that train school-age Fijian rugby players and have links to professional French franchises. More informally, scouts from major rugby league and union teams attend amateur games in Fiji on the lookout for outstanding athletes, run open-call training camps in major population centres to locate potential recruits and have even been known to offer deals to men playing touch rugby on the beaches that flank popular resort hotels (stories of recruitment from obscurity are retold among young men in training in the hope that they too will be chosen). Some of these routes are well established, particularly those to schools, and some young men are well supported and receive an education that can provide opportunities outside of rugby.

Yet, many promises made by recruiters are not fulfilled. Some clubs (from many countries, not just Australia) withhold payments to athletes, do not provide accommodation, employment and transport as promised, and fail to provide exposure to professional rugby opportunities. Moreover, many

---

55   Brett Kimmorley, 'Brett Kimmorley's NRL Round Six Review: Warriors Back to Jungle-Ball, Cronulla Learning How to Win', *Fox Sports*, 9 April 2012, www.foxsports.com.au/nrl/nrl-premiership/brett-kimmorleys-nrl-round-six-review-warriors-back-to-jungle-ball-cronulla-learning-how-to-win/news-story/b8fcc0cca35b005ffdce56e6d2a55223?sv=703b4a65edcc546757b28e896d637a22.
56   Besnier, *On the Edge of the Global.*

Fijians simply do not realise that the remuneration offered will barely cover their basic living costs in another country, let alone allow them to send significant money home to relatives. In recent years, organisations have been formed to protect Pacific Island athletes around the world—for example, the Pacific Island Players Association, which acts as a union; the Pacific Rugby Players Welfare, which focuses on connecting players to reduce isolation and build communities; and the French Fijian Players Association, which does both of these things.

Pacific Islanders have been open to exploitation because of their marginal position in global labour markets—a legacy inherited from colonial times. Pacific peoples' different levels of access to the Australian labour market also reflect colonial legacies, with some Pacific Islanders able to access New Zealand citizenship and the TTTA based on their country of birth while others are excluded. Some Fijian interlocutors claimed that their exclusion was made worse by the preferential hiring of Samoan, Māori and Tongan men. However, the prominence of Fijians in elite Australian rugby, and the emergence of Fijian rugby organisations and teams in Australian cities, could signal that this is changing.

Rugby Futures

Rugby Futures, the organisation mentioned at the beginning of this chapter, exists on the margins of legitimacy. It runs rugby training clinics in several villages and in the major cities in Fiji. The 'futures' part of the training takes the form of a certificate in social work, awarded to attendees for taking part in religiously inflected presentations and discussions about drugs, alcohol and domestic violence. In a country where domestic violence and substance abuse are major problems, and where there is such a passionate interest in rugby among young men, the program has been widely welcomed into many villages.

The program purports to offer young Fijians a route into Australian professional rugby. In partnership with an Australian-based church group, Rugby Futures offers several dozen Fijian participants entry into Australia each year, officially as church workers, unofficially as rugby players. The link with the church means that the selected men are able to access religious worker visas, a special class of visa under the current Australian migration regime, that have far lower thresholds for sponsorship than other classes. However, most of the young men and women who travel this path hope to become professional rugby players through Rugby Futures' connections in the Australian industry. One of the Fijian athletes who arrived in the first year of the program signed a contract with a professional Australian club before moving to a higher-paying contract in Europe. His rapid rise has given the program credibility as a pathway to professional rugby—a reputation that the organisation actively encourages. Yet, the reality is very different, with migrants being forced to work for projects hand-picked by the program head and having little contact with the rugby industry.

Program participants in Australia are reluctant to speak out. Those who have complained in the past have found themselves sent to work as fruit pickers (with their salaries confiscated) in the north of Australia or back to Fiji to explain to family members why they have returned without fulfilling expectations. For voicing concerns about living and working conditions, one man had his passport confiscated. After breaking into the office to reclaim his passport, he ran away from the organisation and hid among the large Fijian community in another major Australian city. With few avenues for complaint, there is little protection given to isolated migrants. The problems are compounded by the fact that the organisation's head also acts as an unofficial agent for the players, making arrangements with amateur clubs in several Australian cities that want talented Fijian recruits in exchange for small unofficial signing bonuses for the players (reportedly up to AU$5,000). However, no players reported receiving any of this money, and clubs that have not been able to pay have not received any players. This results in the majority of Fijians being concentrated in a few clubs.

Aspects of the rugby industry, such as the extremely short careers, possibility of very high wages for manual labour and absence of formal training programs, make it exceptional from the perspective of Australian labour markets and attractive to young *itaukei* men. Athletes at the top of the industry seem to enjoy a different status than other Fijian migrants. Sought out by clubs, fast-tracked for residency and protected by unions, top athletes can be both extremely well paid and secure. Success in rugby transforms the lives of individual players and the broader community in Fiji and Australia through the generous support that athletes give to family, church, villages and other migrants. Further, their success in sport increases the visibility of Pacific Islanders, thereby challenging negative stereotypes of this group. Yet, at the same time, their position is precarious. With one injury, a season without success or the arrival of a new coach, these men can lose their rugby careers. If this occurs, their position in Australian society can also be jeopardised, a precarity faced by other migrants, such as those in the horticultural industry as described by Victoria Stead in this volume.

The majority of young people to pass through the Rugby Futures program remain in Fiji, unable to navigate Australia's or other rugby-playing countries' migration regimes.[57] Very few of those who enter Australia receive any financial benefit from their training and efforts in preparing themselves for a career in rugby. The program disciplines these young men in ways that are designed to make them employable as professional athletes, but opens few other opportunities in Australia. Rarely do they regret their time playing and training for such a culturally important sport as rugby, but the sacrifice of coming to Australia without gaining access to the labour market is a major one. Emanating from a country whose citizens enjoy few rights in contemporary migration regimes and labour markets, and having not been through an elite training program, they are essentially viewed as unskilled.

Conclusion

The coloniality of power is most visible at the margins of Australia's labour industry. The stories of Fijians being exploited while on seasonal work visas in Australia, as told in this chapter and in those by Stead, and Nishitani and Lee (this volume), have broader resonance with the experiences of the would-be professional athletes at the centre of this chapter. The potential rewards attached to short-term migration options for Fijians must be tempered by the existence of untrustworthy agents, confiscated passports and Pacific people isolated in rural and suburban Australia, fearful of reporting their mistreatment to authorities. Rugby migrants share with the majority of Fijian migrants an experience of being caught in a labour market that has historically used Pacific Island people (and Indigenous Australians) for work that white Australians did not want to do, and a migration regime that has long classified Fijians as unfit to live in Australia.

Connections that predate either nations' existence influence the relationship between Australia and Fiji, producing the landscape into which new migrants arrive. Some of these connections take the form of

---

57   For an account of similar dynamics in Samoa see Kwauk, "'Let Them See a Different Path'".

legal and economic frameworks that produce uneven migratory regimes. Others are embodied in the Fijians who reside in Australia, supporting new arrivals and guiding their career trajectories and social lives (sometimes for their own benefit).

The contemporary lines that divide and contour the Australian labour market are influenced by neoliberal logics that dominate economic discussions and migration regimes that prioritise highly skilled migrants. These sets of logic presume the fundamental equality of people—that each individual starts from the same position in society. The success of some Fijians in this system helps to propagate the myth of their efficacy. However, this merely obscures the reality that the majority of Fijian migrants are only able to access certain parts of the economy and are confined to menial labour without any possibility of movement. Australia's colonial history and profound influence on the Pacific region leaves its mark on individuals and nations in ways that are not easily overcome.

Bibliography

Anae, Nicole. '"Very Scanty Covering For the Chocolate Body": The Art of Burlesque and the Fijian Cricket Team in Australia, 1907–1908'. *Australasian Drama Studies* 63 (2013): 33–51.

Andrews, David L. and Michael L. Silk. *Sport and Neoliberalism: Politics, Consumption, and Culture*. Philadelphia: Temple University Press, 2012.

Australian Broadcasting Corporation. 'Seasonal farm workers receiving as little as $9 a week after deductions, investigations reveals'. *7.30*. 25 February 2016.

Banivanua Mar, Tracey. 'Shadowing Imperial Networks: Indigenous Mobility and Australia's Pacific Past'. *Australian Historical Studies* 46, no. 3 (2015): 340–55. doi.org/10.1080/1031461X.2015.1076012.

———. *Violence and Colonial Dialogue: The Australian-Pacific Indentured Labor Trade*. Honolulu: University of Hawai'i Press, 2007.

Bedford, Richard and Graeme Hugo. 'Population Movement in the Pacific: A Perspective on Future Prospects'. Wellington: Labour & Immigration Research Centre, Te Pakapū a Mahi me Te Manene Rangahau, 2012.

Besnier, Niko. *On the Edge of the Global: Modern Anxieties in a Pacific Island Nation*. Stanford: Stanford University Press, 2011.

———. 'Sports, Bodies, and Futures: An Epilogue'. *The Contemporary Pacific* 26, no. 2 (2014): 435–44. doi.org/10.1353/cp.2014.0047.

Besnier, Niko, Daniel Guinness, Mark Hann and Uros Kovac. 'Rethinking Masculinity in the Neoliberal Order: Cameroonian Footballers, Fijian Rugby Players, and Senegalese Wrestlers'. *Comparative Studies in Society and History* 60, no. 4 (2018): 839–72. doi.org/10.1017/S0010417518000312.

Besnier, Niko and Susan Brownell. 'The Untold Story behind Fiji's Astonishing Gold Medal: While Fiji's National Identity Is Deeply Entangled with Rugby, Not Everyone Is Invited to Play'. *SAPIENS*, 19 August 2016, www.sapiens. org/culture/fiji-rugby-racial-sexual-politics/.

Blackledge, Paul. 'Rationalist Capitalist Concerns: William Cail and the Great Rugby Split of 1895'. *The International Journal of the History of Sport* 18, no. 2 (2001): 35–53. doi.org/10.1080/714001551.

Bourdieu, Pierre. *Firing Back: Against the Tyranny of the Market 2.* Translated by Loïc Wacquant. London: Verso, 2003.

'Community Information Summary: Fiji-Born'. Canberra: Department of Immigration and Citizenship, 2014. Accessed 14 March 2019, www.dss.gov. au/sites/default/files/documents/02_2014/fiji.pdf.

Connell, John. 'Emigration from the South Pacific: An Australian Perspective'. In *Immigration: A Commitment to Australia.* Canberra: Committee to Advise on Australia's Immigration Policies, Parliament of Australia, 1988.

Connell, John and Carmen Voigt-Graf. 'Towards Autonomy? Gendered Migration in Pacific Island Countries'. In *Migration Happens: Reasons, Effects and Opportunities of Migration in the South Pacific*, edited by Katarina Ferro and Margot Wallner, 43–62. Vienna: LIT Verlag, 2006.

Gammage, Bill. 'Early Boundaries of New South Wales'. *Historical Studies* 19, no. 77 (1981): 524–31. doi.org/10.1080/10314618108595657.

Gershon, Ilana. 'Neoliberal Agency'. *Current Anthropology* 52, no. 4 (2011): 537–55. doi.org/10.1086/660866.

Gershon, Ilana and Allison Alexy. 'The Ethics of Disconnection in a Neoliberal Age'. *Anthropological Quarterly* 84, no. 4 (2011): 799–808. doi.org/10.1353/ anq.2011.0056.

Grainger, Andrew. 'The Browning of the All Blacks: Pacific Peoples, Rugby, and the Cultural Politics of Identity in New Zealand'. PhD thesis, University of Maryland, 2008.

Grainger, Andrew, Mark Falcous and Joshua Newman. 'Postcolonial Anxieties and the Browning of New Zealand Rugby'. *The Contemporary Pacific* 24, no. 2 (2012): 267–95. doi.org/10.1353/cp.2012.0029.

Guinness, Daniel. 'The Battle for Talent? Sport and Contested Nationality'. GlobalSport, 2016. Accessed 14 March 2019, global-sport.eu/?s=The+Battle+for+Talent%3F+Sport+and+Contested+Nationality.

Guinness, Daniel, and Niko Besnier. 'Nation, Nationalism, and Sport: Fijian Rugby in the Local-Global Nexus', *Anthropological Quarterly* 89, no. 4 (2016): 1109–41. doi.org/10.1353/anq.2016.0070.

Hage, Ghassan. *White Nation: Fantasies of White Supremacy in a Multicultural Society*. Sydney: Pluto Press, 1998.

Hamer, Paul. '"Unsophisticated and Unsuited": Australian Barriers to Pacific Islander Immigration from New Zealand', *Political Science* 66, no. 2 (2014): 93–118. doi.org/10.1177/0032318714554495.

Harvey, David. *A Brief History of Neoliberalism*. Oxford: Oxford University Press, 2005.

Horton, Peter. 'Rugby Union Football in the Land of the Wallabies, 1874–1949: Same Game, Different Ethos'. *The International Journal of the History of Sport* 26, no. 11 (2009): 1611–29. doi.org/10.1080/09523360903169925.

Kadiba, John. 'The Methodist Mission and the Emerging Aboriginal Church in Arnhem Land 1916–1977'. PhD thesis, Northern Territory University, 1998.

Kanemasu, Yoko and Gyozo Molnar. 'Double-Trouble: Negotiating Gender and Sexuality in Post-Colonial Women's Rugby in Fiji'. *International Review for the Sociology of Sport* 52, no. 4 (2015): 430–46. doi.org/10.1177/1012690215602680.

Kwauk, Christina. '"Let Them See a Different Path": Social Attitudes towards Sport, Education and Development in Samoa'. *Sport, Education and Society* 21, no. 4 (2016): 644–60. doi.org/10.1080/13573322.2015.1071250.

Lake, Marilyn. 'The Australian Dream of an Island Empire: Race, Reputation, and Resistance'. *Australian Historical Studies* 46, no. 3 (2015): 410–24. doi.org/10.1080/1031461X.2015.1075222.

Lal, Brij. *Broken Waves: A History of the Fiji Islands in the Twentieth Century*. Honolulu: University of Hawai'i Press, 1992.

Lawson, Stephanie. 'The Military Versus Democracy in Fiji: Problems for Contemporary Political Development'. In *The Military and Democracy in Asia and the Pacific*, edited by R. J. May and V. Selochan (2nd ed.), 132–47. Canberra, ACT: ANU E Press, 2004. doi.org/10.22459/MDAP.03.2004.09.

Mackay, Scott William. 'Australia in the Pacific: The Ambivalent Place of Pacific Peoples within Contemporary Australia'. PhD thesis, University of Melbourne, 2018.

Macpherson, Cluny and La'avasa Macpherson. *The Warm Winds of Change: Globalisation in Contemporary Samoa.* Auckland: Auckland University Press, 2010.

McDonald, Brent. 'Developing "Home-Grown" Talent: Pacific Island Rugby Labour and the Victorian Rugby Union'. *The International Journal of the History of Sport* 31, no. 11 (2014): 1332–44. doi.org/10.1080/09523367.2014.923839.

McDonald, Brent, B Belanji and L Derham. 'It's in the Blood: Negotiations of the Australian Rugby "Field" by Pacific Islanders'. *TASA Conference Referred Proceedings*, 2012.

McGuigan, Jim. 'The Neoliberal Self'. *Culture Unbound*, no. 6 (2014): 223–40.

Miller, Toby, Geoffrey Lawrence, Jim McKay and David Rowe. 'Modifying the Sign: Sport and Globalization'. *Social Text*, no. 17 (1999): 15–33.

Mirowski, Philip. 'Defining Neoliberalism'. In *The Making of the Neoliberal Thought Collective*, edited by Philip Mirowski and Dieter Plehwe, 417 55. Cambridge, MA: Harvard University Press, 2009.

Moore, Clive. *Making Mala: Malaita in Solomon Islands, 1870s–1930s.* Canberra: ANU Press, 2017. doi.org/10.22459/MM.04.2017.

Presterudstuen, Geir Henning. 'The Mimicry of Men: Rugby an Masculinities in Post-Colonial Fiji'. *Global Studies* 3 (2010): 237–48. doi.org/10.18848/1835-4432/CGP/v03i02/40692.

Quijano, Anibal. 'Coloniality and Modernity/Rationality'. *Cultural Studies* 21, no. 2–3 (2007): 168–78. doi.org/10.1080/09502380601164353.

———. 'Coloniality of Power, Eurocentrism, and Latin America'. *Nepantla: Views from South* 1, no. 3 (2000): 533–80. doi.org/10.1177/0268580900015002 005.

Rose, Nikolas and Peter Miller. *Governing the Present: Administering Economic, Social and Personal Life.* Cambridge MA: Polity, 2008.

Scherer, Jay and Steve Jackson. *Globalization, Sport and Corporate Nationalism: The New Cultural Economy of the New Zealand All Blacks.* Oxford: Peter Lang, 2010. doi.org/10.3726/978-3-0353-0000-0.

Schieder, Dominik. 'Fiji Islander Rugby Union Players in Japan: Corporate Particularities and Migration Routes'. *Asia Pacific Journal of Sport and Social Science* 3 (2014): 250–67. doi.org/10.1080/21640599.2014.982339.

Schubert, Mark. 'Griffith's Transnational Fijians: Between the Devil, the Deep Blue Sea … and Their Pastors'. In *Migration and Transnationalism: Pacific Perspectives*, edited by Helen Lee and Steve Francis Tupai, 133–42. Canberra: ANU E Press, 2009. doi.org/10.22459/MT.08.2009.08.

Sharma, Akhilanand, Steven Coombs, Subhas Chandra and Manueli Sagaitu. 'Fiji: Evolution of Education from Colonial to Modern Times'. In *Education in Australia, New Zealand and the Pacific*, edited by Michael Crossley, Greg Hancock and Terra Sprague, 243–64. London; New York: Bloomsbury Academic, 2015.

Stephenson, Peta. 'Beyond Black and White: Aborigines, Asian-Australians and the National Imaginary'. PhD thesis, University of Melbourne, 2003.

Teaiwa, Katerina. *Consuming Ocean Island: Stories of People and Phosphate from Banaba.* Bloomington: Indiana University Press, 2015.

Teaiwa, Teresia. 'Articulated Cultures: Militarism and Masculinities in Fiji during the Mid-1990s'. *Fijian Studies* 3 (2005): 201–22.

Teaiwa, Teresia and Sean Mallon. 'Ambivalent Kinships? Pacific People in New Zealand'. In *New Zealand Identities: Departures and Destinations*, edited by J Liu, T McCreanor, T McIntosh and Teresia Teaiwa, 207–29. Wellington: Victoria University Press, 2005.

Trnka, Susanna. *State of Suffering: Political Violence and Community Survival in Fiji.* Ithaca: Cornell University Press, 2008.

Zavos, Spiro. 'The Browning of the Wallabies'. *The Roar*, 1 June 2007, www.theroar. com.au/2007/06/01/the-browning-of-the-wallabies/.

Newspapers

Fiji Times

Fox Sports

The Sydney Morning Herald

10

Emergent Trends in Indigenous Labour Mobility: Flying to Work in the Nation's Quarry

Sarah Prout Quicke and Fiona Haslam McKenzie

As a phenomenon, contemporary Indigenous mobility and migration resulting from employment in the mainstream labour market is relatively obscured in Australia's public and scholarly consciousness. Given the 'mobile turn' in the social sciences,[1] the 'cultural turn' within migration studies,[2] the long legacy of Indigenous labour mobility and the central, though highly contested, place of mainstream employment in Australia's current Indigenous affairs policy agenda,[3] this obscurity is surprising.

Within a neoliberal political economy, legislative and policy reforms and Indigenous responses to them, have engendered important policy debates with respect to Indigenous economies and broader questions of social and spatial justice.[4] These debates have centred on the role of the state as welfare provider, Indigenous 'mainstreaming',[5] and the relative

---

1   Sheller and Urry, 'The New Mobilities Paradigm'.
2   Blunt, 'Cultural Geographies of Migration'; King, 'Geography and Migration Studies'.
3   Curchin, 'Two Visions'.
4   Altman, 'What Future for Remote Indigenous Australia?'; Altman, 'Indigenous Policy'; Curchin, 'Interrogating the Hybrid Economy Approach'; Curchin, 'Two Visions'.
5   This term refers broadly to the current federal ideological approach to Indigenous affairs policy, characterised by a deliberate shift away from previous approaches that provided for Indigenous-specific services and programs for Indigenous peoples. Many of these programs and services have been discontinued and Indigenous peoples have been incorporated into existing 'mainstream' service delivery models and programs.

'viability' and wellbeing of remote Indigenous communities with limited access to formal educational and market opportunities.[6] These debates and discussions are of critical importance in terms of policymaking. However, their central subjects tend to be Indigenous peoples who are not engaged in mainstream labour markets. The experiences and outcomes of Indigenous peoples who move or migrate because of direct engagement with the mainstream labour market have remained relatively unexamined. That is to say, the contemporary mobile (or migrant) Indigenous labouring subject is rarely the focus of empirical analysis.

This labouring subject has also been largely absent in the Indigenous mobility literature. This literature has addressed important questions of social and spatial justice for Indigenous peoples that revolve around the ways in which Indigenous peoples are often constructed as out of place and/or inauthentic and ungovernable because of their mobility.[7] It surfaces a powerful settler logic that holds that being settled and/or economically productive (narrowly defined within a neoliberal political economy as engaged with mainstream markets) are fundamental pillars of responsible citizenship. In the policy era of neoliberal mainstreaming, remote living can be constructed as a barrier to such citizenship. Geographical movement towards mainstream markets can appear to be an implicit goal of policies and programs that concentrate Indigenous affairs investment and services in larger cities, towns and communities. However, the available evidence suggests that there is no trend of Indigenous peoples moving towards localities with greater employment opportunities.[8]

The Indigenous mobilities literature also traces a range of Indigenous mobility and migration practices associated with customary and cultural activities, as well as the need and desire to access a range of health, housing, education, welfare, recreational and retail services.[9] Of course, if we consider the compelling call of feminist scholars to value processes of social reproduction as forms of real work, many of these movements are, in fact, kinds of labour mobility.[10] Nevertheless, our central point is that the Indigenous mobilities literature seldom, if ever, addresses the more narrow kind of labour mobility with which this chapter is concerned:

6   Biddle, 'Proximity to Labour Markets'.
7   Prout and Howitt, 'Frontier Imaginings'.
8   Biddle, 'Indigenous Migration and the Labour Market'; Taylor, 'Population and Diversity'.
9   Dockery, 'A Wellbeing Approach'; Musharbash, *Yuendumu Everyday*; Prout, 'Interrogating the Image'; Taylor and Bell, *Population Mobility and Indigenous Peoples*.
10   McDowell, 'The Lives of Others'; Silvey, 'Power, Difference and Mobility'.

movement *because of* mainstream labour market employment. Such movements include, but are not limited to, relocating a usual residence to look for or commence a job, long-distance commuting and regular travel associated with mainstream employment.[11]

This chapter seeks to develop the conceptual terrain of these kinds of contemporary Indigenous labour mobilities in Australia by foregrounding the experiences and outcomes of one case study group of Indigenous mobile workers: fly-in fly-out (FIFO) mine employees based at Broome in the West Kimberley region of Western Australia. We make two central, but related, claims. First, there are important similarities and differences between contemporary Indigenous FIFO work and historical Indigenous labour mobility practices. We suggest that Indigenous FIFO mine work is simply a new(er) expression of well-established practices of labour mobility among Indigenous Australians prior to, and since, colonisation. Though, there are also important differences across time and space. Second, Indigenous FIFO workers occupy a unique position on the labour mobility spectrum. Though they often fill lower skilled roles in the sector and thus constitute a precariat of sorts, they do not face the same challenges with respect to exploitation and financial expropriation as many lower skilled transnational labour migrants, including the Pacific Islanders discussed by Stead, and Nishitani and Lee, in this volume.[12] However, neither are their labour mobilities characteristic of the privileged class of highly mobile professionals that Cresswell, Dorow and Roseman refer to as the 'kenetic elite'.[13]

Indigenous FIFO work represents a significant shift from the exploitative and coercive experiences associated with direct colonial subjugation. Today, these labourers are sought after within the resource sector in Australia and have access to the same suite of legislative protections as all other Australians in the mainstream labour market. Nevertheless, their labour mobilities are shaped by a representational politics that is imbued with the coloniality of power.[14] Consequently, FIFO workers still face a unique set of precarities, vulnerabilities and challenges associated with their labour mobility.

---

11 Productivity Commission, *Geographic Labour Mobility*.
12 Buckley, McPhee and Rogaly, 'Labour Geographies'; Preibisch, 'Pick-Your-Own Labour'.
13 Cresswell, Dorow and Roseman, 'Putting Mobility Theory'.
14 Stead and Altman, this volume.

The Historical Legacy of Indigenous Labour Mobility

There is now a rich historical literature, including chapters in this volume (particularly Shino Konishi's), that clearly identifies both pre- and post-settlement practices of Indigenous temporary, circular mobilities related to labour, resource harvesting, management and trade. For example, historians have examined the pre-colonial importance of transnational Macassan[15] and domestic trade networks[16] for Indigenous people living in the country's north. In these systems, Indigenous people were not 'fixed' in time and space, or economically primitive and insular. Rather, in their harvesting and trade practices, mobility and economy were demonstrably enmeshed.

The arrival of British colonists led to the disruption and eventual cessation of some of these practices. It also introduced new forms of Indigenous labour mobility. Roseman, Barber and Nei note that one of the chief historical drivers of labour mobility, particularly under conditions of European colonialism, was the dislocation of people and groups from the homelands from which they had previously derived their livelihoods.[17] Responding to dislocation and opportunity, Indigenous Australians made vital, yet often deeply exploited, contributions to early colonial maritime industries, such as sealing and whaling enterprises in southern Australia[18] and pearling enterprises in the north.[19]

The colonial frontier extended its reach in Western Australia's northern Kimberley region in the late 1800s as pastoral leases were granted and the township of Broome was established as a pearling port. Many Aboriginal people worked both as stockmen and domestic staff for non-Aboriginal pastoralists, sometimes receiving a small wage or basic provisions.[20] Commercial pearling operations were also expanded along the West Kimberley coast with Aboriginal people, especially women, favoured as divers. Malay, Chinese, Japanese, Filipino, Amborese, Koepanger (Timorese) and Macassan divers—many of whom travelled regularly to the region as part of long-standing prior trade networks—

---

15 Lydon, 'Picturing Macassan-Australian Histories'.
16 Redmond, 'Tracking Wurnan'; Redmond and Skyring, 'Exchange and Appropriation'.
17 Roseman, Barber and Nei, 'Towards a Feminist'.
18 Russell, '"The Singular Transcultural Space"'.
19 Keen, 'Introduction'.
20 Bolton, 'Alexander Forrest's Expedition 1879'.

were subsequently exploited, usually coercively through indentured labour arrangements, as divers, deckhands, cooks and onshore workers. By 1910, more than 3,500 people on almost 400 pearling luggers were fishing for pearls and shell around Broome, making it one of the world's largest pearling centres.[21] Pearl diving was dangerous work and these operations sometimes displaced workers thousands of kilometres from their homelands with no promise of eventual safe return.

As the pearling and pastoral industries developed, Catholic missions were also established in three West Kimberley communities: Beagle Bay, Lombadina and Broome. The locally practised Pallotine method of missionary engagement was for clergy and lay people to work in partnership. In some cases, Aboriginal languages, customs and spiritual beliefs coexisted alongside missionary activities that established educational and employment enterprises.[22] Workshops and trade schools were developed to train local Aboriginal men in building skills, farming, shoe making and blacksmithing, while the women were taught to launder, sew and cook and and learned rudimentary skills in Western medical practice. Reading, writing, mathematics, history and music were also an important part of the curriculum.[23] The experiences for mission residents were mixed, but many would later report that the education and skills prepared them for life in a settler-dominant world.[24]

Until the late 1960s, labour opportunities in the emergent pastoral industry (largely unpaid or underpaid)[25] and in building the colony's transport infrastructure (particularly railways and roads) saw large numbers of Indigenous peoples moving regularly across and between pastoral stations, and sometimes to regions a considerable distance from their homelands, to follow available work. Significant changes to Indigenous labour mobility practices in the Kimberley occurred in the 1960s in response to the civil rights movement abroad and domestically. The hard-fought introduction of equal wages for Indigenous people in the pastoral industry[26] in 1968, and the increasing mechanisation of labour

---

21 Hart et al., 'Western Australian Silver-Lipped Pearl Oyster'.

22 Choo, 'Mixed Blessings'; Kelly, *Proud Heritage*.

23 Choo, 'Mixed Blessings'; Lockyer, *Last Truck Out*.

24 Choo, 'Mixed Blessings'; Kelly, *Proud Heritage*; Lockyer, *Last Truck Out*.

25 See, for example, Stevens, *Aborigines in the Northern*; Choo, 'Mixed Blessings'.

26 In 1966, the Commonwealth Conciliation and Arbitration Commission handed down a decision to remove racially discriminatory clauses in the federal pastoral award for station workers, which had allowed station owners not to pay Aboriginal workers the standard award wage (Skyring, 'Low Wages, Low Rents'). These measures took effect in 1968.

in agriculture, transport and maritime industries saw many Indigenous people displaced from the workforce.[27] At the same time, social welfare entitlements were broadened for Indigenous people. Of this period, Skyring comments: 'Increased drinking by people in the reserve camps, unemployment and widespread homelessness all happened at roughly the same time for Kimberley Aboriginal people. These changes conflated as one catastrophe.'[28] She notes that some Aboriginal leaders in the Kimberley describe these reforms as having precipitated a refugee crisis in the region, as many displaced workers moved into larger towns, including Broome.[29] Subsequently, during the 1980s, a federally sanctioned (and funded) outstations movement facilitated the large-scale movement of many Indigenous peoples in the Kimberley back to small homeland communities where there was limited access to an increasingly urbanised and post-industrial mainstream labour market.

This history has produced a contemporary policy emphasis on the failure of past approaches to Indigenous self-determination, the danger of welfare dependence and the economic costs of servicing small remote Indigenous homeland communities in the region. Yet, such policy discourses operate in a relative vacuum with respect to *contemporary* Indigenous experiences of labour mobility, the decision-making processes that underpin employment-related migration and trajectories, and clear evidence regarding their outcomes.

Contemporary Indigenous FIFO arrangements share some characteristics with historical Indigenous labour mobilities. Like Macassan trade networks, and post-settlement work on pastoral stations in north-west Western Australia, they involve frequent circular mobilities (temporary movements away followed by return), but centre around a strong attachment to, and presence on, customary lands. Further, though the underlying political economy that shapes these labour mobilities has changed significantly over time, FIFO mine labour is globally enmeshed in neoliberal, extractive and externally oriented projects, just as these earlier historical mobilities were.

There are also continuities in Indigenous labour subjectivities. These range from essentialising discourses that characterise Indigenous workers as variously unreliable/lazy, naturally talented or highly malleable,

27   Anthony, 'An Anniversary Shrouded in Myths'.
28   Skyring, 'Low Wages, Low Rents', 157.
29   Skyring, 'Low Wages, Low Rents', 157.

to a narrow fixation on the gap between Indigenous and non-Indigenous population-to-employment ratios, and disproportionate welfare dependence.[30] Historically, such subjectivities and discourses produced an under-appreciation of the vital role that Indigenous peoples played in the advancement of the Australian colony. Today, they can be used to de-contextualise, or resist sustained engagement with, the full range of factors driving lower rates of Indigenous labour force participation.[31] They also obscure the lived experiences of the 46.6 per cent of Indigenous peoples aged 15–64 who *are* engaged in mainstream work.

However, there are also important differences between historical Indigenous labour mobility practices and contemporary Indigenous FIFO arrangements. Chief among these are contemporary legal protections for Indigenous workers in respect of remuneration, working conditions, and discriminatory employer behaviours, that did not exist during the early colonial era. Historically, Indigenous people working in maritime industries and on pastoral stations often did so under highly exploitative, abusive and restrictive conditions. Indeed, some scholars have described them as feudalistic and based on semi-slavery arrangements.[32] In many cases, hardship was endured for a range of reasons. Pastoral station work provided an avenue for remaining on country and engendered respect within and outside of the Indigenous community for the skills developed and applied. Other itinerant work provided a means to avoid poverty and/or travel to different regions. However, as a result of a domestic and global civil rights movement in the 1960s, Indigenous peoples today are recognised as equal citizens under the law with the same worker rights, and remuneration standards, as all other citizens when engaged in mainstream employment.

Another significant, and somewhat paradoxical, difference between historical Indigenous labour mobility and contemporary Indigenous FIFO mine work, which we unpack further below, is sector specific and relates to the unique position that Indigenous employees occupy in the Australian mining sector. They are a sought-after, yet often lower skilled, employee sub-population within the industry in Australia. This unique position emerges from a coalescence of differently scaled time and space phenomena. These include global pressures on mining companies to

---

30   See, for example, Commonwealth of Australia, 'Closing the Gap Prime Minister's Report 2018'.
31   See, for example, Gray, Hunter and Lohoar, 'Increasing Indigenous Employment Rates'.
32   Anthony, 'An Anniversary Shrouded in Myths'; Skyring, 'Low Wages, Low Rents'.

secure a social licence to operate on the local territories of Indigenous groups, and national-level legislation in Australia that requires mining companies to negotiate compensation and benefits for Indigenous peoples when mining activities occur on lands over which those groups have a registered or recognised claim to native title.

These two developments have resulted in aspirations and obligations within the mining industry to advance Indigenous employment outcomes, often through FIFO arrangements, which we discuss further below. Also of critical contextual importance here are ongoing, intergenerational experiences of disadvantage wrought by historical processes of colonisation that often sought to dislocate Indigenous peoples from kin and country, and excluded them from mainstream educational and properly remunerated employment opportunities. The result is that many Indigenous mining employees today occupy lower skilled jobs in the industry and face a unique set of challenges associated with maintaining and advancing their career pathways.

West Australian Indigenous Labour Mobility in Context

Data from the 2016 census show that, excluding intra-metropolitan commuting, 13.3 per cent of Western Australia's Indigenous labour force participants worked in a different local government area (LGA) to the one in which they were usually resident.[33] As Figure 10.1 shows, the most significant flows of this form of work-related mobility were towards the mining-intensive shires of Ashburton, Roebourne, Port Hedland and East Pilbara, indicating the predominance of this industry as a driver of Indigenous labour mobility. Indeed, at the 2016 census, mining was proportionally the largest sector of Indigenous employment in Western Australia, and the proportions had increased over that period.[34] However, as Figure 10.2 shows, this predominance of mining as a sector of Indigenous employment is not mirrored more broadly in Australia or, more specifically, in the Shire of Broome where there are no mine sites.

---

33 This figure is based on the authors' calculations using 2016 Australian Bureau of Statistics Census data to compare Indigenous LGA of work with LGA of usual residence. It is, of course, only one measure of labour mobility and does not capture Indigenous peoples commuting beyond Western Australia for work.

34 Australian Bureau of Statistics, 'Indigenous Employment by Industry, 2016'.

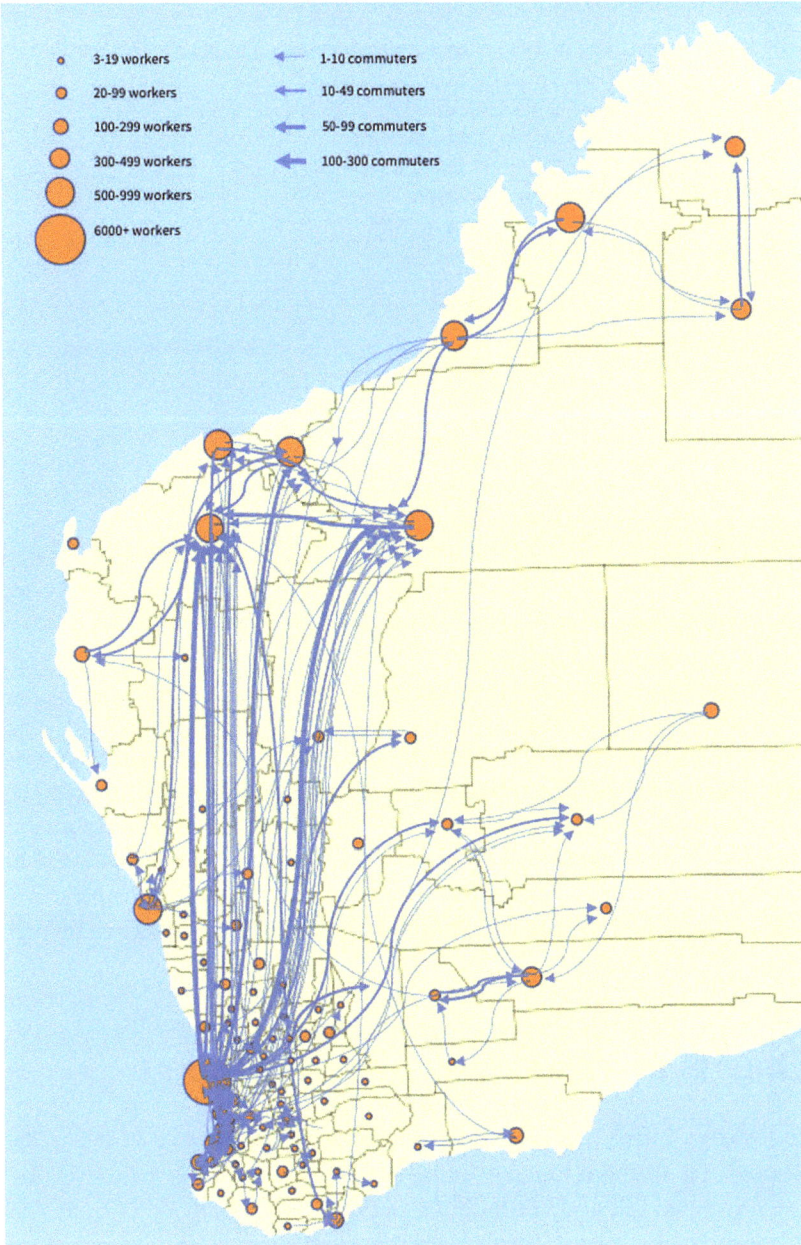

Figure 10.1: Indigenous workforce mobility, 2016.

Note: Arrows and dots are positioned randomly within LGAs on the map to show the flow of movement, not precise locations.

Source: Produced by the authors from 2016 Census data comparing local government area (LGA) of usual residence with place of work LGA.

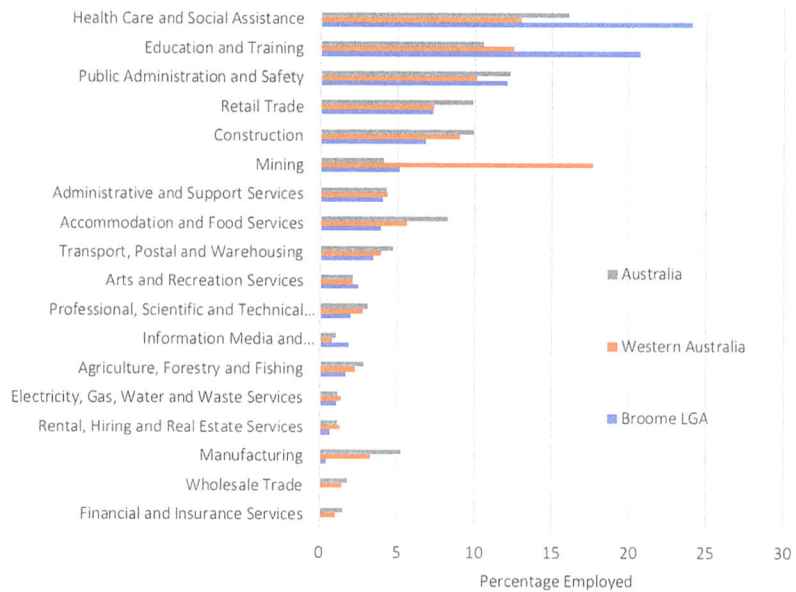

Figure 10.2: Indigenous employment by industry, 2016.
Source: Australian Bureau of Statistics.

Like the rest of Australia, a much higher proportion of Indigenous workers in the Shire of Broome are engaged in the health and education sectors, as well as public administration. This is perhaps partially explained by the fact that Broome is the largest service centre in the Kimberley region and the hub of public and independent health, education and justice services for the entire region. Given that there are no local mining operations within the shire, Indigenous mining employees there are likely to be part of the FIFO workforce.

Origins of Indigenous FIFO in Broome

Indigenous FIFO work is a relatively recent phenomenon in Australia. Though the iron ore industry existed in the country prior to the 1960s, it contributed relatively little to the nation's GDP. After 1976, there was a considerable upsurge in exploration in mining, and this coincided with the introduction of the *Aboriginal Land Rights (Northern Territory) Act 1976*. Cousins and Nieuwenhuysen[35] note that these circumstances

---

35   Cousins and Nieuwenhuysen, *Aboriginals and the Mining Industry*.

began to focus sustained attention on the relationship between Indigenous communities and the extractive industries for, perhaps, the first time. Since then, a large and important scholarly literature has traced the often-fraught relationship between the mining industry and Indigenous peoples rights and interests.[36] Of particular relevance to the present case study is the significant shift that occurred at a national level in respect of the impetus for Indigenous inclusion in the mining workforce following the High Court determination in *Mabo v. Queensland 1992* and the subsequent passage of the national *Native Title Act 1993*.

Though the *Native Title Amendment Act 1998* weakened the provisions of the 1993 Act, these laws require mining companies to negotiate with native title holders and registered claimants, negotiate compensation for loss of native title rights and interests and/or share some benefits with the relevant Indigenous native title group(s).[37] The mining industry was initially antagonistic to the notion of native title,[38] but eventually accepted the obligation to engage with Indigenous peoples.[39] As Langton and Mazel note, mining companies are motivated to 'reach agreement with local traditional Aboriginal owners to avoid costly litigation and delays to exploration and mining projects'.[40]

As these Acts of Parliament began to take effect, resource companies were also facing increasing global pressure to demonstrate a higher standard of ethical engagement with the communities directly affected by their operations. Expensive delays due to local protests and unrest at extraction sites led many mining companies to begin to engage in 'risk mitigation' strategies under the broad banner of 'corporate social responsibility' (CSR). CSR is often couched in terms of companies recognising the 'right

---

36   For example, Altman and Martin, *Power, Culture, Economy*; Weiner and Glaskin, *Customary Land Tenure*; Howitt, Connell and Hirsh, *Resources, Nations*; O'Faircheallaigh, 'Extractive Industries'; Langton, 'The Resource Curse'; Wand and Harvey, 'The Sky Did Not Fall In'.

37   There is significant debate about the effect that native title legislation has had on Indigenous Australians. Some commentators and scholars argue that the effects have been broadly very positive and empowering for Indigenous peoples, providing them with a legitimacy and political voice they previously were not afforded. Others are less convinced. They highlight the deeply colonial premises and processes for claiming and proving the legitimate existence of native title, the grave deficit of resourcing to properly administer native title rights, including negotiation processes with large, multinational mining companies, and the complex local politics of representation and legitimacy that emerge out of the native title process (see Prout Quicke et al., *Aboriginal Assets*, for a recent overview of these concerns).

38   Langton and Mazel, 'Poverty in the Midst of Plenty'.

39   Wand and Harvey, 'The Sky Did Not Fall In'.

40   Langton and Mazel, 'Poverty in the Midst of Plenty', *Poverty in the Midst of Plenty*, 44.

thing to do'; however, as Langton and Mazel,[41] Trebeck,[42] and Harvey[43] explain, this is always envisaged within the context of creating value for shareholders. The new operating paradigm for business, especially publicly listed companies whose practices are more easily scrutinised now than ever before, is profit-making, but within wider prerequisites that satisfy key audiences' perceptions of ethical and responsible corporate behaviours.[44]

In Australia, native title agreement-making processes and CSR imperatives for extractive companies often include Aboriginal employment targets. Resource companies legitimise their 'social licence to operate' by enhancing employment relationships with Aboriginal workers.[45] However, for a number of reasons, these quotas cannot always be fulfilled through local labour. As Haslam McKenzie and Hoath explain, these reasons may relate to reduced employability of local Aboriginal people as a result of the inaccessibility of requisite education and training opportunities; cultural objections to working for extractive industries that 'interfere with country' for which they have spiritual responsibility; a lack of job brokers that strengthen Indigenous linkages with, and within, the mainstream economy; the incompatibility of shift work with cultural obligations; and logistical obstacles such as the lack of a drivers licence.[46] As a result, some companies introduced FIFO operations that target Indigenous peoples living remotely from mine sites to fulfil Indigenous employment quotas or targets.[47]

The Mining Boom and Rio Tinto

The period 2001–14 was characterised by a sustained resources boom in Australia, and Western Australia, as a state endowed with significant mineral deposits, was a major driving force. Over this period, there was a high demand for lower skilled and experienced labour in the mining industry and those industries that service it. Exceptionally strong jobs growth associated with the mining boom progressively and steadily tightened the labour market from 2002. At its lowest point in late 2008, Western Australia's unemployment rate dropped to 2.2 per cent.[48]

41   Langton and Mazel, 'Poverty in the Midst of Plenty'.
42   Trebeck, 'Tools for the Disempowered?'.
43   Harvey, 'Social Development'.
44   Trebeck, 'Tools for the Disempowered?'.
45   Hunter, 'Recent Growth in Indigenous'; Tiplady and Barclay, 'Indigenous Employment'.
46   Haslam McKenzie and Hoath, 'Aboriginal Mine Workers'.
47   Scambary, *My Country, Mine Country*; Taylor and Scambary, 'Indigenous People and the Pilbara'.
48   Australian Bureau of Statistics, 'Unemployment (Cat. 6202)'.

Concentrated extractive operations in the Pilbara region required much larger labour forces than could be supplied from the relatively small local regional populations. FIFO arrangements were intensified to harness larger metropolitan labour markets. In 2006, one transnational mining company, Rio Tinto, pioneered the use of directly flying employees from specific regional Western Australian towns to Pilbara mine sites. Since then, the practice has expanded so that, in 2016, about 16 per cent of the Rio Tinto FIFO workforce commuted directly from a total of eight regional Western Australian centres, including the Shire of Broome, to seven Rio Tinto mining operations in the Pilbara.

The expansion of mining and corporate commitments regarding Aboriginal employment in mining has been instrumental in the increase of Aboriginal employment, especially in remote areas with major mines.[49] From 2001 to 2008, the resources boom saw overall unemployment rates drop dramatically in Western Australia. As Figure 10.3 shows, the trends were similar for both Indigenous and non-Indigenous Western Australians. During the height of the boom, in some remote and very remote areas, and at specific sites, Aboriginal workers accounted for up to 40 per cent of those directly employed or employed through contractors.[50]

However, employment data also show that, while there was a considerable increase in the number of Indigenous people employed in remote mine operations, only a proportion, and often only a small number, of that labour force are local to remote areas.[51] Since filling Indigenous employment quotas from near-mine communities is not always possible, companies can seek to meet their native title Indigenous employment targets, and/or pursue their CSR agendas related to Indigenous employment, by employing Aboriginal people from elsewhere through FIFO arrangements and, specifically, through programs such as Rio Tinto's Regional Workforce Strategy. Aboriginal employees arrive on mine sites after being trained for work in the mining industry through work readiness programs, industry-supported apprenticeships and dedicated training organisations. Increasing Indigenous engagement in *regional* FIFO employment has been a particular focus for Rio Tinto. Today, 23.6 per cent of the company's total Indigenous workforce are from regional towns.

---

49   Hunter, Howlett and Gray, 'The Economic Impact of the Mining Boom'.
50   Australian Bureau of Statistics, 'Labour Force Characteristics'.
51   Australian Bureau of Statistics, 'Labour Force Characteristics'.

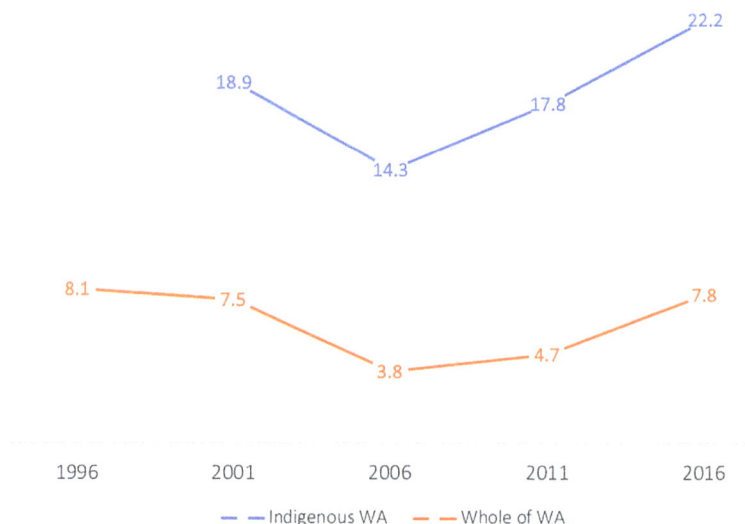

Figure 10.3: Change in unemployment rates, 1996–2016.
Source: Authors' calculations based on 1996–2016 Indigenous Labour Force Status (Usual Residence) census data.

In Broome, 90 per cent of the Rio Tinto FIFO workforce is Indigenous, and usually works two weeks onsite with one week off at home (known as the 2x1 swing) at one of the company's three Pilbara-based mining operations. In the section that follows, we present findings from a 2016 study of Indigenous Rio Tinto FIFO workers and related stakeholders in the Shire of Broome (including the town of Broome and communities along the Dampier Peninsula), which analysed the experience and effects of FIFO work. In total, 32 participants engaged in interviews or focus groups regarding their experiences, interests and concerns with respect to Rio Tinto's FIFO operations out of Broome.

Experiences of Indigenous FIFO Workers in Broome

Historically, mobile Indigenous labourers in Australia experienced financial expropriation and exploitative/abusive working conditions as a matter of course. Such practices were justified, normalised or simply overlooked as frontier development rested on the discourse of Social Darwinism and an absence of legal protections for Indigenous workers. While capitalist accumulation strategies certainly undergird contemporary employee labour mobility practices in the mining sector in Australia, financial expropriation for Indigenous FIFO workers is today comparatively limited. It is a highly formalised, highly regulated and highly paid sector. In Broome, a respected local Indigenous Rio Tinto employee oversees all recruitment, training and ongoing community relations activities for Indigenous employees. Employees and their families identified her as their 'go-to' person for dealing with a range of concerns and problems. They explained that they were comfortable talking to her because 'she is one of us, she understands'.

In addition to managing and funding most recruitment and community relations work internally, Rio Tinto also developed and supports a range of training and skill development programs for prospective employees, as well as mentoring work-ready and apprenticeship employment pathways for local people. Rio Tinto bears most of the cost associated with employment-brokering processes.

Many participants described employment with Rio Tinto as highly sought after by local Aboriginal people in Broome. This favourable disposition is likely, in some measure, a product of the fact that the company's operational 'footprint' in the Shire of Broome is only positive. There are no active mines in the region that have the potential to cause damage to country or produce negative externalities and serious social costs, such as have been experienced in the Pilbara. In Broome, the company financially supports a range of local community initiatives and events. It is also likely due, in some measure, to the company's attempts over several decades to build stronger relationships with local Indigenous communities in the Kimberley through strategic investments and training and employment programs. Employees and their families also described a range of financial and social 'status' benefits associated with working for Rio Tinto. Some noted that working for a large multinational company that has a strong safety record, and a reputation for looking after its employees with high salaries, comfortable accommodation and good industrial conditions, was viewed as a pinnacle employment opportunity. Representatives from training organisations explained that trainees wearing a Rio Tinto high-visibility shirt 'walked taller wearing it'. Aboriginal corporations and other local organisations viewed Rio Tinto employees as potential role models and future mentors for others in the community because they had been well trained and are respected by others in the community.

Further, many research participants claimed that the multicultural history and heritage of long-term Broome residents, and the coexistence of Indigenous cultural practice with mainstream education and employment, has fostered positive attitudes towards mainstream work. A number of interviewees claimed that the influence of mission teaching and the interaction between many cultures, both in the workplace and socially, has produced a strong and enduring work ethic, valuing of reliable work and culture of worker reliability among the multicultural Broome population.

Nevertheless, the fracturing legacies of colonisation are also still evident throughout the Shire of Broome and contribute to certain forms of economic precarity and challenging working conditions that underpin Indigenous FIFO work. Historical experiences of segregation and workplace brutality have promulgated intergenerational disadvantage in Broome. The prevalence of neoliberalism as the prevailing ideology for policy development over the last 30 years has also resulted in the steady withdrawal and rationalisation of numerous government programs that service remote communities across the Kimberley. Broome has consequently become home, if temporarily, to a range of Indigenous people from across the region who have experienced multiple forms of disadvantage and/or disturbance. This includes those that require access to justice, counselling and health services, those dislocated from their customary homelands, and those experiencing conflict within their homeland communities.[52] A lack of suitable accommodation creates additional layers of complexity and hardship, creating opportunities for increased conflict and antisocial behaviour. By comparison to the non-Aboriginal population, health and wellbeing indicators are persistently low. While the physical beauty of Broome and the Kimberley can be mesmerising, there is an undercurrent of disadvantage for many Indigenous people.

The intergenerational effects of living in this (post)colonial landscape mean that many Indigenous people in the region have experienced greater challenges in accessing mainstream education and employment markets. Unsurprisingly then, both in the Shire of Broome and in Western Australia more generally, Indigenous mining employees tend to occupy lower skilled positions within the industry. As Figure 10.4 shows, at the 2016 census, the overwhelming majority of Indigenous mining employees were either machinery operators, drivers, technicians or trade workers and labourers.

52   Prout, 'Urban Myths'.

Less than 10 per cent of the overall Western Australian Indigenous mining workforce were professionals and managers. This profile mirrors that of the Indigenous FIFO workers who participated in the study—most were machinery operators and drivers or mechanics—and also mirrors earlier research findings from Scambary.[53]

While very few jobs in the mining industry could be described as unskilled, and while all of the participants in the study had either undergone a rigorous training program or had prior employment experience in requisite roles, many participants identified a high degree of uncertainty regarding the security of their jobs. As actors in an extractive company operating in a volatile global commodities market, employees of Rio Tinto, and the communities in which it invests, are also subject to a degree of volatility and precarity. For Indigenous FIFO workers, it is the precarity of employment instability in a sector that is both highly sensitive to global market demand and rapidly embracing automation technologies that eliminate the need for lower skilled workers.

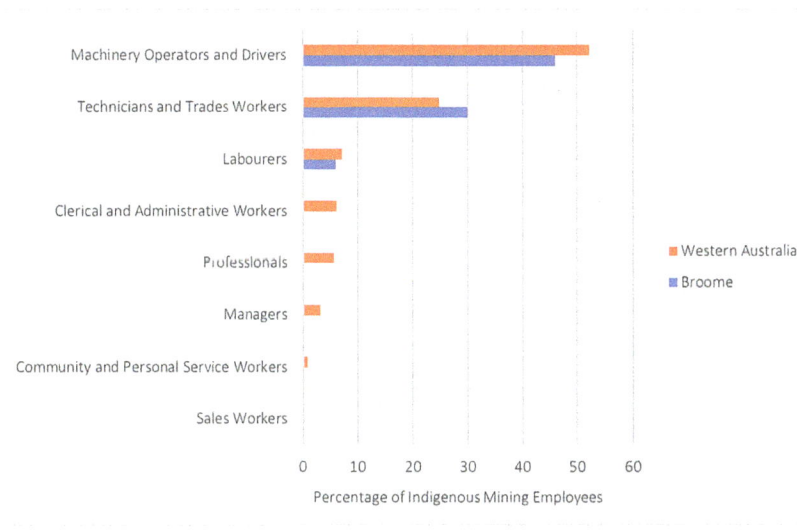

Figure 10.4: Indigenous occupations within the Western Australian mining sector, 2016.
Source: Australian Bureau of Statistics, 'Indigenous Occupations'.

---

53   Scambary, *My Country, Mine Country.*

Numerous participants identified a perception that the pathways to career progression with Rio Tinto were difficult to access. 'The purple circle' has been a recurring theme in research regarding the socio-economic effects of FIFO in regional Western Australia[54] and some participants in the Broome study described a similar phenomenon, in which supervisors used a variety of interpersonal skills and prohibition of opportunities to sideline employees who were viewed to be recalcitrant. These included withholding information, favouritism regarding shifts and rosters, and denying opportunities for promotion and learning new machines. Some Broome-based employees commented on the perceived tolerance of unfair practices, though they did not explicitly attribute these to institutionalised racism or a systemic neo-colonial orientation within the company. Nevertheless, due to their disproportionate occupation of lower skilled jobs with the company, Indigenous employees can be disproportionately affected by these practices when they occur.

Many participants felt vulnerable to automation and redundancy during the period of downturn that has characterised the post-2014 resources sector in Western Australia, and this has inhibited their ability to plan for their futures. For example, those who start their employment term in public housing quickly find their salary moving them above the eligibility threshold to remain tenants of the state. When this occurs, they must find new housing arrangements. However, housing costs in Broome are extraordinarily high and there is a limited private housing market. Further, Indigenous peoples often face discrimination within the housing market. Where employees have secured housing in the private market, the risk of redundancy increases their vulnerability to housing cost pressures. Public housing waiting lists are long and, in small communities within the shire, alternative housing is not easily attained and household crowding is a common problem. This uncertainty can extend to other avenues of expenditure and investment and work against long-term planning. Will school fees become unaffordable? Can the vehicle finance continue to be serviced? While many of these uncertainties are common to mining employees regardless of their Indigenous status, discrimination and cultural attachments to country and kin can add additional layers

---

54   Haslam McKenzie, 'Are There Enduring'; Davies, Maru and May, 'Enduring Community Value'; Heiler and Pickersgill, 'Shiftwork and Rostering Arrangements'.

of complexity to answering these kinds of questions for Indigenous FIFO employees. They may feel less able or inclined to simply relocate to larger job markets in search of alternative employment.[55]

Other significant onsite challenges associated with FIFO work were also identified.[56] Some of these are common to all FIFO workers and some are unique to Indigenous workers. Rostered FIFO swings on long shifts (usually 12 hours) in male-dominated mining camps located in remote areas with arid climates are exacting for all workers. Indigenous employees and their families interviewed in this study had differing perspectives on what kind of roster rotation they felt best served their circumstances. However, all described it as physically, emotionally and mentally challenging. While most employees interviewed believed they had been adequately prepared for the mine site, all agreed that nothing can prepare an employee for 12-hour shifts, the number of unknown people or the scale of the mine site. The training programs, they indicated, did not adequately prepare for fatigue management.

Rio Tinto has argued that fierce competition for labour within the industry has generated vastly improved camp conditions for employees and generous remunerations packages, and that longer shifts allow employees more time at home with their families at the end of their intensive swings.[57] While market competition may have produced some improvements in conditions for workers, the make-up of swings, shift lengths and mine site worker conditions all remain the purview of the company, and many employees who participated in the study described the levels of mental, physical and emotional fatigue associated with these arrangements as acute.

A second key challenge at the employee–employer interface that Indigenous workers identified related to managing and maintaining their cultural obligations while in the employment of a multinational mineral extraction company. For most, these challenges manifest in respect of obligations to their home communities. Compassionate leave and cultural leave were important for meeting bereavement and ceremonial obligations. Indigenous employees appreciated that this was accepted as

---

55   Hunter, Howlett and Gray, 'The Economic Impact of the Mining Boom'; Haslam McKenzie and Hoath, 'Aboriginal Mine Workers'.
56   In this chapter, we focus in particular on the employee/employer interface, though we note that a range of off-site challenges associated with social reproduction were also raised.
57   Rio Tinto, 'Submission to the House of Representatives'.

legitimate leave. However, many considered three days per year inadequate, especially as flights in and out of Broome were not likely to coincide with the times of bereavement, meaning that employees must take additional time as annual or unpaid leave. Further, employees noted that family members did not always understand that company policy cannot be bent or changed for individuals, which sometimes caused heightened tension within families already dealing with loss and associated trauma.

Some participants described a level of cultural distress related to being involved in extractive activities on the customary homelands of other Indigenous peoples. Disturbing the ground is an activity considered particularly culturally sensitive within Indigenous relational ontologies that encompass country. Where employees reported related concerns, Aboriginal support officers (ASO) and mentors onsite played a critical role. Several interviewees recounted an experience in which Aboriginal employees regularly saw a spirit person and felt a negative spiritual presence. The ASO helped to explain the situation to the company and organised a smoking ceremony. The company was reported to have taken these concerns very seriously and senior management supported the necessary cultural protocols to appropriately respond. Other interviewees described the significance of smoking ceremonies onsite and the role of ASOs in not only organising them, but also communicating the importance of these rituals to others in the company.

Conclusion

We commenced with the assertion that Indigenous labour mobility has received marginal (at best) scholarly attention in Australia. It has been under-examined and under-theorised by economists, geographers and other social scientists. This study begins the process of exploring the costs and benefits associated with one type of work-related mobility for Indigenous people. The empirical findings presented highlight the uniqueness of Indigenous FIFO work as a form of Indigenous labour mobility within Australian history. It is distinct from the precarious and often-exploitative unskilled labour mobilities characteristic of much labour mobility in the early colonial period. Indigenous employment in this case study is politically important to Rio Tinto and, therefore, labour mobility is intentionally facilitated, and paid for, by the company. Indigenous mainstream labourers now have protections under Australia's legal code, unlike many international labour migrants.

However, Indigenous FIFO work is inextricably linked to the coloniality of power in at least two key ways. First, this kind of labour is politically important to resource companies not just because of their need, and even desire, to secure a social licence to operate, but also because of a legal apparatus in Australia—the native title system—that requires companies to negotiate compensation and benefits, such as employment opportunities, with native title groups. However, the native title system is a function of Crown law, and requires Indigenous peoples to represent themselves in ways that are legible to the settler state, while, at the same time, proving cultural distinctiveness. Even when such proofs have been accepted by the Crown, the very reality of FIFO work is evidence that agreement-making processes are not always able to secure employment benefits for the native title groups with whom such agreements are made. Second, evidence suggests that many FIFO workers are lower skilled employees who are most vulnerable to increases in technological automation and fluctuations in global commodity prices. Arguably, a large part of the reason for this is that Indigenous Australians tend to have lower levels of educational attainment and higher levels of overall disadvantage. Such circumstances link directly to colonial processes of dislocation, marginalisation and exclusion.

Bibliography

Altman, Jon. 'Indigenous Policy: Canberra Consensus on the Neoliberal Project of Improvement'. In *Australian Public Policy: Progressive Ideas in the Neoliberal Ascendency*, edited by L. Orchard and C. Miller, 115–32. Bristol: Policy Press, 2014. doi.org/10.2307/j.ctt1ggjk39.13.

——. 'What Future for Remote Indigenous Australia? Economic Hybridity and the Neoliberal Turn'. In *Culture Crisis: Anthropology and Politics in Aboriginal Australia*, edited by J. Altman and M. Hinkson, 259–80. Sydney: UNSW Press, 2010.

Altman, Jon and D Martin, eds. *Power, Culture, Economy: Indigenous Australia and Mining*. CAEPR Research Monograph No. 30. Canberra: ANU E Press, 2009. doi.org/10.22459/CAEPR30.08.2009.

Anthony, T. 'An Anniversary Shrouded in Myths'. *Analysis & Policy Observatory*, 22 August 2006, apo.org.au/node/5924.

Australian Bureau of Statistics. 'Indigenous Employment by Industry, 2016'. Canberra: Australian Bureau of Statistics, Tablebuilder, 2017.

———. 'Indigenous Occupations – Broome and Whole of WA, 2016'. Canberra: Australian Bureau of Statistics, Tablebuilder, 2017.

———. 'Labour Force Characteristics of Aboriginal and Torres Strait Islander Australians, Estimates from the Labour Force Survey 2011'. Canberra: Australian Bureau of Statistics, 2012.

———. 'Unemployment (Cat. 6202)'. Canberra: Australian Bureau of Statistics, 2009.

Biddle, N. 'Indigenous Migration and the Labour Market: A Cautionary Tale'. *Australian Journal of Labour Economics* 13, no. 3 (2010): 313–30.

———. 'Proximity to Labour Markets: Revisiting Indigenous Employment through an Analysis of Census Place of Work Data'. *Australian Journal of Labour Economics* 13, no. 2 (2010): 75–89.

Blunt, A. 'Cultural Geographies of Migration: Mobility, Transnationality and Diaspora'. *Progress in Human Geography* 31, no. 5 (2007): 684–94. doi.org/10.1177/0309132507078945.

Bolton, G. 'Alexander Forrest's Expedition 1879 and Early Development of the Cattle Industry'. In *Kimberley History: People, Exploration and Development*, edited by C. Clement, J. Gresham and H. McGlashan, 101–10. Perth: Kimberley Society, 2012.

Buckley, M., S. McPhee and B. Rogaly. 'Labour Geographies on the Move: Migration, Migrant Status and Work in the 21st Century'. *Geoforum* 78 (2017): 153–58. doi.org/10.1016/j.geoforum.2016.09.012.

Choo, C. 'Mixed Blessings: Establishment of Christian Missions in the Kimberley'. In *Kimberley History: People, Exploration and Development*, edited by C. Clement, J. Gresham and H. McGlashan, 195–214. Perth: Kimberley Society, 2012.

Commonwealth of Australia. 'Closing the Gap Prime Minister's Report 2018'. Canberra: Commonwealth of Australia, 2018.

Cousins, D. and J. Nieuwenhuysen. *Aboriginals and the Mining Industry*. Sydney: Allen and Unwin, 1984.

Cresswell, Tim, Sara Dorow and Sharon Roseman. 'Putting Mobility Theory to Work: Conceptualizing Employment-Related Geographical Mobility'. *Environment and Planning A: Economy and Space* 48, no. 9 (2016): 1787–803. doi.org/10.1177/0308518X16649184.

Curchin, K. 'Interrogating the Hybrid Economy Approach to Indigenous Development'. *Australian Journal of Social Issues* 48, no. 1 (2013): 15–34. doi.org/10.1002/j.1839-4655.2013.tb00269.x.

———. 'Two Visions of Indigenous Economic Development and Cultural Survival: The "Real Economy" and the "Hybrid Economy"'. *Australian Journal of Political Science* 50, no. 3 (2015): 412–26. doi.org/10.1080/10361146. 2015.1049976.

Davies, J., Y. Maru and T. May. 'Enduring Community Value from Mining: Conceptual Framework'. In *CRC-REP Working Paper CW007*. Alice Springs: Ninti One Limited, 2012.

Dockery, M. 'A Wellbeing Approach to Mobility and Its Application to Aboriginal and Torres Strait Islander Australians'. *Social Indicators Research* 125, no. 1 (2016): 243–55. doi.org/10.1007/s11205-014-0839-8.

Gray, M., B. Hunter and S. Lohoar. 'Increasing Indigenous Employment Rates: Issues Paper No 3'. In *Closing the Gap Clearinghouse*, edited by Australian Institute of Health and Welfare. Canberra: Commonwealth of Australia, 2012.

Hart, A., K. Travaille, R. Jones, S. Brand-Gardner, F. Webster, A. Irving and A. Harry. 'Western Australian Silver-Lipped Pearl Oyster (Pinctada Maxima) Industry'. In *Western Australian Marine Stewardship Council Report Series No. 5*. Perth: Government of Western Australia Department of Fisheries, 2016.

Harvey, Bruce. 'Social Development Will Not Deliver Social Licence to Operate for the Extractive Sector'. *The Extractive Industries and Society* 1, no. 1 (2014): 7–11. doi.org/10.1016/j.exis.2013.11.001.

Haslam McKenzie, F. 'Are There Enduring Community Values from Mining for Aboriginal People in the Pilbara?'. *Journal of Australian Indigenous Issues* 17, (2014): 91–107.

Haslam McKenzie, F. and A. Hoath. 'Aboriginal Mine Workers: Opportunities and Challenges of Long Distance Commuting'. In *Labour Force Mobility in the Australian Resources Industry: Socio-Economic and Regional Impacts*, edited by F. Haslam McKenzie, 157–70. Singapore: Springer, 2016. doi.org/10.1007/978-981-10-2018-6_9.

Heiler, K. and R. Pickersgill. 'Shiftwork and Rostering Arrangements in the Australian Mining Industry: An Overview of Key Trends'. *Australian Bulletin of Labour* 27, no. 1 (2001): 20–42.

Howitt, R., J. Connell and P. Hirsh, eds. *Resources, Nations and Indigenous Peoples*. Melbourne: Oxford University Press, 1996.

Hunter, B. 'Recent Growth in Indigenous Self-Employed and Entrepreneurs'. In *CAEPR Working Paper No. 91*. Centre for Aboriginal Economic Policy Research, The Australian National University, 2013.

Hunter, B., M. Howlett and M. Gray. 'The Economic Impact of the Mining Boom on Indigenous and Non-Indigenous Australians'. In *CAEPR Working Paper No. 93*. Canberra: Centre for Aboriginal Economic Policy Research, The Australian National University, 2014.

Keen, I. 'Introduction'. In *Indigenous Participation in Australian Economies: Historical and Anthropological Perspectives*, edited by I. Keen, 1–23. Canberra: ANU E Press, 2010. doi.org/10.22459/IPAE.12.2010.01.

Kelly, S. *Proud Heritage*. Broome: Kimbooks Publishing, 1999.

King, Russell. 'Geography and Migration Studies: Retrospect and Prospect'. *Population, Space and Place* 18, no. 2 (2012): 134–53. doi.org/10.1002/psp.685.

Langton, M. 'The Resource Curse'. In *The Griffith Review* 28, griffithreview.com/articles/the-resource-curse/.

Langton, M. and O Mazel. 'Poverty in the Midst of Plenty: Aboriginal People, the 'Resource Curse' and Australia's Mining Boom'. *Journal of Energy & Natural Resources Law* 26, no. 1 (2015): 31–65. doi.org/10.1080/0264681 1.2008.11435177.

Lockyer, B. *Last Truck Out*. Broome: Magabala Books, 2009.

Lydon, J. 'Picturing Macassan-Australian Histories'. In *Indigenous Networks: Mobility, Connections and Exchange*, edited by Jane Carey and Jane Lydon, 140–66. Hoboken: Routledge, 2014. doi.org/10.4324/9781315766065-7.

McDowell, L. 'The Lives of Others: Body Work, the Production of Difference, and Labour Geographies'. *Economic Geography* 91, no. 1 (2015): 1–23. doi.org/10.1111/ecge.12070.

Musharbash, Y. *Yuendumu Everyday: Contemporary Life in Remote Aboriginal Australia*. Canberra: Aboriginal Studies Press, 2008.

O'Faircheallaigh, C. 'Extractive Industries and Indigenous Peoples: A Changing Dynamic?'. *Journal of Rural Studies* 30, (2013): 20–30. doi.org/10.1016/j.jrurstud.2012.11.003.

Preibisch, K. 'Pick-Your-Own Labour: Migrant Workers and Flexibility in Canadian Agriculture'. *International Migration Review* 44, no. 2 (2010): 404–41. doi.org/10.1111/j.1747-7379.2010.00811.x.

Productivity Commission. *Geographic Labour Mobility*. Canberra: Commonwealth of Australia Productivity Commission, 2014.

Prout, S. 'Interrogating the Image of the Wondering Nomad'. In *Aboriginal Populations: Social, Demographic, and Epidemiological Perspectives*, edited by F. Trovato and A. Romanuik, 381–414. Edmonton: University of Alberta Press, 2014.

——. 'Urban Myths: Exploring the Unsettling Nature of Aboriginal Presence in and through a Regional Australian Town'. *Urban Policy and Research* 29, no. 3 (2011): 275–91. doi.org/10.1080/08111146.2011.578300.

Prout, S. and R. Howitt. 'Frontier Imaginings and Subversive Indigenous Spatialities'. *Journal of Rural Studies* 25, (2009): 396–403. doi.org/10.1016/j.jrurstud.2009.05.006.

Prout Quicke, S. M. Dockery and A. Hoath. *Aboriginal Assets: The Impact of Major Mining Agreements Associated with Native Title in Western Australia*. Curtin University and the University of Western Australia, 2017.

Redmond, A. 'Tracking Wurnan: Transformations in the Trade and Exchange of Resources in the Northern Kimberley'. In *Indigenous Participation in Australian Economies II: Historical and Anthropological Perspectives*, edited by I. Keen, 57–72. Canberra: ANU E Press, 2012. doi.org/10.22459/IPAE.07.2012.03.

Redmond, A. and F. Skyring. 'Exchange and Appropriation: The Wurnan Economy and Aboriginal Land and Labour at Karunjie Station, North-Western Australia'. In *Indigenous Participation in Australian Economies: Historical and Anthropological Perspectives*, edited by I. Keen, 73–90. Canberra: ANU E Press, 2010. doi.org/10.22459/IPAE.12.2010.05.

Rio Tinto. 'Submission to the House of Representatives Standing Committee on Regional Australia'. In *Inquiry into the Use of Fly-In Fly-Out (FIFO) and Drive-In Drive-Out (DIDO) Work Practices in Regional Australia*. Canberra: Parliament of Australia, 2011.

Roseman, S., P. Barber and B. Neis. 'Towards a Feminist Political Economy Framework for Analyzing Employment-Related Geographical Mobility'. *Studies in Political Economy* 95, no. 1 (2016): 175–203. doi.org/10.1080/19187033.2015.11674951.

Russell, L. '"The Singular Transcultural Space": Networks of Ships, Mariners, Voyagers and "Native" Men at Sea, 1790–1870'. In *Indigenous Networks: Mobility, Connections and Exchange*, edited by Jane Carey and Jane Lydon, 97–113. Hoboken: Routledge, 2014. doi.org/10.4324/9781315766065-5.

Scambary, B. *My Country, Mine Country: Indigenous Peoples, Mining and Development Contestation in Remote Australia*. CAEPR Monograph No. 33, Canberra: ANU Press, 2013. doi.org/10.22459/CAEPR33.05.2013.

Sheller, M. and J. Urry. 'The New Mobilities Paradigm'. *Environment and Planning A* 38, (2006): 207–26. doi.org/10.1068/a37268.

Silvey, R. 'Power, Difference and Mobility: Feminist Advances in Migration Studies'. *Progress in Human Geography* 28, no. 4 (2004): 490–506. doi.org/10.1191/0309132504ph490oa.

Skyring, F. 'Low Wages, Low Rents, and Pension Cheques: The Introduction of Equal Wages in the Kimberley, 1968-1969'. In *Indigenous Participation in Australian Economies II: Historical Engagements and Current Enterprises*, edited by N. Fijn, I. Keen, C. Llyod and M. Pickering, 153–69. Canberra: ANU E Press, 2012. doi.org/10.22459/IPAE.07.2012.08.

Stevens, F. *Aborigines in the Northern Territory Cattle Industry.* Canberra: Australian Nationa University Press, 1974.

Taylor, J. and M. Bell, eds. *Population Mobility and Indigenous Peoples in Australasia and North America*. London: Routledge, 2004.

Taylor, J. and B. Scambary. 'Indigenous People and the Pilbara Mining Boom: A Baseline for Regional Participation'. In *Research Monograph No. 25*. Canberra: Centre for Aboriginal Economic Policy Research, The Australian National University, 2005.

Taylor, J. 'Population and Diversity: Policy Implications of Emerging Indigenous Demographic Trends'. Canberra: Centre for Aboriginal Economic Policy Research, The Australian National University, 2006.

Tiplady, J. and M. Barclay. 'Indigenous Employment in the Australian Minerals Industry'. St Lucia: Centre for Responsible Mining, University of Queensland, 2007.

Trebeck, K. 'Tools for the Disempowered? Indigenous Leverage over Mining Companies'. *Australian Journal of Political Science* 42, no. 4 (2007): 541–62. doi.org/10.1080/10361140701513604.

Wand, P. and B. Harvey. 'The Sky Did Not Fall In? Rio Tinto after Mabo'. In *The Limits of Change: Mabo and Native Title 20 Years On*, edited by T. Bauman and L. Glick, 289–309. Canberra: Australian Institute for Aboriginal and Torres Strait Islander Studies Press, 2012.

Weiner, J. and K. Glaskin, eds. *Customary Land Tenure and Registration in Australia and Papua New Guinea: Anthropological Perspectives*. Canberra: ANU E Press, 2007.

11

Mysterious Motions: A Genealogy of 'Orbiting' in Australian Indigenous Affairs

Timothy Neale

There are several signs that we are between distinct periods in federal policy in relation to Aboriginal and Torres Strait Islander peoples in Australia. Following its emergence in 2015, the first and second Turnbull administrations demonstrated an acute case of policy *aporia*, lacking direction or vision in relation to Indigenous policy. Faced with the Uluru Statement from the Heart in May 2017—the outcome of deliberations by over 250 Aboriginal and Torres Strait Islander representatives from across Australia—the Turnbull Government rejected its modest plans as 'too ambitious'.[1] This included the proposal for an elected 'First Nations Voice' that would act as an advisory body with far less institutional power than its predecessors, such as the Aboriginal and Torres Strait Islander Commission (ATSIC) abolished by the Howard Government in April 2004. Since the Uluru Statement, the various federal policy processes built around a proposed referendum on the constitutional recognition of Indigenous peoples have come to a grinding halt. The 'Recognise' advocacy body established to foster public support for such a referendum was quietly folded after receiving $25 million in federal funding over

---

1   McKenna, *Moment of Truth*; Calla Wahlquist, 'Turnbull's Uluru Statement Rejection Is "Mean-Spirited Bastardry" – Legal Expert', *The Guardian*, 26 October 2017, www.theguardian.com/australia-news/2017/oct/26/turnbulls-uluru-statement-rejection-mean-spirited-bastardry-legal-expert.

four years.[2] Subsequently, in 2018, the Turnbull Government announced a 'refresh' of the Closing the Gap strategy, which sought to improve the lives of Indigenous peoples by focusing upon quantifiable quality of life measures such as life expectancy and school completions. This was the first indication of a potential move away from a policy approach that has enjoyed bipartisan favour since its initiation in 2008.

Another sign of a possible epochal shift is the recent downturn in the political fortunes of individuals I have described elsewhere as 'executive advocates'.[3] These are people who, subsequent to the dissolution of ATSIC, sought to 'navigate the space between the settler state and specific Indigenous communities and regions' by acting as de facto representatives in federal and state politics. As policy consultants, media personalities and business executives, these individuals have endeavoured to 'make Indigeneity and Indigenous peoples legible' to government while themselves remaining separate from government institutions, 'discursively fluid, and sometimes conceptually contrary'. This 'advocate' finds its archetype in the lawyer and policy consultant Noel Pearson. Subsequent to his rise to national prominence during the tense negotiations over native title legislation in the early 1990s, Pearson became a major voice in policy debates during the early 2000s on the basis of his bold assertions about Indigenous peoples' 'right to take responsibility' for their socio-economic situation.[4] Funding and widespread political favour followed in the next decade, to the point that it was quite reasonable to state, in 2011, that he was 'undoubtedly the most influential person in Indigenous policy making in Australia today'.[5] However, like other advocates who rose to prominence during the same period (e.g. Warren Mundine, Marcia Langton and Bess Price), Pearson has recently been sidelined from the federal and state policy circles that once supported him. This culminated in Pearson's (2017) public declaration that he had been cruelly 'betrayed' by the conservative politicians with whom he had been previously been allied.[6]

---

2   Latimore, 'Jumping the Gate'.
3   Neale, *Wild Articulations.*
4   See Pearson, *Up from the Mission.*
5   Altman, 'Noel Pearson's Policies'.
6   Pearson, 'Betrayal'.

This is not to suggest, in any way, that Pearson and other similar executive advocates will not find equal political favour again. Rather, as part of broader consideration of shifts in Australian Indigenous policy,[7] this seems an apt time to reconsider the cultural and political influence of executive advocates, such as Pearson, who became nationally prominent over the past two decades.[8] In this chapter, I would like to contribute to such a review by giving a brief genealogy of Pearson's concept of 'orbiting', revisiting its practical instantiations, discursive framing in news media, international parallels and academic reception. As I explain, Pearson's proposal that remote-living Indigenous peoples should 'orbit' in and out of their remote communities presents many conceptual issues, and there is little empirical evidence to suggest Indigenous peoples have followed his advice. What is important to understand, I argue, is how the celebration of the 'orbiting' idea in news media and policymaking has helped sediment certain precepts or assumptions into Australian political discourse about Indigenous peoples, their communities and their futures.

What is Pearsonian Orbiting?

As anthropologist Paul Burke states, Pearson's idea of orbiting 'could be minimally defined as an alternative to irreversible migration to urban centres':

> [It] encourages Aboriginal people in remote settlements to take up distant educational and employment opportunities, but with the expectation of return to the home settlements for culturally significant events.[9]

In other words, the capacities of remote Indigenous communities are best grown by encouraging individuals with significant future earning potential to leave them because, avowedly, they may then return at some point. While, as Burke notes, 'the concept has never been fully developed in easily accessible documentation', it is nonetheless worth surveying the thin explanations of this influential concept. An early version appears in a speech Pearson delivered in 2000, later published in his collective writings, in which he posed his problem as 'the social and economic incorporation'

---

7   For example, Altman, 'In the Name of the Market?'; Maddison, Clark and de Costa, *The Limits;* Strakosch, *Neoliberal Indigenous Policy.*

8   See also Klein, 'The Curious Case'; Watt, 'Debating Decentralisation'.

9   Burke, 'Indigenous Diaspora'.

of 'the most marginalised underclass in Australian society'.[10] The answer, Pearson stated, was that 'we have to get educated', which would occur by sending Aboriginal children in remote regions 'into orbits into the wider world' and their mainstream educational institutions. These children would become 'completely bicultural' and periodically 'come back to their home base' in remote communities, enriching those communities with the skills, resources and financial capital acquired elsewhere. It was entirely possible, Pearson insisted, for Aboriginal people to maintain 'our culture' and connection to 'home' after being embedded in and enculturated by the (white) sites of late capitalism. Thinking in opposition, Pearson was arguing against the possibility that the integration of Aboriginal people raised in Aboriginal-majority communities into the lifestyles and practices of cities—'Perth or New York or Singapore'—would negatively affect them in any way or make them reluctant to return to their places of birth. It would be transformative, but only in benevolent ways that did not taint the individual's 'cultural' core.

As I have discussed elsewhere, the first decade of the new millennia was a period in which Pearson built a political and organisational empire in Australia.[11] He established Cape York Partnerships (CYP) in 2000, which then became the coordinating agency for a range of other companies delivering a spectrum of social services independently and in collaboration with government departments. In the following years, these networks implemented disciplinary measures such as alcohol restrictions and welfare quarantining in a range of Cape York communities, all couched in the language of 'grassroots change', alongside capacity-building programs in bicultural schooling, parenting skills, financial management, home improvement and much more. Recalling this period, Pearson later remembered how he had been guided by the contention that 'under no scenario were any of these communities viable without a significant proportion hitting the road in search of jobs'.[12] By the close of 2011, $100 million in state and federal government funds had been spent on four communities targeted by most of these programs—Hopevale, Aurukun, Mossman Gorge and Coen—amounting to over $36,000 per Indigenous resident. In 2010, one of the Pearson-led companies began administering schools in three of these communities before, in 2012, taking over the management of a secondary school named Djarragun College near

---

10   See Pearson, *Up from the Mission*.
11   Neale, 'Staircases, Pyramids'; Neale, *Wild Articulations*.
12   Pearson, 'Remote Control'.

the city of Cairns. These attempts at educational administration received significant criticism in the years that followed due to their use of an expensive United States literacy program, highly publicised outbreaks of violence and the 'inconclusive' results of government audits.[13] In November 2016, after complaints by community members and threats by state government overseers to void these administration contracts, Pearson's company forfeited the management of the Aurukun school.

Through this period, Pearson and his allies continued to propagate the 'orbiting' concept without clarifying it.[14] Pearson frequently appeared in the nation's newspapers insisting that remote Indigenous communities 'cannot be parochial', lambasting politicians who doubted his vision and proclaiming his belief 'in the need for mobility for Cape York Peninsula youngsters'.[15] Young people must 'have the confidence and capacity to orbit between two worlds and enjoy the best of both'.[16] Yet, what of the practical measures? One early CYP trial program, documented in a series of unpublished papers, involved temporarily placing an unknown number of Indigenous youth offenders with Indigenous families in distant towns and cities. These 'young people who need to be removed from their environment' were avowedly an instance of 'orbiting',[17] as was the group of 16–25 year olds that CYP transported over 3,000 kilometres to south-eastern Australia to pick fruit for three months, 'well away from distractions and interference of families'.[18] The latter received significant media attention, with journalists eager to celebrate how seasonal labour 'offers [these young men] the chance to build a life' and 'an introduction (in some cases a rude one) to the individualism and competition that underpin the prosperity of mainstream Australia';[19] they were 'valuing money because they had earned it, and not had it handed to them'.[20]

13   Joshua Robertson, 'Noel Pearson Under Fire from All Sides over Aurukun School Experiment', *The Guardian*, 7 July 2016, www.theguardian.com/australia-news/2016/jul/07/noel-pearson-under-fire-from-all-sides-over-aurukun-school-experiment; Leisa Scott, 'What's Being Done to Save Cape York's Troubled Communities?', *The Courier-Mail* (Brisbane), 20 July 2016; Jamie Walker, 'Noel Pearson Teaching Model to Get $22m', *The Australian*, 1 July 2014.
14   For example, Ah Mat, 'The Moral Case'; Pearson, 'Man Cannot Live'.
15   Noel Pearson, 'Labor's Ideas Mature', *The Australian*, 9 December 2006, www.theaustralian.com.au/opinion/noel-pearson-labors-ideas-mature/news-story/b39be24b54b5bf90f4e1cbbe391b0cd1.
16   Tony Koch, 'Out on a Limb', *The Weekend Australian*, 20 November 2004, magazine section, 23.
17   James, 'Petrol Sniffing'.
18   James, 'A Report on the Trial'.
19   Michael Duffy, 'The Welfare Trap That Denies the Right to Self-Improvement', *The Sydney Morning Herald*, 23 December 2006, www.smh.com.au/national/the-welfare-trap-20061223-gdp42u.html.
20   Tony Koch, 'Indigenous Pickers Grab Job Chance', *The Australian*, 23 March 2005, 1.

In internal reports too, these programs approached orbiting as a remedial or preventative disciplinary technique applied to young people with emerging drug and alcohol issues. During this period, Pearson also appeared in the national news publicising a five-year 'orbiting' program funded by Macquarie Bank, called 'Higher Expectations', through which 'the top' Cape York high school students were given scholarships to attend prestigious boarding schools in metropolitan centres.[21] Such projects excelled in attracting publicity but were subject to little scrutiny or assessment. The first comprehensive federal government review of Pearson's social welfare program noted in 2013 that, while having 'people increasingly "orbit" from [their home community] for work' was a key aim, 'there is no evidence to indicate that more residents are taking up the opportunity to leave or "orbit"' either organically or through the program's inducements.[22]

Surveying its various articulations, there seem to be five key precepts to Pearsonian orbiting, all of which are clearly contestable. First, *the capital deficit precept* asserts that remote-living Aboriginal people need to acquire labour skills and financial and cultural capital that they currently do not have to thrive both individually and collectively. Second, *the capital supply precept* claims that these labour skills and financial and cultural capital are solely available in urban and regional centres and, ideally, from certain mainstream educational institutions. Third, *the return precept* assures doubters that Aboriginal people who venture to urban and regional centres will go back to their home communities at some undefined point, whether permanently or periodically, necessarily enriching those communities. They will do this, Pearson has argued, because of their 'strong and continuing cultural connection to ancestral lands'.[23] Fourth, *the cultural stability precept* insists that these 'orbiters' will remain culturally Aboriginal regardless of how prolonged or in-depth their engagement with the dominantly non-indigenous institutions, cultural norms and social networks of urban or regional life. Fifth, *the beneficence precept*, which I infer from the breeziness with which Pearson describes orbiting practices, implies that the different stages of adaptation and adjustment encountered by these individuals will be relatively easy. As I discuss in the following section, all five of these precepts have been contested by

21   Smith, 'Cape York Student'.
22   FaHCSIA, *Cape York Welfare*.
23   Noel Pearson, 'In Search of a Sustainable Future', *The Australian Financial Review*, 15 November 2005, 23.

activists and scholars in Australia. They are also entirely contrary to what we know of other peoples' parallel journeys in other countries, travelling routes often described as 'circular migration'.

Circulating Orbits

Discourses, policies and studies of circular migration have led curious parallel lives in international diplomacy and Australian policymaking. Without attempting to give an exhaustive account, it is worth taking a brief look at these different contexts and tracing some of their political and conceptual interrelations. While clearly linked to earlier forms of journeying and migration, the phrase 'circular migration' became prominent among migration researchers and diplomats in the late 1960s and 1970s as a way of describing repeated seasonal or life cycle migrations. Early studies were interested in measuring the phenomenon of 'short-term, repetitive or cyclical' movements of people within nations, seeking to track, rather than necessarily explain, how people moved between different sites of residence.[24] Arguments about the forces propelling these individuals were, and typically remain, derived from the five approaches that have shaped studies of labour migration more generally since the late nineteenth century, synthesised by Gidwani and Sivaramakrishnan as two approaches: 'dual economy' understandings that focus on individual rational actors, variously taking advantage of wage or cost of living differences in different sites; and Marxian understandings that privilege the pressures of uneven development, mapping migration onto the differences between processes of modernisation and capitalist production in different sites.[25] As Gidwani and Sivaramakrishnan suggest, the 1990s and early 2000s witnessed a significant push in international scholarship to respect both migrants' agency and the impersonal structures shaping their lives, attending to the personal advantages of migration, the harmful social implications for families and communities, the occasions of extreme exploitation and the 'modest origins of counterhegemony' in their movement between social worlds.

24 Hugo, 'Circular Migration'.
25 Shrestha, 'A Structural Perspective'; Gidwani and Sivaramakrishnan, 'Circular Migration'. See also Jokisch, 'Migration and Agricultural Change'.

In the past two decades, talk of circular migration has become 'the rage in international policy circles' due to its ostensible 'win-win-win' labour outcomes.[26] Avowedly, 'receiving' countries gain comparatively cheap labourers with limited political rights, 'sending' countries receive remittances from that labour, and migrants and their families receive comparatively higher wages. Much ink has been spilled by institutions such as the World Bank and European Commission on the appropriate management of these flows—particularly between Eastern and Western Europe—one outcome of which has been robust data suggesting that the individuals involved are neither truly returning or temporary migrants, but rather engaged in 'a continuing, long-term and fluid movement'.[27] Circulation between economies leads to a life of interminable parallel circulations. Does this international literature therefore conform with Pearson's vision? Not quite, as many of the factors that keep migrant labourers circulating across national borders do not apply to Indigenous peoples living in remote Australia. To simplify: Indigenous peoples' legal rights to reside and work do not differ between urban and remote contexts, and their origin in a relatively affluent 'receiving' nation is a barrier to their being attractive to other 'receiving' nations. In short, the spatialised disparities between rights and economies that are central to circular migration internationally do not hold. As Basok has shown, migrants 'orbit' between their 'sending' and 'receiving' contexts because they cannot remain permanently in the latter, perpetually circulating in part to maintain their relative affluence in their 'home' context; this ensures that they remain highly vulnerable to abusive employment.[28]

If there is something to draw from this literature, it is arguably that the third and fourth precepts of Pearsonian orbiting are unsound. While part of what has been celebrated about circular migration has been its role in the growth of official and unofficial remittances back to comparatively less affluent 'sending' regions, far exceeding levels of international aid, the return of financial capital is not necessarily correlated to the return of human capital.[29] When migrants have the ability to remain (legally or illegally) in contexts where they have greater earning potential, but limited social networks, they often do so. Pearson has suggested that Aboriginal peoples will necessarily return 'home' because of their cultural ties that,

---

26 Vertovec, 'Circular Migration'.
27 Agunias and Newland, *Circular Migration and Development*.
28 Basok, 'He Came, He Saw'; Basok, 'Post-National Citizenship'.
29 Vertovec, 'Circular Migration'.

according to the fourth precept, will not be transformed by their travels. It takes little effort to see this is a ridiculous assertion, not only because people have historically sought travel precisely because of its transformative effects, but also because it contradicts Pearson's own narrative.[30] Orbiting is imagined to initiate a singular revolution in an individual's skills, norms and values, but without affecting their 'culture'. This paradox parallels another in Pearson's schema, which is that he imagines young Aboriginal people to be sufficiently rationalist self-serving actors that they pursue individual gains, leaving their families and social worlds, while remaining sufficiently communally minded as to be willing to forfeit or redistribute those gains at a certain point.[31] Such contradictions are arguably a feature of, rather than a glitch in, his arguments.[32] Insisting on both incorporation into mainstream education and employment institutions and the value of cultural continuity provides considerable rhetorical space in which to manoeuvre as required.

Possibly due to its vagueness, academic assessments of Pearson's orbiting proposal have been relatively slow to develop in Australia. In the wideranging *Black Politics,* political scientist Sarah Maddison critiqued Pearson's account as founded in a false idea of Aboriginal people as 'atomized individuals' rather than embedded members of dense social networks.[33] This discursive move, Maddison suggests, is linked to other attempts to re-imagine and re-territorialise communally held Aboriginal lands as individual private property. Meanwhile, seasoned anthropologists pointed out that neither the theory or practice of orbiting was wholly novel. As Peter Sutton noted, during the 1960s, missions in South Australia and the Northern Territory had sent, or encouraged, their Aboriginal residents to travel hundreds of kilometres to acquire skills and market capital by becoming seasonal fruit pickers in the continent's south-east.[34] Merlan has similarly stated that Katherine-area Aboriginal people were orbiting during the 1960s, 'long before' Pearson coined the term, when 'a quite active system of managed, and often mobile, labour policy' allowed, and sometimes forced, them to work far from home for varying periods of

30 Clifford, *Routes.*
31 Demographic evidence suggests that employment prospects may actually decline for some Aboriginal and Torres Strait Islander peoples with migration. See Biddle, 'Indigenous Migration and the Labour Market'.
32 Neale, 'Staircases, Pyramids'.
33 Maddison, *Black Politics.*
34 Sutton, *The Politics of Suffering.* See also Sharp and Tatz, *Aborigines in the Economy*; Prout Quicke and Haslam McKenzie, this volume.

time.[35] Crucially, these people could legally (and illegally) be forced to both leave their home communities and to also return.[36] Surveying the myriad subsequent policy interventions that have shaped the lives of remote-living Aboriginal peoples, Morphy has suggested that the 'anchored kin-based network has proved to be extremely resilient, adaptive and persistent' in forestalling migration out of the places in which they were raised.[37] When people do migrate from remote communities, Coulehan and Gaykamaŋu write, 'the movement … to the city is more complex, contentious and open-ended than Pearson's vision'.[38]

Reproof to Pearson's beneficence precept, among others, can also be found in Paul Burke's attempts to study the 'diaspora' of Walpiri peoples between 2009 and 2012. During this time, as Burke explains, many factors pressured Walpiri peoples living in central Australian remote communities to migrate out, including not only the restrictive social policies of the Northern Territory Emergency Response (the 'Intervention') beginning in 2007, but also longer-term histories of social tensions and violence within their immediate environs.[39] Among the diaspora, Burke found that only 'a tiny minority' resembled the Pearsonian ideal of socially and spatially mobile persons with full-time employment, and that, in fact, for the overwhelming majority, the basis of economic life remained the same outside remote communities as it was inside them; namely, government welfare payments and public housing.[40]

Burke is nonetheless careful to note that social and cultural transformations are occurring. While they do not conform to the 'orbiting' ideals found in policy advocacy, a subsection of middle-aged Walpiri women have established new lives and social networks outside central Australia, many entering into long-term relationships non-Walpiri men. In their movements, these women are not motivated by aspirations of careerism or communal development, but by a shared critique of the gender relations and social conditions of their home communities. Discussing this same context, notably through the experiences of one particular Walpiri woman, Melinda Hinkson has recently described such trajectories in

---

35   Merlan, 'Anthropology and Policy-Preparedness'.
36   See also Beckett, 'From Island to Mainland'; Collmann, *Fringe Dwellers and Welfare*.
37   Morphy, '(Im)Mobility: Regional Population'.
38   Coulehan and Gaykamaŋu, 'Family Matters'.
39   Burke, 'Indigenous Diaspora'.
40   Burke, 'Indigenous Diaspora'.

terms of *eviction* and *exile* rather than diaspora or orbiting.[41] In using this language, Hinkson draws attention to the ways in which 'leaving' irrevocably transforms interpersonal relationships, the factors (some potentially lethal) that keep people from returning 'home' and the personal placemaking that necessarily occurs away from 'home'. One could well argue, based on the diverse literatures surveyed in this section, that the lives of actual 'orbiting' Aboriginal peoples likely neither remain stable nor change in the ways Pearson has proposed.

A Looping Discourse

There appears to be little evidence in Cape York Peninsula or elsewhere to indicate that Pearson's idea of 'orbiting' has been taken up by Indigenous peoples living in remote or rural areas. Census data suggest that in the Cape York Peninsula communities targeted by Pearson's social reform agenda, populations have neither shrunk nor grown dramatically between 2006 and 2016, whereas unemployment rates have ballooned.[42] This is not to suggest, though, that 'orbiting' has not been influential. Rather, as I will argue in this closing section, Pearson's descriptions of 'orbiting' and its celebration by journalists, politicians and others have played an important role in shaping Indigenous policy debates. 'Orbiting' is fundamentally focused on those Indigenous peoples born in remote and regional communities and their future prospects. For many decades, the viability of life in exactly these communities has been a focus of Indigenous policy in Australia. During the so-called 'self-determination' era (c. 1972–98), federal agencies, in particular, sought to fund multiple programs that would enable the continuation of Indigenous life and cultural practices in these places.[43] Such initiatives were later criticised for 'failing' to create long-term economic support for these communities, though this was not their objective, and taken as examples of unsustainable policy. Thus, in the 1990s, conservative political voices began to speak of the 'failure' of self-determination policy, variously framing the living conditions and economic disadvantage of remote and regional communities as a result of inappropriate social policy rather than settler colonial dispossession,

---

41   Hinkson, 'At the Edges'; Hinkson, 'Precarious Placemaking'.
42   For example, unemployment in Coen (3.5 per cent in 2006 and 31.5 per cent in 2016), Aurukun (9.5 per cent in 2006 and 48.8 per cent in 2016) and Hopevale (5 per cent in 2006 and 41.8 per cent in 2016) increased through this decade. See also Altman, 'Searching for the "Real"'.
43   Myers and Peterson, 'The Origins and History'.

exploitative resource extraction, insubstantial land rights, institutional racism, predatory business practices or the many other causes one might reasonably identify.[44] The problem, they argued, was too much 'culture' and not enough economy. In the early 2000s, Pearson stepped into these debates by first proclaiming Indigenous peoples' 'right to take responsibility' for their socio-economic positions and futures, and then insisting they 'orbit' into capitalist geographies.

In doing so, Pearson has helped sediment several 'orbiting' precepts within Australian policy. Pearson was not the originator of these ideas, of course, as there is a long history of bureaucrats and others making similar discursive divisions. For example, understandings of remote and regional Indigenous communities as sites of endemic capital deficit, and urban centres as singular sites of capital supply, were foundational to the era of assimilation policy (c. 1951–72) and its strategies of removing Indigenous peoples—particularly children—from their remote and regional homes. Thus, when journalists, policy advocates and politicians began to use this pattern of reasoning again in the early 2000s, they were criticised as endorsing a 'new' assimilationism. In this new iteration, Indigenous communities were frequently described as 'cultural museums' or 'lands of shame' in which there was little to no formal employment.[45] Rather than having 'real jobs' in the 'real economy' of market employment, the residents of these communities were depicted as avowedly engaged in 'pretend jobs' in the 'gammon economy' of government welfare.[46] Journalists could be found regularly describing remote Indigenous communities as 'abject failures', with incredibly high rates of unemployment and living conditions 'worse than those in Rwanda and South Africa'.[47] Such accounts reached fever pitch around the time of the 2007 Intervention and have continued through the subsequent years. For example, in 2014, the Western Australian premier described remote communities as 'not viable' and 'not sustainable'.[48] The following year, the prime minister, Tony Abbott, drew both criticism and support after he claimed that Indigenous peoples in remote communities were making

44 See Austin-Broos, *A Different Inequality*. For example, Sutton, 'The Politics of Suffering'.
45 For example Hughes, *Lands of Shame*.
46 See Jordan, *Better than Welfare?*; Kowal, 'Responsibility, Noel Pearson'.
47 Neale, *Wild Articulations*.
48 Dan Harrison, 'Remote Indigenous Communities Under Threat', *The Sydney Morning Herald*, 14 November 2014, www.smh.com.au/politics/federal/remote-indigenous-communities-under-threat-20141114-11myb9.html.

a 'lifestyle choice' that could not be supported indefinitely by taxpayers.[49] More recently, in 2018, commentators on national television called for 'another stolen generation' to remove Indigenous children from remote communities.[50] While Pearson has criticised the language used in many of these comments, his work has nonetheless been important in supporting the spatial and discursive divisions that underpin them.

Figure 11.1: Noel Pearson with Australian prime minister Tony Abbott in the Northern Territory, September 2014.

Source: Tracey Nearmy, AAP Image.

Perhaps the most important, though less obvious, effect of Pearson's work has been its mobilisation of the language of 'choice' in relation to remote and regional Indigenous communities. Precept four of 'orbiting', as I outlined earlier, involves the contention that Indigenous peoples can exit their home communities without changing their 'cultural' identity. They remain culturally whole even as, following Pearson, they become 'completely bicultural'. From this (contradictory) point of view, Indigenous peoples who are born remote from the 'opportunities' of urban education and employment appear to be faced with a kind of choice in

49   Shalailah Medhora, 'Remote Communities are "Lifestyle Choices", says Tony Abbott', *The Guardian*, 10 March 2015, www.theguardian.com/australia-news/2015/mar/10/remote-communities-are-lifestyle-choices-says-tony-abbott.
50   Josh Dye, 'Sunrise Investigated over "Racist" Aboriginal Segment', *The Sydney Morning Herald*, 30 March 2018, www.smh.com.au/entertainment/tv-and-radio/sunrise-investigated-over-racist-aboriginal-segment-20180330-p4z71s.html.

which their Aboriginality, connection to kin or cultural identity is not at stake. Remote-living Indigenous peoples, Pearson has written, need to acquire 'the capabilities to choose a life that they have reason to value', namely a life of wage labour and wealth accumulation.[51] Indigenous peoples' 'traditional cultural forms', as Pearson has said, appear to be 'a choice rather than a necessity' in capitalist modernity.[52] It is not a coincidence that, in the years after Pearson first used such language, conservative politicians have spoken of Indigenous peoples needing to be given 'a genuine choice' about where they live,[53] framing life in remote community as a 'lifestyle choice', and conservative policy advocates, such as the mining magnate Andrew Forrest, have represented their programs to encourage Indigenous employment in mainstream economies in terms of creating 'healthy lifestyle choices'.[54] Using 'orbiting' reasoning, a chorus of politically conservative voices have repeatedly and successfully lobbied for the end of various remote services, including the Community Development Employment Projects scheme, criticising anything that does not directly or indirectly coerce people from their remote and regional homes.[55] For such commentaries, the 'orbiting' concept is a crucial discursive foundation. Using it, residents committed to living in remote Indigenous communities are able to be re-positioned as errant subjects, making an 'unhealthy' choice to delay their inevitable exit.

As I wrote at the beginning of this chapter, it is premature for any retrospective summary of Pearson's influence on Indigenous politics and policy in Australia.[56] However, there are clear and present signs of a transition in the language and paradigms underpinning federal and state policy, moving from a post-ATSIC moment in which Pearson and other 'executive advocates' held significant sway over the terms of debate. This provides an important opportunity to reconsider these terms and their practical effects. Existing research by myself and others' suggests that the practical effects of 'orbiting' initiatives have been marginal, contrary or virtually impossible to detect, and that their underlying precepts do not align with research in Australia or internationally. What is also apparent, I have argued, is that the 'orbiting' idea has helped sediment

51   CYI, *From Hand Out to Hand Up*.
52   Pearson, 'Pathways to Prosperity'.
53   Eastley, 'Vanstone Says'.
54   Andrew Forrest, 'We Have a Mutual Obligation to End the Welfare Trap', *The Australian*, 2 August 2014, 4.
55   See Altman and Klein, 'Lessons from a Basic'.
56   However, also see Watt, 'Pearson's Mission'.

certain discursive constructions of Indigenous lives in remote and regional Australia within political and policy contexts. In short, 'orbiting' has helped many to (re)imagine these lives outside local context and communal relations, staging them as individualised actors who should choose the only sound 'lifestyle choice' in capitalist modernity: the life of a migrant labourer.

Bibliography

Agunias, Dovelyn Rannveig and Kathleen Newland. *Circular Migration and Development: Trends, Policy Routes, and Ways Forward.* Washington, DC: Migration Policy Institute, 2007.

Ah Mat, Richie. 'The Moral Case for Indigenous Capitalism'. *Native Title on the Ground Conference.* Alice Springs, NT: AIATSIS, 2003.

Altman, Jon. 'In the Name of the Market?'. In *Coercive Reconciliation: Stabilise, Normalise, Exit Aboriginal Australia*, edited by Jon Altman and Melinda Hinkson, 307–21. Fitzroy, Vic: Arena, 2007.

——. 'Noel Pearson's Policies Embraced by White Australia, but How Effective Are They?'. *The Conversation*, 9 August 2011, theconversation.com/noel-pearsons-policies-embraced-by-white-australia-but-how-effective-are-they-2226.

——. 'Searching for the "Real" Economy on Cape York'. *Crikey*, 3 June 2013. www.crikey.com.au/2013/06/03/searching-for-the-real-economy-on-cape-york/.

Altman, Jon and Elise Klein. 'Lessons from a Basic Income Programme for Indigenous Australians'. *Oxford Development Studies* 46, no. 1 (2018): 132–46. doi.org/10.1080/13600818.2017.1329413.

Austin-Broos, Diane. *A Different Inequality: The Politics of Debate about Remote Aboriginal Australia.* Sydney, NSW: Allen & Unwin, 2011.

Basok, Tanya. 'He Came, He Saw, He Stayed: Guest Worker Programmes and the Issue of Non-Return'. *International Migration* 38, no. 2 (2000): 215–38. doi.org/10.1111/1468-2435.00108.

——. 'Post-National Citizenship, Social Exclusion and Migrants Rights: Mexican Seasonal Workers in Canada'. *Citizenship studies* 8, no. 1 (2004): 47–64. doi.org/10.1080/1362102042000178409.

Beckett, Jeremy. 'From Island to Mainland: Torres Strait Islanders in the Australian Labour Force'. In *Indigenous Participation in Australian Economies,* edited by Ian Keen, 63–72. Canberra, ACT: ANU E Press, 2010. doi.org/10.22459/ IPAE.12.2010.04.

Biddle, Nicholas. 'Indigenous Migration and the Labour Market: A Cautionary Tale'. *Australian Journal of Labour Economics* 13, no. 3 (2010): 313–30.

Burke, Paul. 'Indigenous Diaspora and the Prospects for Cosmopolitan "Orbiting": The Warlpiri Case'. *The Asia Pacific Journal of Anthropology* 14, no. 4 (2013): 304–22.

Clifford, James. *Routes: Travel and Translation in the Late Twentieth Century.* Cambridge, MA: Harvard University Press, 1997.

Collmann, Jeff. *Fringe Dwellers and Welfare: The Aboriginal Response to Bureaucracy.* St Lucia, Qld: University of Queensland Press, 1988.

Coulehan, Kerin and Waymamba Gaykamaŋu. 'Family Matters: Yolŋu Women and Children and Rural–Urban Mobility'. In *Exploring Urban Identities and Histories,* edited by Christine Hansen and Kathleen Butler. Canberra, ACT: Australian Institute of Aboriginal and Torres Strait Islander Studies, 2013.

CYI. *From Hand Out to Hand Up: Cape York Welfare Reform Project.* Cairns, 2007.

Eastley, Tony. 'Vanstone Says Remote Indigenous Communities Becoming "Cultural Museums"'. *ABC Local Radio,* 9 December 2005, www.abc.net.au/ am/content/2005/s1527233.htm.

FaHCSIA. *Cape York Welfare Reform Evaluation 2012.* Canberra: Department of Families, Housing, Community Services and Indigenous Affairs, 2013.

Gidwani, Vinay and K. Sivaramakrishnan. 'Circular Migration and the Spaces of Cultural Assertion'. *Annals of the Association of American Geographers* 93, no. 1 (2003): 186–213. doi.org/10.1111/1467-8306.93112.

Hinkson, Melinda. 'At the Edges of the Visual Culture of Exile: A Glimpse from South Australia'. In *Refiguring Techniques in Digital Visual Research*, edited by Edgar Gamez Cruz, Shanti Sumartojo and Sarah Pink, 93–104. London, UK: Springer, 2017. doi.org/10.1007/978-3-319-61222-5_8.

——. 'Precarious Placemaking'. *Annual Review of Anthropology* 46 (2017): 49–64. doi.org/10.1146/annurev-anthro-102116-041624.

Hughes, Helen. *Lands of Shame: Aboriginal and Torres Strait Islander 'Homelands' in Transition.* Centre for Independent Studies, 2007.

Hugo, Graeme, J. 'Circular Migration in Indonesia'. *Population and Development Review* 8, no. 1 (1982): 59–83. doi.org/10.2307/1972690.

James, Milton. 'Petrol Sniffing on Cape York Peninsula: An Intervention Strategy'. Lecture. Cape York Partnerships, unpublished, 2004. Accessed 10 March 2018, www.fromthebush.org/uploads/1/9/9/7/19974045/petrol_sniffing_on_cape_york_peninsula.pdf.

——. 'A Report on the Trial of Placing Young Indigenous People from Cape York Peninsula Region into Private Sector Employment Picking Fruit in Southern States'. Cape York Partnership, 2005. Accessed 20 January 2017, www.capeyorkpartnerships.com/downloads/placing-young%20Indigenous-cape-york-into-employment-161106.pdf (site discontinued).

Jokisch, Brad. 'Migration and Agricultural Change: The Case of Smallholder Agriculture in Highland Ecuador'. *Human Ecology* 30, no. 4 (2002): 523–50. doi.org/10.1023/A:1021198023769.

Jordan, Kirrily, ed. *Better than Welfare? Work and Livelihoods for Indigenous Australians after CDEP*. Canberra: ANU Press, 2016. doi.org/10.22459/CAEPR36.08.2016.

Klein, Elise. 'The Curious Case of Using the Capability Approach in Australian Indigenous Policy'. *Journal of Human Development and Capabilities* 17, no. 2 (2016): 245–59. doi.org/10.1080/19452829.2016.1145199.

Kowal, Emma. 'Responsibility, Noel Pearson and Indigenous Disadvantage in Australia'. In *Responsibility*, edited by Ghassan Hage and Robin Eckersley, 43–56. Melbourne, Vic: Melbourne University Press, 2012.

Latimore, Jack. 'Jumping the Gate'. *Inside Story*, 23 August 2017, insidestory.org.au/jumping-the-gate/.

Maddison, Sarah. *Black Politics*. Crows Nest, NSW: Allen & Unwin, 2009.

Maddison, Sarah, Tom Clark and Ravi de Costa. *The Limits of Settler Colonial Reconciliation: Non-Indigenous People and the Responsibility to Engage*. New York: Springer, 2016. doi.org/10.1007/978-981-10-2654-6.

McKenna, Mark. *Moment of Truth: History and Australia's Future*. Melbourne, Vic: Black Inc., 2018.

Merlan, Francesca. 'Anthropology and Policy-Preparedness'. *The Asia Pacific Journal of Anthropology* 14, no. 4 (2013): 323–38. doi.org/10.1080/14442213.2013.804869.

Morphy, Frances. '(Im)Mobility: Regional Population Structures in Aboriginal Australia'. *Australian Journal of Social Issues* 45, no. 3 (2010): 363–82. doi.org/10.1002/j.1839-4655.2010.tb00184.x.

Myers, Fred and Nicolas Peterson. 'The Origins and History of Outstations as Aboriginal Life Projects'. In *Experiments in Self-Determination: Histories of the Outstation Movement in Australia,* edited by Nicolas Peterson and Fred Myers, 1–22. Canberra: ANU Press, 2016. doi.org/10.22459/ESD.01.2016.01.

Neale, Timothy. 'Staircases, Pyramids and Poisons: The Immunitary Paradigm in the Works of Noel Pearson and Peter Sutton'. *Continuum* 27, no. 2 (2013): 177–92. doi.org/10.1080/10304312.2013.766317.

——. *Wild Articulations: Environmentalism and Indigeneity in Northern Australia.* Honolulu: University of Hawai'i Press, 2017. doi.org/10.21313/hawaii/9780824873110.001.0001.

Pearson, Noel. 'Betrayal'. *The Monthly*, December 2017, www.themonthly.com.au/issue/2017/december/1512046800/noel-pearson/betrayal.

——. 'Man Cannot Live By Service Delivery Alone'. *Opportunity and Prosperity Conference.* Melbourne, 13 November 2003.

——. 'Pathways to Prosperity for Indigenous People'. *Sir Ronald Trotter Lecture 2010.* Auckland, New Zealand: New Zealand Business Roundtable, 2010.

——. 'Remote Control'. *The Monthly*, May 2015, www.themonthly.com.au/issue/2015/may/1430402400/noel-pearson/remote-control.

——. *Up from The Mission: Selected Writings* (2nd ed.). Melbourne, Vic: Black Inc., 2011.

Sharp, Ian Gordon and Colin Tatz. *Aborigines in the Economy: Employment, Wages and Training.* Melbourne, Vic: Jacaranda Press, 1966.

Shrestha, Nanda R. 'A Structural Perspective on Labour Migration in Underdeveloped Countries'. *Progress in Human Geography* 12, no. 2 (1988): 179–207. doi.org/10.1177/030913258801200202.

Smith, Suzanne. 'Cape York Students Apply for Prestigious Boarding Schools Positions'. *ABC Lateline*, 31 July 2007.

Strakosch, Elizabeth. *Neoliberal Indigenous Policy: Settler Colonialism and the 'Post-Welfare' State.* London: Palgrave Macmillan, 2015. doi.org/10.1057/9781137405418.

Sutton, Peter. 'The Politics of Suffering: Indigenous Policy in Australia since the 1970s'. *Anthropological Forum* 11 (2001): 125–73. doi.org/10.1080/00664670125674.

——. *The Politics of Suffering*. Carlton, Vic: Melbourne University Press, 2009.

Vertovec, Steven. (2007) 'Circular Migration: The Way Forward in Global Policy?' *COMPAS Working Paper 4*, Oxford.

Watt, Elizabeth. 'Debating Decentralisation'. *The Australian Journal of Anthropology* 28, no. 1 (2017): 120–24. doi.org/10.1111/taja.12221.

——. 'Pearson's Mission: Revisiting Noel Pearson's Revisionist History of Hope Vale'. *Journal of Australian Studies* 42, no. 1 (2018): 34–50. doi.org/10.1080/14443058.2017.1414072.

Newspapers

The Australian
The Australian Financial Review
The Courier-Mail (Brisbane)
The Guardian
The Sydney Morning Herald
The Weekend Australian

12

Of Pizza Ovens in Arnhem Land: The State Quest to Restructure Aboriginal Labour in Remotest Australia

Jon Altman

Preamble

In contemporary Australian policy, and especially Indigenous policy, little distinction is made between labour, work, employment and jobs. In fact, most of the focus is on formal or paid employment. Consequently, in the last decade, we have seen the emergence of employment policy with the overarching goal to 'close', or at least reduce, the gap in formal employment outcomes between Indigenous and non-Indigenous Australians. As the 10th annual Closing the Gap report recently tabled in the Australian Parliament clearly demonstrates, this goal—first articulated by Kevin Rudd in 2008 as an element of the National Apology to the Stolen Generations and then adopted by the Council of Australian Governments that year—has failed. The goal was to halve the gap at the national level in what is technically termed the 'employment to population ratio' between 2008 and 2018.[1] This goal has not only failed nationally, but also, and most spectacularly, in the 86 per cent of the Australian continent that is defined officially as remote and very remote; the latest census of 2016 indicates

---

1   Commonwealth of Australia, *Closing the Gap*.

that, in very remote Australia, only three in 10 Indigenous adults are in some form of paid employment compared to eight in 10 non-Indigenous adults. This is not a gap, it is a gulf.

In a 30-year period from the early 1970s, the unusual circumstances of remote Indigenous Australia were recognised by policymakers and, consequently, some programs were designed to accommodate the absence of formal commercial and employment opportunity. However, in the twenty-first century, as neoliberal thinking and associated valorisation of the free market became ascendant, policy discourse and practice changed. There is a growing expectation that remote-living Indigenous people will find mainstream employment and that the welfare dependency and social dysfunction attributed to such dependency will decline and disappear. This expectation accelerated rapidly after the Northern Territory National Emergency Response (the 'Intervention') in 2007 and governmental insistence that the norms and values of remote-living Aboriginal people should alter to embrace mainstream values of neoliberal individualism. It was never made clear how such an embrace of Western norms would generate paid employment in remote places, but the logical options are threefold: local Aboriginal people would take the jobs held by non-local, non-Aboriginal people; remote economies would grow and so generate more paid employment; jobless people would move to places where there are more jobs (see Prout Quicke and Haslam McKenzie, and Neale, in this volume).

In this chapter, I home in on the last issue of anticipated labour mobility for employment as the least likely option for the Aboriginal people with whom I have worked over the past four decades in very remote localities where there are few or no paid jobs. I know one place, an outstation in western Arnhem Land in the Northern Territory called Mumeka, extremely well. I lived there in 1979 and 1980 and have visited almost every year since. Much of my work as an anthropologist has been with people who constitute a community defined, in part, by their traditional ownership of the area around Mumeka and, in part, by their shared use of Kuninjku, a dialect of a regional pan-dialectical language called Bininj Kunwok.[2] The only paid employment at Mumeka for a long time now has been for a teaching assistant. To get paid employment, Mumeka residents

---

2   Garde, *Culture, Language and Person Reference.*

have either to migrate to the nearby township of Maningrida, where there are few available jobs, or further afield, or somehow economically develop their outstation and surrounds to generate jobs.

I begin this chapter by revisiting some observations on a brief visit to Mumeka in July 2012 that, six years on, I interpret as a pivotal moment when I saw a particular form of economic development being introduced. I have made several presentations between 2012 and 2014 using this ethnographic material but, for a variety of reasons that will become apparent as the narrative unfolds, including disbelief at what I was observing, I have not published this material until now.[3]

I commence with an observation about remote development for employment and then try to make some analytic sense of this. I look to provide some historical and regional contexts for what I saw. I then explore Kuninjku regimes of work under colonial conditions and in the postcolonial present, and examine some possible explanatory theories for interpreting a form of recolonisation that is occurring in the name of modernising development and employment creation. I end with a postscript that provides a brief update of the consequences that have unfolded since that pivotal moment to which I now turn.

Mumeka, July 2012

As I thundered along the bone-jarring dirt road officially classified as a 'flat-bladed track' (that had clearly not seen a blade for some time) towards the Aboriginal township of Maningrida in west Arnhem Land, I pondered what issues might await me in this region where I had worked since 1979. As usual, my head was full of ideas and too many projects.

3   I have circled around these issues elsewhere in Altman, 'Bawinanga and CDEP'; Altman, 'Basic Income for Remote'; Altman, '"The Main Thing"'. This chapter builds on collaborations with the UK Economic and Social Research Council funded 'Domestic Moral Economy' project based at the University of Manchester, from 2011 to 2015. I would like to foremost thank many Kuninjku people in the Maningrida region for their collaborations over many years; Elisabeth Yarbarkhsh for research assistance; Jörg Wiegratz and Chris Gregory for stimulating interactions; and Murray Garde, Chris Haynes, Tim Rowse and especially Melinda Hinkson, as well as many others for stimulating comments and challenges during various presentations made in Cairns, Canberra, Brisbane, Tokyo and Wellington.

This was my 48th visit to the region in 33 years (1979–2012). Increasingly, my so-called 'field work' involved catching up with old friends and their families, commiserating about departed relatives, and just talking in very concrete ways, as is local custom, about family (theirs and mine), ceremony, places and hunting, and the latest manifestation of settler colonial incursion into the Kuninjku community. I was undertaking what I increasingly think of as random 'spot check' field work reminiscent of some of the time allocation techniques I used when I was a doctoral student residing at Mumeka.

I pulled into Mumeka and parked my vehicle where I always stop, a safe and courteous distance from the house of senior traditional owner Iyuna (now deceased) and was warmly greeted as always. I looked around. There is always something happening at Mumeka, and I saw that the outstation surrounds had been drastically cleared, not by fire as is the usual practice in the dry season, but by some flat-bladed instrument attached to a tractor.

I asked my friends what was going on here. There were numerous flat packed cardboard boxes neatly stacked, mudbricks, a brand-new ride-on lawnmower, rakes, brooms, plastic wheelie bins, a generator and manifestations of construction. 'We are all on "new CDEP"' my friends cheerily told me, referring to the Community Development Employment Projects (CDEP) scheme that many had engaged with for over a decade and that was currently being unilaterally and radically reformed by the Australian state. 'We are making vege [vegetable] gardens and barbeques, [a] pizza oven and chicken houses [coops]'. 'To eat?' I asked, for these are extraordinary meat-eating hunters. '*Kayakki, dabuno* [no way, for eggs!]', they answered. 'We are getting five new houses' (to supplement two modern houses at Mumeka shared by about 30 people), added Jimarr, 'and a service station to provide diesel for overland travellers' (as a new enterprise). 'Really', I said, '*waybukki*, true story?' '*Yo, waybukki*', was the reply. Development, it seemed, was coming to Mumeka.

I drove on to Maningrida, the regional township and services centre, with some trepidation. While I know many people there, this larger township is never as serene as Mumeka and can often be politically turbulent. My point of articulation with Maningrida is the Bawinanga Aboriginal Corporation (BAC) that I have worked with since its establishment as an outstation resource agency in 1979. BAC has been extremely successful as an Aboriginal organisation. It is the largest in the Northern Territory; however, since the Intervention, it has struggled, experiencing four changes of CEO, with the latest having just been sacked by the all-Aboriginal board, and an unprecedented turnover of staff. In an organisational and historical sense, I probably knew more about BAC than any of its current staff or board. Whatever was happening at Mumeka would be driven by BAC and I braced myself to explore the thinking behind this latest development—the notion that highly mobile people could be transformed to tend gardens, raise chickens and even run service stations, all forms of labouring that required sedentary living and labouring.

Policy and Regional Contexts

My visit to Mumeka coincided with the completion of the five-year Intervention that sought to morally restructure the norms and values of remote-living Aboriginal people. In June 2012, when this project neared its end date without having achieved its aims, it was extended for a further 10 years and rebadged as Stronger Futures for the Northern Territory.[4] This is an ongoing paternalistic effort to align Aboriginal ways of living with those of the dominant mainstream. The public discourse around Aboriginal dysfunction and subsequent associated policy settings were the culmination of a fundamental policy shift that effectively declared self-determination dead and mainstreaming or assimilation as the way ahead for Aboriginal people.[5]

This project of moral restructuring was also encapsulated from 2008 in a policy framework called Closing the Gap. Although promulgated as a national project, the policy was poorly conceptualised for remote circumstances and took little account of history or possible Aboriginal responses and resistance to it. It was the latest in a long line of visionary social engineering exercises that looked to discipline the behaviour of Aboriginal workers, parents and welfare recipients to ensure greater employment participation, higher school attendance, better parenting and more responsible spending patterns.[6] Clearly, in such impositions,

---

4   The *Stronger Futures in the Northern Territory Act 2012* is available at www.legislation.gov.au/Details/C2012A00100 (accessed 15 March 2019). In 2015, with a change of federal government, anew National Partnership Agreement on Northern Territory Remote Aboriginal Investment (NTRAI) from 2015–16 to 2021–22 replaced the National Partnership Agreement on Stronger Futures in the Northern Territory.

5   Strakosch, *Neoliberal Indigenous Policy*.

6   Hinkson, 'Introduction: In the Name'.

there are deeply embedded contests about ways of living and being, with the powerful state machinery discursively asserting the superiority of Westerns norms and values over Aboriginal ones.

I focus here on the Maningrida regional setting in west Arnhem Land and deploy my points of regional articulation with the Kuninjku community of about 300 people and with BAC to say something about transformations and political contestation with a focus on contested regimes of working. In situations of economic plurality or hybridity—entangled relations between Kuninjku people who strive to maintain elements of their customary hunting and gathering economy and a neoliberal state and market capitalism—different regimes of labouring—characterised as Balanda (non-Aboriginal) and Bininj (Aboriginal) or formal and informal/paid and unpaid—have been evident since state colonisation. What is distinctive and at stake in the latest transformation is an increasing gulf between Bininj and Balanda perspectives even as the state is determined to close the employment gap.

One reason for this, in my view, is that, in looking to transform the labour relations of people like the Kuninjku, the state and its agents are oblivious to the extraordinary transformations that have already occurred as a result of Kuninjku adaptations to regional manifestations of state colonisation and capitalism. Further, in looking to statistically 'close the gap' between Indigenous and other Australians, there has been little attention paid to the actual nature of the local economy or its long-standing ethnic duality, or to the risk that, in aiming to close statistical gaps, local livelihoods and wellbeing might, in fact, be put at risk and decline.

The overarching observation that I develop below focuses on the growing incommensurability between the state's goal for remote-living Aboriginal people like the Kuninjku and what is desired by them and might be regionally possible. There is an intensifying political struggle underway about values and ways of living that I examine by focusing on the quest to transform residents of places like Mumeka into employed labour. In the context of this volume's focus on labour mobility (see especially Chapters 10 and 11), there is an ongoing struggle between the state and its agents looking to convert flexible and highly regionally mobile Kuninjku into regimented and sedentary workers, and Kuninjku responses to this imposition.

Kuninjku Labour Regimes: Pre- to Postcolonial

Kuninjku people were among the last Aboriginal groups to be colonised in remote Australia; their pre-colonial lives in Arnhem Land residing in an Aboriginal reserve were only partially disrupted by occasional expeditions onto their traditional lands and the establishment of a mission at Oenpelli 200 kilometres to the west where some resided from the early twentieth century. It was the establishment of the more proximate Maningrida as a colonial outpost that directly affected their way of living.[7]

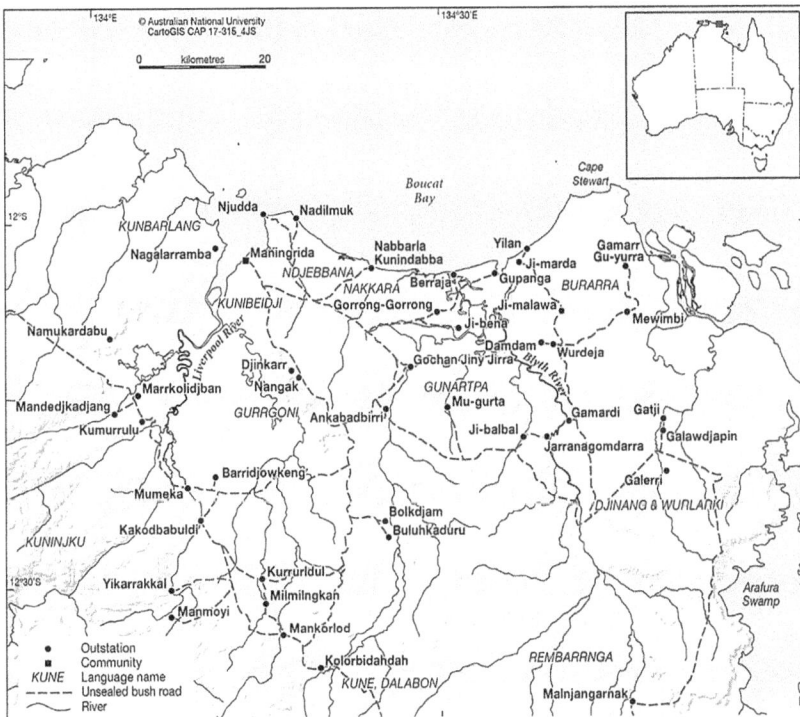

Figure 12.1: Map of the Maningrida region.
Source: CartoGIS, College of Asia and the Pacific, The Australian National University.

In 1949, a trading post was established at Maningrida by what was then the Native Affairs Branch of the Northern Territory administration as an instrument of controlling colonial policy. It was abandoned in 1950. In 1957, it was re-established, this time as a Welfare Branch settlement to create a colonial presence in a region of 10,000 square kilometres

---

7   Altman and Hinkson, 'Mobility and Modernity'.

where none had previously existed. Government policy at that time was shifting from protection within a closed-off gazetted reserve to a quest to transform Aboriginal people to mainstream subjects via assimilation. Maningrida slowly developed into a township where Aboriginal people, as wards of the state, were to be trained for such assimilation through education, training and jobs, and the adoption of Western ways of living.

Historically, Maningrida failed as a project of assimilation for two main reasons. First, counter to capitalist logic, the settlement was established without any assessment of commodities that might flow from the hinterland. As it turned out, there were very few of any commercial value. Second, and again counter to capitalist logic, a series of development projects were established including forestry, cattle and buffalo raising, dairy, market gardens, orchards, flower propagation, fishing and fish processing, a piggery and chicken raising without any realistic appraisal of commercial viability or comparative advantage. All failed.[8]

Since 1957, Maningrida has had both Balanda and Bininj populations; it is a place of dual ethnicity but multiple language communities (see Figure 12.1). Up until the early 1970s, power was legally vested with Balanda officials as agents of the colonial state. In 1972, policy shifted dramatically from imposed assimilation to decolonising self-determination, which was initially viewed with great optimism by government as a way to empower Aboriginal people and to overcome earlier development failures. This history is important given that what I observed at Mumeka in July 2012 was arguably a microscopic simulacrum of what had occurred at Maningrida in the 1960s.

My focus on the Kuninjku mainly reflects my long-term research relationship with this group. Key distinguishing features of the Kuninjku community are that many of its members had late contact with the colonial state with some not moving to Maningrida until 1963. Kuninjku adapted poorly to settlement life and so, from the early 1970s, were among the first to decentralise and move to live on ancestral lands at tiny communities called outstations. Over time, their forms of residence have become more complicated and increasingly many live between the township and hinterland on a seasonal basis. In the last two decades, a number of Kuninjku people have settled at Maningrida on a more permanent basis for a range of reasons, such as employment, education for

---

8   Much of this history is available in expanded form in Altman, *Hunter-Gatherers Today*.

children and access to health services; however, the permanence of such residential choice is difficult to assess given historic residential mobility—bush to town and vice versa.

Prior to their contact with the Australian colonial state, Kuninjku people mainly survived by highly mobile hunting, fishing and gathering, utilising what has been termed a kin-based domestic mode of production.[9] Kuninjku adapted badly to Maningrida in part because they resisted, more actively than other groups, the expected transformation to Western forms of sedentary labouring for training allowances. Colonial officials frequently complained about their hyper-mobility back and forth from their traditional lands for ceremony and wildlife harvesting, sometimes instigated because of hunger in the government settlement. Their only notable employment success in those colonial times occurred when a perceptive superintendent realised that sociable group work was important to Kuninjku. Provided with a blue tractor and trailer, a work crew productively collected rubbish from the communal kitchen and dumped it into a nearby creek.

In the early 1970s, with the change of policy from assimilation to self-determination (as defined by the state) and land rights, most Kuninjku people moved back to live and work on their country. When I lived with a small group averaging just 32 people at Mumeka in 1979 and 1980, they clearly differentiated their own work from Balanda forms. Their work was highly flexible, unsupervised and pleasurable; the latter was supervised, subject to relations of white domination and generally to be avoided on an ongoing basis. Indeed, Kuninjku were, and remain, happy for Balanda to undertake certain forms of work that require skills that they do not possess and that require hierarchical forms of organisation and the exercise of workplace authority.

I collected information over one annual seasonal cycle about work effort (using time allocation techniques), the organisation of labour, dietary intake, sources of market and non-market income and expenditure patterns.[10] This research greatly augmented earlier experimental research undertaken by Fred McCarthy and Margaret McArthur in 1948 at nearby Fish Creek (or Kunnanj) with a group of related Aboriginal people. These earlier data were used by Marshall Sahlins to make his influential argument

---

9   Sahlins, *Stone Age Economics*; Altman, *Hunter-Gatherers Today*.
10   Altman, *Hunter-Gatherers Today*.

that the hunter-gatherer domestic mode of production was the original affluent society.[11] While, like McCarthy and McArthur, I documented that all adults worked three to four hours per day, I also showed that this work extended over seven days a week and was an average across all adults. Hence, I made the case that, as a group, Kuninjku labouring effort was the equivalent of full-time by broader societal standards.

I cannot explore in any detail the Kuninjku mode of production here; however, as an aside, I note the following features that are immediately salient to the issues raised in this chapter. When at Mumeka, I quantified that hunting and gathering was the mainstay of the economy, hence the title of my book *Hunter-Gatherers Today*. This form of production in turn required people to live in a highly mobile manner, and I documented regular seasonal residential shifts between resource bases. It also required periods of extraordinary hard labouring—work density in hunting, fishing and gathering in hot tropical conditions could be very arduous, as I discovered quickly through participant observation. As I have documented elsewhere, over time, the overall contribution of hunting to livelihood has declined as other sources of cash income from art sales and transfer payments from the state have increased.[12] Yet, self-provisioning dependent on mobility has remained a crucial aspect of Kuninjku subjectivity. Access to vehicles for mobility for economic, social and cultural reasons is of the highest priority for Kuninjku after meeting immediate survival needs, and earning cash and saving for vehicles is a major motivation for engagement with market capitalism via arts manufacture.[13]

I also examined the organisation of work and showed that it was undertaken in two broad but highly interchangeable forms: individually or with kin, with the latter more common. Everyday work was, and remains, organised by negotiated consensus. Only in ceremonial work was there a willing acceptance of the domination of 'managers' (*djunkkay*) who organised ritual workers and still do; people work at ceremony for the ceremonial boss and also today, at Christian Fellowship, people work hard with song and dance for a new additional boss 'Jesus'.

---

11   Sahlins, *Stone Age Economics*.
12   Altman, 'From Kunnanj'.
13   Altman and Hinkson, 'Mobility and Modernity'.

In the last 30 years, labour arrangements have changed in many ways; however, for Kuninjku, effective work is still organised either on one's own or with one's immediate family or in small groups, preferably of other Kuninjku. The former is especially evident in arts practice; in the last three decades, arts production has grown rapidly, with Kuninjku being the most prolific and successful artists in the region. The latter is evident in hunting for food in the bush, but also in Maningrida. For example, a group of Kuninjku women dominate at the local Babbarra Women's Centre and form a sociable team of closely related and successful textile screen printers. At outstations, there are almost no formal jobs beyond a handful of part-time teaching assistants.

My focus in this chapter is on materially productive forms of labour, mainly because this is the point of articulation with policy concerns about formal employment. Yet, from the emic Kuninjku perspective, such labour is little differentiated from spiritual work at ceremonies and reproductive and nurturing labour. What is important is that acceptable labour for Kuninjku has some prerequisites if it is to be sustainable: it must be flexible, allowing high rates of residential mobility; negotiated (with supervisors, Bininj or Balanda); and secondary to family and ceremonial obligations. This could be termed the Kuninjku work values regime. It is a regime that is based on positive reciprocity with kin and 'balanced' exchange with the market (i.e. art for cash, which is often influenced by the soundness of social relations with the arts manager), and seeks to avoid negative reciprocity and exploitative relations. To deploy David Graeber's schema explaining the moral grounds of economic relations, Kuninjku labouring is based on everyday sharing and avoids hierarchy and domination.[14]

From 1979, this flexible Kuninjku labouring regime has been strongly supported by BAC, especially since 1989 with its application of rules for managing the CDEP scheme in a suitably flexible manner. BAC's goals include the maintenance of language, culture and traditional practice; community development; promoting the welfare of its members; and services provision. BAC deployed its corporate capacity to assist Kuninjku mainly by using the CDEP scheme to provide a form of unconditional income support when people were at outstations, and by effectively marketing Kuninjku art via Maningrida Arts and Culture, the main

---

14   Graeber, *Debt*.

regional institution for productive (rather than consumptive) engagement with global capitalism. Coincidentally, it also provided considerable logistical support for ceremonial work.[15]

Following the Intervention in 2007, BAC's capacity to support flexible labouring declined markedly—the CDEP scheme came under discursive attack and unhelpful reform, and BAC's main export enterprise, the globally renowned Maningrida Arts and Culture, declined in profitability in the wake of the global financial crisis. Simultaneously, local forms of political representation were systematically diluted—an Australian Government official was installed as the supreme regional political authority and agent of surveillance for Canberra.

From the late 1990s, the Australian Government has increasingly represented remote-living Aboriginal people like the Kuninjku as welfare dependent, passive and in social and moral decline. These people have been framed in national discourse and the popular media as savage and primitive and as problematic parents. This was part of the rationale for the 'national emergency'. Hence, they needed strict policing and disciplining in work, education, expenditure of welfare income, ordered housing and so on if they were to be human in the same way as other citizens within Australia's late liberal order.[16] Simultaneously, the language of rights and responsibilities has emerged; however, it is applied to people who regard the rich Australian state as responsible for their wellbeing and have no notion of reciprocity as being a part of any regionally recognised social compact.

Subsequently, a neoliberal trope has emerged that emphasises the need for greater exposure to market capitalism, individualism, entrepreneurship and private accumulation. Places like Maningrida have been identified for special attention because of their relative size and associated visibility. Maningrida, with just over 3,000 residents, is one of the largest Aboriginal townships in the Northern Territory. In early 2009, it was defined for a short time as a 'Territory Growth Town' by the Northern Territory Government.[17]

---

15 Altman, 'Bawinanga and CDEP'.
16 Macoun, 'Aboriginality and the Northern Territory Intervention'; Anthony, *Indigenous People, Crime*; Checketts, 'The Pulse of Policy'.
17 Sanders, 'Working Futures'.

To qualify for development assistance, BAC has increasingly been required to actively participate in this project of improvement. This requirement was resisted for a time; however, more recently, with a change of CEO in 2010, there has been acquiescence.[18] Like the Australian Government, BAC does not currently recognise or strongly advocate for Kuninjku notions of labour; instead, it mainly subscribes to the state requirement to assist in closing the gaps, and the rhetoric that people on 'sit down' money (i.e. welfare) need to learn to 'stand up', as one BAC manager explained it to me in July 2012.

In the post-Intervention environment, we have seen a twin perspective that is increasingly shared by political and bureaucratic elites residing far away in Canberra and Darwin, and recent powerful Balanda arrivals at Maningrida who occupy managerial and professional positions. First, the promulgation of the myth that there just might be sufficient paid jobs for all to be employed within the region if it were rapidly developed. Second, and alternatively, that there are prospects for people to be trained for employment elsewhere, for example in mines (see Prout Quicke and Haslam McKenzie, this volume). Such perspectives fly in the face of both commissioned consultancy research and census data that document the excess supply of labour in the region.

Therefore, in July 2012, because of a loss of corporate memory and an ignoring of documented history, there was a return to a version of the developmental approach of the 1960s, with a host of small speculative ventures (that failed then) to be revisited—like the chicken and egg farming and vegetable gardens that I observed being developed at Mumeka (as well as other outstations). In the quest to demonstrate that formal labour is being undertaken, workers at Mumeka were all issued with high-visibility work wear, boots and safety sunglasses, illustrative, perhaps, of hard industrial work and a demonstration of modern compliance with occupational health and safety standards, and worn by Kuninjku so that they could be *seen* labouring. What is more, these new 'development' projects were being incubated on a highly speculative basis without any commercial business planning or assurance that state support would continue. Yet, BAC managers presented these as enterprises with mixed objectives, including training hunter-gatherers in horticulture and

---

18   This change can be linked in part to the appointment of a developmental CEO who had been actively involved as a government business manager during the Intervention and was a senior member of the Australian Federal Police; he is the CEO who was sacked in July 2012.

animal husbandry to ensure the 'food security' (a new buzz term) that seasonal hunting and fishing predicated on high labour mobility could not deliver, according to BAC staff. Then there was environmental health improvement, another buzz term in Canberra, hence funding for the pizza ovens and mudbrick barbeques for cooking to replace 'unhygienic' open fires and ground ovens, as explained to me by another Balanda manager.

Figure 12.2: The Mumeka work crew, July 2012.
Source: Photograph by Jon Altman.

I visited Mumeka several times during my regional field work in July 2012 to observe and discuss progress. As some members of the Mumeka work crew (and a Balanda tradesman) needed to daily commute an hour each way from Maningrida, only two or three hours a day were devoted to actual labouring in these new ventures. Kuninjku people at Mumeka were thrilled by the largesse that was provided with public funds but were not convinced about the likely sustainability of any of the projects; they were just going with the flow. I observed on several occasions that as soon as formal labouring was completed, people headed off to hunt and fish, which they did with success—long-necked turtles, barramundi, pig, buffalo, file snakes and ibis were evident—while the work crew that had driven out rushed back to Maningrida to their families and to shop, participating in speculative hunting and fishing on the way. Paradoxically, and likely unintentionally, in looking to 'develop' Mumeka and impose Western forms of labouring on Kuninjku, both the state and BAC were facilitating hyper-mobility funded by a government program. Members of the work crew who lived at Mumeka assured me that the high-visibility clothing was removed for after-hours hunting, not a bad idea with dangerous feral water buffalo and pigs a common target as a food source.

Interpretative Frames for Understanding Recolonisation

The Australian state is deploying a mix of old colonial and new market mentalities as it looks to recolonise remote Aboriginal spaces, sponsor 'new' development projects, and attempt new ways to immobilise people and their labour. Yet again, a pathway to late modernity for remote-living Aboriginal people is being charted by distant political and bureaucratic players using local agents to implement somewhat fanciful employment-creation projects. These untrustworthy trustees who always promise, but rarely deliver, seek to render deep development problems technical, to paraphrase James Ferguson,[19] choosing to turn a blind eye to past and present failures as the ideological rationales for improvement schemes become entangled with a messy world.

I have used the prism of labouring here to examine the political struggle to reshape norms and values away from what is perceived as the unstable, communal Aboriginal fix, to the stable, Western market fix, as Tania Murray Li might say,[20] except that no one seems to know what the market fix might look like in this region, and no one who exercises power really seems to know what people actually do. For Kuninjku, occupationally flexible labouring in hunting and fishing and arts production—activity that is unrecognised as 'real' work—greatly improves the quality of people's lives and livelihoods. However, official employment statistics are constructed in a manner incapable of reflecting such regional realities and thus reflect instead the urgent discursive goal to close employment gaps.

---

19 Ferguson, *The Anti-Politics Machine.*
20 Li, *The Will to Improve.*

Neoliberal Governmentality

Loic Wacquant has argued, persuasively in my view, that neoliberalism is not an economic but a political and cultural project.[21] In Arnhem Land we see the political rationality of governmentality looking to improve social conditions by seeking to alter Kuninjku conduct and habits, deploying new technologies, institutions and forms of knowledge seeking to create self-interested subjects with a progressive desire for industry (be it chicken eggs or market gardens); stable formal employment and regular work patterns; and individual, not group, accomplishment. It is no coincidence in this reading that there are many more police deployed in Maningrida and that regulatory barriers are placed in the way of those who wish to pursue other ways of being; getting a gun licence or getting a driving licence or registering a vehicle essential for hunting are all bureaucratic nightmares in remote outposts like Maningrida.

Wacquant sees neoliberal governmentality as the art of shaping populations and the self to conform to the market, even if the market might be miniscule as in 'Territory Growth Towns' like Maningrida or even more so at Mumeka: its institutional core consists of an articulation of state, market and citizenship that harnesses the first to stamp the second on the third. I do not explore Wacquant in any detail here, but there is much in his framework that resonates strongly with what the state is looking to implement in remotest Australia: liberty for those at the top, punitive paternalism for those at the bottom; idleness as a perceived social problem for the unworthy unemployed; ethnic disciplining; and the communicative mission of projecting asserted sovereignty into previously under-governed geographic spaces.

James Ferguson also interprets neoliberalism as a political project, but he challenges progressive anthropologists (such as myself) to turn neoliberal logic to progressive practical use.[22] In urban southern Africa, Ferguson suggests that black populations are not, and are unlikely to become, formal wage labourers; local livelihoods are being decimated owing to the valorisation of formal work and the conditional provision of supervised workfare and endless training sponsored by the state that clings to the

21 Wacquant, 'Three Steps'.
22 Ferguson, 'The Uses of Neoliberalism'.

false hope that trained people will somehow magically find suitable employment irrespective of politico-economic structural constraints. His observations resonate with the Arnhem Land case examined here.

What is especially revealing in the Maningrida situation is how the powerful Australian state based in Canberra, the national capital, wields authoritarian managerialism to directly influence development in remote regions. Yet, the responsibility for implementing this impossibly difficult governmental policy is devolved to local organisations like BAC.

From its formation in 1979 to 2007, BAC occupied a difficult position, trying to constantly mediate between the state and its Aboriginal members over the delivery of contested forms of development and labouring. This tension was managed relatively successfully for a variety of reasons including an ability to attract committed senior staff who stayed for long periods of time and were sympathetic to the priorities of local people. However, in the post-Intervention era, the culture of the organisation has shifted as it has increasingly adopted a bureaucratic rationality that locally mirrors the policies of the state. In recent years, it has attracted a revolving door of staff, many of whom lack a commitment to local control and are far more self-interested than they were in the past; most only last a short time and some even fly-in and fly-out from Darwin, where BAC established an ancillary office for a time. In general, most people working for BAC today are more interested in the jobs package and less interested in local histories, complexities and cultures. This has resulted in considerable conflict, with the sacking of the CEO by the all-Aboriginal board in July 2012 being just one example. As the state promulgates 'false capitalist' solutions to deeply entrenched development challenges, it is complicit in attracting (and aiding and abetting) managers who seek to riskily mimic state ideology and put forward proposals for risky projects like vegetable gardens, chicken coops and pizza ovens.

Moral Economy

The concept of moral economy, as Chris Hann reminds us, has been applied to criticise economism and highlight the values that have provoked sections of society to resort to political action and behaviour that puts the long-term values of community before the short-term value of individual utility.[23] In his early work, James Scott argues that peasants have a strong conservative ethic that prioritises the subsistence needs of all members of local communities. Scott suggests that peasants in South-East Asia are risk averse and driven by a safety-first principle, and that they have strongly held beliefs in the moral right to subsistence and equitable access to land; yet, he is at pains not to romanticise such economic relations.[24] Initially, Scott argued that, in situations in which this moral economy was threatened, peasants were likely to rebel; however, in later work, he demonstrated that more subtle forms of resistance might be deployed.[25] More recently, Scott has argued that some groups maintain a high degree of mobility and move to ungoverned spaces when their 'subsistence ethic' ideology is threatened by authority.[26]

Following Scott, I deploy the concept of moral economy as one analytical means to explain the historic transformation of Kuninjku labouring and what is occurring in the present. I do this in part by using a model of hybrid economy that illustrates how Kuninjku people have simultaneously balanced their domestic mode of production based on subsistence with the requirements of market capitalism and the state. My local theorisation looks to transcend what I see as the false dichotomy between customary economy and market economy, the former embedded and ruled by consensual social norms, the latter disembedded and ruled by impersonal market forces in a distinction reminiscent of that made by Karl Polanyi.[27] The contemporary Kuninjku economy is thoroughly transformed from any 'traditional' or 'pre-colonial' form. Yet, this economy remains fundamentally organised by normative rules that emphasise mobile forms of labour that allow hunting, sharing with kin and responsiveness to ceremonial obligations. The everyday application of such rules is not free of tensions and conflict.

Returning to the central issue of labouring; the state is looking to impose individual forms of regulated work on Kuninjku people even as its own statistical collections demonstrate that there is insufficient work for everyone, and even as Kuninjku (and others) engage in formal employment in very particular and highly flexible ways. The attempted imposition by the state and its local agents of formal Western work

---

23   Hann, 'Moral Economy'.
24   Scott, *The Moral Economy*, 5, 33.
25   Scott, *Weapons of the Weak*; Scott, *Domination and the Arts*.
26   Scott, *The Art of Not Being Governed*.
27   Polanyi, *The Great Transformation*.

patterns and rigidity threaten the moral foundations of Kuninjku notions of community and proper behaviour based on a valorisation of family, sharing and participation in ceremony—all actions associated with unpredictable availability for work and residential fluidity. It also threatens the foundations of the hybrid economy that is predicated on the maintenance of customary links to the land for sustenance, and a high degree of continual occupational mobility between formal and informal work activities rather than the expected commitment to sustained employment and occupational specialisation.

As I noted earlier, there is an underlying dominant assumption by the state and its agents of imagined inactivity, whereas Kuninjku life is teeming with economic and social activity and ceremonial life, all being inseparable in the Kuninjku world view. There is also an underlying assumption that Kuninjku and other people in Maningrida are unaware of the global and local manifestations of market capitalism, even though Kuninjku have been acutely observing the comings and goings of Balanda and their demanding labouring regimes for a long time. Increasingly, Kuninjku people watch television, engage with social media and, occasionally, travel, both domestically and internationally, and so they have an acute awareness of different forms of work and which forms they desire and do not.

In Maningrida, Kuninjku see a dual economy demarcated mainly by ethnicity with a growing number of Balandas holding professional and managerial jobs, living in small family units, earning a lot of money, enjoying an endless supply of cash, fully (if not over-) employed and living in a hyper-mobile manner; in recent years, some, especially contractors, fly-in and fly-out like mine workers (see Prout Quicke and Haslam McKenzie, this volume). All this has a different logic to the priorities of Kuninjku. Census data in recent years show that the median Balanda income is over four times that of local Aboriginal people.[28] Yet, almost without exception, Balanda today do not stay for long—government officials come and go, as do most employees of Aboriginal organisations, some of whom are even foreign backpackers and holders of temporary 457 work visas. Unsurprisingly, such transient visitors lack understanding of local economic history or regional cultural practices, and do not

---

28   At that time, median individual income for Indigenous adults was $268 per week and for non-Indigenous adults $1,167 per week. See '2011 Census, Community Profile', Australian Bureau of Statistics, accessed 31 March 2018, www.censusdata.abs.gov.au/census_services/getproduct/census/2011/communityprofile/IARE704003?opendocument.

have any deep local social relationships. While local information on remittances out of Maningrida is not available, one suspects much wealth is transferred out of the region by Balanda even as they participate in the project to fix 'the Aboriginal development problem'. When I asked Kuninjku if they desired to live and work in this way, the response was invariably 'no'—such work represents an unacceptable regulation of life. As one (now deceased) friend, Joshua Jununwangga, put it to me: 'I am far too busy for a full-time Balanda job.'

Conclusion

A moral panic, the reported abuse of children, accompanied the Northern Territory Intervention; consequently, issues of morality now permeate all aspects of policy, including an emerging intolerance of culturally different ways of labouring. There is much here that is reminiscent of Charles Fourier's nineteenth-century critique of the resistance by wage labourers to the boring, repetitive work of early capitalism versus the flexible, attractive labour that could provide greater freedom if accompanied by a guaranteed income (that the CDEP scheme at outstations used to provide). Fourier insisted that only free work can be pleasurable.[29] Kuninjku would agree. What is clear today is that the state is looking to construct subjectivity for Kuninjku by deploying the tropes of rigid paid work and responsibility. Implementation of this paternalistic project is being devolved in large measure to local organisations, like BAC. In the process, a historically successful Aboriginal organisation is being coopted and depoliticised because of its financial dependence on the state.

The growing space that is being created (rather than reduced) between Bininj and Balanda views on labouring in remote places like Maningrida is concerning, as it inadvertently allows for what can be termed reckless use of public funds; more harshly, it enables a form of petty corruption and waste that is state sanctioned. Pursuit of the state's quest to close the employment gap leaves much room for the promotion of false capitalist endeavours. Those who quietly acquiesce to the state project can be rewarded with largesse, while those who challenge its validity are punished—a form of moral hazard that resonates with what some have observed in weak states, not in supposed 'strong' states like Australia.[30]

---

29 Spencer, 'Work in Utopia'.
30 Weigratz, 'Fake Capitalism'; Ferguson, 'The Uses of Neoliberalism'.

Maningrida is becoming a more permissive place, with more and more outsiders coming and going and fewer checks and balances today than during the 'self-determination' era when a legally enforced permit system could be deployed to monitor the movements of outsiders. Kuninjku are, at times, bewildered when in Maningrida by the comings and goings of unknown people with unknown purposes and sometimes are keen to escape for a sojourn at outstations, just for some welcome bush order; when in town, they are becoming less visible, often working indoors on arts production to avoid recruitment for some well-intentioned training program to equip them for forms of labour for which they have no desire.

What is missing in much of this debate is recognition that groups like the Kuninjku have made extraordinary transformations in a very short time. For over a decade, they were responsible for the bulk of the region's only commodity exports: art. As such, they were the ones most engaged with global capitalism. However, they did this in their own way and with a degree of sensible caution, ensuring that the other key sector of their domestic economy, self-provisioning, remained intact.

In July 2012, Kuninjku were willing to don high-visibility safety clothing symbolic of hard work, hoping, perhaps, that they might be sighted from the nearby flat-bladed vehicular track by visiting officials. They struggle to retain key elements of their plural economy even when facing requirements to engage in monochromic forms of Western labour; their early response to the 'new' development approach and its labouring requirements is highly pragmatic and adaptive, even humorous. Yet, it also demonstrates a resignation that enhanced engagement with the dominant state is currently required.

In the longer term, if one is to see a regional *développement durable*, a form of development that is beneficial and lasts,[31] local political institutions will need to be reactivated to challenge destructive forms of neoliberal state-sponsored economism. One interpretation of my analysis is that it provides some semblance of hope because, even after 55 years of colonisation, decolonisation and, since 2007, attempted recolonisation (to 2012), Kuninjku people have managed through their agency and alliances to mould forms of hybrid economy and associated flexible labour relations that accord with their desires to remain at home and near, or on, ancestral lands. The Kuninjku case that I present here is not intended as

---

31 Hart and Padayachee, 'Development', 61.

some heroic tale of the destruction of the hegemony of neoliberal ideas as recently described by David Graeber.[32] To the contrary, what I have described as governmental overreach can have, as has subsequently become apparent, deeply destructive consequences with human casualties.

Postscript: March 2018

I have been back to the Maningrida region nine times since July 2012, the visit during which I observed what I now interpret as a tipping point in the absurd neoliberal governance of remote places like Mumeka. There have been two federal elections and the policy landscape has worsened quite significantly in my view. BAC has been in and out of special administration; it ran into financial difficulties owing to developmental overreach and wasteful projects that meant it could not meet its obligations to creditors.

It is difficult to explain why the Australian Government, with all its surveillance apparatus, would have allowed the situation at BAC—one of the largest and most successful Indigenous corporations in remote Australia—to eventuate. It seems to me that there is a brutal political conflict underway, driven by the deployment of excessive state power, that is looking to escalate the project of behavioural modification on people like the Kuninjku using community-based organisations like BAC as the local blunt instrument to oversee the transformation of what is perceived as unproductive welfare-dependent labour into imagined paid employment or, at the very least, to discipline the jobless.

From 1 July 2013, the CDEP scheme was incorporated into the new Remote Jobs and Communities Program launched by the Gillard Government in its dying days. Then, with a conservative government elected in September 2013, the remnants of the scheme that had been 'grandfathered' were swept away. First, there was a review of Indigenous employment and training programs headed by a mining magnate, Andrew Forrest, to plough the turf for reform.[33] Next, there was implementation of his recommendations, which included the end of the flexible CDEP

32   Graeber, 'The Shock of Victory'.
33   Forrest, *Creating Parity*.

scheme for all on 1 July 2015 and its replacement by the cynically renamed Community Development Program (CDP) that has little similarity to the old scheme.[34]

A combination of special administration and policy reform has seen BAC become more and more an 'employment and training' provider selected by competitive tender, and less an outstation resource agency that delivered forms of appropriate development to support flexible ways of living and labouring to its membership. BAC's financial rehabilitation appears successful. However, as with all structural adjustment and financial bailouts, this has come at a cost: loss of organisational autonomy, new externally imposed modes of operation and requirements to comply with CDP guidelines that focus on paid employment and the omnipresent Closing the Gap paradigm.

CDP is a 'work for the dole' scheme that requires able-bodied people aged 15–49 years to work five hours a day, five days a week in a range of work-like activities with Newstart Allowance (the dole) as remuneration. Such stringent work requirements eliminate other livelihood possibilities, especially self-provisioning on country away from Maningrida. BAC is paid a bonus if it places jobless participants in sustainable mainstream employment (defined as 13- and 26-week outcomes). BAC is also paid for alerting Centrelink if participants fail to turn up for make-work, training or designated appointments—welfare payments are docked one day's pay for each 'no-show' occurrence. To date, BAC, like other providers distributed across regional and remote Australia, has been more effective in alerting Centrelink about no-shows than in delivering jobs to a massive caseload of nearly 1,000 jobless adults in a regional economy that has few jobs.[35]

The old colonial logic of the 1960s has re-emerged in a punitive and impoverishing manifestation. Using a stick-and-carrot[36] behavioural approach, it is assumed that surplus Aboriginal labour can be disciplined and trained to make it job ready. Alternatively, it is assumed that people will migrate for employment even if only to escape this paternalistic regime. In a highly contradictory and destructive manner, politicians and their

---

34 These recommendations were implemented despite a robust critique of the review process and its recommendations, see Klein, 'Academic Perspectives on the Forrest Review'.

35 See Jordan and Fowkes, 'Job Creation and Income Support'.

36 The normal order of this phrase has been intentionally reversed to indicate that there is currently plenty of stick and little carrot.

officials in Canberra are promoting an employment pathway for jobless Aboriginal people like the Kuninjku that recent official information from the 2016 Census clearly informs them does not exist.[37] At the same time, the mainstream media and policy discourse laments the destructive effects of inactivity and the consequences for wellbeing of deepening poverty. Again and again the assumption is made that the relational norms and values adhered to by people like the Kuninjku will be broken and will dissipate when confronted by a powerful discursive trope that promises much and delivers little other than punishment in the form of 'no-show' penalties. There is currently no basis for the belief that market capitalism will blossom in the Maningrida region with employment for all and associated wealth creation. This is just an imagined procedural fix based on ideological blind faith that has no basis in regional reality.

The modern state and its bureaucratic apparatus might look to depoliticise and control local organisations like BAC and people like the Kuninjku but, as Tania Murray Li has illustrated with her work in Indonesia, local groups remain deeply political and capable of subverting imposed plans.[38]

This raises two important questions: How might maladapted Western institutions, like punitive welfare to move people to rigid formal employment, be refigured to facilitate more effective flexible forms of livelihood? The CDEP scheme, which was replete with postcolonial possibility, has now been eliminated by the settler colonial state.[39] The second question is, to paraphrase Erik Olin Wright, how might 'real utopias be envisioned' for people like the Kuninjku? My research for the last three decades has focused on the deployment of local Kuninjku labour for livelihoods that accord with their aspirations. I end by pondering how a livelihoods approach might be restored for the Kuninjku community and other Aboriginal people living in very remote parts of Australia.

---

37   A summary of employment data for the three census, 2006, 2011 and 2016, shows that the Indigenous employment/population ratio declined from 26 per cent in 2006 to 18.4 per cent in 2016, having risen slightly to 34 per cent in 2011. The comparative non-Indigenous figures are 95.5 per cent, 91.4 per cent and 88.9 per cent. The Indigenous unemployment rate rose from 17.2 per cent in 2006 to 34 per cent in 2016, even as the labour force participation rate declined from 31.4 per cent to 22.6 per cent. All figures from 'Community Profiles', Australian Bureau of Statistics, accessed 15 March 2019, www.abs.gov.au/websitedbs/censushome.nsf/home/communityprofiles?opendocument&navpos=230.

38   Li, *The Will to Improve.*

39   Jordan, *Better than Welfare?*

A first requirement is for outsiders to recognise local economic realities and the political imperative to restore social power to community organisations. A second might be to recognise the sociological reality that locally dominant non-capitalist imperatives, so evident in flexible labour arrangements, persist—they cannot just be wished or assumed away, as inconvenient as this may be to the state project of disciplining and neoliberalising labour.

My latest visits to Mumeka were in July 2017 and July 2018. The pizza oven was still there, in sound condition and still unused, a fixture embedded in the landscape. The market gardens are overgrown and the trickle irrigation irreparable. The wooden chicken coops, reputed to have been made in Denmark, are in fragments. There were no people at Mumeka; the residents were scattered, some living in Maningrida, some elsewhere at ceremony. Mumeka was a small flourishing place when I first went there in 1979; in 2012 it was abuzz with developmental excitement. It is now just seasonally occupied.

Figure 12.3: The pizza oven at Mumeka, July 2017.
Source: Photograph by Jon Altman.

In the present, the disjunctures between Kuninjku and Western notions of what constitutes acceptable forms of labour, and the roles that labour mobility and migration might play, are wider than ever. The Australian state is looking to close statistical employment gaps and reduce welfare dependency. This goal requires that people like the Kuninjku either reduce their regional mobility (especially between the township of Maningrida and outstations) and participate in Western forms of formal employment when it is available or migrate for employment. Neither option is currently acceptable to Kuninjku. Paradoxically, it is Balanda and, to a far lesser extent, non-local Indigenous people who migrate to Maningrida to take up employment, but then demonstrate their mobility by only staying for a short time before leaving.

Tragically, the recolonisation project has been highly destructive of the regional forms of plural economy that were evolving. Kuninjku people today are more welfare dependent and impoverished than at any time since the colonial state came to stay in central Arnhem Land in 1957, despite state investment in development paraphernalia like pizza ovens, chicken coops and market gardens. The state's agents and personnel come and go, like its policies, which, arguably, have had more adverse effects than ever on people like the Kuninjku who have stayed.

Bibliography

Altman, Jon. 'Basic Income for Remote Indigenous Australians: Prospects for a Livelihoods Approach in Neoliberal Times'. In *Basic Income in Australia and New Zealand: Perspectives from the Neoliberal Frontier*, edited by Jennifer Mays, Greg Marston and John Tomlinson, 179–205. Basingstoke: Palgrave Macmillan, 2016. doi.org/10.1057/9781137535320_9.

——. 'Bawinanga and CDEP: The Vibrant Life and Near Death of a Major Aboriginal Corporation in Arnhem Land'. In *Better than Welfare? Jobs and Livelihoods for Indigenous Australians after CDEP*, edited by Kirrily Jordan, 175–217, Canberra: ANU Press, 2016. doi.org/10.22459/CAEPR36.08.2016.07.

——. 'From Kunnanj, Fish Creek, to Mumeka, Mann River: Hunter-Gatherer Tradition and Transformation in Western Arnhem Land, 1948–2009'. In *Exploring the Legacy of the 1948 Arnhem Land Expedition*, edited by Martin Thomas and Margo Neale, 113–34. Canberra: ANU E Press, 2011. doi.org/10.22459/ELALE.06.2011.

———. *Hunter-Gatherers Today: An Aboriginal Economy in North Australia*. Canberra: Australian Institute of Aboriginal Studies, 1987.

———. '"The Main Thing Is to Have Enough Food": Kuninjku Precarity and Neoliberal Reason'. In *The Quest for the Good Life in Precarious Times: Ethnographic Perspectives on the Domestic Moral Economy*, edited by Chris Gregory and Jon Altman,163–96. Canberra, ANU Press, 2018. doi.org/10.22459/QGLPT.03.2018.08.

Altman, Jon and Melinda Hinkson. 'Mobility and Modernity in Arnhem Land: The Social Universe of Kuninjku Trucks'. *Journal of Material Culture* 12, no. 2 (2007): 181–203. doi.org/10.1177/1359183507078122.

Anthony, Thalia. *Indigenous People, Crime and Punishment*. Milton Park, Abingdon: Routledge, 2013. doi.org/10.4324/9780203640296.

Checketts, Juliet. 'The Pulse of Policy: Mapping Movement in the Australian Indigenous Policy World'. PhD thesis, The Australian National University, 2016.

Commonwealth of Australia. 'Closing the Gap Prime Minister's Report 2018'. Canberra: Department of Prime Minister and Cabinet, 2018.

Ferguson, James. *The Anti-Politics Machine: 'Development', Depoliticisation and Bureaucratic Power in Lesotho*. Minneapolis: University of Minnesota Press, 1994.

———. 'The Uses of Neoliberalism'. *Antipode* 41, S1 (2009): 166–84.

Forrest, Andrew. *The Forrest Review: Creating Parity*. Canberra: Department of Prime Minister and Cabinet, 2014.

Garde, Murray. *Culture, Language and Person Reference in an Australian Language*. Amsterdam: John Benjamins Publishing Company, 2013.

Graeber, David. *Debt: The First 5,000 Years*. New York: Melville House Publishing, 2010.

———. 'The Shock of Victory'. In *Revolutions in Reverse: Essays on Politics, Violence, Art, and Imagination*, 11–30. Minor Compositions, London 2011.

Hann, Chris. 'Moral Economy'. In *The Human Economy: A Citizen's Guide*, edited by Keith Hart, Jean-Louis Laville and Antonio David Cattani, 187–98. Cambridge: Polity, 2011.

Hart, Keith and Vishnu Padayachee. 'Development'. In *The Human Economy: A Citizen's Guide*, edited by Keith Hart, Jean-Louis Laville and Antonio David Cattani, 51–62. Cambridge: Polity, 2011.

Hinkson, Melinda. 'Introduction: In the Name of the Child'. In *Coercive Reconciliation: Stabilize, Normalise, Exit Aboriginal Australia*, edited by Jon Altman and Melinda Hinkson, 1–12. Melbourne: Arena Publications, 2007.

Jordan, Kirrily, ed. *Better than Welfare? Jobs and Livelihoods for Indigenous Australians after CDEP*. Canberra: ANU Press, 2016. doi.org/10.22459/CAEPR36.08.2016.

Jordan, Kirrily and Lisa Fowkes. 'Job Creation and Income Support in Remote Indigenous Australia: Moving Forward with a Better System'. CAEPR Topical Issue No. 2/2016. Canberra: Centre for Aboriginal Economic Policy Research, ANU, 2016.

Klein, Elise, comp. 'Academic Perspectives on the Forrest Review: Creating Parity'. CAEPR Topical Issue No. 2/2014. Canberra: Centre for Aboriginal Economic Policy Research, ANU, 2014.

Li, Tania Murray. *The Will to Improve: Governmentality, Development and the Practice of Politics*. Durham: Duke University Press, 2007. doi.org/10.1215/9780822389781.

Macoun, Alissa. 'Aboriginality and the Northern Territory Intervention'. PhD thesis, University of Queensland, 2012.

McCarthy, Frederick and Margaret McArthur. 'The Food Quest and the Time Factor in Aboriginal Economic Life'. In *Records of the American-Australian Scientific Expedition to Arnhem Land*, Volume 2, Anthropology and Nutrition, edited by Charles Mountford, 145–94. Melbourne: Melbourne University Press, 1960.

Northern Territory Government. *Maningrida: Jobs Profile 2011*. Darwin: Department of Business and Development.

Polanyi, Karl. *The Great Transformation*. New York: Fararr and Rienhart, 1944.

Sahlins, Marshall. *Stone Age Economics*. Chicago: Aldine and Atherton, 1972.

Sanders, W. 'Working Futures: A Critique of Policy by Numbers'. CAEPR Working Paper No. 72/2010. Canberra: Centre for Aboriginal Economic Policy Research, ANU, 2010.

Scott, James. *The Art of Not Being Governed: An Anarchist History of Upland Southeast Asia*. New Haven: Yale University Press, 2009.

——. *Domination and the Arts of Resistance: Hidden Transcripts*. New Haven: Yale University Press, 1990.

———. *The Moral Economy of the Peasant: Rebellion and Subsistence in South East Asia.* New Haven: Yale University Press, 1976.

———. *Weapons of the Weak: Everyday Forms of Peasant Resistance.* New Haven: Yale University Press, 1985.

Spencer, David. 'Work in Utopia: Pro-Work Sentiments in the Writings of Four Critics of Classical Economics'. *The European Journal of the History of Economic Thought* 16, no. 1 (2009): 97–122. doi.org/10.1080/09672560802707449.

Strakosch, Elizabeth. *Neoliberal Indigenous Policy: Settler Colonialism and the 'Post-Welfare' State.* Basingstoke: Palgrave Macmillan, 2015. doi.org/10.1057/9781137405418.

Wacquant, Loic. 'Three Steps to a Historical Anthropology of Actually Existing Neoliberalism'. *Social Anthropology* 20, no. 1 (2012): 66–70. doi.org/10.1111/j.1469-8676.2011.00189.x.

Wiegratz, Jörg. 'Fake Capitalism? The Dynamics of Neoliberal Moral Restructuring and Pseudo-Development: The Case of Uganda'. *Review of African Political Economy* 37 (2010): 123–37. doi.org/10.1080/03056244.2010.484525.

Wright, Erik Olin. *Envisioning Real Utopias.* London: Verso, 2010.

An Afterword

Lynette Russell

It is a rare joy to be asked to comment on a collection of papers as thoroughly important as those contained in this volume. Although I might be quick to characterise these as 'labour history' they are, in fact, much more than that; while most have a historical element to them, all contributions are also deeply and completely contemporary, topical and political. History—good and meaningful history—must, I believe, embrace interdisciplinarity. To understand Indigenous peoples, their historical specificity and their varied responses to contact and colonialism, we need to engage with historical texts, ethnography, anthropology, material culture studies as well as politics. As an experiment in interdisciplinary studies, these authors weave an intellectual dialogue across, between and within the disciplines of history, ethnography, anthropology, human geography, cultural and Indigenous studies. By taking a regional Pacific-wide approach, *Labour Lines and Colonial Power* offers up both parallels and significant contrasts between Pacific Islander and Indigenous Australian labour mobility experiences.

Transnational and multi-site histories,[1] along with studies in Indigenous labour and mobility, have recently experienced something of a resurgence.[2] Building on foundational early work, such as that by Clive Moore, Regina Ganter and, more recently, Julia Martinez and Adrian Vickers, John Maynard and my own offerings, the maritime industries have provided

---

1   I am thinking here of Wolfe, *Traces of History*, and others works including Edmonds, *Urbanizing Frontiers*.
2   Carey and Lydon, *Indigenous Networks*; Banivanua Mar, *Decolonisation and the Pacific*; Chappell, *Double Ghosts*; Shineberg, *The People Trade*. See also contributors in Standfield, *Indigenous Mobilities*.

the most visible location for studies of native labour and mobility.[3] The chapters in *Labour Lines* take this starting point and move beyond it in exciting, surprising and revelatory ways.

I am going to resist reiterating the content of each chapter; however, I do note that, taken in its entirety, these authors speak to and with each other, showing the power and importance of a collected volume of essays. Those of us in universities are being actively discouraged from producing edited collections, especially ones published by 'local' presses as we strive for new nebulous targets of 'excellence' and 'impact'. This collection is a perfect demonstration of why this is a flawed idea. Emerging out of a symposium hosted by Deakin University, the essays here have all the hallmarks of having been thoroughly discussed, workshopped, digested and reformed. It is telling that there is a mixture of senior scholars and up-and-coming early career researchers. Even more importantly, there is a diversity of approaches, with Indigenous and settler writers complementing, contrasting and challenging each other. Perhaps the greatest strength of this approach is the time periods covered: the past, the recent past and the present.

Too often the concept of Indigenous labour history is male focused—images of hard male bodies doing physically demanding work not fit for a 'white man' predominate. As Haskins and Scrimgeour have powerfully shown us, from 1900 to the mid-twentieth century, domestic labour in Australia was widely regarded as not *real* labour, as it was conducted by women and often women of colour.[4] It is revealing that, within this collection, serious scholarly attention is paid to women's labour as well as men's and the role gender plays is considered and developed. *Labour Lines and Colonial Power* is a potent reminder of how a collection can be so much more than the sum of its parts. Like the labour it describes, the essays here are wide ranging, complex and layered.

Finally, while I resisted the urge to describe individual contributions, I would like to comment on one essay: Chapter 3, '"Boyd's Blacks": Labour and the Making of Settler Lands in Australia and the Pacific', by Tracey Banivanua Mar. This is undoubtedly the last time any of us will read new and fresh insights from Tracey, highlighting her brilliance and the tragedy

---

3   Moore, 'Revising the Revisionists'; Ganter, *The Pearl-Shellers;* Maynard, *Fight for Liberty;* Maynard, 'Transcultural/Transnational'; Russell, *Roving Mariners;* Martinez and Vickers, *The Pearl Frontier.*
4   Haskins and Scrimgeour, '"Strike Strike, We Strike"', 89.

of her loss. As ever, she elucidates the complexity of transnational histories and demonstrates the intersectionality of the early colonial labour trade. With her eye firmly on Pacific Islander experiences of trade, labour and mobility, she takes the reader on an insider's journey presented within an activist-historian's framework. This chapter is extremely important; indeed, it is set to be a classic piece of historical literature. It serves as a stark reminder of how vital it is to have Indigenous/Pacific Islander and/or 'native' scholars speaking to, and 'talk'ng up' to, our collective histories.[5]

Bibliography

Banivanua Mar, Tracey. *Decolonisation and the Pacific: Indigenous Globalisation and the Ends of Empire*. Cambridge: Cambridge University Press, 2016.

Carey, Jane and Jane Lydon, eds. *Indigenous Networks: Mobility, Connections and Exchange*. London: Routledge, 2014. doi.org/10.4324/9781315766065.

Chappell, David. *Double Ghosts: Oceanian Voyagers on Euroamerican Ships*. London, England: M. E. Sharpe, 1997.

Edmonds, Penelope. *Urbanizing Frontiers: Indigenous Peoples and Settlers in 19th-Century Pacific Rim Cities*. Vancouver: UBC Press, 2010.

Ganter, Regina. *The Pearl-Shellers of Torres Strait: Resource Use, Development and Decline, 1860s–1960s*. Melbourne: Melbourne University Press, 1994.

Haskins, Victoria and Anne Scrimgeour. '"Strike Strike, We Strike": Making Aboriginal Domestic Labor Visible in the Pilbara Pastoral Workers' Strike, Western Australia, 1946–1952'. *International Labor and Working-Class History*, 88 (2015): 87–108. doi.org/10.1017/S0147547915000228.

Martinez, Julia T. and Adrian Vickers. *The Pearl Frontier: Indonesian Labor and Indigenous Encounters in Australia's Northern Trading Network*. Honolulu: University of Hawai'i Press, 2015. doi.org/10.21313/hawaii/9780824840020.001.0001.

Maynard, John. *Fight for Liberty and Freedom: The Origins of Australian Aboriginal Activism*. Aboriginal Studies Press, 2007.

---

5   I am borrowing the term 'talk'ng up' from the hugely influential Moreton-Robinson, *Talkin' Up to the White Woman*.

———. 'Transcultural/Transnational Interaction and Influences On Aboriginal Australia'. In *Connected Worlds: History in Transnational Perspective*, edited by Ann Curthoys and Marilyn lake, 195–208. Canberra: ANU E Press, 2005.

Moore, Clive. 'Revising the Revisionists: The Historiography of Immigrant Melanesians in Australia'. *Pacific Studies* 15, no. 2 (1992): 61.

Moreton-Robinson, Aileen. *Talkin' Up to the White Woman: Aboriginal Women and Feminism*. St Lucia: University of Queensland Press, 2000.

Russell, Lynette. *Roving Mariners: Australian Aboriginal Whalers and Sealers in the Southern Oceans, 1790–1870*. New York: SUNY Press, 2012.

Shineberg, Dorothy. *The People Trade: Pacific Island Laborers and New Caledonia, 1865–1930*. Honolulu: Center for Pacific Island Studies, University of Hawai'i Press, 1999.

Standfield, Rachel. *Indigenous Mobilities: Across and Beyond the Antipodes*. Canberra: ANU Press and Aboriginal History, 2018. doi.org/10.22459/IM.06.2018.

Wolfe, Patrick. *Traces of History: Elementary Structures of Race*. London: Verso Books, 2016.

www.ingramcontent.com/pod-product-compliance
Lightning Source LLC
Chambersburg PA
CBHW050807270326
41926CB00026B/4589